The World of Wu Zhao

The World of Wu Zhao
Annotated Selections from Zhang Zhuo's *Court and Country*

N. Harry Rothschild

ANTHEM PRESS

Anthem Press
An imprint of Wimbledon Publishing Company
www.anthempress.com

This edition first published in UK and USA 2025
by ANTHEM PRESS
75–76 Blackfriars Road, London SE1 8HA, UK
or PO Box 9779, London SW19 7ZG, UK
and
244 Madison Ave #116, New York, NY 10016, USA

First published in the UK and USA by Anthem Press in 2023

© 2025 N. Harry Rothschild

The author asserts the moral right to be identified as the author of this work.

All rights reserved. Without limiting the rights under copyright reserved above, no part of this publication may be reproduced, stored or introduced into a retrieval system, or transmitted, in any form or by any means (electronic, mechanical, photocopying, recording or otherwise), without the prior written permission of both the copyright owner and the above publisher of this book.

British Library Cataloguing-in-Publication Data
A catalogue record for this book is available from the British Library.

Library of Congress Control Number: 2024945419
A catalog record for this book has been requested.

ISBN-13: 978-1-83999-393-0 (Pbk)
ISBN-10: 1-83999-393-6 (Pbk)

Cover Image: Wu Zhao going out with her retinue (唐後行從圖).
Attributed to Zhang Xuan of the Tang. Colored painting on silk.
With the kind permission of Mr. Lu Zhong.

This title is also available as an e-book.

I dedicate this book to my wife, Chengmei, and my two children, Viola and Liu.
I love you all tons and will miss you immeasurably.

Contents

Acknowledgments ix

Figures xi

Map xii

Tables xiii

Weights and Measures xvi

Introduction 1

CHAPTER 1
Wu Zhao: her inner palace, her inner circle 23

CHAPTER 2
The culture of the court 45

CHAPTER 3
"Cruel officials": Wu Zhao's "teeth and horns" 71

CHAPTER 4
Beyond court and capital: local officials 87

CHAPTER 5
The common people 99

CHAPTER 6
Relationships: men, women, and family in the time of Wu Zhao 119

CONTENTS

CHAPTER 7
Generals and military men 135

CHAPTER 8
The frontier and beyond: foreigners and others during Wu Zhao's reign 151

CHAPTER 9
Religion and the supernatural world 171

CHAPTER 10
Flora, fauna, and the natural world 197

Afternote 223

Appendix: People and Places 227

Notes 241

Bibliography 279

Index 295

Acknowledgments

This manuscript was assembled late in the throes of a six-year struggle with metastatic gastroesophageal cancer. There were days when I had to climb up the stairs to my office on hands and knees—days that I didn't make it. If my doctors are right, I will not live to see this book's publication. Copious gratitude goes out to my oncologists—Jaffer Ajani, Leanne Fox, and Roger Inhorn—for keeping me alive just long enough to complete this project.

I have long loved the peculiar characters, strange quirks, and unusual events in Zhang Zhuo's *Court and Country*. *The World of Wu Zhao*, whatever its flaws and blemishes, is a labor of love and will, but there is no way that I could have completed this project alone as my illness progressed and my physical condition deteriorated. I am truly fortunate to be surrounded and supported by my family during this difficult and painful time.

Loving thanks to my brother, Amos, and my father, Michael, for their countless hours of sustained work to help me edit and fine-tune the manuscript of this book, particularly in its later stages, as my illness worsened. Without them, this project would not have been completed.

Gracious thanks to Wang Hongjie, my brother, for generously, time and again, helping me with subtle details and minutiae in Zhang translations, and for the dozens of "quick questions" about this book that he patiently fielded. Deep thanks as well to Keith Knapp for his friendship and generous spirit, going far above and beyond, helping me find images and secure permissions in the later stages of this project—when I lacked the acumen and energy to do so myself. Both have helped me avoid errors and have made this manuscript better.

Thank you to the Tang Studies Society for their generous $1,500 Research Grant in 2020 that enabled the purchase of otherwise hard-to-locate materials that helped bring this project to fruition.

Abundant thanks are also due to my colleagues at UNF, who have helped me so often during these difficult years. In addition to being a sounding board for ideas in the book, David Sheffler, in his capacity as department chair, has shown tremendous friendship, kindness, generosity, and patience, going far

ACKNOWLEDGMENTS

out of his way to help diminish course loads. Thanks also to Sarah Mattice, Stephanie Smith, and Paul Carelli, for stepping up during my illness to cover courses. And an emphatic thank you to Marianne Roberts for helping me navigate Human Resources and bureaucracy—and life in general.

Any mistakes are, of course, my own.

Postscript—Dr. N. Amos Rothschild, brother of the author:

I would like to thank the following people for their help and generosity in securing or granting permissions for the images that appear in this book: Mr. Lu Zhong, Dr. Vladimir Belyaev, Professor Jiang Sheng of Sichuan University, Professor Han Yuxiang of the Nanyang Han Art Museum, Professor Lidu Yi of Florida International University, and Professor Huang Xiaofeng of the Central Academy of Fine Arts. Special thanks are due to Professor Keith Knapp, who fulfilled his promise to my late brother with tremendous patience and persistence.

Figures

Figure 1 A woodblock print of Wu Zhao from a Ming dynasty encyclopedia	24
Figure 2 A Tang dynasty bronze fish tally	48
Figure 3 A Zhou dynasty bronze turtle tally	49
Figure 4 A Qing dynasty painting of Yu Qianlou, a filial son who tastes his father's feces	79
Figure 5 An ink rubbing of two men playing pitch pot (*touhu*)	111
Figure 6 A Ming dynasty painting of Emperor Taizong	136
Figure 7 A Tang dynasty porcelain camel and groom	163
Figure 8 A Qing dynasty woodblock print of a qiu'er beast	201

Map

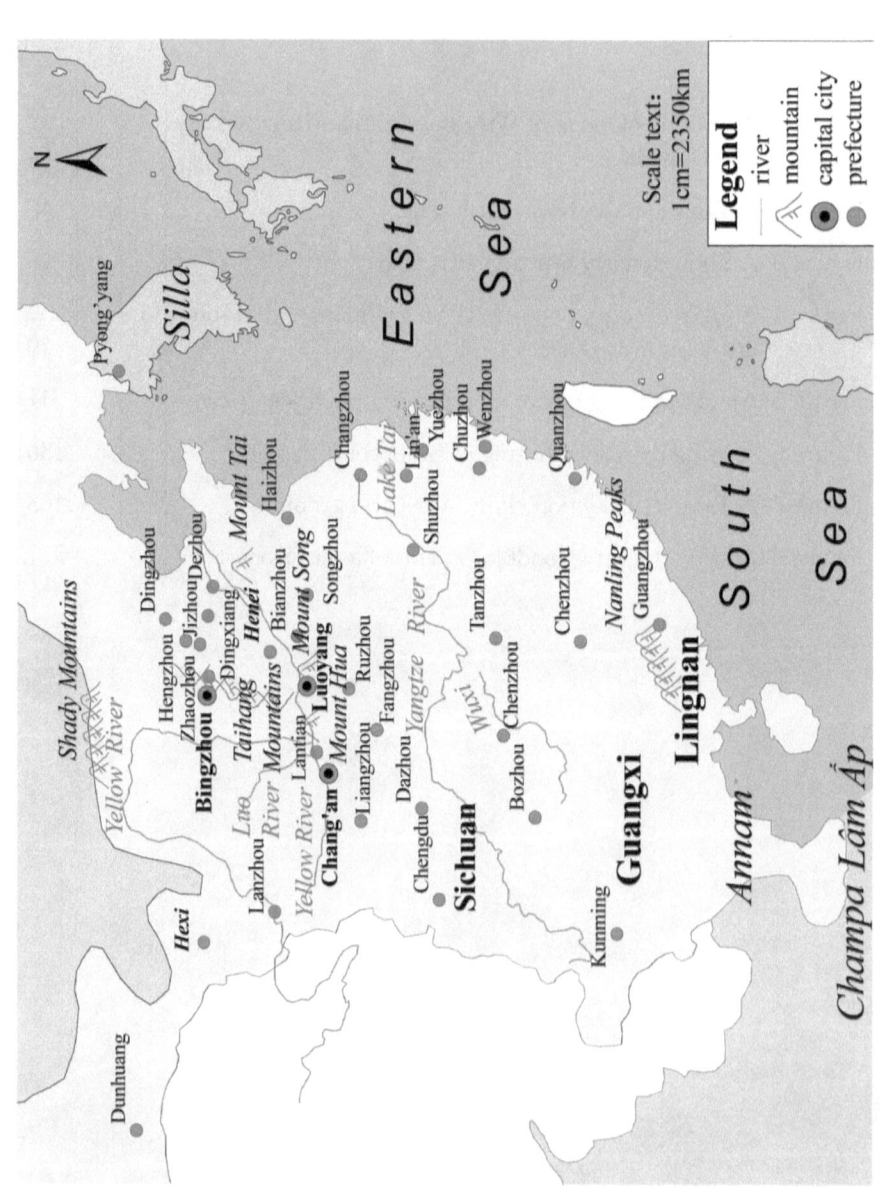

Tables

DYNASTIES AND RULERS MENTIONED HEREIN

Xia 夏 (2200–1766 BC)
  Yu 禹 the Great
Shang 商 (1766–1045 BC)
  Zhou 紂
Western Zhou 周 (1045–221 BC)
  King Wen 文王
  King Wu 武王
Eastern Zhou
  Spring and Autumn era 春秋時代 (771–481 BC)
  Warring States 戰國時代 (481–221 BC)
Qin 秦 (221–206 BC)
Western Han 西漢 (206 BC to AD 8)
  Gaozu 高祖 (r. 206–195 BC) and Empress Lü 呂后 (regent, 195–180 BC)
  Wudi 武帝 (r. 141–86 BC)
Xin 新 (AD 8–23)
Eastern Han 東漢 (24–220)
Cao Wei 曹魏 (220–265)
Jin dynasty 晉 (265–420)
  Wudi 武帝 (r. 266–290)
Northern (386–581)   and   Southern (420–589) dynasties 南北朝
Northern Wei 北魏, Toba Wei (386–534)   Liu Song 劉宋 (420–479), Mingdi 宋明帝
Northern Qi 北齊 (550–577)   Southern Qi 南齊 (479–502)
Northern Zhou 北周 (557–581)   Liang 梁 (502–557)
Sui 隋 (581–618)
Tang 唐 (618–690 and 705–907)
  Gaozu 高祖 (r. 618–626)
  Taizong 唐太宗 (r. 626–649)
  Gaozong 唐高宗 (r. 649–683), Li Zhi 李治

Zhongzong 中宗 (684, 705–710), Li Xiǎn 李顯
Ruizong 睿宗 (r. 684–690, 710–712), Li Dan 李旦
Xuanzong 玄宗 (r. 712–756), Li Longji 李隆基
Zhou 周 (690–705)
    Wu Zhao 武曌 (r. 690–705), also Wu Zetian 武則天, Celestial Empress 天后, and Empress Wu 武后
Five Dynasties and Ten Kingdoms 五代時潮
Song 宋
Yuan 元
Ming 明
Qing 清

REIGN ERAS FROM 655 TO 756[1]

Reign Era	Translation	Date of Inauguration
Gaozong's Reign (begins July 15, 649), Son of Taizong (r. 626–649)		
Yonghui 永徽	Eternal Banner	February 7, 650
Xianqing 顯慶	Manifest Felicitation	February 7, 656
Longshuo 龍朔	Draconic Conjunction	April 4, 661
Linde 麟德	Unicorn Virtue	February 2, 664
Qianfeng 乾封	Supernal *Feng* rite	February 14, 666
Zongzhang 總章	(a chamber in Bright Hall)	April 22, 668
Xianheng 咸亨	Total Efficacy	March 27, 670
Shangyuan 上元	Highest Origin	September 20, 674
Yifeng 儀鳳	Phoenix Regulator	December 18, 676
Diaolu 調露	Harmonious Dew	July 15, 679
Yonglong 永隆	Forever Eminent	September 21, 680
Kaiyao 開耀	Dawning Brilliance	November 15, 681
Yongchun 永淳	Eternal Purity	April 2, 682
Hongdao 弘道	Amplifying the Dao	December 27, 683
Zhongzong's First Reign		
Sisheng 嗣聖	Heir to the Sage	January 23, 684
Ruizong's First Reign/Wu Zhao Acts as Regent		
Wenming 文明	Cultured Luminosity	February 27, 684
Guangzhai 光宅	Illuminated and Filled	October 19, 684
Chuigong 垂拱	With Hanging Robes and Folded Hands	February 9, 685
Yongchang 永昌	Eternal Prosperity	January 27, 689
Zaichu 載初	Great Beginning	December 18, 689
Wu Zhao's Zhou Dynasty, 690–705		
Tianshou 天授	Heaven Bestowed	October 16, 690
Ruyi 如意	At Will	April 22, 692
Changshou 長壽	Protracted Longevity	October 23, 692

Yanzai 延載	Extension of an Era	June 9, 694
Zhengsheng 證聖	Verification of Sagehood	November 23, 694
Tiance wansui 天冊萬歲	Appointed by Heaven for 10,000 Years	October 22, 695
Wansui dengfeng 萬歲登封	Forever Ascending to Perform the *Feng* Sacrifice	January 20, 696
Wansui tongtian 萬歲通天	Communing with Heaven for 10,000 Years	April 22, 696
Shengong 神功	Divine Merit	September 29, 697
Shengli 聖曆	Sage Calendar	December 20, 697
Jiushi 久視	Distant Vision	May 27, 700
Dazu 大足	Great Footprint	February 15, 701
Chang'an 長安	Enduring Security	November 26, 701

Restoration of the Tang Dynasty. Zhongzong's Second Reign

Shenlong 神龍	Divine Dragon	January 30, 705
Jinglong 景龍	Scintillating Dragon	October 5, 707

Brief Reign of Shaodi (Li Chongmao, Zhongzong's Youngest Son, Wu Zhao's Grandson)

Tanglong 唐隆	Ascendancy of the Tang	July 5, 710

Ruizong's Second Reign

Jingyun 景雲	Scintillating Cloud	August 19, 710
Taiji 太極	Great Ultimate	March 1, 712

Reign of Xuanzong, Ruizong's Son and Wu Zhao's Grandson

Yanhe 延和	Extended Harmony	June 21, 712
Xiantian 先天	Preceding Heaven	September 12, 712
Kaiyuan 開元	Opening of an Era	December 23, 713
Tianbao 天寶	Heavenly Treasure	February 10, 742

Weights and Measures[1]

LENGTH/DISTANCE

10 *cun* 寸 is one *chi* 尺 (just less than a foot; roughly 29.5 cm).
Ten *chi* (just short of ten feet) is one *zhang* 丈.
1800 *chi* is one li 里 (roughly one-third of a mile).

VOLUME

1 *sheng* 升 (roughly 1.25 pints); 10 *sheng* is a *dou* 斗 (12.5 pints; .175 bushels).

WEIGHT

Sixteen *da-liang* 大兩 (a bit more than an ounce) equaled a *jin* 斤.
One *jin* equaled 1.35 pounds.
Tang coins weighed about 4.2 grams each. A string of 1,000 bronze coins weighed roughly 9.3 pounds. A *shi* 石 is 133 pounds.

CLOTH MEASURES

One *p i* 批 (measure) of silk is about 21 inches wide and four *zhang* (38 feet) long.

Introduction

THIS BOOK OFFERS READERS A FIRSTHAND glimpse of China in the late seventh and early eighth centuries. It is based upon more than 200 translated, annotated, and contextualized vignettes from Zhang Zhuo's eighth-century miscellany, *Collected Records of Court and Country* (*Chaoye qianzai* 朝野僉載; hereafter *Court and Country*). Few sources can deliver such an immediate and authentic sense and feel for the empire during the reign of Wu Zhao 武曌 (624–705, also known as Empress Wu and Wu Zetian), China's first and only female emperor.

Beginning from Wu Zhao's inner palace, this book expands in ever-wider concentric circles. While the opening chapter centers on the woman sovereign's inner quarters, where her male favorites dressed up in polychrome garments and rode wooden cranes, the second chapter moves to the outer court, examining the culture of the elite officials charged with administering the government. From Zhang Zhuo, we learn how these court denizens devised derisive nicknames for each other and tried to one-up one another at intricate word games. The third chapter looks at Wu Zhao's "cruel officials" (*kuli* 酷吏), henchmen who took an aesthetic delight in their bloodsport. Next, we leave the capital and travel into the prefectures and counties in a chapter that examines a full gamut of local officials—from conscientious magistrates to clerks who preyed on the citizens in their jurisdictions. Subsequently, a chapter on the common people surveys a wide range of clever artisans (including a master painter whose trompe l'oeil birds of prey were so realistic they scared pigeons from roosting on the rafters of a Buddhist temple), wealthy merchants literally risen from the muck, hospitable peasants, gamesmen, day laborers, and street performers. Chapter 6 investigates stories of men, women, and relationships—many featuring contraventions or abuses of patriarchal and Confucian norms—with a close eye on gender and power dynamics. The ensuing chapter explores accounts of generals and military men charged with defense against border threats from the Turks, the Khitan, and the Tibetans; these defenders ranged from men with consummate martial skill, to brilliant strategists, to craven and incompetent leaders who brought down disasters upon their men. Chapter 8 features accounts of foreigners and sojourners in the greater realm that comprised seventh-century China—not just the aforementioned bordering peoples, but others as well, including Sogdians, Jihu, and even a description of the marital practices of the people of Champa in Southeast Asia. The ninth chapter shares excerpts concerning religion, popular and elite, orthodox and unorthodox—from stories of Daoist masters and Buddhist monks, including a Chan master who converts an alligator to the Buddhist faith, to more folksy tales of lute-strumming diviners, dream interpreters, faith healers, and *yin-yang* masters; this chapter also contains selections culled from Zhang's assorted ghost stories, tales of the supernatural, and eerie, prophetic ditties. The final chapter scrutinizes flora, fauna, and the larger natural world, from stories of winged and watery tribes to legends engraved on the landscape. There is a special section on Lingnan, literally "the land south of the peaks," chock-full of stories of toxic vegetation and venomous creatures.

ZHANG ZHUO'S LIFE AND OFFICIAL CAREER

Sources providing material on the life and career of *Court and Country*'s author, Zhang Zhuo, have left a trail of sporadic, incomplete, and contradictory evidence. These piecemeal traces offer glimpses of a figure almost too intriguing and multifaceted to be credible; however, as Herman Melville remarks in *The Confidence-Man*, "no writer has produced such inconsistent characters as nature herself has." Melville elaborates by recounting a story about the platypus: "When the duck-billed beaver of Australia was first brought stuffed to England, the naturalists, appealing to their classifications, maintained that there was, in reality, no such creature; the bill in the specimen must needs be, in some way, artificially stuck on."[1]

In reassembling the fragments and shards that remain to us, I have come to see Zhang Zhuo as a supremely duck-billed character. That he survived in the treacherous world of Wu Zhao was a testament to his multitudinous skills; he was at once a sly poet; an ingenious yet self-defeating academic; a diplomat; an intrepid travel writer of great penetration, scope, and imagination; an inventor of fictional genres (including the novelette and erotic fiction); and an audacious political schemer and gadfly. Indeed, perhaps it is because Zhang is such an original that he is able to convey something intact and genuine about the alien world of Emperor Wu Zhao.

Zhang Zhuo was born in 658, during the early years of the reign of Tang emperor Gaozong,[2] shortly after the ruler elevated Wu Zhao to become his empress. Zhang came from Luze in Shenzhou (in modern-day Hebei). His life and career spanned the reigns of Gaozong, Wu Zhao, Zhongzong, Ruizong, and the first half of the lengthy reign of Xuanzong.[3]

INTRODUCTION

Zhang Zhuo's polite name (*zi* 字), the name men took upon reaching their maturity, was Wencheng, meaning Literary Success or Literary Fruition. His pen name (*hao* 號) was Fu Xiuzi, Master Who Drifts then Rests. This pen name—meant to suggest the peripatetic nature of his checkered career—is drawn from a passage in which the Daoist sage Zhuangzi articulates the nature of a Daoist sage: "In life it is as if he drifts along, in death it is as though he is merely resting."[4] *Court and Country* relates the story behind his peculiar given name, Zhuo 鷟. Young Zhang Zhuo

> *dreamed that a huge purple bird patterned in five-colors descended in the family's great hall. He informed his grandfather, who explained, "This is an auspicious sign. In the past, Eastern Han scholar Cai Heng said, 'There are five kinds of phoenixes. The vermilion one is known as the patterned phoenix. The black one is called the simurgh. The yellow one is the yuanchu* 鵷鶵 *, the male phoenix from the Southern Seas. The white one is the honghu* 鴻鵠 *, a high-soaring swan phoenix. And the purple one is called the yuezhuo* 鸑鷟 *.' This purple bird assists the supreme phoenix. This dream presages your aid and support of the emperor."*[5] (3.61)

Here, as with so much else of what we know about Zhang Zhuo, information about Zhang's life and career comes from Zhang himself! His grandfather's (obviously flattering) interpretation of his dream furnishes the lucky name that he hopes might help his precocious and highly intelligent scion rise to aid the emperor as a chief minister, just as the colorful *yuezhuo* helps the regal phoenix. These aspirations seemed attainable when the prodigy Zhang passed the "presented scholar" (jinshi 進士) examination at 17 and was formally introduced and recognized before Tang emperor Gaozong and his consort, Wu Zhao, in the mid-to-late 670s. As he traveled to the capital, *Court and Country* tells us that he "dreamt that he was enveloped by a felicitous cloud" (3.61), auguring success. Sure enough, he then passed a series of eight special examinations, scoring highest marks on every one. His answers on these examinations were especially brilliant, prompting Examiner Qian Weidao to affirm that Zhang's answers were "first in the entire empire" (3.61).[6] This stunning success on examinations showed Zhang's tremendous potential, and seemed to suggest that the young *yuezhuo* was poised for flight. Shortly thereafter, Zhang was awarded the position of Defender of Xiangle County in Ningzhou, in modern-day Gansu, along the Hexi Corridor at the start of the Silk Road. Despite this promising beginning, however, his half-century official career was unremarkable—full of low-to-mid-ranking positions, ups and downs, and demotions after locking horns with the powerful.

At some juncture, around the time Zhang Zhuo was 20, he sought to marry into the Su family. The Su patriarch sized him up as a prospective son-in-law and remarked, "While you, Sir, have talent, you will never gain wealth and influence. You'll perish after reaching fifth rank." The Su father then married his daughter off to another official—one of Zhang's colleagues from the same hometown, Luze—with greater promise of future rank and wealth, despite the man's swarthy complexion and diminutive size.[7]

During Gaozong's final years and Wu Zhao's regency (684–690), Zhang made no real career progress, but remained a local official, apparently moving laterally between posts as a low-ranking Defender in different counties. He served as a Defender in Heyang County, closer to Wu Zhao's capital, Luoyang.[8] While there, he solved several cases. When a counterfeiter forged the seal of a warehouse supervisor and used it to sell grain, he tricked the man into incriminating himself. In another case,

> a donkey had been stolen then recovered, but its valuable saddle, worth 5000 cash, remained missing. Zhang Zhuo released the donkey, covering its head. The beast wandered straight back to the homestead where it had been kept; the valuable saddle was found hidden beneath a haystack. (5.109–10)

The thief was brought to justice. These cases made manifest Zhang's cleverness as an investigator and problem-solver. Such experiences doubtless inform Zhang's accounts of local officials (included in Chapter 4) whose shrewd detective work solved crimes and helped maintain a sense of peace and justice in their jurisdictions.

One of the official histories records that Zhang served as Defender of Chang'an, the capital. A Tang source reports his service as Defender of Luoyang, Wu Zhao's capital. He wrote a verse, "Cry of the Swallows," which includes a final stanza that reads,

> My alexandrite body, like a cumbersome weight.
> Dragged through the muck, my strength is slight.
> Yet I always surge to first place.
> Two rise, the pair flying off into space.

At the time, this poem was widely circulated; it seems to refer to Zhang's attainment of the foremost position on the examinations.[9]

Perhaps the proximity of these positions to Chang'an and to the Divine Capital (Shendu 神都)—as Wu Zhao dubbed her religiopolitical center, Luoyang—allowed Zhang Zhuo to network. Eventually, another official recommended him for the position of investigating censor during the Changshou era (692–694) or Zhengsheng era (694–695) of the female emperor's Zhou dynasty.[10] Though Zhang became part of the central bureaucracy for the first

INTRODUCTION

time, this was still not a high-ranking post, and he was soon demoted. A Tang source records that

> In the time of the Celestial Empress, when Turkish Khan Qapaghan captured emissary Ma Xiantong, he asked, "Where is Zhang Wencheng?"
> Ma answered, "He was recently demoted and sent off."
> Qapaghan answered, "If your country has a man of such mettle and fails to use his talents [...] the Han people are doomed."[11]

Sources place this conversation—which indicates that the Turkish khan knew of and revered Zhang Zhuo—in 700, during the later stages of Wu Zhao's reign. It is not clear that Zhang Zhuo held all of the aforementioned low-ranking county defender and county magistrate positions between the late 670s and 695; in addition, he may have held several of these offices between his dismissal from the Censorate in 701 and 711.

Court and Country contains a record of several low-level prefectural positions that Zhang Zhuo held late in Wu Zhao's reign. In 701, he was demoted from his position as censor to serve as a granary supervisor in Chuzhou in modern-day Zhejiang. Half a year later, as predicted by a diviner, he was transferred to become a revenue manager in Liuzhou (2.37), a remote prefecture in faraway Lingnan in the malarial south. Thereafter, he was recalled to serve as a district magistrate in Dezhou.[12]

Shortly after Wu Zhao's death and deposal, Zhang Zhuo re-emerged to pass two additional administrative examinations in 706.[13] In 711, excelling as always on the tests that comprised the state examination curriculum, Zhang Zhuo passed yet another exam, "virtue and worthiness," finishing third among the 28 successful candidates.[14] He was appointed as an Adjutant in a princely establishment charged with helping prepare Emperor Ruizong's fourth son, Prince of Qi Li Longfan, for future responsibilities involving rites, music, and other matters. This was still not a high-ranking position; he was probably seventh-ranked (of the nine ranks). Shortly, though, he was promoted to a position as Aide in the Court of State Ceremonial (sixth rank), a division of the Ministry of Rites charged with receiving foreign diplomats. There are several curious passages about this promotion in *Court and Country*:

> When Zhang Zhuo was an Adjutant in the establishment of the Prince of Qi, he dreamed that he was astride a donkey wearing crimson robes. Even in his sleep, he felt this peculiar, musing, "How is it that as a green-clad official I'm riding a horse, but, promoted to the ranks of the crimson-clad, I'm riding a donkey?" That year, after sitting for and passing the examination, he was promoted to a fifth-ranked position, Aide in the Court of State Ceremonials. (3.61)

Homophones for the first two characters in the Department of State Ceremonials (*Honglusi* 鴻臚寺) are "red" (*hong* 紅) and donkey (*lu* 驢). Thus, his dream of riding a donkey while clad in red robes proved prophetic.[15] This story may have marked a promotion from seventh to sixth rank, as an official Tang history indicates that the position of Aide in the Court of State Ceremonials is a sixth-ranked position.[16]

Another passage from this same year—which arguably marked the pinnacle of Zhang Zhuo's political career—recounts a strange incident that augured further good fortune for the Zhangs in 711:

> *When Wencheng was Aide in the Court of State Ceremonial, rats gnawed on his cap, belt, and green robes. A large, chestnut-sized spider hung down from his bedroom doorframe. Several days later, there was an amnesty and his rank was raised to fifth. His son, after considering killing the creatures, had not, and the rats almost gnawed through his belt, too. Shortly thereafter, the son was appointed Boye County Defender.*[17] (1.18)

Emperor Ruizong issued an amnesty that elevated officials of fourth rank and below by one grade in the summer of 711.[18] The decision of Zhang Zhuo's son to spare the rats (just as Ruizong would spare lives by issuing the amnesty) is linked to the family's good fortune: Zhang's promotion to fifth rank and his son's appointment.

Court and Country contains yet another account of a strange omen from this period of Zhang's career. From the passage, we learn that Zhang held the title Director of the Court of Watches, an office responsible for supervising the establishment of the heir apparent:[19]

> *When Zhang Wencheng became Director of the Court of Watches, his wife heard an owl hooting in a tree in the courtyard at dawn and, taking it as an evil omen, spat toward the creature. Wencheng simply said, "Hurry up and clean the floors. I'm about to be promoted." Before he'd finished speaking, guests arrived at the gate to offer congratulations.* (1.18)

Director of the Court of Watches, a fourth-ranked position, was the highest position and rank Zhang Zhuo reached. This achievement indicates he had been promoted and transferred to the princely establishment of Li Longji, the future Emperor Xuanzong. It is not clear why and how Zhang Zhuo knew the owl's usually ominous call was auspicious in this instance.

While Zhang Zhuo was briefly part of Xuanzong's princely establishment, it most certainly did not help his career once Xuanzong became emperor. In the early years of Xuanzong's reign (712–756), Zhang Zhuo faced several crises. He was nearly killed and twice banished from the capital. When Censor and "cruel official" Li Quanjiao impeached Zhang in 714 and Zhang was exiled, the family hired several Daoists to determine his fate. The incident is described in *Court and Country*:

> *Liang Xuzhou, a Daoist from Liangzhou, used the "nine palaces" astrological method of fortune-telling to determine Zhang's fate.*[20] *The Daoist said, "The Five Demons of the lunar lodges have extended their lifespans, though the handle of the Northern Dipper nears its demise: Zhang is confronting a great crisis of his life. Following the divination of the Zhou Book of Changes he will encounter great terror and distress, but because the divination also shows dispersion, so, like wind on water, this crisis will ultimately pass." The Zhangs also asked a second Daoist from Anguo Monastery, Li Ruoxu—only telling him Zhang Zhuo's horoscope.*[21] *The Daoist investigated and said, "This year this individual is entrapped in the Celestial Prison. He will first be sentenced for a capital crime but will avoid death. Otherwise, he may succumb to an incurable illness and perish." As predicted, Censor Li Quanjiao impeached him and he was sentenced to death by imperial order. But Minister of Justice Li Rizhi, and other officials like Zhang Tinggui, Cui Xuansheng, and Cheng Xingmou all interceded on his behalf, petitioning for a reduction of sentence. In the end, his death sentence was commuted to distant banishment in Lingnan. This is proof that the predictions of this pair of Daoists were credible.* (1.2)

Only after Zhang's son memorialized, begging to take his father's place, did several officials convince the sovereign to be lenient and reduce Zhang Zhuo's sentence to distant exile.

Apparently, Zhang was recalled fairly soon. Two years later, he provoked the ire of Yao Chong, a powerful chief minister in the court of Xuanzong, and was again sentenced to death. Tang histories record damning characterizations of his personality. One records that "Zhang Zhuo's character was high-strung and impetuous, a nature ill-suited to literati–officials. Upright gentlemen loathed him; Yao Chong found him particularly insufferable."[22] Another describes him as "excitable and impetuous, dissolute and unrestrained, unfit for the company of proper gentlemen."[23] Based on such descriptions, Howard Levy opines that Zhang "must have had a sharp and critical pen; he incurred the wrath of influential officials and was known for the tendency to make extremely humorous remarks, presumably at the expense of others. He was demoted during the reign of [Wu Zhao], whose administration he criticized, and was later exiled during […] Xuanzong's Kaiyuan era."[24] Tony Qian points out one further reason for Yao Chong's animosity: Zhang Zhuo wrote a literary judgment (*pan* 判: discussed below) criticizing a 705 coup which Yao Chong backed—the coup that removed Wu Zhao from power and restored the Tang. Zhang Zhuo claimed that the trespass of the coup members and the imperial bodyguards—using numerous florid examples from canonical literature to corroborate his argument—was technically not authorized under Tang law.[25]

Another reason underlying Zhang's dispute with Yao Chong may have been a debate over the best way to manage the plague of locusts that beset the North China Plain in 715 and 716.[26] Zhang's criticism of the chief minister's proactive measures to rid the country of the scourge—aggressively catching and destroying the crop-devouring insects—appears in *Court and Country*:

> *In the 4th year of Kaiyuan, in Henan and Hebei locusts became a pestilence. Each big as a finger, their flying swarm blocked out the sun, eating every sprout, blade of grass, tree leaf and even roots, leaving nothing at all. By imperial order, emissaries were dispatched to advise prefectural and county officials on how to get rid of them. Those who caught a shi of locusts were given a shi of grain in return; those who caught a* dou *of locusts were likewise given a* dou *of grain. Holes were excavated to bury them, but for every shi of grasshoppers buried, ten shi were born. Grasshopper eggs covered the ground, each the size of a grain of panicled millet, half a cun thick. The Master Who Drifts then Rests said, "In the past, under the Martial and Civil Sagely August Emperor Taizong, a great swarm of locusts settled over greater Chang'an. At his order, some locusts were gathered so that he might observe them. He seized a large one from his bodyguard and cursed the creature: 'It is Our policy and punishments that are out of kilter, Our benevolence and faith that do not yet warrant confidence. Therefore, it is suitable that you devour my heart rather than harm the sprouts and grain of the people.' He then swallowed them. Almost immediately, a flock of a million crane-like birds descended and ate all of the locusts within a single day. This was a spiritual response to his virtuous action. If heaven's response was merely incidental, this wouldn't happen. If heaven decides to be punitive, even if you bury locusts, more will be born. It is suitable that you cultivate illustrious virtue and prudently mete out punishment in order to respond to heaven's censure. How is it that you do not cultivate virtue in order to avert disaster, but simply presume that by killing the locusts you might avert calamity? This path recommended by chief minister Yao Chong lacks harmonious principle."* (Sup., 169)

Zhang ultimately lost this debate. His argument does not appear in any of the dynastic histories. Presumably, he simply included his own argument in *Court and Country* for posterity. Though elsewhere Zhang expressed skepticism about auspicious and inauspicious omens, in this instance he subscribed to the logic that, since the locusts were a heaven-sent calamity, the ruler's cultivation of virtue, not human action, was the best response to avert the crisis.

He lost more than the debate. Yao Chong accused Zhang Zhuo of administrative malfeasance in Jiangnan. Zhang was sentenced to death. Following a long and storied stylized tradition of extreme self-denigration in such cases, Zhang wrote a plea to the emperor, Xuanzong, claiming he was "a piece of excrement who deserves ten thousand deaths" and comparing himself to an insect; he begged for 100 more days to finish up his writings—a lifetime of "poems, rhapsodies, memorials, records, and other works"—so that he might present them to court.[27] Xuanzong's personal intervention does not seem to have been necessary; after several officials interceded on Zhang's behalf, his punishment was reduced to banishment to Lingnan.[28]

In a diminished role in exile, he served as an administrative aide for several years in Gongzhou Prefecture, in what is today an autonomous region of the Zhuang minority in Guangxi Province.[29] Eventually, after political allies disputed the severity of his punishment, Zhang was recalled and given the position of supernumerary official in the Transit Authorization Bureau, a branch of the Ministry of Justice charged with monitoring movement through ports and city gates. Such supernumerary positions were half-salaried, an indication that Zhang may have had few bureaucratic responsibilities in his later years. Zhang died in this position in 731 at the age of 73.

ZHANG ZHUO'S LITERARY CAREER: FRAMING *COURT AND COUNTRY*

The *Old Tang History* relates that Zhang Zhuo's literary fame reached such proportions that "all in the realm knew his name, and even the lowly and unlearned had memorized and could recite his works."[30] In addition, he was known for his literary prowess by other luminaries. Poet–official Yan Banqian remarked, "The words of Master Zhang are as precious as bronze cash, always right on the money: ten thousand arrows fired, ten thousand on target." People of the time called him the "Bronze Cash Scholar."[31] His works—particularly his first work, *Grotto of a Playful Goddess*—were propagated far and wide; Zhang enjoyed a lofty reputation in the Korean kingdom Silla and in Japan. Every time these "eastern barbarians" would send emissaries to the Chinese court, the ambassadors brought gold to purchase his work. In this manner, word of his talent and reputation had spread afar. Yet Zhang Zhuo had his detractors. One of the Tang state histories offers the following literary criticism: "In writing prose, every character Zhang wrote was accurate; yet his words, while elaborate and florid, were short on principle. His works were satirical and slanderous, ornate and vulgar, but they were widely circulated in his period and in later eras his works circulated widely."[32]

Zhang Zhuo is not the most reliable narrator. He was the smartest guy in the room who all too often, sometimes to his detriment, felt the need to show off his intelligence. From his beginnings as a young prodigy and a brilliant writer, he was never able to parlay his literary talent into the highest rank and status. One gets the impression that he was vainglorious and took delight in using his keen wit to slice colleagues to ribbons.

Steeped in Confucian learning from an early age, he and other Confucian literati had to come to terms with the anomaly of having a female ruler presiding over the empire. Compiled after Wu Zhao's death, Zhang's *Court and Country* consistently depicts the female sovereign in an ugly light. He devotes an inordinate amount of time and space to passages delineating the violence and savagery of her "cruel officials," and spins detailed stories of her garish male favorites. Such accounts purport to expose a pervasive culture of sycophancy that, at every turn, arouses Zhang's contempt, mockery, and censure.

While several other works are attributed to Zhang, the three most significant are *Grotto of a Playful Goddess* (*Youxianku* 游仙窟), *Judgments on Dragon Sinew and Phoenix Marrow* (*Longjin fengsui* 龍筋鳳髓), and *Court and Country*. A brief exploration of Zhang Zhuo's other works will help further illuminate this curious man and his character.

Likely written when he was a young man, *Grotto of a Playful Goddess* features the beau ideal pair in premodern China—the handsome and gifted young scholar (*caizi* 才子) and the beauty (*mei nü* 美女)—the archetypal couple in later romances and novels. In what Howard Levy terms "China's first novelette,"[33] Zhang Zhuo's *Grotto* helped define this genre of romance stories, which paired promising young scholars and examination candidates with beauties. Back in premodern times, it was for this work—considered humorous and provocative at best, frivolous and salacious at worst—that Zhang Zhuo was best known. Yao Ping classifies *Grotto* as "part of the first wave of erotica in Chinese history."[34]

The plot of *Grotto* follows a young scholar as he travels through the rugged and mountainous Northwest, where Zhang took his first position as Defender of Xiangle County. He ends up staying a most memorable night in the compound of a lovely young widow. Indeed, there is more than a bit of autobiography and fanciful aggrandizement in *Grotto*: the young libertine protagonist of this amorous adventure is named Zhang and at one point the beauty, Tenth Lady, addresses him as Wencheng, Zhang's polite name.[35] Flirtation and titillation arise not from long moonlit strolls along sandy beaches, but from an artful exchange of lofty aristocratic lineages as the scholar woos his intended paramour through the performance of literary prowess and familiarity with the classics. The protagonist eloquently displays that these canonical works could be artfully and poetically redeployed as titillating double entendres, a fact that the well-educated gentlelady grasps and volleys back to the handsome young official, displaying her own literary skills and willingness to play the game. To further set the mood and ambience, after prolonged badinage they engage in drinking games, partake of rare delicacies, and watch and participate in dances, all amid silk brocaded rugs and serenaded by a dulcimer. In some respects, their courtship is not so different from some modern romance: mood is set with music, delicious food, and artfully suggestive repartee. Blunt expression of one's desire would be witless and vulgar. The erotic is discovered, by and large, in mutual teasing, titillation, and flirtatious wordplay. Such intellectual foreplay far exceeds the consummation. As the evening progresses, the lyrical sparring continues as "[b]oldly suggestive verse about writing brushes, wine vessels, and wine ladles raise emotional temperatures."[36] Finally, as the two match wits playing "double-six" (*shuangliu* 雙六), a form of backgammon, the scholar proposes a win-win wager: if Tenth Lady wins, she gets to sleep with him; if he wins, he gets to sleep with her.

Tenth Lady, the woman the scholar woos, is described as an elegant and ethereal, divine presence. This was a time-honored form of flattery: long before the Tang, there were stories of hierogamous dalliances with goddesses. Tang poets often employed this tactic, waxing rhapsodic by comparing the prospective courtesans or paramours for whom they yearned to female deities or lovely fairies. The endurance of this poetic device suggests such verbal stratagems must have proven effective.

While Zhang's *Grotto* possesses and sustains the aesthetic verve and sensual energy of Tang poetry, Levy praises the complete absence of "Confucian didacticism" and moralizing in the text, remarking,

> the roles of the sexes were described in original imagery which was in sharp contrast to the stereotyped expressions used mechanically by countless generations of Chinese writers and copied from the *Book of Odes* and other revered classics. The only ethical imperative in the T'ang novelette was the subtle reminder to the reader of the inevitability of parting and of the pain which parting brings.[37]

The text enjoyed greater fame abroad than at home—particularly in neighboring Korean kingdoms and on the Japanese archipelago. The first novel of any sort introduced in premodern Japan, *Grotto* exerted a tremendous influence on the literary imagination, and spawned numerous imitations in the centuries that followed.[38]

Probably written shortly after Wu Zhao's death, *Judgments on Dragon Sinew and Phoenix Marrow* was a collection of "literary judgments" (*pan* 判)—a category of test-texts written in a "highly stylized prose, rather than technical legal" jargon that candidates composed as part of the civil service exams. The perfect "literary judgment" should feature an "exhaustive accumulation of literary, historical, and cultural" precedents to showcase the breadth of the writer's classical learning, all rendered with an eloquent flourish.[39] Zhang was known for writing "the most ornate and erudite" literary judgments; thus he left a collection of his meticulously crafted, persuasive literary judgments—all couched in florid language and studded with a dazzling array of classical allusions—for posterity.⁴⁰ His literary and aesthetic skill amplified the rhetorical force of his essays.

Not everyone was impressed. Southern Song chronicler and intellectual gadfly Hong Mai found Zhang's judgments tedious and "unreadable," opining that Zhang "only knows how to accumulate stories from the past, but when it comes to sentencing or discussions of the law, [his work] is shallow and without substance."⁴¹ In his study of this text, Tony Qian remarks that Zhang's judgments reflect a "lack of restraint and pride in showing off his erudition," providing a glimpse of the "cantankerous and haughty attitude that must have made Zhang hard to get along with."⁴² To Zhang, literary style (the deft use of the calligraphy brush) was more important than the substance of the case at hand. He played fast and loose, and rarely let the facts of a case obstruct a good historical or literary allusion. One can assume that Zhang followed a similar path in *Court and Country*: he never allowed facts to interfere with lewd gossip, juicy anecdotes, and good storytelling.

Court and Country was compiled decades after Wu Zhao's death, its vignettes and anecdotes garnered during Zhang Zhuo's half-century of peregrinations across the empire during his lengthy, if relatively inglorious, official career. Jack Chen has remarked that the sort of anecdotes that Zhang Zhuo gathers "represent items of interest that are not integrated into larger narrative structures, but are dispersed or freely circulating, necessitating the work of an editor or compiler who will collate them into publishable form."⁴³ Zhang Zhuo clearly felt up to this task, confident that he possessed both the knowledge and intellectual gravitas to craft a curious and worthwhile assemblage of stories. Ellen Cong Zhang has illustrated that the miscellanies and notes of Song scholars "celebrated the role of extensive travel, social gathering, and personal exploration" that helped define these men as cosmopolitan "erudite scholars."⁴⁴ A prototype to these later works, *Court and Country* enabled Zhang Zhuo to record the breadth of his knowledge and experience with signature panache. As the narrator of these anecdotes, Zhang also interprets them and sometimes offers his thoughts, assuming a measure of intellectual and moral authority.⁴⁵ This work was also connected to Zhang Zhuo's reputation and his legacy. Anna Shields points out that "literati chroniclers" like Zhang Zhuo "lived in a world where writing, politics, and social status were inextricably intertwined."⁴⁶

"To rule the world," Robert Campany observed in his investigations of early medieval China, "was to collect the world. Governance entailed [...] placing the periphery, especially that which was anomalous in the periphery, into some systematic relationship with the center [...] Once things were collected, writing enabled them to be situated and depicted in a unified taxonomic field [...] structured according to proper moral principles and correlative categories." To an extent, *Court and Country*—with its accounts of the supernatural, of the flora and fauna of remote regions, and of the cultural Other—can be understood as part of what Campany terms the "cosmographic enterprise" of the center.[47] Zhang Zhuo, in a sense, was continuing a long tradition of collecting accounts of the strange and peculiar and rendering them into a culturally legible form for his primary audience, fellow literati in the political center.

There are some significant problems with *Court and Country* as a historical document. First and foremost, the original version composed by Zhang Zhuo has not survived. *Court and Country*, recorded in subsequent state histories as part of the lexicon of books in the Tang imperial library, originally had 20 chapters and three supplemental chapters.[48] The six-chapter version of the text that we have inherited first appears in a late Ming dynasty source, Chen Jiru's *Secret Satchel from the Hall of Precious Colors* (*Baoyantang miji* 寶顏堂秘笈). In the Qing, this abbreviated version is included in Emperor Qianlong's massive Four Warehouses project to gather (and selectively censor) all past knowledge. More recently, scholars have salvaged a seventh, supplemental chapter comprised of fragments not included in the six surviving chapters that have been culled from other sources in which Zhang Zhuo is cited as the author of a passage. Passages have been recovered from Duan Chengshi's *Miscellaneous Morsels of the Youyang Region* (*Youyang zazu* 酉陽雜俎) from the late Tang, Li Fang's 李方 early Song-era *Extensive Records of the Taiping Era* (*Taiping guangji* 太平廣記; hereafter *Extensive Records*),[49] Tao Zongyi's 陶宗儀 fourteenth-century anthology *Tales from Beyond the City Walls* (*Shuofu* 説郛), and other sources. Perhaps the 20-chapter original was topically organized, but the inherited, woefully incomplete version—six chapters plus assembled scraps gleaned from other sources—lacks any clear or coherent structure:

Six chapters plus additional fragments; a total of 416 passages.
Chapter 1: 78 passages
Chapter 2: 61 passages
Chapter 3: 66 passages
Chapter 4: 47 passages
Chapter 5: 60 passages
Chapter 6: 58 passages
Supplemental*: 86 passages

*Cobbled together in modern editions from passages attributed to *Court and Country* in later sources, but not included in the six-chapter versions that appear in *Baoyantang miji* or Four Warehouses.

Furthermore, the text is clearly corrupt. Passages come from the Tianbao era (742–756) of Xuanzong's reign, which began a decade after Zhang Zhuo's death. On several occasions, Xuanzong's posthumous name is used—possibly an error of careless later copyists and compilers reassembling the text from other texts. Other passages come from the late Tang, a century after Zhang's death! As Levy frames it, "The original composition must have been lost after which someone else, centuries later, perhaps toward the end of the Tang, gathered records together and compiled the work under the same name."[50]

There are still other peculiarities. *Court and Country* refers to Wu Zhao's Zhou dynasty roughly 50 times; however, in three cases—two of which appear in the supplemental final section of fragments culled from a wide range of later texts—it is called the "illegitimate Zhou" (*wei* Zhou 偽周). If Zhang Zhuo were trying to drive home a point that the woman emperor's dynasty was spurious, he could routinely use the *wei Zhou* label to call attention to its lack of legitimacy. Moreover, there is an odd inconsistency to authorial self-reference in the work. The name Zhang Zhuo is used 20 times; his pen name, Master Who Drifts then Rests, appears five times; and his polite name, Zhang Wencheng, shows up six times.

Despite these doubts about the text, *Court and Country* provides more than 400 stories and fragments reputedly drawn from things that Zhang Zhuo heard and saw, many illuminating regional customs, folklore, or the lives of otherwise unknown individuals. While he failed to reach the highest echelons of court and to have an impactful political career, Zhang Zhuo blazed an incandescent path across the literary world, writing China's first novel (arguably the world's first novel), his works creating a buzz well beyond court-literati circles, so that he became something of an international celebrity, known in the Luoyang marketplace, among the Tujue Turks, and in Nara Japan.

EMPEROR WU ZHAO AND THE EMPIRE OVER WHICH SHE PRESIDED[51]

The emperor was the epicenter of the Chinese medieval mind. It is necessary, therefore, to provide in this Introduction a brief biography of the central and recurring figure in *Court and Country*: female emperor Wu Zhao. Zhang Zhuo served under Wu Zhao until he was an official with grizzled whiskers. His vignettes offer a first-person witness of her realm.

In patriarchal medieval China, a society where "men were venerated and women denigrated" (*nanzun, nübei* 男尊女卑), it took a favorable confluence of circumstance, opportunity, ambition, and prodigious talent for Wu Zhao to ascend the throne. Emerging from provincial obscurity, Wu Zhao, the second daughter in the second marriage of a Taiyuan lumber magnate and regional official, remarkably ascended to become the first and only female emperor in China's 5000-year history. Prior to inaugurating her reign as emperor, Wu Zhao had three decades of political seasoning, becoming intimately familiar

INTRODUCTION

with court politics and administration. First, she ruled in tandem with her husband Gaozong (r. 655–683), then presided over the court as Grand Dowager (684–690) after his death. In 690, she established her own Zhou dynasty, which lasted until 705. Though in the patriarchal Confucian historiography she is often dismissively portrayed as a cruel, lascivious, unprincipled, and manipulative usurper, closer scrutiny reveals a nuanced historical personage possessed of a peculiar sense of humor and a staggering political acumen, a woman keenly aware of the impediments imposed upon her gender, and sensitive to the myriad challenges of governing a multiethnic, religiously pluralistic empire.

Central Asian steppe culture and Buddhism played significant roles in her improbable rise. Wu Zhao was born into the dawning Tang dynasty, a sprawling cosmopolitan empire arising from four centuries of chaos and warfare to encompass many lands, peoples, and religions. A ceaseless flow of Silk Road caravans carried new fashion, goods, and ideas from Persia and Central Asia, and the resultant mélange of nomadic steppe and sedentary, agrarian Chinese heartland formed a cultural hybrid that loosened the hold of Confucian mores upon women of the early Tang. Undoubtedly, this hybrid culture enabled the germination of Wu Zhao. In addition, Buddhism—the "most popular and influential faith" in early Tang China[52]—was wildly popular among commoners and elites. This pan-Asian religion crossed ethnic and cultural boundaries, linking India, Southeast Asia, Central Asia, China, Korea, and Japan. Buddhist temples, pagodas, and statuary filled the twin capitals, Luoyang and Chang'an, and dotted the surrounding countryside. An ardent sponsor and patron of the Buddhist faith, Wu Zhao funded the Buddhist establishment, which reciprocated with support for her ascendancy and sovereignty.

As a child, Wu Zhao followed her parents through a series of provincial official appointments; her mother was a devout Buddhist and scion of the hybrid Chinese–Central Asian family that had ruled the short-lived Sui dynasty (581–618). After her father's death, Wu Zhao left her widowed mother to enter the imperial harem of the second emperor of the Tang, the celebrated Taizong, as a fifth-ranked concubine.[53] The scanty records of the dozen years she languished in his seraglio indicate that she neither gained Taizong's favor nor advanced in rank. After a series of succession disputes, a weary and dying Taizong settled upon his ninth son—the youngest of his three sons with his consort, Empress Changsun—the future Gaozong, and instructed the ill-prepared young man in the art of statecraft. While the heir apparent spent more time in the inner quarters with the convalescing ruler, Wu Zhao developed a deep bond with him. After Taizong's death in 649, Wu Zhao and the other concubines were sent to a Buddhist convent. Shortly thereafter, Gaozong recalled her to the inner palace and promoted her to second-ranked concubine, a Lady of Luminous Deportment. After she bore several sons, Gaozong elevated Wu Zhao to empress in 655, removing barren Empress Wang, a woman of eminent background.

Less than a decade into his reign, in his early thirties, Gaozong suffered a serious stroke. No longer capable of managing affairs of state, he began to share imperial responsibilities with Wu Zhao. Beginning in 660, she jointly deliberated upon administrative decisions with her imperial husband from behind a curtain in the audience hall. People of the time called the co-ruling husband-and-wife team the "Two Sages" (*Ersheng* 二聖). Over time, it became increasingly apparent that Wu Zhao—four years her husband's elder—was the alpha sage, the stronger voice in this seventh-century power couple. The *Comprehensive Mirror* records that,

> When the emperor held an audience, the empress sat to his rear behind a curtain, listening to all affairs of state, large and small. Every decision— demotion and promotion, life and death—issued from the mouth of the empress. The Son of Heaven merely sat with folded hands.[54]

To normalize her presence outside of the inner palace, Wu Zhao staged numerous spectacular ceremonies. During her first decades as empress, she occasionally performed a vernal sacrifice to the Silk Goddess, paralleling the emperor's spring plowing rites. She led eminent ladies of the state to garner mulberry leaves to feed silkworms.[55] Silk weaving was the quintessential vocation for women—as a maxim manifesting the gendered division of labor in traditional China says, "men plow and women weave."[56] Her central role in such public and visible rites marked Wu Zhao as "First Lady" of the Empire. She also repurposed other major ceremonies of state, fashioning for herself a significant public role where formerly the empress had played no part. In the grand *feng* and *shan* (*feng shan* 封禪) rites—the rarest and grandest of all rites of state where the emperor would broadcast harmony and order with Heaven and Earth from one of the sacred marchmounts of China—Wu Zhao convinced Gaozong to allow her to perform an offering at Mount Tai in 666.[57] Her ongoing engagement both in routine governance and in rituals of state acclimated court and country to her presence.

By the mid-670s, when an aspiring, adolescent Zhang Zhuo first sat for examinations in hopes of becoming an influential court official, Wu Zhao had almost two decades of court experience. When her son, heir apparent Li Hong, died of tuberculosis in 676, ailing Gaozong offered to abdicate the throne to her. While Wu Zhao turned down the offer, she assembled an informal group of literary masters committed to bolstering her anomalous political authority.

After Gaozong's death in late 683, the eldest remaining son of the Two Sages, Zhongzong, took the throne and rapidly proved himself an incompetent and incapable emperor. Less than two months into his feckless reign, widowed empress Wu Zhao deposed and banished him. Subsequently, she assumed the role of grand dowager-regent. She designated her tractable youngest son emperor even as she relegated him to the palace of the crown prince. Removing the curtain that had concealed her as Gaozong's co-ruler, Wu Zhao "oversaw the court and issued edicts" (*linchao chengzhi* 臨朝稱治) just like an emperor.[58] To show the empire that she was the new ruler presiding over a new era, she changed the court colors and altered names of offices to follow ornate, archaic precedent of the past Zhou dynasty, revered as a halcyon age of perfect government. Furthermore, she designated Luoyang as her Divine Capital, establishing a new seat of power away from the Tang capital, Chang'an.[59]

Though Wu Zhao had not formally declared the advent of a new dynasty, these steps alarmed the Li family, the dynastic founders of the Tang. However, separate uprisings led by Li princes in 684 and 688 sputtered and failed. During her regency, to curb further rebellions and silence potential rivals, she utilized a notorious group of "cruel officials" (see Chapter 3). Feared and loathed by the Confucian court, these men perfected the art of fabricating conspiracies to ensnare potential challengers, devising elaborate tortures to extract confessions. While Wu Zhao disbanded these men once she felt secure in her power as emperor in the late 690s, Zhang Zhuo and others cited this reign of terror, the atrocities and torments that these men perpetrated, as evidence of the woman emperor's unconscionable cruelty.

For six years as grand dowager-regent, Wu Zhao tactfully delayed the fateful step of declaring herself emperor and launching her own dynasty. Along the way, she took incremental steps toward assuming the throne *de jure*. In accord with a time-honored tradition of gathering auspicious omens to augur the rise of a worthy new sovereign, a white stone with amethyst characters that read "When the Sage Mother is among the people, the realm will enjoy eternal prosperity" was "discovered" by her supporters in the Luo River in 688. Later, with due pomp and fanfare, Wu Zhao held a gala ceremony, assuming the title "Sage Mother, Divine Sovereign"; "Sovereign" (*huang* 皇) was part of the compound for emperor (*huangdi* 皇帝). To mark the occasion, she stood atop an altar on the banks of the Luo River, as court ministers, military officers, and foreign dignitaries paraded past, gifting her a trove of splendid birds, miraculous beasts, precious jewels, and other wondrous rarities.[60] This was a pivotal intermediate step.

THE WORLD OF WU ZHAO

In autumn 690, Wu Zhao ascended the throne as the first and only female emperor in Chinese history. For her dynasty's name she chose Zhou, echoing the idealized remote past era of King Wen, King Wu, and the Duke of Zhou, sage rulers long honored for transcendent virtue and perfect administration. She transformed Luoyang into an international cosmopolis rivaling Chang'an, mobilizing migrations of people and pushing an effort to build up new palaces and walls, vibrant markets to serve the growing population, and scores of canals for the increased traffic on waterways.

Recognizing the precarious position in which a woman with the effrontery to declare herself emperor placed herself, Wu Zhao creatively mustered a magnificent armature of symbols, omens, titles, and rites to substantiate her unusual political presence, all presented in a sensational, public style that became her trademark. In staging and representing such spectacles, Buddhism figured prominently. Decades before she became emperor, Wu Zhao had fostered deep connections with the Buddhist community. Her unstinting patronage won the support of the Buddhist establishment, which saw in her a charismatic champion to propagate their faith. At the same time, it infuriated many in the Confucian court, who felt their normative authority undermined and challenged. One of the Buddhist marvels was a spectacular ritual complex described in *Court and Country*, a cloud-piercing Buddhist pagoda nearly 1000 feet tall, housing a giant, lacquered 880-foot Buddha. This edifice was linked to another 300-foot building crowned by a ten-foot, gold-plated phoenix, a symbol of female imperial power, set above a celestial observatory with rooms representing the seasons and months (5.115). In 695, Wu Zhao erected a towering, octagonal Buddhist pillar surrounded by mysterious guardian beasts and topped by a scintillating fire pearl set on a cloud canopy and held aloft by a quartet of dragons. Shortly after her death, in an effort to restore a normative androcentric order, her grandson Xuanzong ordered this monument to international Buddhist pacifism pulled down and melted into weapons.[61] These monuments stood as signatures of her distinctive rule.

In military affairs and foreign relations, Wu Zhao took pains to prove that she was anything but soft or weak. With a surname Wu 武 meaning "martial," Wu Zhao attached great importance to recruiting capable generals—both Han Chinese and foreign. In 692, her forces defeated the Tibetans and reclaimed the Four Garrisons and its rich oases, which strengthened Chinese control over Silk Road commerce. Late in her reign, she also created the military examination (*wu ju* 武舉) to foster the development of capable and talented military officers.[62]

Bone-weary after a half century of governing, Wu Zhao's final years were unremarkable. In 698, recognizing that her Wu nephews were universally loathed, she named her son heir apparent, a decision that meant the Zhou dynasty would not outlive her reign. In her senescence, she lost, by degrees, the unrelenting strong will and acumen that had enabled her to control the court. Increasingly, she retreated to her inner palace, taking refuge with male favorites, the Zhang brothers, an exquisitely handsome pair of youths who turned her inner palace into a theatrical paradise. Nearing 80, she also turned to Daoism, like many Chinese emperors before and after her, seeking immortality. To this end, leaving her fractured court, she often headed for the hot springs and Daoist temples of Mount Song, south of Luoyang.

In 705, resenting the waxing political influence of the Zhangs and exploiting the infirmities of the aging emperor, a group of court ministers and imperial bodyguards staged a coup, butchering the Zhangs and forcing Wu Zhao into retirement. The Tang dynasty was restored. Wu Zhao died later that year and was interred with her husband, Gaozong, at Qianling, the only tomb in Chinese history to house two emperors.

In the didactic Confucian historiographical narrative that runs through subsequent imperial Chinese history, Wu Zhao is consistently demeaned and demonized. She is generally referred to as Grand Dowager or Empress Wu, and rarely acknowledged as emperor. Her dynasty is often called the "illegitimate Zhou." Moreover, she is accused of inhuman, barbarous acts of suspect historical accuracy: smothering her infant daughter and blaming it on Empress Wang, killing several of her sons, or practicing witchcraft to incapacitate her husband Gaozong. In assessing Wu Zhao's reign, Liu Xu, a Confucian historian of the Five Dynasties era, framed her in just such negative terms:

> Empress Wu's conspiracy to seize the position of Gaozong's legitimate wife by choking the breath from her own swaddling infant; her mincing and pickling of enemies, grinding their bones into pepper dust—who would not claim this to be egregious? This is the disposition of a licentious and jealous woman![63]

In short, she has long been judged a wicked woman, an anti-heroine, regicidal where the ideal male ruler was duly filial, volatile while he showed equanimity, corrupt where he was virtuous, lewd where he was the epitome of moderation, self-aggrandizing where he was austere. In literature, too, Wu Zhao has been reimagined in salacious caricature. In a Ming dynasty novella, *The Lord of Perfect Satisfaction*, she is cast as lust-driven, insatiably wanton, relentlessly seeking pleasure from her prodigiously endowed lover—his "meaty implement" could allegedly support a 45-pound rice bucket—while neglecting matters of state.[64] In Li Ruzhen's mid-Qing novel *Destinies of Flowers in the Mirror*, a hedonistic fox spirit in the guise of capricious Wu Zhao orders all of the flowers in the imperial garden to blossom in the dead of winter and is outraged when the fractious peony fails to bloom.[65] These hyperbolic, ero-grotesque representations of Wu Zhao are extensions of the long-standing Confucian depiction of a whimsical, willful, self-indulgent, and unnatural woman in power.

Yet even Confucian historians allowed Wu Zhao a certain grudging admiration for her statecraft and governance. Song dynasty historian Ouyang Xiu observed that, "Although she expelled the legitimate emperor and changed the dynastic name, still she alone issued rewards and punishments and did not surreptitiously delegate authority to ministers, allowing them to usurp power from above and govern from beneath."[66] Another Song historian, Sima Guang, similarly projected reluctant respect in his observation that,

> Even though the Grand Dowager excessively used emolument and rank to gain the hearts of the people, those not responsible in office were eventually dismissed and punished. The Grand Dowager grasped the handle of punishment and reward in order to administer the empire. Government issued from her alone. She possessed enlightened oversight and good judgment of character. Therefore, at that time outstanding and sagely men competed to be employed by her.[67]

These more generous assessments tally with historical reality: by most objective criteria, Wu Zhao's rule was successful. Economically and culturally, her achievements rival those of the best Tang emperors. There were no major peasant rebellions. She played a seminal role in the growth of East Asian Buddhism. She held on to the vast territories of the Tang empire, staving off powerful enemies. The significant growth in the registered population—from 3.8 million family households (19 million people) in 652 to 6.15 million (roughly 31 million people, assuming five persons per household) in 705—reflects administrative stability and economic prosperity.[68] With neither precedent nor sequel, Wu Zhao's remarkable achievement of becoming China's lone woman emperor stands as testament to her historical significance. She was an eminently capable ruler and a shrewd politician who dominated the Chinese court for the better part of a half-century.

ZHANG ZHUO'S REPRESENTATION OF WU ZHAO IN *COURT AND COUNTRY*

David McMullen characterizes the framers and jealous keepers of the Chinese historiographical tradition as a class of men who, wielding "enormous authority" and employing a "particularly high-sounding language," carefully cull and curate "the facts," in pursuit of their solemn mission of crafting moral narratives that tend to "reward the good and sort out the evil";

thereby, their enterprise can "demonstrate concisely, definitively, and for all time the truth of the Confucian political and ethical code."[69] A woman in the preeminent position of political power was anathema to Confucian traditions and values. Wu Zhao represented an unnatural anomaly, an abomination, an eclipse of the sun, a hen crowing to greet the dawn. After Wu's deposal, the restoration of the Tang dynasty, and her death in late 705, Confucian court officials and historians launched a campaign to systematically delegitimize and efface many political and personal vestiges of the female sovereign.

Zhang Zhuo's *Court and Country* was part of this early eighth-century revisionism, a kind of "cancel culture": his writings on Wu Zhao's person and court are geared toward denigrating the woman emperor and pointing out the corruption, arbitrariness, incompetence, and malfeasance that riddled her reign. Zhang also provides anecdotes of exemplary, principled Confucian officials who possessed the conviction and courage to remonstrate with Wu Zhao—often to their own detriment. In this sense, following a long, patriarchal historiographical tradition, Zhang provides a didactic morality play pitting avaricious, extravagant, corrupt, and callous sycophants against righteous, benevolent Confucian men of principle.

Knowing how problematic the re-assembly of *Court and Country* has been, I can only say I hope that the original 20-chapter version is discovered and that many of the passages on Wu Zhao from the extant version prove to be significantly corrupted. I express this hope not as a biographer and an apologist for Wu Zhao seeking her further historical rehabilitation, but based upon appreciation of Zhang Zhuo's prodigious literary and aesthetic talent. Despite ridicule and criticism from the prudish court, his early work enjoyed tremendous popularity in China and throughout Central and East Asia. Though not known as a poet, his verse stuck a chord in winding alleys, marketplaces, and taverns, and was recited everywhere. Many aspects of his life show that he was an intellectual maverick. Zhang Zhuo had a complicated and thorny relationship with the elite mandarins in the court—before, during, and especially after Wu Zhao's reign. His gifts far exceeded those of the men he often held in contempt. Clearly, he was never fully accepted or given his due within these claustrophobic circles. The negative assessments of his character in official histories tell the story of an enfant terrible, a contrarian whose penchant for mockery, casual arrogance, mercurial rashness, and caustic humor—which he often failed to keep concealed—chafed others greatly in the staid and modulated confines of the court. His early work was not Confucian-approved in tenor or substance, and his character marked him as a free-spirited misfit in the court, where on multiple occasions he antagonized the powerful. But passages on Wu Zhao and her minions that we find in

Court and Country, almost without exception, are boilerplate Confucian characterizations, devoid of Zhang's characteristic spark of quirky genius—as will become apparent in the following chapter. Many passages in his work are lively and idiosyncratic, not these flattened, stale, prepackaged cautionary tales about how women and power don't mix.

1

Wu Zhao: her inner palace, her inner circle

A WOODBLOCK PRINT OF Wu Zhao crowned with an elaborate imperial phoenix headdress appears in the section on "historical personages" in the early seventeenth-century Ming dynasty *Illustrated Encyclopedia of Heaven, Earth, and Man* (*Sancai tuhui* 三彩圖會; see Figure 1). While the broad forehead and square face of the grand dame depicted fit earlier descriptions of Wu Zhao appearing in standard histories, this conventionalized depiction of a cinch-lipped matron clad in ceremonial imperial regalia—and sporting an expression between irked and dour beneath her long, arched brows and above her rounded chin—does little to capture the robust personality and idiosyncratic character of China's only female emperor.

Predominantly negative in tenor, standard historical accounts of Wu Zhao nonetheless reflect a grudging appreciation of her far-reaching intellect and enormous capacity for subtle machinations. The *Old Tang History* characterizes her as "intelligent and tactful, possessing vast literary and historical learning."[1] Attesting to her *weiqi* master's ability to calculate and strategize, the *New Tang History* remarks that she "possessed a diverse repertoire of means for wielding power and was capable of countless tactical changes and permutations."[2]

Though Zhang Zhuo spent much of his career outside of the capitals, he served as a Censor in Wu Zhao's court. As mentioned in the Introduction, his characterization of the female emperor and her close adherents is congruent with a wider Confucian historiography that systematically demonizes her person and denigrates her reign. While passages in *Court and Country* offer glimpses of her character and personality, they also emphasize Wu Zhao's volatile swings between delight and rage, her uncritical acceptance of auspicious omens, and her penchant for luxury and excess. Most of these anecdotes lack the idiosyncrasies and nuance of Zhang's other stories. It is likely they were altered and flattened, retrofitted to Confucian precepts at some point between Zhang's death and the reappearance of an abridged *Court and Country* in the Ming, 800 years later.

Figure 1 A woodblock print of Wu Zhao from a Ming dynasty encyclopedia. This image is reproduced here with the generous permission of Shanghai guji chubanshe, which published a photographic reproduction of the *Sancai tuhua* in 1998.

OMENS AND SYMBOLS

Symbols and omens exercised an inordinate power in the world of Wu Zhao. Take, for example, this story from *Court and Country* of a staged cat-and-parrot show gone terribly awry:

> *In the time of Zetian, the Grand Dowager had a cat and a parrot trained to eat from a single vessel. The emperor ordered Censor Peng Xianjue to supervise a display of the unusual*

> *harmony between the two to a congregation of court officials. Before the display formally began, however, the famished cat tore the parrot asunder with its jaws and devoured it. Zetian was greatly embarrassed. Wu was the name of the ruling family of state, marking this incident as a dangerous and inauspicious harbinger.* (5.117)

Behind this anecdote, there is a complex backstory four decades in the making. In the mid-650s, not long after Wu Zhao had been elevated to empress, her formal rivals, displaced Empress Wang and Gaozong's erstwhile favorite Pure Consort Xiao, had been detained in a forsaken corner of the palace, where they were fed through a slit in the door. Learning that Gaozong had been in contact with these two, a wary Wu Zhao—only recently ensconced as empress—took callous and drastic measures to silence the women once and for all. After being beaten one hundred strokes and having their hands and feet severed, the pair were plunged into vats of fermented wine. Witnessing their painful death, Wu Zhao reputedly exulted, "Now you crones can get drunk to your very marrow!" In the final throes of lingering agony, Pure Consort Xiao uttered a dying imprecation: "Only because Little Miss Wu is an enchantress of a fox spirit have things reached this juncture! I shall be reincarnated as a cat and Little Miss Wu as a mouse, so that I can pounce on her and tear her throat out in vengeance."³ Learning of this curse, superstitious Wu Zhao banished cats from the imperial palace. It was presumably to publicly exorcise these demons that, 35 years later, Wu Zhao had the cat and parrot exhibition set before her court to broadcast to everyone that the old curse had been lifted amid the prosperity and harmony of her reign.⁴ The Chinese term for parrot, *wu* 鵡, is homophonous with and shares a common element with the Wu 武 in Wu Zhao's surname. Therefore, the parrot was readily understood as a representation of Wu Zhao.⁵

Court and Country repeatedly emphasizes that Wu Zhao was beholden to signs, symbols, and omens of all sorts. As such, Zhang's text presents the female emperor as prone to manipulation, an easy mark for hustlers and grifters seeking rapid advancement. She was profoundly concerned with collecting and displaying tokens of Heaven's validation of her reign. During her six years as grand dowager and in the first years of her Zhou dynasty, she meticulously accumulated and cataloged an impressive symbolic repertoire of auspicious portents, augural stones, and apocrypha, all carefully geared to legitimize her unprecedented ascent to the pinnacle of political power.

Wu Zhao's preoccupation with auspicious omens was not in the least uncommon. Erik Zürcher remarks that "signs and happenings reported" as auspicious omens were understood as "amazing, exceptional, and charged with deep significance […] but […] very much part of the natural order of things," "spontaneous reactions to the ruler's (or potential ruler's) virtue."⁶

In her study of auspicious omens and miracles in early and early medieval China, Tiziana Lippiello notes that "already in Han times (206 BC–220 AD), the need was felt of systematizing and cataloguing the great number of anomalous phenomena which, from time to time, were witnessed in all the prefectures and commanderies of the empire, and then reported to the central court where historians scrupulously recorded them."[7] In the late fifth or early sixth century, Shen Yue wrote a three-chapter treatise, part of his *History of the Liu Song Dynasty*, cataloging 94 different kinds of auspicious omens—ranging from the appearance of dragons, phoenixes, and numinous turtles, to auspicious clouds, miraculous herbs, plants, and mushrooms.[8] There were also evil omens that presaged disaster. "Anomalies," as Sarah Schneewind frames it, "were meaningful messages that signaled rightful retention or impending transfer of the Mandate of Heaven."[9] In fact, in times of dynastic change, contenders invariably mustered omens to make manifest Heaven's sanction; many emperors—especially at the outset of new dynasties—gathered auspicious omens as evidence that they were the rightful possessors of Heaven's mandate. Wu Zhao's father, Wu Shihuo, had furnished Tang founder Li Yuan, Gaozu, with a compendium of auspicious tokens demonstrating that Heaven, nature, and the cosmos, legitimated and sanctioned his rule.[10] Therefore, *Court and Country*'s criticism of Wu Zhao's fondness for auspicious signs and omens represents a starkly biased narrative; indeed, as we will see in Chapter 9, Zhang Zhuo himself was hardly skeptical of omens, and attached inordinate significance to dreams and signs.

The following passage from *Court and Country* contains a pair of anecdotes that also focus on Wu Zhao's predilection for omens:

> *Zetian was fond of auspicious signs. Low-level official Zhu Qianyi claimed that he had a dream that Zetian's white hair had turned black and that her missing teeth had regrown.*[11] *He was thereupon promoted to a position in the Ministry of Justice.*
>
> *The Court of Judicial Review had imprisoned more than 300 people. After the autumn equinox, in a corner of the prison yard they fashioned a five-foot long footprint of a divine being. In the middle of the night, they cried out in unison, then told the wardens that a golden-faced god standing thirty feet tall had proclaimed, "Fear not, though all of you have grievances and have been wrongly accused, the emperor, with her boundless graciousness and clemency, will grant you an amnesty." With a torch, they then illuminated the giant footprint. Wu Zhao issued an empire-wide amnesty and changed the reign era to Great Footprint.* (3.72–73)

In the latter anecdote, Wu Zhao alters the name of her reign era and issues a general amnesty in response to a manufactured omen. She frequently took such steps to accentuate auspicious occasions or commemorate personal triumphs. The group of prisoners—clearly aware of this predisposition—successfully engineered a hoax that prompted her to issue an amnesty, saving them from imprisonment.

In the former anecdote, credulous to a fault and susceptible to flattery, Wu Zhao promotes Zhu Qianyi, a low-ranking official, for reporting a dream about her personal rejuvenation. Such dreams were considered fit to be placed under the category of auspicious omens: the "Treatise on Auspicious Omens" (*Xiangrui zhi* 祥瑞志) in the *History of the Southern Qi* (*Nan Qi shu* 南齊書) records a number of the ruler's dreams and accompanying interpretations.[12] *Court and Country* later offers a more extensive account of Zhu Qianyi's alleged omens and Wu Zhao's responses thereto:

> *Zhu Qianyi was shallow and dull-witted, lacking in discernment; in appearance, he was hideous in the extreme. He forwarded a petition [to Wu Zhao], claiming, "Your humble minister has dreamed that Your Majesty will live 800 years." The emperor appointed him to the office of reminder, then he soon rose to an even higher position. When he returned from an assignment, he again forwarded a petition reading, "I have heard Mount Song chanting 'May the Emperor live Ten Thousand Years!'" Thereupon, the emperor gifted him a fish tally in a crimson purse, though he had not yet reached fifth rank.*[13] *When he wore the crimson fish purse on his green robes, there were none in court and abroad who didn't think it gauche and mocked him. Later, when the Qidan rebelled, an imperial edict stated that officials who furnished the military with a team of horses would be rewarded with fifth rank. Zhu purchased and presented a team of horses. Unable to wait, Zhu filed a memorial requesting crimson robes. The emperor was furious, and, responding to his case, wrote: "Release him from service! Send this bumpkin back to his rustic hovel at once." Outraged and filled with resentment, Zhu Qianyi died.*[14] (4.92)

As in the prior passage, Wu Zhao is depicted here as an aging, gullible ruler whose yearning for longevity enabled a status-seeking sycophant to climb the ranks by fabricating flattering dreams and omens. The ruler's shortcomings led to disruption at court, as Zhu was clearly out of place after his unwarranted promotions. Gifted a vermilion silk purse—an accessory usually reserved for high officials—he wore it anyway, though it clashed with his green robes: a fashion and sumptuary faux pas (for more on the significance of robe colors and fish tallies at court, see Chapter 2). Ultimately, his impatience to obtain a red robe to match his tally-bag proved his undoing. In the middle of a fierce war against the Qidan to the northeast, he had the short-sighted temerity to present a memorial before the court formally requesting advancement, thereby earning a temperamental rebuke and demotion from Wu Zhao. Like the story of the "Great Footprint," this one is intended to demonstrate that Wu Zhao's proclivity for uncritically believing and accepting omens led to poor decision-making, the trademark of a muddle-headed ruler (*hunjun* 昏君).

INTEMPERATE GRANNIE

Zhang Zhuo's *Court and Country* is full of maxims, aphorisms, and folk sayings that prove to be wise and prophetic. Take, for example, the following:

> *From the Xianheng era forward, people all said,*
>
> > Don't speak recklessly or Grannie will get riled.
> > When Third Uncle hears, he'll kill with a smile.
>
> *Later, as the saying predicted, Zetian took the throne and Filial and Harmonious succeeded her. Grannie is Zetian. Third Uncle means Filial and Harmonious, because he was her third son.* (1.12)

This little rhyme-chant implies that "Grannie" Wu Zhao possessed a volatile and mercurial temperament that one would be wise not to provoke. Though her son, Zhongzong, might wear a simpering smile, he could prove lethally unpredictable in his own right. Filial and Harmonious (Xiaohe 孝和) was his posthumous title. This historical allegory is intended to reflect, to an extent, popular perception among the denizens of Luoyang and Chang'an about the character of Wu Zhao and her son. One of the few cathartic outlets for the overworked and overtaxed commonfolk dwelling in the shadows of the palaces was the opportunity to lampoon or caricature rulers. Clever epithets like "Grannie" or "Third Uncle" enabled merchants manning their market stalls, manure collectors scouring the streets, or ironmongers at their forges to poke fun at the wealthy and powerful without explicitly naming names.

Yet such doggerel also had a darker aspect. Much like the ominous meanings underlying nursery rhymes like "London Bridge" in Western culture, folk ditties in medieval China carried sinister or prophetic undertones and held disconcerting hidden meanings. Like the rumblings of child sacrifice and the shadowy fear of being immured alive that cling to the ostensibly upbeat and lilting "London Bridge," the threat of running afoul of riled-up Grannie was dangerously real![15]

AN ALTERNATIVE PERSPECTIVE

Not every passage on Wu Zhao in *Court and Country* is categorically negative. One odd story reflects her fearlessness:

> *In the time of the Celestial Empress, Chief Steward Zhang Sigong presented beef jerky on top of which was a centipede as long as a chopstick. The Celestial Empress stored it in a jade box. The following day, she summoned Sigong and showed him, remarking, "This extremely*

toxic creature was on yesterday's jerky. Recently, a rooster ate a similar hundred-legged black insect and suddenly died. Its stomach was opened and inside was a house centipede. All of the other insects the rooster had eaten were digested, only this creature remained intact. Ever since yesterday We[16] have been nauseated and unable to eat." Sigong bowed his head and begged for death. She spared Sigong, but banished him and the cooks to Lingnan. (Sup., 169)

From this morsel of narrative, it would seem that Wu Zhao personally picked up the writhing centipede with her chopsticks and placed it in a jade container. Rather than furiously summoning the steward in the immediate aftermath of the discovery, she waited until the following morning. Then, having had time to reflect, she coolly determined that this was likely not an intentional attempt to poison her. Her remark about the intact centipede inside the rooster is intended to indicate that, among insects, this centipede was singularly poisonous and formidable. Nonetheless, she consequently chose to spare Zhang Sigong. The episode reveals a certain calculating patience on her part. Still, a centipede garnish atop the sovereign's morning jerky was an oversight that could not go unpunished: she banished Zhang and the entire kitchen staff to Lingnan, the lands south of the peaks.

Meats were more often consumed by high officials and rulers. In the era before refrigeration, techniques of preservation like pickling, salting, and jerking meat were essential. Remarking on the last of these three, Charles Benn observes, "Jerky had a long history in China, and during the medieval period the process was applied to beef, mutton, venison, and wild and domestic pigs."[17]

MALE FAVORITES: XUE HUAIYI AND THE ZHANG BROTHERS

Several passages in *Court and Country* condemn Wu Zhao for keeping male favorites (*nan chong* 男寵) in her inner palace. One account emphasizes her unwillingness to heed remonstrance from the Confucian court, particularly when it came to such personal and intimate matters:

By nature, Master Xue was deviously clever. He often entered the inner quarters of the palace. Official Wang Qiuli sent a memorial that read, "In the time of Taizong, Luo Hei excelled at playing the pipa and subsequently was castrated and made a eunuch in order to instruct the palace women. Now Your majesty wishes to have Huaiyi enter the inner quarters. Your humble official requests that he be castrated so that chaos will not be sown." The memorial was shelved and not circulated. (Sup., 172)

In this account, set in 686, when Wu Zhao was grand dowager presiding over court, one official—taking umbrage at the frequent comings and goings of Wu Zhao's reported monk-lover Xue Huaiyi—issues a memorial, citing precedent to show that it is not suitable for ungelded men to enter the private, inner precincts of the Forbidden City.[18] Wu Zhao ignores the moral protestations of this Confucian minister, who wants to maintain an appearance of propriety by keeping the male outer sphere and the female domestic sphere discrete. As a standard of correct behavior, minister Wang Qiuli cites an example from earlier in the Tang, when Emperor Taizong castrated a master musician, Luo Hei (elsewhere Luo Heihei; see Chapter 8), before bringing him into inner quarters to teach *pipa* lute to the concubines. Wu Zhao ignored Wang Qiuli and allowed "Master Xue" to continue to move in and out of the inner quarters. Though Zhang's language is not particularly judgmental in this passage, impropriety and sexual transgression are strongly insinuated.

While Xue Huaiyi was a "male favorite," he also worked outside of the palace in various capacities—as a general, an architect, and a Buddhist monk. One of the Tang histories reports that Wu Zhao, "wishing to hide [Xue Huaiyi's] tracks and facilitate his entry and exit from the 'forbidden inside,' had him tonsured as a monk."[19] The aforementioned Ming dynasty novella, *Lord of Perfect Satisfaction*, describes Master Xue as "a mountebank who sold pharmaceuticals" in the market of Chang'an. He was said to use aphrodisiacs to enable him "to copulate all night without getting tired. The empress loved him utterly."[20]

After Xue Huaiyi's death, the woman emperor's favorites in the final years of the seventh century and the dawn of the eighth century were Zhang Yizhi (d. 705) and Zhang Changzong (d. 705). These two elegantly perfumed, vermilion-rouged, white-skinned, twenty-something brothers spent most of their time in the inner palace under the aegis of their powerful matron-protector, septuagenarian Wu Zhao. In the final years of her reign, this duo improbably became the most powerful, despised, and feared figures in the empire.

In the later stages of Wu Zhao's reign as emperor, she had already redesignated her son Li Xian as heir apparent, a decision that meant the end of her rule would mark the end of the Zhou dynasty and the restoration of the Tang and the Li family. Rather than deal with the constant pressures of court, she preferred to retreat to her mountain villas or to the flamboyant gaiety that the Zhangs provided in her inner palace. However, the scandalous ascendancy of the Zhangs overshadowed the reinstallation of the Li clan. A brief passage from *Court and Country* explains,

> *In the time of the Celestial Empress, a folksy saying that circulated went, "When Lord Zhang imbibes liquor, Lord Li gets drunk." "Lord Zhang" was a disparaging reference to Zhang Yizhi and his brothers. "Lord Li" indicates the Li family.* (1.12)

Needless to say, such mocking placement of the Zhangs on equal—or superior—footing to the once and future ruling dynastic family rankled many.

Lin Yutang, with typical snarling disapprobation, casts the Zhangs as "male mistresses" (*nan qingfu* 男情婦), part of a "rear palace full of male beauties."[21] Dora Shu-fang Dien speculates that the duo, "who powdered and rouged their faces like female impersonators in Peking opera, [...] were most likely gay."[22] Framing the biased manner in which the Confucian narrative casts the reviled brothers, Rebecca Doran notes that the Zhangs are "constructed as the ultimate emasculated male pets."[23] Other scholars have referred to them as Wu Zhao's "friends and confidants,"[24] "favorites" (*pixing* 嬖幸),[25] "male favorites,"[26] or as "unconventionally talented pretty-boys."[27] In a passage below, *Court and Country* refers to them as "palace intimates" (*neibi* 內嬖). The text chronicles that a popular ditty circulated in the mid-to-late 680s, predating Zhang Yizhi's rise to eminence in Wu Zhao's court by a decade:

> From the Chuigong era forward, in the Eastern Capital[28] a song called "Qi'bir" circulated; all of the lyrics were lascivious and flamboyant. Later, when Zhang Yizhi and his brother were palace intimates, Yizhi's pet name was Qibi. (1.12)

Qibi is both the name of a Turkish tribe from the northwest of the empire that submitted to the Tang in 632 and the name of the dominant family from that tribe. A general named Qibi Heli remained loyal to Tang Taizong even when other Qibi chieftains switched their allegiance to a rising Turkish khanate in 642.[29] Apparently, a folk dance of the Qibi Turks—considered by the Chinese to be playful and obscene, tantalizing and salacious—circulated in Wu Zhao's capital, Luoyang, and was transformed into popular doggerel. This ribald song's popularity may also reflect the tendency of centrist/Han Chinese attitudes to exoticize and sexualize the cultural Other during the Tang.[30] Thus, this account illustrates that the very name of Wu Zhao's male favorite Zhang Yizhi epitomized lewd extravagance. In the open, cosmopolitan Tang, these brothers were an integral part of an emergent celebrity culture; they were conduits for popular outrage, commanding fascination and notoriety. The incandescent loathing directed at the Zhang brothers was magnified precisely because of reversed gender roles and gender politics at the unique historical moment.

The inherited version of *Court and Country* has helped shape this narrative of an era where gender norms were turned topsy-turvy. A female ruler presided over the empire and kept a stable of male favorites and other adherents. These men are, relentlessly and without exception, cast in a negative light and freighted with a litany of pejorative associations. The scene below can be viewed as an example of the ugly excess, callousness, and waste that *Court and Country* frequently assigns to the Zhangs and Wu Zhao's other adherents:

> *In the time of the Zhou, Zhang Yizhi was made Director of the Reining Cranes Institute, Zhang Changzong was designated Vice Director, and Zhang Changyi, Luoyang Head. They competed in extravagance and excess. Yizhi fashioned a huge iron cage into which he put many ducks and geese. There was a charcoal fire-pit set in the bottom and a bronze basin filled with five-flavored juice. The geese and ducks walked around the fire. When thirsty, they drank juice from the basin. Meanwhile, they were slow roasted alive as they painfully revolved around the fire, until outside and inside they were cooked through, and their feathers all dropped out. When the meat was roasted to a deep red, the fowl died.*
>
> *Changzong bound a donkey alive in a small room similarly equipped with a charcoal fire and a bronze basin full of five-flavored juice—and let it roast alive. Zhang Changyi pounded an iron post into the ground. He bound the four feet of dogs together and suspended them from the pole. Then he released kestrels and falcons who rent them alive. When much of the flesh was torn off, the dogs were still alive. They dubbed the practice "Bitter Anguish," because no one could bear listening to the clamor of torment.*
>
> *Once when Zhang Yizhi was visiting his brother Zhang Changyi, they had a yearning for horse intestine, and appropriated the horse of one of the attendant riders in their entourage. They disemboweled it alive, leaving the creature to die a lingering death.*
>
> *Later, when Zhang Yizhi, Changzong and the rest of the lot were executed, the common people minced them into pieces, fried and roasted them, and devoured them; they had white, marbled fat like plump hogs. When Zhang Changyi fell, breaking both ankles, people gouged out his heart and liver. They decapitated him and carried the head to present at the capital. Folks called Changyi's end "The Cavalry Horse's Retribution."* (2.31–32)

Perhaps these gruesome vignettes might best be comprehended as misguided assertions of masculinity by the kept men serving in Wu Zhao's harem. They demonstrate the perverse delight that the Zhang brothers took in devising ornate and outlandishly cruel entertainments while hosting drinking parties and banquets. Pretending to be austringers, the Zhangs loose falcons to rend bound dogs. Though elites had practiced falconry for more than two millennia in imperial China, Leslie Wallace has shown that this sport—once sanctioned as a display of imperial authority—evolved, in the centuries leading up to the Tang, into a pastime that showcased "waste, excess, and ritual impropriety," making manifest the dubious moral fiber of young profligates.[31] Finding sport in releasing famished raptors upon bound prey, the Zhangs took the already-tarnished reputation of this once noble art to a shocking and perverse new nadir. When it came to devising elaborate means of inflicting pain upon living creatures, the brothers staged an elaborate competition. The passage ends with what might be understood as karmic retribution. Mirroring the suffering and pain that the brothers inflicted upon sentient beings, they perished in grisly and lingering fashion, a terrible yet warranted justice meted out by the common people.

The Zhangs parlayed the influence of being the attractive young playthings of the senescent emperor into wealth, rank, power, and influence. *Court and Country* describes the opulence that the brothers enjoyed and their unsettling sense of the transience of their favor. They occupied

> a *huge, beautiful mansion costing several millions strings of cash, replete with columns of carved cypress, Central Asian glazed tiles, and Malaysian gharuwood accents.*
> *On the front façade of the mansion, a ghostly hand wrote, "How long can this last?" When he ordered it scraped off, the ghost calligraphed the same message again. This message reappeared for seven days in succession, after which Zhang Yizhi wrote beneath it, "A month is sufficient."* (6.146)

Zhang Yizhi's premonition that such overweening opulence and indulgence would not endure came to pass. The passage in *Court of Country* concludes with a matter-of-fact assertion that, six months later, Zhang Yizhi indeed met his demise, and his wealth was confiscated (6.146).[32]

In addition to Zhang Yizhi and Zhang Changzong, there were other Zhang brothers who availed themselves of favor, leading lives of unrestrained profligacy with a cavalier and bumptious swagger. Accounts indicate that they seized whatever human and material resources they desired—because they could! The following excerpt from *Court and Country* depicts two of the lesser Zhang brothers, Changqi and Changyi:

> *Overbearing in their eminence, Zhang Yizhi and his brothers seized estates and residences, male and female slaves, and courtesans and concubines of others in numbers beyond reckoning. When Zhang Changqi was walking along the street in Wannian County*[33] *he encountered a woman, whose husband was trailing close behind her carrying their child. Changqi used his riding crop to knock off her headscarf. The woman then swore at him. Changqi then instructed his servant, "Lay her across the horse's rump." He then rode off with her. On three or four occasions, the husband lodged complaints in the bronze tattling box,*[34] *but she was not returned. Later, Changqi was seized and taken to the Wannian government offices after being accused of other crimes and sentenced to death. Zhang Changyi once said to a friend, "Being this kind of manly man is truly living of the edge: Right now, if a thousand men wanted to topple me, they couldn't take me down; once I fall though, even if ten thousand men come to support me, I'll never be able to rise again." Soon thereafter, the Zhang brothers met their demise and were all cut down.* (Sup., 161)

Under the extended aegis of Wu Zhao, Changqi assumed and enjoyed impunity. The latter brother, Changyi, is depicted as possessing a greater degree of self-awareness about the transient nature and fragility of their power: he astutely recognizes that the seemingly limitless influence that renders them unassailable for the moment cannot last, and that a terrible reckoning ultimately awaits. The Zhang brothers were slaughtered in the coup that removed Wu Zhao from power in 705.[35]

If we are to believe Zhang Zhuo and the general tenor of the Confucian histories, the aura of "gender anarchy" (to borrow Rebecca Doran's term) lingered even after the death of the Zhangs and Wu Zhao's deposal. Wu Zhao's daughter, daughter-in-law, and granddaughter dominated the court, while her son Zhongzong proved himself a feckless and incompetent ruler.[36] Zhang Zhuo characterized the court in the wake of the Zhang brothers' degradations as a place where an upside-down culture eroded the mettle of good men:

> *Wei Yuanzhong butted heads with the Two Zhangs, and was demoted to Commandant of Gaoyao County in Duanzhou. When the Two Zhangs were executed, he re-entered court as Minister of War, Grand Secretary, and President of the Department of State Affairs, and yet he was not as straightforward as before in his words. The ancients had a saying: "When the wife is in control, filial piety declines."*[37] (Sup., 173–74).

The notion that "when the wife is in control, filial piety declines" is axiomatic Confucian boilerplate suggesting that when normative patriarchal mores are compromised or contravened, the fabric of society becomes unraveled. Even good men of Confucian substance like Wei Yuanzhong (see Zhang Zhuo's assessment of Wei in the following chapter) were irreparably damaged by the reign of Wu Zhao and the insidious presence of the Zhang brothers—and specifically by the subversive assault of her reign on core Confucian virtues like loyalty and filial piety.

In an earlier work, I pointed out the egregious, if predictable, Confucian double standard that the harsh judgment of Wu Zhao's male favorites reveals:

> [C]ompared with male emperors who routinely enjoyed harems of hundreds, even thousands, of women [...] Wu Zhao's handful of male favorites shows not unbridled sexual appetite, but tremendous restraint. [...] It was both accepted and expected that every male emperor would have a seraglio in the Inner Palace with nine ranks of concubines, yet Wu Zhao is often demonized because she took several male lovers over her twenty years of widowhood.[38]

Xue Huaiyi and the Zhang brothers, whose services did not overlap, do not exactly comprise a harem.

WU KINSMEN AND RELATIVES

A grandmaster of nepotism, Wu Zhao installed numerous kinsmen in positions of influence and power during her regency and reign, most prominent among them her nephews, Wu Chengsi and Wu Sansi.[39] Nepotism extended into the past as well. She ennobled her lineage of Wu ancestors to help elevate herself and her living kin, liberally bestowing lofty imperial titles upon foremothers and forefathers, while granting high offices and noble titles to current relatives. She also quickly removed kinsfolk from office when they proved incompetent or incapable, though she would often give them second or third chances.

When Wu Zhao became emperor in 690, she designated Wu Chengsi and Wu Sansi as princes. Their sons and daughters, too, were given noble titles.[40] Shortly thereafter, Wu Chengsi and his supporters bid to establish him as Crown Prince; Wu Zhao deliberated, but, seeing the vehement opposition this proposal met in her court, decided against it.[41] Still, during her grand New Year's rites of 693, amid a musical spectacle featuring legions of dancers, her Wu nephews—rather than her sons—performed the secondary and tertiary rites, indicating that Wu Zhao favored the elevation of a Wu as Crown Prince.[42] When making her final selection in 698, however, Wu Zhao conferred with trusted court minister Di Renjie, who posed the ominous question, "Which is the more intimate bond: aunt-to-nephew or mother-to-son?" He continued, "If Your Majesty bequeaths the empire to Li Xian, the ancestral temple will prosper for ten thousand years. If Your Majesty passes the throne to Wu Sansi, the tablet of the aunt is not to be attached to the ancestral temple."[43] In Chinese tradition, a nephew does not present offerings to a deceased aunt. To a septuagenarian, the prospect of becoming a wandering, hungry ghost, cast out by her descendants, was terrifying. Ultimately, she recalled her son from exile and made him heir apparent as she found her kinsmen unworthy, matter-of-factly declaring to Di Renjie in a judgment recorded in *Court and Country*, "*Chengsi and Sansi are like scrofulous ringworms*" (3.60). This decision determined that the Zhou dynasty would end with Wu Zhao's reign.

Not surprisingly, Zhang Zhuo's assessment of the characters of Wu Zhao's nephews was also scathingly negative. *Court and Country* depicts the Wu nephews as behaving with a high-handed impunity, particularly in their dealing with people of lower status. Wu Chengsi, in the following passage, shows no regard for the law whatsoever:

> *In the time of the Celestial Empress, Ji Xi, the father of Erudite of the Court of Imperial Sacrifices*[44] *Ji Xu, was Prefect of Yizhou.*[45] *He was sentenced to death for bribery. South of Heaven's Ford Bridge, Ji Xu begged the Royal Secretary, Prince of Wei Wu Chengsi, prostrating himself and saying that he had committed a capital crime. When Chengsi asked him about it, Ji Xu said, "I have two younger sisters who are worthy of serving you, Great Prince." Chengsi assented and subsequently sent an oxcart to transport them to his compound. For three days, neither of the sisters spoke. Feeling this to be peculiar, Chengsi asked why.*

> The two responded, "Our father has violated the laws of the realm and we are grieving for him and have no one we can trust or depend upon." Because of the favor he enjoyed, Chengsi had their father pardoned from his death penalty and subsequently had Ji Xu promoted to Head of the Court of Imperial Stud,[46] then rapidly moved to become Vice Censor-in-Chief and Vice Minister of Personnel. His ascendancy through the ranks was due not to his talent, but to his two younger sisters entreating Wu Chengsi. (5.124–25)

The passage is designed to demonstrate that licentious Wu Chengsi's fondness for women informed his casual and private style of managing matters of court and state. This predilection was apparently widely known; appealing to influential Chengsi for the life of his corrupt father, the supplicant proffers his two younger sisters as concubines. The father was pardoned. Showing themselves to be filial daughters and good sisters, the two girls from the Ji family parlayed their newfound favor with Wu Chengsi into rapid career advancement for their brother. The Ji sisters' machinations to secure their father's life and rapidly advance their elder brother's political career show how women within the inner quarters could leverage favor into a degree of influence. Ji Xu ultimately rose to become a chief minister, though the final line in the passage shows clear disapprobation both for Ji and for the culture of Wu Zhao's court: he rose to eminence not based upon talent, but through a sort of sexual networking in a court where promotion was based on favor, sycophancy, influence-peddling, or acting as an informant. This is another passage calibrated to depict Wu Zhao's court as woefully dysfunctional and un-Confucian. Of course, ascending the ranks through connections (*guanxi* 關係), toadying, bribery, or official profiteering was a well-established part of the culture of the court long before Wu Zhao, and has remained an enduring and vital canker at the heart of Chinese politics ever since. In any era of Chinese history, one could cherry-pick myriad examples of official corruption, malfeasance, license, and callousness.[47] This example is geared to showcase the vileness of the reprobate Wus, the high-handed arrogance and lawlessness of the female emperor's kinsmen, particularly when dealing with those of lesser status.

While the Wus may have been indomitable tigers in dealing with the lowly, appropriating women and property with presumptuous rapacity, *Court and Country* also suggests another facet of the Wu nature: when dealing with those who enjoy greater favor (favor being the ultimate currency in Wu Zhao's court), their innate cringing nature and servile character surfaces. Thus, they are exposed as sycophants in their willingness and eagerness to flatter Wu Zhao's male favorites. The following passage from *Court and Country* intimates that real power in Wu Zhao's Zhou dynasty issued from private channels and intimacies rather than from public office:

WU ZHAO

Prince of Liang Wu Sansi wrote a biography for Zhang Yizhi, saying that he was the reincarnation of Wang Zijin and on Mount Goushi erected a temple. Men of literary talent and flatterers vied to write poems in order to recite them—among them Cui Rong was the finest. Later, Yizhi's entire clan was exterminated, and the sycophants attached to him were all banished to Lingnan. (5.125)

Wu Zhao's nephew Wu Sansi pens a fulsome biography for her favorite Zhang Yizhi, claiming he was the reincarnation of a crane-riding, syrinx-playing Daoist immortal.[48] The account ends with the reassuring assertion that justice was ultimately served: the male favorites were killed, and their hangers-on were banished.

Wu Sansi exhibits a similarly flattering approach to eunuchs, a group that enjoyed significant access and influence. *Court and Country* details Wu Sansi's sycophantic treatment:

When eunuchs visited Wu Sansi's residence, he was accommodating and reverent, allowing them to do whatever they pleased. He dressed up young lads in lavish silks, rushing hither and thither offering the eunuchs such a succession of toasts that they didn't have time to eat. Enjoying the singing boys, awash in lascivious disport, they nearly forgot to return to the palace. The eunuchs vied to lavish praise on Wu Sansi's loyalty and his principled morality and lauded his talent and virtue. In reality, outside the palace he was as callously treacherous as Auntie Lai,[49] and in the inner palace he colluded in Traitor Wei's disgrace. (Sup., 178)

Eunuchs, like male favorites, enjoyed a private access to the emperor's person that was denied to court officials. With the exception of attendant eunuchs, no man other than the emperor had access to the inner palace and the harem. Eunuchs, often southern tribesmen castrated as very young boys, were considered safe companions because they were incapable of fathering children. Sequestered within the inner palace, women in the harem needed eunuchs to run errands in the outer court or marketplace. Accordingly, eunuchs were the main conduit between women in the harem and the outside world. In return for a small jade pendant, a eunuch might help a concubine obtain aromatic incense of Bornean camphor and patchouli from the Western market to burn in the palace temple. In exchange for a precious bauble, a eunuch who held the emperor's ear might sing the praises of a lonely woman. Eunuchs also carried tidings from a concubine's family to their natal kin—for a price. In this manner, many eunuchs accumulated great fortunes. Confucian officials, frustrated that the eunuchs possessed an access to the emperor's private world that they lacked, contemptuously referred to them as "wood-worms"—a reference to the manner in which eunuchs insinuated themselves into the vermiculated structure of the palatine culture they undermined. By the mid-Tang, there were tens of thousands of eunuchs in the palace.⁵⁰ J. K. Rideout makes note of "the bias of the official historians against a class from whom they were divided not merely by political rivalry, but also by differences of education, religion and place of birth"; with their subterranean access and networking, these "rats beneath the floor" posed, from the Confucian vantage, a "grave political menace."⁵¹

This anecdote displays the willingness of Wu Sansi to curry favor with the eunuchs by hosting banquets featuring gaudily clad youths and sensuous music. In return for the hospitality, eunuchs returning to the palace gushed copious praise for Wu's impeccable character, propping up his campaign to gain his aunt's favor and, thereby, even greater political sway. The whole exchange constituted a repugnant quid pro quo from the Confucian vantage. The Confucian establishment found the alliance between eunuchs, favorites, and Wu family members nauseating, contemptible, and hypocritical in the extreme. The passage ends by linking Wu Sansi to Lai Junchen ("Auntie Lai"), the head of Wu Zhao's "cruel officials" (see Chapter 3), and Empress Wei, with whom he had an affair after Wu Zhao's death. Clearly, the objective of Zhang Zhuo's sketch is to represent a depraved individual who was part of a toxic culture.

According to another account, one of Wu Zhao's more distant relatives, Zong Chuke, the son of the woman emperor's paternal aunt,⁵² was promoted to Royal Secretary, becoming a chief minister due to his composition of a text framing her monk-lover Xue Huaiyi as a Buddha reincarnate:

> By nature, Royal Secretary of the Heavenly Empress Zong Chuke was a sycophant and a flatterer. At the time, Master Xue had gained favor of a sort akin to that enjoyed by Lao Ai, so Zong wrote a two-chapter biography that claimed Master Xue was a sage who had descended from heaven, from a remote era that no man knew—that he was Sakyamuni reincarnate, Guanyin reborn. Within a year, Zong was elevated to Royal Secretary. (5.125)

Zong Chuke gained this position at the very dawn of Wu Zhao's Zhou dynasty in 690.⁵³ The politics in the court rewarded his fawning and servility with high rank! Alternatively, Zong's ascendancy could have been linked to nepotism. After a brief tenure as Royal Secretary, he was banished to Lingnan in the distant south for rape and taking bribes.⁵⁴ Zong was quickly recalled, and he subsequently offered Wu Zhao useful counsel. On one occasion, he helped prevent a border conflict by informing her that reports of a Turkish vassal's rebellion were false; the vassal had not plotted to rebel, his scheming nephew had filed misleading reports.⁵⁵

Undermining Zong's fawning effort likening Xue Huaiyi to a Buddhist divinity, *Court and Country* places "Master Xue" in the ignominious company of Lao Ai, a notorious and well-endowed impostor eunuch who rose to prominence in the Kingdom of Qin through his relationship with the queen dowager, the mother of the First Emperor of Qin (Qinshi Huangdi 秦始皇帝). To make him better resemble a eunuch, the queen dowager had Lao Ai's beard and eyebrows plucked out and bribed officials to stage a fake castration. Thereafter, she enjoyed his company and clandestinely bore him two children. Eventually, the First Emperor of Qin learned of their subterfuge and Lao Ai and his entire clan were exterminated.[56] Lao Ai is a cautionary tale; by the Tang, his name was a Confucian codeword for the moral chaos caused by the inversion of gender norms when noblewomen bring men into the inner palace!

Wu Yizong was another kinsman of Wu Zhao—grandson of her uncle, a first cousin once removed. Under her Zhou dynasty, he received the nobility title Prince of Henei and served in a number of civil and military positions, wherein he gained a well-founded reputation for cowardice, ineptitude, cruelty, and avarice. As we shall see in a later chapter, when appointed as a general to lead troops against the Khitan on the northeast, he lost courage before the enemy appeared and abandoned the prefectural center, leaving it to be pillaged. In the following anecdote from *Court and Country*, Wu Yizong is depicted as a buffoon bereft of all social graces:

> *In the Zhou, once when Wu Zetian was throwing a banquet in the inner palace and in extremely high spirits, Prince of Henei Wu Yizong suddenly rose and presented a formal proposal, "When an official has an urgent notification for the ruler; it is like a son bringing an urgent matter to the attention of his father." Greatly alarmed, Zetian asked what this matter involved. Wu Yizong answered, "Your Official's investiture income used to be directly levied by my household, but now, by Your Majesty's imperial edict, prefectural and county authorities levy taxes and then disburse the investiture income. This is causing me great loss." Utterly furious, Zetian gazed upwards at the rafters for a long spell before rounding on Yizong and saying, "We are in the midst of a delightful banquet surrounded by family and intimate friends. And then you, a prince by blood, over the trifling matter of a couple hundred houses of income investiture rights, scare me half to death! You are unworthy to bear the title prince!" She ordered that he be dragged from the premises. Removing his official headgear, Yizong prostrated himself, and paid obeisance. The other princes intervened, saying, "Yizong is foolish and obtuse! It's just a stupid mistake on his part!" Zetian then relented and let him off.* (4.93)

The primary point of this passage from *Court and Country* is that Wu Yizong is an individual possessed of no redeeming qualities whatsoever, an acquisitive donkey who covets wealth and rank, but is altogether devoid of any sense of propriety. However, the account also reveals Wu Zhao's sense of decorum, the proper time and place for everything. Violation of that decorum was a grave transgression. If an official had the temerity to bring a formal proposal before the emperor at a festive banquet, she would naturally assume that the intrusion was a pressing matter of state. Her disgust at discovering that her relaxation and pleasure had been rudely interrupted over a relative's cupidity (his desire to secure a greater cut of the investiture income that members of the imperial family and those with nobility titles enjoyed) is readily apparent. Indeed, she threatens to strip him of his title then and there, prompting the offender to grovel before the congregated revelers. Realizing that meting out punishment would only further kill the mood of the occasion, Wu Zhao softened, and let the party presumably continue into the night.

HANGERS-ON OF MALE FAVORITES

The only men that the Confucian establishment found more despicable than male favorites were the parasitic individuals who curried favor with those male favorites. Some Wu kinsmen attached themselves to Master Xue and the Zhangs, cloyingly heaping praise upon them in hopes of augmenting their influence, but *Court and Country* also targets another group of lesser adherents, the fawning court officials who desperately sought the potential benefits of joining this entourage.

This first account derisively characterizes Zheng Yin as a serial hanger-on, attaching himself to one favorite or powerbroker after another:

> *Initially, Vice Minister of Personnel Zheng Yin was an appendage of Lai Junchen. After Lai's execution, he attached himself to Zhang Yizhi. After Yizhi was massacred, he relied upon Commoner Wei. Later he placed his trust in Prince of Qiao.*[57] *In the end he was beheaded.* (5.123–24)

First, Zheng Yin appended himself to "cruel official" Lai Junchen (see Chapter 3), then to the Zhang brothers, and later to Empress Wei, a major power-player in the ceaseless palace intrigue for the five years following Wu Zhao's deposal and death. The passage concludes with a fitting Confucian moral ending when the repeat-offender sycophant is executed. In the following chapter, Zhang Zhuo offers a highly critical and negative opinion of Zheng Yin, remarking that he is a *"crafty and vulgar"* fellow who *"squats like a fox at the heels of the eminent and respectable, hunching down like a pheasant before the gates of the powerful"* (4.98).

Another serial hanger-on, Cui Shi—albeit a gifted poet–aesthete and "famous partisan of female rulers"—is also skewered in *Court and Country*:[58]

> *Cui Shi sycophantically served Zhang Yizhi and Commoner Wei.*[59] *When Miss Wei was killed, he attached himself to the Taiping Princess and enjoyed the sort of favor once lavished upon Feng Zidu and Dong Yan. His wife was beautiful; along with Cui's two daughters, she*

entered the Crown Prince's apartments. Cui was made Vice Minister of the Secretariat and served as a chief minister. Someone lampooned him on a placard, writing, "This mediocre talent dwelled at the residence of the ruler because he presented his voluptuous wife at the spring palace."[60] (5.125)

Both Feng Zidu and Dong Yan were male favorites from the Western Han: the former was the intimate of general Huo Guang, and the latter was the younger lover of a Han princess.[61] They are mentioned to suggest that Cui Shi belongs in the ignominious company of these past men who curried favor with women to advance their careers. In state histories, handsome Cui was reputedly the lover of both Shangguan Wan'er and Wu Zhao's daughter, the Taiping Princess.[62] Rebecca Doran provides an incisive analysis of the passage above, noting that it

> condemns Cui for engaging in exchanges that violate accepted gendered and moral hierarchies. [...] The disdain for Cui Shi stems from his flagrant disregard for sexually encoded gender protocol. Cui Shi doubly forfeits his manhood, first by adopting the female-identified, inferior position of sexual servant and second by violating his duty as husband and father. [...] [G]iving one's wife to the harem was highly unusual and would have been deemed shameful.[63]

Doran sums up the historiographical narrative on this rogues' gallery of cosseted favorites, sycophants, and Wu kinsmen:

> In literary-historical accounts, men such as the Zhang brothers, Xue Huaiyi, [...] Cui Shi, Zong Chuke [...] and high-ranking members of the Wu clan are immortalized as the emasculated lackeys of un-feminine women: male concubines who are fully controlled by their mistresses politically, financially, and sexually. They are the perfect foil for women who appropriate the roles of men. These narratives are driven by the rhetorical use of inverted gender behaviors, whereby the female usurps the "male" position forcing the male into the inferior "female" position of concubine or dependent.[64]

In the Introduction to this book, I voice serious reservations about corruptions or alterations of fragments from *Court and Country*. Nevertheless, if most of these passages (with their scathing tone) indeed derive from Zhang Zhuo in the early eighth century, then he played an undeniable role in shaping a longer Confucian narrative strategy for delegitimizing and denigrating women in power.

HOW TO DISPARAGE WU ZHAO'S KINSMEN AND FAVORITES: FRAME THEM AS ILLITERATE LOUTS!

One of the sharpest insults that Confucian literati, the proud keepers of the *wen* cultural and literary heritage, foisted on their enemies was the accusation of illiteracy or stupidity. In this tradition, *Court and Country* characterizes Wu Zhao's nephew Helan Minzhi (d. 670)—the son of her elder sister—as a literary impostor, claiming his work was actually authored by Zhang Changling, an essayist and poet who gained some eminence late in Taizong's reign:[65]

> *The stele inscription for the Feng Sacrifice on the Eastern Peak that Helan Minzhi wrote was actually written by Zhang Changling.* (Sup., 173)

This accusation that a ghostwriter authored a stele inscription on his behalf was perhaps the lightest in the litany of accusations levied against Helan Minzhi—a rakish scoundrel, by all accounts, charged with incest, rape, lewd conduct, and misappropriation of official funds. Eventually, he was banished to Lingnan; along the road, he hanged himself with his mount's reins.[66]

To brand the Zhang brothers, scions of an elite aristocratic family, as illiterate was more difficult. Nonetheless, a passage from the supplemental part of *Court and Country*—harvested from Liu Kezhuang's 劉克莊 Southern Song work, *A Continued Collection of Poetry and Words from the Rear Village* (*Houcun shihua xuji* 後村詩話續集)—bluntly indicts the notorious duo's illiteracy and ignorance:[67]

> *Zhang Yizhi and Zhang Changzong were illiterate and unable to wield a calligraphy brush, so all of their dispatches to superiors and imperial orders were written by their sycophantic hangers-on.* Pearls and Flowers of the Three Teachings *that they presented was the work of Cui Rong, Zhang Yue, and others, yet Zhang Yizhi surreptitiously took credit for authorship.*[68] (Sup., 172–73)

Early in the second half of Wu Zhao's Zhou dynasty, the Zhangs had been placed in charge of an ambitious project, compiling the 1300-chapter *Pearls and Blossoms of the Three Faiths* (*Sanjiao zhuying* 三教珠英), a broad-reaching anthology that sought to systemically gather the sum total of Buddhist, Daoist, and Confucian wisdom. Literary masters like Song Zhiwen and Cui Rong were the true authors. State histories all contend that the project was little more than an elaborate aesthetic gloss to conceal the riotous carousing, boisterous feasting, and lascivious entertainments in the inner palace, and muffle the cacophony of ugly rumors outside.[69] In *Court and Country* and in official histories, any scholarly endeavor in which the Zhangs engage is summarily presented as plagiarism and clumsily wrought fraud.

TRANSGRESSIVE WOMEN IN WU ZHAO'S AFTERMATH

The seven-year period following Wu Zhao's death was dominated by a quartet of women: her daughter-in-law Empress Wei; her daughter, the

Taiping Princess; her granddaughter, the Anle Princess, and her protégé and secretary, Shangguan Wan'er. In historiographical reconstructions of this era, these women—heirs to Wu Zhao's "unnatural" transgressions upon the patriarchal, male order—are consistently critiqued through descriptions of their lavish estates, their unapologetic conspicuous consumption, their self-indulgent destruction of nature, and their elaborate, self-aggrandizing monuments. This wanton female excess is set in stark contrast to the good governmental moderation of male rulers, who put the common people first.[70]

The narratives in *Court and Country* on Wu Zhao and these other women in the early eighth century feature what Rebecca Doran characterizes as "a combination of fascination and antipathy for the profligate and exotic behaviors of female power-holders and members of their factions."[71] Zhang Zhuo's passage below describes an ornate incense burner that the Anle Princess had crafted for a Buddhist Temple:

> *In Luozhou prefecture, the Anle Princess had a "Hundred Treasures Incense Burner" built for Zhaocheng Buddhist Temple. It was three feet tall, with four gates and a surrounding railing with mahogany balusters adorned with grasses and flowers, flying birds and walking beasts, apsaras and female musicians, qilins and phoenixes, white cranes and soaring immortals flowing like silk or gauze, moving gently and gracefully in fine relief—the extraordinary sort of vessel that a demon or ghost might fashion. Pearl, agate, lapis lazuli, amber, glass, coral, inlay from the shell of the southern giant clam, lustrous jade, and glittering gems—at a cost of 30000 cash, treasures of every sort from the household of the Anle Princess were exhaustively used in fashioning this precious incense burner.*[72] (3.70)

Here, negative characteristics like wasteful excess and extravagance are linked to women and Buddhism; tacitly, judicious restraint and thrift are connected to male Confucian ministers. From the perspective of the Anle Princess, this valuable gift to the temple would help her gain Buddhist merit and accumulate positive karma that could help her in this life and in future incarnations. Her gift-giving was not necessarily motivated by selfishness: this karmic merit could also be transferred to living or deceased parents and relatives.[73]

According to standard histories, after a slew of affairs, Empress Wei conspired to poison her husband Zhongzong and installed a puppet emperor, plotting deviously as her mother-in-law Wu Zhao had before her.[74] In subsequent tradition, she is branded with the disparaging epithets "Traitor Wei" (*Ni* Wei 逆韋) or "Commoner Wei" (Wei shuren 韋庶人). In the following excerpt from *Court and Country*, contempt for Empress Wei is obvious not only in the label "Traitor," but also in the choice to emphasize her embarrassing literary incompetence, so unbecoming in an empress, and the antipode to Shangguan Wan'er's mastery of numerous forms:

> All of Traitor Wei's poems and miscellaneous writings were written by Lady of Bright Countenance Shangguan.[75] Rivalling Lady of Handsome Fairness Ban and Western Jin Concubine Zuo, the Lady of Bright Countenance, the granddaughter of Shangguan Yi,[76] had a vast and profound grasp of the classics and the histories as well as a style of writing and literary expression that penetrated the essence. (Sup., 173)

The Lady of Bright Countenance, Shangguan Wan'er, is not only lauded for her scintillating writing and mastery of canonical works, but also compared to exemplary female writers, historian-advisor-poet Ban Zhao of the Eastern Han and Zuo Fen of the Western Jin. In a milieu where *wen* culture was tantamount to power, Shangguan Wan'er, given her admirable poetic and literary prowess, has been judged far more gently than the Empress Wei, the Anle Princess, and the Taiping Princess. Ban Zhao is best known for *Lessons for Women* (*Nü jie* 女戒), which emphasized the importance of a woman's adhering to her Confucian role of obedience, duty, and reverence toward her in-laws.[77] Zuo Fen was a talented poet, scholar, calligrapher, and embroiderer who served as a concubine in the harem of Emperor Wu of Jin.[78] Though Shangguan Wan'er had an affair and plotted intrigues with Wu Zhao's nephew, Wu Sansi, amid the turbulent coups in 710, she ultimately used her influence to keep power in the hands of the Li family, the Tang dynasts.[79] For this reason, in addition to appreciation for her literary talent, Confucian historiography has cast her in a relatively kind light. The contrast between this admiration for hyper-literate Shangguan Wan'er and the bald contempt directed toward the Zhang brothers and Wu Zhao's kinsmen Helan Minzhi—all of whom had ghostwriters compose their work, exposing an unforgivable lack of cultural competency—is worthy of note.

2

The culture of the court

IN STAFFING HER COURT, WU ZHAO abruptly appointed men and quickly promoted them; however, she removed or demoted with equal alacrity officials who proved venal, inept, or worse, disloyal. Though unpredictable and at times arbitrary, she sought and assembled men of talent. She was an enthusiastic patron of institutes of learning and played a significant role in the early development of the examination system.[1] One of her reforms to the system was ordering that the names of test-takers be covered, so that examiners would not be influenced by family pedigree or connections, a practice that continued in later eras.[2] One motive underlying Wu Zhao's dramatic expansion of the examination system was to curtail the influence of great aristocratic clans, who, through long-established networks of privilege and nepotism, filled the upper ranks of the court. Even as empress, she sponsored reforms that greatly increased the volume of successful examination candidates and provided them a fast-track to bureaucratic positions. These new candidates, often men of more humble background, felt beholden to Wu Zhao rather than to highborn relatives and friends in court.[3] Under her patronage and support, the examination system grew dramatically during her half-century as empress, grand dowager, and emperor.

Though wary of the prestige of the old aristocracy that had sought to hinder her ascendancy, Wu Zhao was no social revolutionary; her court was anything but a simple meritocracy. She bolstered her own position while grand dowager and emperor, liberally awarding Wu kinsmen titles and offices as she diligently fashioned an elaborate aristocratic backstory to elevate herself and her clan (see Chapter 1). One episode in *Court and Country* clearly displays Wu Zhao's deep-seated classism, describing her reluctance to allow a man who had risen from a position outside the nine ranks to enter the uppermost echelons of the bureaucracy:

> In the Zhou, Zhang Heng, rising from a background of Clerk, reached a position of fourth rank. When he was advanced a grade, it was suitable that he enter third rank and he began to wear the insignia. Upon returning from an audience with the emperor, he saw some newly

cooked steamed cakes along the roadside and bought one. As he was eating the steamed cake on horseback, a Censor impeached him for official misconduct. Zetian sent down an edict reading, "Those born outside the official ranking system are not allowed to enter the three ranks of chief ministers." Thereupon, Zhang was stripped of his insignia. (4.94)

A mere clerk—no less the sort of fellow who stopped by roadside vendors for steamed cakes on the way home from work—had no place among the purple-clad ranks of chief ministers! Indeed, while Wu Zhao helped refresh the bureaucratic ranks with an infusion of new blood, the woman emperor was deeply preoccupied with status and its perks.

Of course, this abiding concern with status and position extended beyond the person of the ruler; it was an integral aspect of the court and wider society. Another episode in *Court and Country* from late in Wu Zhao's Zhou dynasty also shows how deeply this system of ranking was embedded in the collective consciousness:

Shortly after Vice Minister of Heaven[4] Gu Zong obtained third rank, his son-in-law came to visit. At the time, the construction of the grand gate was just completed. When Gu Zong rode up to the gate, his horse snorted and stumbled to the ground, refusing to cross the threshold. Only when Gu whipped the horse did it reluctantly lurch forward and enter. His retinue then followed. Shortly thereafter, the gate collapsed. Gu Zong was displeased and fell sick. When the directors and vice directors came to inquire about his illness, Gu said, "I was ill-suited to enter the third rank. I owe my success to all of Your Excellencies. I know that I'm not worthy." Within the ten-day xun week[5] he passed away. (6.145–46)

On the threshold of the hall where the emperor and chief ministers deliberate, the horse of Gu Zong, sensing its rider did not belong, stubbornly balked. After Gu insisted on entry, the gate collapsed: his very presence seemingly undermined the solemnity and dignity of the office. Like the horse, the stonework could not countenance such a man holding such a lofty position. Rejected by creatures and elements alike, Gu Zong fell ill. Ultimately, on his deathbed, Gu Zong himself humbly acknowledged his unworthiness.[6]

SIGNS OF STATUS AND SERVICE IN THE COURT

Officials in the courts of the Tang and Wu Zhao's Zhou wore silken robes color-coded according to rank. Silk was, as Chen BuYun frames it, a fabric of "political legitimacy" that manifested court privilege and social status. "Textile production," she claims, "was both the root of imperial power and the driving force of fashion." Ministers of third rank and higher wore purple robes (there was no honor greater than having the emperor gift a purple robe); fourth and fifth ranked officials wore red; sixth and seventh, green;

eighth and ninth, blue. Officials outside of the nine ranks and commoners could only wear coarse, drab-colored silk and lesser fabrics. Moreover, Wu Zhao's court had a particular aesthetic flair. Certain high-ranking officials sported robes inscribed with palindromes and adorned with elaborate animal motifs—dragons, deer, and phoenixes for civil officials; tigers, leopards, and eagles for imperial bodyguards.[7]

Tang officials also wore fish tallies as emblems of service (see Figure 2).[8] These tallies were kept in decorative bags affixed to the belts of officials. Many passages in *Court and Country* reflect the degree to which court officials were conscious of status and capable of reading at a glance a courtier's rank and office. For instance, the following snippet reflects the importance of such status symbols and indicates that rulers developed distinctive personal styles:

> *In the Shangyuan era, by order officials of ninth rank and higher wore knives, whetstones, and other accoutrements from their belts along with colored fish-shaped handkerchiefs made of knotted silk. This fish shape was considered to be a powerful auspicious sign. In the court of the Celestial Empress, this practice was discontinued. In the Jingyun era, the practice was resumed. Knotted white fish were fashioned as embellishments.* (3.68–69)

The fish—a carp (*li* 鯉)—was a homophone for the surname of the Li family that founded and ruled the Tang. Accessorizing with various sorts of silken, jade, and bronze carp was a way that an official might display loyalty and alignment with the ruling dynasts while showcasing both taste and wealth. The character for fish (*yu* 魚) is also a homophone for plentitude (*yu* 餘); even today, when the Chinese New Year is celebrated, people offer a felicitous "May you enjoy fish/plenty year after year! (*Niannian youyu* 年年有餘)." Thus, these fish were auspicious tokens.

Another passage in *Court and Country* also examines these tallies in Wu Zhao's era:

> *In the Han, when troops were dispatched, a bronze tiger tally was used. At the beginning of the Tang, a silver rabbit was utilized because the rabbit was considered a token of good fortune. And, because a carp was considered auspicious, subsequently a bronze fish tally was worn as an ornament/tally. In the spurious Zhou dynasty, because the Wu surname was part of the Xuanwu, bronze was fashioned into turtle tallies.* (Sup., 178)

Among the four cardinal directions in traditional China, the Xuanwu 玄武 (literally the Dark Warrior)—its emblem a snake coiled round a turtle—symbolized the north. The Vermilion Bird was the icon of the south; the White Tiger emblemized the West; and the Azure Dragon represented the East. Wu Zhao's surname, meaning "warrior," was the same Wu used in the iconic Xuanwu; the turtle thus saw use as a tally form during her reign (see Figure 3).[9]

Figure 2 A Tang dynasty bronze fish tally.

Official Tang histories corroborate this account—though they only mention the chelonian component of the tally, perhaps failing to mention the Xuanwu because it was an emblem associated with Wu Zhao. One passage in the *Old Tang History*, a state history written shortly after the fall of the Tang, refers to sumptuary laws established in the latter stages of Wu Zhao's Zhou dynasty. These laws dictated that the highest-ranking court ministers could embellish their bags with gold, those of fourth rank could decorate with silver, while those of fifth rank and below could only adorn with bronze.[10]

THE CULTURE OF THE COURT

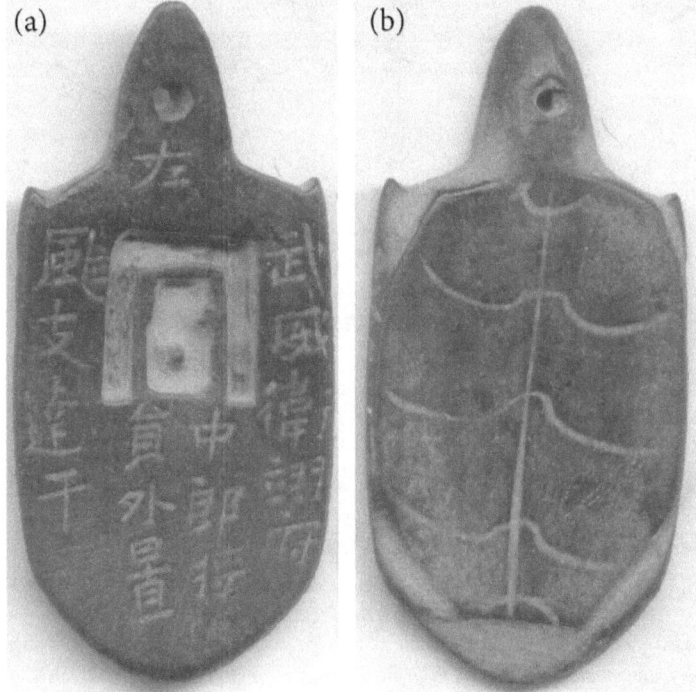

Figure 3 (A & B): A Zhou dynasty bronze turtle tally.

HUMOR IN THE COURT

Mention of the imperial court and bureaucracy in medieval China invariably summons a vision of austere men gathered in audience before the presiding emperor, all clad in color-coded formal robes corresponding to their rank as they engaged in grave matters of state. In its examinations of the culture of the court during the reign of Wu Zhao, Zhang Zhuo's work provides a far more nuanced picture. In addition to furnishing intriguing information about the court's other signs of status and allegiance examined above, accounts from *Court and Country* also reveal an assortment of court cliques with varied and conflicting interests, men with distinct personalities and peculiar characters. Moreover, Zhang's text offers glimpses of officials at leisure, casually lampooning each other's appearances or mannerisms.

The comic savagery of Zhang Yuanyi

The following lengthy passage features a court wag named Zhang Yuanyi, with whom Wu Zhao clearly enjoyed a relaxed and informal badinage. She asks for news from Zhang, prompting a witty and gossiping response:

Under the court of Zhou emperor Zetian, when barbarians appealed to request investiture, many were given official positions and rewards, including one who was designated Censor of the Right. Once, Zetian[11] asked Court Gentleman Zhang Yuanyi, "Outside the palace what sort of amusing tidings are there?"

Yuanyi responded, "Zhu Qianyi is wearing green, while Lu Renjie is wearing vermilion. Lü Zhiwei rides a horse, while Ma Jipu rides a donkey. Li Qianli wishes his given name was his surname; Wu Xiwu wishes his surname was his given name.[12] In the Left Censorate there's a Hu the Censor, in the Right the Censor's a hu!" "Hu the Censor" meant Hu Yuanli; "Censor's a Hu" meant one of the Censors of the Right was a Sogdian. Soon, Zetian shifted the Sogdian to a different official position.

When the Zhou dynasty severed the Tang's mandate, there was a Censor from Beizhou, Zhao Kuo, a man extremely diminutive in stature. He rose to become Investigating Censor. People of the time called him "Terrace[13] Dregs"; Li Zhaode contemptuously called him "Frostbitten Sheaf of Grain" and Yuanyi, at a single glance, dubbed him "Stunted Owl on a Falcon's Roost."

At the time, Kong Luqiu of Tongzhou was serving as low-ranking official; he adopted the air of a martial man. People of the day called him "Field Commander-in-chief." Yuanyi, at a glance, dubbed him "Adjutant Stork in the Phoenix Pool."[14]

Su Weidao possessed a talent and learning, a breadth of knowledge and magnanimity of spirit, admired by all. In body and spirit, Wang Fangqing was ugly and shallow. His expressions were vulgar and obtuse. In knowledge and talent he failed to rise above the ordinary and mundane. And yet both men served as Vice Ministers in the Secretariat. Someone asked Yuanyi, "Who is more worthy, Su or Wang?" He answered, "Su is like one who obtains a gyrfalcon in the ninth month; Wang is like one covered with frozen flies in the tenth month." The person asked what he was talking about. And Wang responded, "To catch a gyrfalcon takes outstanding agility. To be covered with frozen flies requires a certain stubborn timorousness." People of the time admiringly remarked upon his capacity to penetrate to the heart of matters.

When Qidan rebel Sun Wanrong raided Youzhou prefecture, Prince of Henei Wu Yizong was made commander-in-chief. When the soldiers Yizong marshalled reached Zhaozhou, he heard that rebel Luo Wuzheng was coming from the north with several thousand cavalry; the prince promptly abandoned horses and soldiers and fled south to Jingzhou prefecture, leaving resources and vessels along the road in his wake. Only when he heard that the enemy had withdrawn, did he advance once more. But when the troops returned to the capital, a banquet was laid and liquor was set out. Right in front of the emperor, Yuanyi mocked Yizong,

> *Fired from his great bow the arrow little distance flies,*
> *He clambers up steps to mount his stumpy Shu pony and ride.*
> *When the rebels are far away, full 700 li up to the north,*
> *From behind city walls to battle themselves, his troops storm forth.*
> *Then in reckless retreat, armor and weapons aside are cast,*
> *See the general mount a hog and flee due south mighty fast.*

THE CULTURE OF THE COURT

The emperor asked, "As Yizong has a horse, why would he ride a pig?" Zhang Yuanyi responded, "He rode a pig—just wrapped his legs around a hog and took off." The emperor roared with laughter. Wu Yizong complained, "That wasn't spontaneous. Yuanyi had that zinger planned ahead of time." The emperor then said, "Choose a rhyme and give it to him." Yizong said, "I request that he use 'disarray' for the rhyme." In a trice, Yuanyi bounced back,

> *His hair ever in disarray,*
> *Threadbare sideburns no floral spray.*
> *His face is a peach blossom—not*
> *And eyes vainly fail to match the apricot.*

Zetian was delighted and the Prince was greatly humiliated. Thereafter he was known as "Great Bow with Short-Flying Arrow."[15]

Wu Yizong was short of stature and ugly in appearance. In the Zhou, Yizong's younger sister, the Jingle County Princess, was likewise short and ugly. Though Miss Wu was the eldest in the Wu clan, people of the time called the homely Jingle County Princess "Big Brother." When the County Princess and [Emperor] Zetian were riding together, the ruler ordered Yuanyi to write a poem.

> *Horse caparisoned in peach flower embroidery pass*
> *The trains of her silken dress fresh as green grass.*
> *Ah, 'neath the gauzy veil of her hat a visage like no other:*
> *Such a lovely countenance, that of Big Brother!*

Zetian laughed loudly and the County Princess was deeply humiliated.

High official Lu Shide was large, tall, and swarthy, with a lame foot. Yuanyi, at a glance, called him "Undertaker Walking a Rutted Track" and also called him "Duke Ling of Wei," meaning he resembled the undertaker who protected the coffin.[16]

Vice Minister of Heaven Ji Xu was large and tall, and liked to incline his head upward as he walked, as though peering at something lofty and distant. Zhang Yuanyi dubbed him the "Willow-Gazing Camel."

Palace Vice Censor Yuan Bensong was humpbacked, swarthy, and scrawny. Yuanyi dubbed him "Stooped Scribe of Lingnan."[17]

Court Gentleman Zhu Qianyi was stout and swarthy, fat and short. His body was filthy and greasy. Yuanyi called him "Table Maiden of the Court of Imperial Entertainments."[18]

Dongfang Zha was tall, and his robe was short; he had a bony face and thick eyebrows. Yuanyi called him "Field Commandant."

Tang Boruo was dwarfish in height; Yuanyi dubbed him "Hunched and Stumpy Sichuan Pony."

Court scholar Ma Jipu had only one eye. Yuanyi called him the "Squinting Archer."

> *Court Gentleman Zhang Ruzi often gazed skyward. Yuanyi designated him "Vinegar Guzzler."*
>
> *Sishui County Head Su Zheng was a frivolous gadabout. Yuanyi called him "Rat Without a Hole."* (4.87–88)

Many of Zhang Yuanyi's jokes are based on puns and homophones. For instance, when he says Zhu Qianyi is wearing green and Lu Renjie is wearing red, it is because Zhu 朱, in addition to being a surname, means "vermillion," and the family name Lu 逯 is a proximate homophone for "green" (*lü* 綠). Thus, the tongue-in-cheek pun might be rendered, "Mr. Red is wearing green, while Mr. Green is wearing red." Fifth-ranked officials wore red, while sixth and seventh-ranked officials were clad in green. Thus, there is an implicit class/rank consciousness built into the joke. The next joke is also connected to surnames; the common surname Ma 馬 also means "horse," while the family name Lü 閭 is a homophone for donkey (*lü* 驢). Thus, the second joke in Zhang Yuanyi's response to Wu Zhao's request for new humorous tidings might be rendered as follows: "Well, Sir Donkey is bestride a horse while Mister Horseman is mounted on a donkey." Zhang Yuanyi's opening salvo on news of the court ends with further wordplay. In the Left Tower of the Censorate, there is a "Hu the Censor" (a man with the surname Hu who held that post); in the Right Tower there was a "Censor who's a *hu* 胡," a Sogdian or "Western barbarian" (see Chapter 8). Wu Zhao had assigned this non-Han Chinese official to the position. However, the passage reveals that the female emperor was receptive to a certain subtle remonstrance sugarcoated in humor: gathering from Zhang's quip that the Sogdian Censor was unpopular, she transferred this non-Chinese officer to another position.

Thereafter, the bulk of the passage enumerates derogatory nicknames that Zhang Yuanyi bestowed upon various civil and military officials. Wu Zhao's own family members—including her sadistic and buffoonish cousin Wu Yizong, whom we encountered making a spectacle of himself in the previous chapter—were not spared; indeed, the nimble-tongued quipster reserved some of his choicest barbs and most caustic mockery for the female emperor's own kinsmen, showing little concern that it might rouse her anger or compromise his personal safety. His gibe targeting Wu Yizong is based on "hog" (*shi* 豕) being a homophone for "turd" (*shi* 屎)—the implication being that, when the enemy was still afar, the craven general from the Wu family, literally scared shitless, retreated pell-mell. In addition to allowing brazen criticism (which if levied seriously in another forum would provoke conflict and outrage), humor offered a platform where one had to check one's status at the door, as the high-ranking and powerful were fair game for a piercing riposte or a scalding lampooning. Zhang Zhuo's anecdotes also reveal the humiliating

THE CULTURE OF THE COURT

survival strategies of an inept figure like Wu Yizong: just as his comic groveling saved him from Wu Zhao's wrath after his offense at the banquet (see Chapter 1), so his begrudging willingness to play along with being the butt of another courtier's mockery enabled him to side-step the consequences of his cowardice and disastrous failures as a military commander. Graham Sanders aptly observes that Wu Zhao's "appreciative guffaw" afforded Zhang Yuanyi protection against Wu Yizong's wrath.[19]

The playful bestowal of satirical nicknames

Clearly, there was great social currency in being capable of encapsulating another court member's appearance or character in a malicious four-character sketch. The wide inclusion of such passages in *Court and Country* attests both to the fact that the practice was ubiquitous in the court and to the fact that Zhang Zhuo personally took delight in these attacks upon the court's eminent and powerful members—particularly given his own inability to enter the highest ministerial echelons.

The following two anecdotes from *Court and Country* further illustrate the popular convention of assigning nicknames in Wu Zhao's time:

> *In the Zhou, Zhang Yuanyi had a thick midsection, a scrunched-up neck, and lopsided eyes. Ji Xu sized him up and called him "Toad Swimming Against the Current." (4.88)*

> *In the Tang, Yuzhang[20] Clerk He Ruojin had bulging eyes and a thick neck. Zhang Zhuo called him the "Suckling Calf." (4.89)*

In the first anecdote, Zhang Yuanyi falls victim to the convention that he himself used to skewer so many fellow officials when Ji Xu—the "Willow-Gazing Camel" himself—coins a devastatingly apt four-character sobriquet to mock his odd appearance. In the latter, Zhang Zhuo himself delivers a comic and evocative nickname at the expense of a local leader from Jiangxi.

Wang Jishan—a veteran official who served in the Tang and the Zhou for decades, rising to chief minister—had the dubious distinction of earning multiple disparaging sobriquets:

> *In the Zhou, Vice Minister of the Secretariat Du Jingxian, because of his outstanding literary erudition and vast breadth of his knowledge, was dubbed "Crane Calling from a Roost of Cockerels."[21] In the Tang, Wang Jishan was a man of mediocre talent and trivial character. In temperament he was obtuse, and in spirit he was muddle-headed. When he was Royal Secretary, people called him "Pigeon Congregating at the Phoenix Pool." Soon he was promoted to Left Minister of the Department of Culture and Prosperity. He didn't have any*

administrative responsibilities, but he did not allow the donkeys of any of the clerks to enter the precincts of the Terrace, driving them off all day without taking time to rest. People of the time called him "Chief Minister of Donkey-Rousting." (4.92)

In other sources, Wang Jishan is described as an upright and conscientious official, though decidedly lacking in classical learning.[22] Though Zhang Zhuo clearly does not hold Wang Jishan in high esteem, perhaps this depiction of the gray-bearded chief minister as a feckless buffoon with no administrative responsibilities, reduced to corralling donkeys, is really targeting Wu Zhao herself. This account might be understood as an effort to make her court appear as a carnivalesque Festival of Fools where *éminence grises* end up as mule tenders.

Chen Ximin, a lesser official who does not appear in the dynastic histories, also earned a pair of demeaning nicknames for his inefficiency and incompetence:

In the Court of Official Review, because Rectifier Chen Ximin lacked the talent to fulfill his official responsibilities, he would get bogged down and delayed. Other officials in the court coined the nickname "Master of the Lofty Brush" because he would hold his calligraphy brush to his forehead for half a day without setting it to paper. Playing on the homophone between "hole" and "Confucius," and punning on the word an 按 *which can mean "follow" or "press," Chen was also called "Presser of Holes" because he edited and emended drafts so often that he wore a hole through the paper. (6.132)*

This passage uses homophones to poke fun at the inept official: an expert or a master is called a *gaoshou* 高手, literally "elevated hand," a term used here to mock the waffling Chen Ximin, who sits for long stints, paralyzed by bureaucracy, his hand held aloft. His second nickname, "Follower of Confucius" (an Kong 按孔子), could also be understood—especially given his predilection for editing drafts so frequently that he wore through the paper—as "Presser of Holes."

As in the case of Du Jingxian's moniker "Crane Calling from a Roost of Cockerels"—a nickname acknowledging a man of superior mettle surrounded by lowly peers—these labels were not always employed for mockery. When he was chief minister, Vice Director of the Department of State Affairs[23] Liu Rengui commanded great respect. Under the Two Sages, he proved himself a successful general during the Korean campaigns and established a reputation as a loyal, competent, and principled voice in the court. A snippet in *Court and Country* reveals his sobriquet:

When Liu Rengui was Left Charioteering Archer, everyone in the realm called him the "All-knowing Charioteering Archer." (Sup., 174)

THE CULTURE OF THE COURT

Proficient in both martial and civil arts, Liu Rengui was perhaps the most highly esteemed general/statesman of the era. His nickname reflected the high esteem in which he was held.

Numerous other epithets abound, but one peculiar example in particular warrants clarification:

> In the Tang, minister Zhu Qinming immersed himself in the classics and histories, not spending any time on current events. With a massive bulbous head, he was stubborn, inflexible, and suspicious. The lesser functionaries all called him "Old Baggage." An "old baggage" (ao) was the chunk of meat without the seven openings—the nostrils, eyes, ears, mouth—obtained by a wild man in the time of Duke Mu of Qin. (4.90)

A passage from a fourth-century text, Gan Bao's *Search for the Supernatural* (*Soushen ji* 搜神記), helps to shed light on Zhang Zhuo's passage. In an account in Gan Bao's work set in the Spring and Autumn period (seventh cent. BC), a man unearthed an animate, lumpish, female object that "resembled a goat but was not one, looked like a pig but was not a pig." The man thought to present the grotesque and amorphous creature as tribute to Duke Mu of Qin, but on the trip he encounters two pheasant-children—one male and one female—who inform the man that his strange companion is an *ao* 媼, an "Old Baggage," a devourer of corpse brains who could only be slain with a cypress stake. The "Old Baggage," in turn, tells the man that the one who possesses these bird-children can gain control over the realm. Naturally, when the discoverer of the "Baggage" reaches Duke Mu, the ambitious ruler is far more interested in capturing the pheasant-children than in receiving the proffered she-lump.[24] Needless to say, likening the bulbous-headed Zhu Qinming to a corpse-eating *ao* was less than flattering.

A joke 1,300 years in the making!

Court and Country also records a witticism often repeated by an otherwise unknown acquaintance of Zhang Zhuo's, Yi Shentong:

> Yi Shentong often told a story of how Bole ordered his son to seek a horse like the horses he described in the Equestrian Canon. For a year, the son sought out a horse resembling the superior horses drawn in the book, but, unable to find a worthy specimen, returned and reported to his father, who promptly told him to head out again to seek the horse.
> As he was leaving, they saw a huge toad and the son turned to Bo Yue and said, "I just saw a horse that nearly fit the description [...] but not quite."
> Bole answered, "Why?"
> Looking down at the toad, the son said, "He had a massive head, bulging eyes, and a bumpy, ridged back. It also seems that his hooves aren't built for speed and endurance."

Bole replied, "Indeed, though this 'horse' may be good at hopping and jumping, it doesn't quite measure up."

The son then laughed, and thus ended his quest to find the perfect horse. (6.134)

The joke is set 1,300 years in the past. The *Equestrian Canon* is an actual text; silken fragments were found in the famous Eastern Han Mawangdui tomb in Changsha, Hunan.²⁵ Bole (also known as Sun Yang 孫陽), who served as a retainer of Duke Mu of Qin in the seventh century BC, was famous for being able to judge a horse based on its physiognomy and confirmation. At a glance, this equine savant could gauge a horse capable of galloping 1000-*li* in a single day.²⁶ "Obtaining ten good horses," it was said, "is not as good as obtaining one excellent physiognomist of horses, like Bole."²⁷ This putative author of the *Equestrian Canon* sent his son to find a horse that equaled the perfect equestrian specimens described in his text. The joke demonstrates the comic gap that often exists between the ideal and the actual.

Zhang Zhuo composes humorous ditties with a colleague and mocks inept test-takers

In some stories in *Court and Country*, Zhang Zhuo plays a prominent role. Almost invariably, his observations prove to be deadly accurate or prescient. Wielding his deft calligraphy brush and clever wit, he was unwilling to leave the comic glory to others. In the following account, Zhang and a colleague make up a doggerel to poke fun at Wu Zhao's excessive appointment of officials:

When Zetian severed the Tang's mandate, all candidates were granted positions without taking the examination. As soon as they left home to seek fortune in the capital, candidates beyond count were made Censors, Case Reviewers, Reminders, and Rectifiers of Omission. Zhang Zhuo made up a little ditty:

> *Rectifiers coming by the cartload,*
> *Reminders measured by the bushel coming to 'work'*
> *Vice Censors plentiful as the teeth of a push-rake*
> *Like bowls from a mold, her army of Clerks*

At the time, Shen Quanjiao, overbearing and unbridled, was ever showing off and flaunting his talents. He wore his official headpiece high and his cloth gown long. Reciting verses in the Southern Court, he added four lines of his own:

> *Overseeing Reminders who don't review statutes,*
> *court scholars who can't write prose,*

> and paste-headed Relief Commissioners—
> Bleary-eyed Sagely Divine August[28] can't see beyond her nose.
>
> Thereupon, Shen was seized by the "rake-pushing" Censor Ji Xianzhi and taken to the Left Tribunal, where he was formally charged and brought before the court to face the accusation that he had slandered the court and undermined the customs of the state. Ji petitioned that Shen be flogged before the court then punished according to law. Zetian merely laughed and said, "As long as you ministers are not excessive in wielding power, what does it matter what the people of the realm say? In this case, it's not necessary to mete out punishment. Release him." At this, all the color drained form Censor Ji's face. (4.89)

It is both amusing and telling that Zhang describes his colleague as "overbearing and unbridled, ever showing off and flaunting his talents," yet he has no reservations about showing off his own. Though Zhang side-steps official sanction, his colleague Shen Quanjiao—perhaps because he directly mentions Wu Zhao's title in his verse—was accused by a Censor of slandering the court and subverting the state. Rather than showing outrage, a bemused Wu Zhao, showing magnanimity of spirit, merely dismissed the charge with a laugh.

Though the examination system in imperial China (mentioned in the anecdote above) did not reach its pinnacle until the subsequent Song dynasty, it provided an important vehicle for recruiting talent in the Tang and during Wu Zhao's Zhou. Zhang Zhuo was a brilliant test-taker. His excellence on the examinations gained him fame as a young prodigy; however, not unlike a high-school student who is feted for scoring a perfect 1600 on the SATs but never translates that test-taking aptitude into college success, Zhang spent his career foundering as a mid-level bureaucrat. Not surprisingly, he found a certain amusement in the shortcomings of others who struggled on the examinations. Zhang Zhuo's account of a candidate's struggle and subsequent self-justification reflects the sort of story that prompted mirth among the literati:

> In the Zhou, when the Ministry of Personnel held an examination, Shen Zirong, though there were two hundred different topics, never put his calligraphy brush to paper. When people asked him why, he answered, "It's nothing but fate. Not one topic suited me well. There was one that tallied rather well, but people's names were different." The following year, once again Shen failed to set brush to paper. When people inquired, he explained, "My topic was a watermill's grindstone. If only it were a Lantian millstone, but today they asked about a Fuping millstone. How am I supposed to write about that?" When people heard, not a one but clapped their hands in derision. (4.93)

The idea that either the made-up names used in a sample case or a millstone's place of origin might hinder a candidate's ability to respond and prompt writer's block is, of course, comic and absurd. Sometimes the human capacity for self-justification and the ability for rationalizing defeat is truly astounding!

Many of these jokes contained in *Court and Country* are not congenial to modern eye or ear. Part of the challenge and fun is trying to explore and make sense of customs and humor that are incongruous with modern and Western norms.

MASTERY OF LANGUAGE: JUDGE DEE SWAYS THE EMPEROR AND SHARES DOGMEAT WITH A COLLEAGUE

Di Renjie is perhaps the most famous official in the entire Tang dynasty. Gaining notoriety for his capacity to get to the bottom of cases as a local magistrate, he was featured in detective novels in late imperial China as a crime-solving magistrate. China scholar Robert van Gulik has written a number of novels about mysteries and crimes solved by "Judge Dee." Recently, several big-budget movies in China have featured Di Renjie's stunning aptitude for solving mind-bending cases.

Di Renjie served as one of Wu Zhao's chief ministers. The female emperor developed an abiding trust in, and had a personal rapport with, her minister, referring to him affectionately as the "Nation's Elder."[29] An account in *Court and Country*, set at a critical juncture in the middle of her Zhou dynasty, contains Di Renjie's interpretation of Wu Zhao's dream about a splendid parrot with broken wings:

> The *wu* 鵡 of parrot is homophonous with Your Majesty's surname Wu 武 . The two wings represent your two sons. If you elevate them, the two wings will be whole and flap again. (3.60)

Aware that Wu Zhao was profoundly superstitious and placed a high premium on dreams and omens, Di—who played an integral role inside and outside of court in persuading her to return power to the Li family after her reign—interpreted her dream in a manner that nudged her toward the decision to bequeath the empire to her sons from the Li family. A master in dream glyphomancy, the mystic art of using characters that appear in elements of a dream to interpret its meaning, the clever minister deftly persuaded Wu Zhao to restore her sons and the Tang.[30]

Another episode in *Court and Country* not only displays Di Renjie's grasp of deconstructing language and characters but also shows a more light-hearted aspect of the minister:

> Vice Minister of Justice Di Renjie mockingly said to Vice Minister of Justice Lu Xian, "Sir, if I yoke a horse 馬 to your name Lü 盧 , you become a donkey 驢 ."

THE CULTURE OF THE COURT

> Lu answered, "If we split Your Excellency's surname Di 狄 in half, then we have a pair of hounds 犬 ."
> Di Renjie retorted, "No, in the character Di, beside the hound radical there is fire."
> Lü quipped, "Well, if there's fire beside a hound, then let's enjoy the boiled dog meat."
> (6.133–34)

This vignette shows Di deploying his knowledge in a far more playful manner with a colleague, reflecting the lively intellectual banter of the day. He corrects a friend's error, and his friend playfully recovers.

GOOD OFFICIALS

Court and Country offers a number of other anecdotes about good court officials. Though the following passage is set after the female emperor's death, the focal figure, Li Rizhi, also served as a low-level official under Wu Zhao:[31]

> When Minister of Justice Li Rizhi was in charge of metropolitan counties near the capital, he never meted out the punishment of flogging by rod, yet managed affairs successfully. During his tenure as Minister of Justice, there was a clerk who received an imperial order to perform a duty but forgot and didn't perform his charge for three days. At that point, Minister Li had the clerk strip off his clothing and summoned all of the clerks, claiming that he wished to punish the man. Li scolded, "I'd like to give you a good round of scourging, but I'm afraid that if I did, people of the realm would say that you were able to rouse Li Rizhi's ire and had a taste of Li Rizhi's beating stick. Anyway, you're hardly even human—even your wife and son have no respect for you." He then released the man. Thereafter, none of the clerks dared to commit any offense. If anyone committed the slightest fault, all of his colleagues would jointly censure him. (5.113)

Early in Xuanzong's reign, Li rose to become a prominent minister. The Song source *Extensive Records*—borrowing this same passage from Zhang Zhuo—situates the anecdote in a chapter devoted to officials who have a "tolerant and measured" (*qiliang* 器量) approach.[32] Unlike the "cruel officials" featured in the following chapter, Li—both as a magistrate overseeing counties in the capital region and as Minister of Justice supervising subordinates—managed to strike the difficult balance between strictness and forbearance. He flogs an errant underling not with a whip, but with public shaming. This strategy helped foster an exacting and efficient culture of self-policing among the clerks on his staff. Zhang Zhuo presents Li's strategy of cultivating a principle-driven culture of shame without resorting to corporal punishment as a leadership style worthy of emulation.

In another passage from *Court and Country*, Zhang Chujin embodies the good official when he performs some cerebral detective work to rescue a prefect from wrongful implication and execution. He cleverly exposed the fraud of a low-level official who hoped to parlay a false accusation (that his superior had ties to the leader of a 684 rebellion against Wu Zhao) to his advantage:

> In the Chuigong era when Zetian administered the state, the net of false accusations and framing began. Huzhou Assistant Jiang Chen took Prefect Pei Guang's dossier of cases and cut out characters to create a fraudulent new document connected to the Xu Jingye rebellion, which he used to lodge an accusation against Pei. The officials appointed to investigate Pei found that the script on the document was in his writing, but they were dubious as the expressions used were not his. Three different officials examined the document, but none could decide. An imperial order requested that the officials find someone who could examine the document and find the truth in the matter. All unanimously said, "Zhang Chujin can!" They sent for him. Gloomy and weighed down with anxiety, Zhang lay supine on a couch under a west-facing window. When the sun was high, he held the document up to the sunlight and examined it, discovering that the characters seemed to have little seams. Looking at the document under ordinary light one couldn't see it, but, holding it up to the sunlight, the seams of the patched-on characters were visible. He ordered all of the prefectural officials to gather and demanded an earthenware basin of water. He ordered Jiang Chen to drop the document on the surface of the water. When he did, the characters peeled off one by one. Jiang Chen kowtowed and confessed his guilt. By imperial order, he was caned one hundred times with a stick, then beheaded. Zhang Chujin was rewarded with 100 bolts of silk. (5.109)

Perhaps Zhang's saturnine disposition and anxiety stemmed from his knowledge that the deadly net cast by the "cruel officials" was already tightening around him. In 689, Zhang and several others were accused by Zhou Xing, a leader among these "cruel officials," of helping to shelter rebel leaders from the Xu Jingye rebellion of 684—the same charge that Zhang had helped Pei Guang avoid. Zhang Chujin was sentenced to death.[33] There is a dramatic passage about Zhang's would-be execution in the late Tang *Records of the Censorate*:

> In the Tang dynasty court of Zetian, Minister of Justice Zhang Chujin was framed by "cruel official," Zhou Xing. When he was about to be sentenced, he raised his head and sighed, "Ah, heaven above and earth below: How could it be that you don't see my loyalty and filial piety? How can you allow the innocent to be so wrongly charged with a crime?" Tears streamed from his eyes, prompting people watching in the marketplace to sob along with him. Suddenly, dark clouds crowded from every quarter, as though attuned to Zhang's agony. At the last moment, Zetian sent an imperial pardon. As soon as the proclamation was read, the dark clouds cleared from the heavens, replaced by a profusion of auspicious rainbow clouds. At the time, the buzz among people was that this was the result of Zhang's loyalty and uprightness.[34]

This is an example of the "mutual resonance of Heaven and Earth" (*tianren ganying* 天人感應), the notion that nature and the cosmos are in sympathetic harmony, both responsive to the realm of men.[35]

However, another excerpt from *Court and Country* makes one question whether Zhang Chujin was, in truth, a good official:

> In the Tang, Vice Minister of Justice Zhang Chujin memorialized the emperor proposing that even if rebels and traitors to the state already had been given a special amnesty from death, their family members should still be executed by beheading or strangulation, or exiled to face penal servitude, stripped of all official titles and made into servants or slaves. Later, when Chujin was implicated and accused of rebellion, although he held an amnesty from the death sentence, all of the male members of his family aged fifteen or older were executed, and his wife was exiled into penal servitude. One of his acquaintances remarked, "Snared by his own law…this is what's called retribution." (Sup., 157)

This passage suggests that Zhang Chujin had a complicated relationship with the court and the "cruel officials." On the one hand, Zhou Xing, one of the leading "cruel officials," sought to punish Zhang, as we saw above. On the other hand, Zhang proposed a draconian measure that, when implemented, increased the number of executions, thus aligning it (and Zhang) with the practices and directives of the "cruel officials." The passage emphasizes the brutal karmic retribution evident in the fact that Zhang's family was eradicated because of his own policy. Zhang himself was banished to the southern hinterlands, where he was murdered in 690, just before Wu Zhao ascended the throne.[36] This anecdote was salvaged from the chapters on "Retribution" in *Extensive Records*.[37]

THE FILIAL AND THE UNFILIAL

Filial piety (*xiao* 孝) was a signal virtue of Confucianism and in Chinese culture. Keith Knapp terms it "the paramount cultural value" which "shaped nearly every aspect of Chinese social life: attitudes toward authority, patterns of residence, conceptions of self, marriage practices, gender preferences, emotional life, religious worship, and social relations."[38] Failure to abide by the tenets of filial piety marked one as a miscreant, incapable of adhering to fundamental bonds of blood and society. The *Tang Code*, compiled by Taizong and promulgated early in Gaozong's reign, categorized a lack of filiality as one of the "Ten Abominations," ranking it alongside treason, rebellion against the state, depravity, and incest, on the short-list of the most heinous crimes.[39] Being unfilial—the ultimate manifestation of a man's deficient character—was a charge able to destroy one's reputation and career. The following account from *Court and Country* delineates four examples of the dereliction of filial devotion:

> In the Zhou, Vice Minister of Summer[40] Hou Zhiyi was old; the emperor issued an edict requesting that he retire from service. Hou presented a memorial saying that he was unwilling. In the audience hall he leapt up and down, rushing about to display his sprightliness.
>
> After mourning a parent's death, Zhang Cong requested that he be recalled to serve in his former post.
>
> When the mother of Secretary of the Ministry of Personnel Gao Jun passed away, his relatives were organizing her funeral. Gao Jun said, "I'm unable to return and act as a filial son."
>
> When Vice Director Zhang Qizhen was accused of falsely claiming to mourn his mother's death as a filial son, he refused to respond to the charge.
>
> At the time, those in the Secretariat said of these four, "Hou Zhiyi is unwilling to retire, Zhang Cong requests to be recalled and restored to his post, Gao Jun is unwilling to act as a filial son in mourning, and Zhang Qizhen wishes for a parent's death. None of these men conformed to norms of Confucian teaching; all strayed from the noble path. Are they not like beasts with the hearts of men?" (4.93)

Among the four unfilial acts delineated in this passage, the aging general's frisky display of vigor, while perhaps indecorous, seems the least offensive. To some extent, the unfilial behavior of this quartet is intended to illustrate that such reprehensible behavior—while still prompting a harsh rebuke from the Confucian gentlemen in the Secretariat—was no anomaly in Wu Zhao's court.

Zhang Zhuo proffers these four anti-exemplars in diametric opposition to Cui Hun, who served in the court immediately following Wu Zhao's deposal and death. Salvaged from the section on "Filial Sentiment" in an early Northern Song encyclopedia,[41] this account details Cui's profound devotion and filial angst:

> In the Tang, Censor Cui Hun, by nature warm and reverent, conscientiously attended his parents with the utmost filiality. Whenever his parents felt the slightest discomfort, he would beg the spirits to let him take their place. Once when his mother was sick, Hun knelt and entreated the illness to strike him instead. Shortly thereafter, he felt sickness enter through his ten fingers and spread through his entire body. Subsequently, all of his mother's suffering was alleviated. His distress was so keen when he was mourning his mother's passing that even a spoonful of liquid could not pass his lips. Ravaged by sorrow, he fell ill. Unable to bear it and to overcome his grief, Cui Hun expired. People far and wide lamented his passing. (Sup., 174)

One of the truest measures of character was the degree to which a man displayed filial devotion to his parents. Cui Hun was thus honored and immortalized as a filial son.

THE CULTURE OF THE COURT

Another anecdote in *Court and Country*, salvaged from the same encyclopedia under the general rubric "Filiality," tells of the profound grief that gripped Su Ting after the death of his father:[42]

> When Su Ting was Secretarial Drafter, his father Left Archery Commandant Su Gui passed away.[43] Grieving Su Ting grew emaciated and wasted away beyond the prescription of rites. When an imperial order came commanding him to return and resume office, Su memorialized, steadfastly declining. The emperor sent Vice Director of the Chancellery Li Rizhi to Su Ting's residence with an imperial order requesting that Su return to office. But the entire time Li was present, Su simply sat without speaking. When Li returned, he reported in his memorial, "When I saw Su Ting in such a state of exhaustion and emaciation, almost unable to overcome his grief, I couldn't bear to speak for fear that it would push him too far and he would perish." Feeling compassion for Su Ting, the emperor did not force him to return to office.
> People of the time said, "Su Gui had a true son; Li Qiao had no son." (Sup., 154)

As a Censor late in Wu Zhao's reign, Su Ting gained a reputation as a principled minister by sending a memorial calling for cases involving Wu Zhao's "cruel officials" (see next chapter) to be redressed. During the second reign of Wu Zhao's youngest son Ruizong (710–712), Su Ting stepped away from official duties to return to his hometown and properly mourn his deceased father. Before the three-year mourning period was up, Ruizong sought to recall him to government service and assigned another chief minister, Li Rizhi, the errand of retrieving the capable minister. While Li Rizhi returned empty-handed, Su Ting eventually completed his mourning and went on to serve Xuanzong as a chief minister.

A source contemporary to *Court and Country* provides clearer context regarding the final sentence of the passage above: *"Su Gui had a true son; Li Qiao had no son."* Wu Zhao's son Zhongzong—possibly in 684, during his brief first reign—summoned the young sons of two high-ranking officials with great literary talent, Su Gui and Li Qiao, requesting that the two display their learning.[44] Su Gui's son, the future filial paragon Su Ting (who would have only been four or five at the time) quoted time-honored Confucian advice from the *Book of History*: "If wood is cut following a plumb line, it will be straight; so it is that a lord who follows wise counsel can become a sage ruler."[45] Su Ting's son drew upon the same text, citing a warning from the reign of the notorious Zhou, the tyrannical final king of the Shang dynasty: "Break not the ankles of those crossing rivers, nor should you dissect the hearts of the worthy."[46] Both children urged the emperor to heed cautionary wisdom from the *Book of History*: the only difference is that Su Ting quoted the wise minister of a good ruler, while Li Qiao's child issued an admonition from an evil king's rule. Zhongzong, a vapid ruler who lacked classical learning—perhaps considering Li Qiao's son insolent for selecting a quote that tacitly associated him with a negative paragon—proclaimed, "Su Gui has a true son! Li Qiao has no son!"

By attributing that utterance to *"people of the times"* instead of to Zhongzong, Zhang Zhuo—with his manifest dislike of Li Qiao—purposefully shifted the context; he made it seem as though it was widely understood that Li Qiao's son (instead of having been misunderstood after proffering timeless counsel) was unfilial, a product of bad parenting from a covetous careerist who attached himself to Wu Zhao and her favorites.

Li Qiao was a gifted poet–official and rhetorician who served under Wu Zhao. Zhang Zhuo's claim that his son was "no son" is a clear slight. We will see later in this chapter that when asked about Li Qiao, Zhang Zhuo promptly launches into a character assassination. Zhang paints Li as one who *"loves glory and official advancement, but hates to see the ascent and promotion of others"*; is skilled in *"literary writing and essays, but loathes others who wield a calligraphy brush with talent"*; and is *"greedy and covets ill-gotten gains, yet despises it when others receive presents or bribes"* (4.98; see below). Zhang concludes that Li Qiao—glory-seeking, treacherous, and inured to luxury—was cut from the same cloth as the *"former female ruler"* whom he served: Wu Zhao.

FROM THE PERSPECTIVE OF THE CENTER

In this passage from *Court and Country*, an officious chief minister in Wu Zhao's court creates a complex and ridiculously bureaucratic new system of rural checks and balances to control, supervise, and regulate local responsibilities on a sub-county level:

> *In the Zhou, Lu Renjie of Heyang rose from lowly rank to enter the Secretariat as a chief minister. In this capacity, he altered the form of tax receipts empire-wide. His new system was complex, fraught with minutiae, proliferating with innumerable laws and statutes. Every village had to establish a local field official and also three elders charged with maintaining honesty and straightforwardness. They administered even the most trivial cases and set up a system of locks and keys. For every ten sheep, there were nine shepherds. Locals all dispersed, seeking to evade the consequences, but the chief ministers felt this was a new system for the ages that could be implemented, and Lu Renjie was promoted. After several years of the common people suffering, his new regulations were put to rest.* (4.92)

In any large bureaucracy, there is often a disconnect between the metropolis and the periphery, between the plans mapped out in the audience hall of the court and the ground-level reality in a county 1000 miles away. As one who served both in central and local government, Zhang Zhuo was keenly aware that the best-laid plans of court ministers for managing country and village agriculture rarely suited varying climates and landscapes. The passage above, no doubt containing a bit of hyperbole (Lu Renjie did not actually propose a nearly one-to-one shepherd-to-sheep ratio), reflects this awareness. From the foundation of the Chinese empire to the Great Leap Forward, rash application of one-size-fits-all policy over a diversity of regions, cultures, and peoples almost invariably has proved a recipe for administrative waste and failure. Chapter 4 will examine more closely some of the issues and problems that local officials confronted because of the vast spaces between center and circumference.

When a court official was demoted or banished from the capital cities, Chang'an and Luoyang, sent down to the malarial swamps of the south or some rocky borderland, it was like being expelled from the shining capital and cast into the benighted unknown. Many never returned. Former colleagues would hold drinking banquets and write poems to "send off" an unfortunate friend. Close friends might even accompany them for the first few stages of the journey. This account from *Court and Country*, set a decade after Wu Zhao's deposal and death, features a governor of Chang'an who had small empathy for families' prolonged and sentimental separations from banished men:

In the Tang, Metropolitan Governor of the Capital Region Cui Rizhi punished those banished or demoted from Chang'an, Wannian, and all the other counties in the capital region, never allowing them to delay or remain in the region. Anyone who delayed or broke the rule was beaten with a rod. Soon thereafter, Cui Rizhi had his rank decreased to a junior official in She County[47]*, and, when pressured by the county head, begged for more time to part with his wife. It was not granted.* (Sup., 157)

Cui is described in unflattering terms in one of the Tang histories as "avaricious, violent, and lawless."[48] Zhang Zhuo delights in stories of just retribution that feature harsh or inflexible men getting their well-earned due. This tale is no exception: Cui Rizhi meets his deserved fate when he is subjected to his own harsh rule denying banished and demoted officials time to say good-bye to friends and family!

ZHANG ZHUO PROVES TO BE A FLAWLESS JUDGE OF CHARACTER (IF HE SAYS SO HIMSELF)

A lengthy passage presented as a dialogue between a "guest"—an interlocutor whose sole function is to pose questions about different men in Wu Zhao's court—and Zhang Zhuo affords the author occasion to flaunt his linguistic dexterity and wit while displaying his nuanced insights about the personalities and characters of various ministers:

> *In the Tang, Lu Shide of Rongyang served as Chancellor. A guest asked Master Who Drifts then Rests, "What sort of man is Chancellor Lu?"*
>
> *He answered, "The Chancellor is direct yet warm-hearted, broad-minded yet serious, on the exterior muddle-headed yet clever on the inside, superficially obscure yet crystal clear in essence. Much like the waves on a vast sea, he is turbid but not muddied; like a blade that has been through a hundred smeltings, he's whetted and ground to a keen edge yet not blunted by use. One might say that Lu is a true gentleman of substance and virtuous character, one of the great men of the era.*
>
> *The guest asked, "What about Di Renjie as Chancellor?"*
>
> *The Master Who Drifts then Rests answered, "In observing the classics and the histories, his knowledge is rough. His grasp of calligraphy and essays is cursory, yet in his sincere adherence to regulations and willingness to offer cutting, blunt remonstrance to the ruler, he has an air of one of the ancients. With the recklessness of a fiery hero, he razed the licentious cults. In heart and spirit, he is upright and direct. He can wade through the muck of court without getting sullied. His courageous spirit is resolute and unyielding. He is decisive and clear in rendering decisions. In his later years, however, he craved wealth, like a disciple of He Qiao[49]!"*
>
> *The guest asked, "Could Vice Minister of the Secretariat Li Zhaode become a famous minister?"*
>
> *The Master Who Drifts then Rests responded, "Li Zhaode has grand ambitions, yet he is a small vessel, a man who puts on lofty airs but possesses paltry knowledge. He hides behind his authority to control matters and uses pressure points to threaten people. He is excessively obdurate and headstrong, yet insufficiently respectful and tolerant. This is not a proper path for one to last long in court." Soon Li paid the price and was punished by law.*
>
> *The guest also inquired, "Luoyang officer Lai Junchen is graceful, poised, and handsome. Do you consider him an unswervingly loyal minister?"*
>
> *The Master Who Drifts then Rests answered, "Junchen has a gentle face but a cruel heart—a man of treacherous character and paltry virtue. His clever sophistry mimics wisdom; his deft flattery counterfeits loyalty. He subverts and undermines the foundation of state, slandering and framing good, respectable people. He is a disciple of Jiang Chong.[50] He injures the people like a venomous wasp or scorpion, but he shall meet a grievous end at the hands of the people!"*
>
> *In the end, Lai was made Chief Minister of the Court of Imperial Stud, then massacred in the Western Market.*
>
> *The guest asked, "Can Wu Sansi be considered a prince of high repute?"*
>
> *The Master Who Drifts then Rests responded, "Availing himself of nepotism, Sansi has reached a position of power exceeding that of the Three Dukes.[51] He appears respectful and deferential, but his heart is treacherous and cruel. Superficially, he projects public-mindedness and directness; within, he fabricates murky schemes, manipulating laws of state to wreak personal vengeance, arrogating court authority to inflict great damage. Later, he was invested as Prince of Dejing. This man is a thief of the tripods of state. He shan't perish of old age!"*
>
> *In the end, he was killed in the palace coup of Crown Prince Jiemin.[52]*

THE CULTURE OF THE COURT

The guest then queried, "Secretariat Director Wei Yuanzhong is staunchly loyal and straight-forward. Can he be considered a worthy minister of this era?"

The Master Who Drifts then Rests answered, "Yuanzhong is deficient in both the civil and military arenas; by reputation and in substance, he is empty. On the surface, he appears principled and resolute, but in his bosom he's a favor-currying lackey. In confronting and denouncing Zhang Shiqi's clique, he was as courageous as a savage bear; in fawningly casting his lot with Wu Shikai's band, he was as craven as a sickly cur. As a warrior he was indecisive as a mouse, alternately advancing then scurrying backward; as a man, he's no different than a viper or poisonous lizard. He adhered to Wu Sansi's clique and denounced the revolt of the Five Princes. It's precisely this sort of man who fosters a chaotic court with corrupt politics. When I carefully mull over his career, he will not come to a good end."

Not unexpectedly, because of an offense Wei was exiled to distant Sizhou, where, fraught with anxiety and filled with resentment, he perished.

The guest also queried, "What about Secretariat Director Li Qiao?"

The Master Who Drifts then Rests answered, "His Excellency Li has three faults: by character he loves glory and official advancement, but hates to see the ascent and promotion of others; by disposition he is fond of literary writing and essays, but he loathes others who wield a talented calligraphy brush; he is greedy and covets ill-gotten gains, yet despises it when others receive presents or bribes. In this respect, he's just like a former female ruler: By nature she craved rich and succulent viands, yet she prohibited the people from eating meat; by disposition she loved colorful and elegant silks, yet she imposed strict sumptuary laws on the people; by character she was lascivious and wanton, but hated it when others enjoyed music and sex. This is the path of His Excellency Li."

The guest then asked, "What about Director of Corporal Punishments Xu Yougong?"

The Master Who Drifts then Rests answered, "Yougong is a loyal and straightforward gentleman. He is intelligent with conviction, resolute and decisive. Situated in a fallen, decadent time, he never resorted to flattery to gain an advantage. Amidst a tumultuous court, he never sought recourse in obsequious expressions in order to avoid confrontation. He managed to secure the release of those implicated in Lai Junchen's net of accusations and freed Yuan Zhihong from his trial by fire. When the tiger's tail swooshed past, he never flinched; when the dragon's scales brushed by, he remained unafraid. He was a phoenix roosting among stunted owls; his directness allowed him to keep his body intact. Because he was a leopard among jackals and wolves, his loyalty kept harm at bay. If only he had lived in a peaceful and uncorrupted age, he might be spoken of in the same breath as Zhang Shizhi and Ding Yuguo.[53]*"*

The guest also queried, "What about Chief Minister of the Court of Imperial Granaries Zhao Luwen?"

The Master Who Drifts then Rests answered, "Luwen's mind is not focused on knowledge and his eyes fail to recognize literature. Superficially, he appears respectful, but his nature is treacherous. He is a man of little wisdom but many schemes. He slopes along in faltering steps like a skulking cur, then makes a sudden move like a greedy swine. Like a suckling lamb lured out of the pasture in the morning, unaware of its imminent doom, or a moth at night about to alight on a candle flame yet not cognizant of its forthcoming immolation, how can such a man hope to keep his head on his neck for long?"

Later, because Zhao was implicated for sedition with Commoner Wei, all three sets of his kinsmen were exterminated.

> *The guest also asked, "What about when Zheng Yin was appointed Vice Minister of Personnel?"*
>
> *The Master Who Drifts then Rests answered, "Yin is a rascal capable of unbridled violence, a crafty and vulgar fellow, a man of shallow learning and superficial words, light on talent and deficient in virtue. He squats like a fox at the heels of the eminent and respectable, hunching down like a pheasant before the gates of the powerful. Initially, he relied upon Lai Junchen; later, he attached himself to Zhang Yizhi. He cringed fawningly in the rooms of Prince of Dejing[54] and served as a hemorrhoid-lapping lackey in the court of the Anle Princess. He's like a wren perched precariously on swaying reeds and rushes, or a catfish swimming in a boiling cauldron. Such a man—lacking in magnanimity of spirit and, in the end, made of mediocre substance, using his paltry qualities to seek to flourish—can only meet with the good fortune of death."*
>
> *Not unexpectedly, Zheng Yin was executed for conspiring to rebel.* (4.97–98)

While the precise timing of this alleged conversation is unclear, it is written as though these questions were asked late in the reign of Wu Zhao. There is a brief afterword to each of Zhang Zhuo's thumbnail descriptions to indicate that his analysis was invariably spot-on—a clever device for enhancing authorial credibility.

Zhang Zhuo's assessments of these men—all high-ranking court officials in Wu Zhao's Zhou dynasty—divide them into "good guys," characterized as imperturbable paragons of Confucian virtue, and "bad guys," oily and callous, self-serving and sycophantic. Lu Shide, Di Renjie, and Xu Yougong fall into the former category. The five men who fall decisively into the latter category represent different groups that Zhang Zhuo and Confucian historians of subsequent eras hold in particular contempt: Lai Junchen was one of Wu Zhao's "cruel officials"; Wu Zhao's nephew, Wu Sansi, is the final consequence of extreme nepotism; Li Qiao is a literary master who lent his talents to glorifying Wu Zhao (and later her daughter-in-law Empress Wei); Zhao Luwen is a "skulking cur"; and Zheng Yin is an obsequious hanger-on.

Two curious cases are more ambiguous. Both Li Zhaode and Wei Yuanzhong are characterized in the official histories as upright and principled chief ministers with impressive, if checkered, careers. Li Zhaode had the courage to challenge Wu Zhao's cruel officials and remonstrated against Wu Zhao when she planned to name her nephew Wu Chengsi heir apparent.[55] Wei Yuanzhong, whom the interlocutor describes as "loyal and straight-forward," had a lengthy and distinguished civil and military career dating back to when Gaozong was still alive. He also locked horns with Wu Zhao's cruel officials and clashed with her male favorites, the Zhang brothers.[56] Because these men resisted Wu Zhao's political allies, Confucian histories regard them in a relatively favorable light. However, Zhang Zhuo dismisses Li Zhaode as a hard-headed man of small talent. Moreover, because of Wei Yuanzhong's

THE CULTURE OF THE COURT

allegiance to Wu Zhao's nephew, Wu Sansi, Zhang relegates the erstwhile chief minister to the ranks of the curs and lackeys, framing him as a vacillating incompetent while disparaging both his civil and military career.

Still, Zhang Zhuo and later Confucian historians agreed about the other five men and the types they embodied. Men from these groups, in the Confucian narrative, all facilitated Wu Zhao's unnatural rise to power; as such, they were impediments to the restoration of the normative Confucian patriarchal order. For this parade of degenerates, lugubrious fates are meted out in case after case. Such fates are presented as richly deserved—the final outcomes of lifetimes of corruption, hypocrisy, and transgressive cruelty. Thus, invariably, they all met exile, misery, or violent death. These men violated a natural sense of proportion. The judgment of their unnatural, twisted lives is linked until they seem a collective emanation of Wu Zhao herself, as though she spawned this brood of amoral and unnatural children.

3

"Cruel officials": Wu Zhao's "teeth and horns"¹

DONALD WYATT OBSERVED THAT "WU ZHAO's own propensity for the wanton perpetration of violence against her perceived domestic enemies [...] helped clear her path of real and imagined obstructers by the thousands."² Wyatt is right: her "cruel officials" (*ku li* 酷吏) were an essential part of her political authority, the umbrageous *yin* that complemented the sunny *yang* of aesthetes eloquently singing her praises and colorful ceremonies staged to validate her power. Therefore, any effort to scrutinize the dark countenance of the Janus-faced female sovereign needs to examine the *modus operandi* of these brutal henchmen; they helped Wu Zhao quash her opposition and consolidate power, particularly in the years immediately before and following her establishment of the Zhou dynasty in 690.

Wu Zhao was certainly not the first ruler to ruthlessly deploy strongarms to gain and consolidate power: prior to her reign, records attest to more than a millennium of draconian punishments exacted by countless "cruel officials" throughout early and early medieval Chinese history. Sima Qian began cataloging the careers of such men in *Records of the Grand Historian*, the template for later dynastic histories. Explaining his rationale for including biographies of such individuals, he wrote, "When the people turn their backs on what is basic and are too ingenious, they ravage traditions and play with the laws, so that even the good among them cannot be transformed and only a thorough severity can return them to good order. Thus, I wrote 'The Cruel Officials.'"³ While acknowledging their drawbacks, the celebrated annalist recognized, despite (or, arguably, because of) their cruelty and violence, a certain constructive value, a political utility, in the actions of these men. Toward the end of their collective biography, the Grand Historian observed, "The virtues of these ten men can be taken as models, their vices as a warning. These men, by their schemes and strategies, their teaching and leadership, restricted wickedness and ended evil. Although harsh, these men did what their duty prescribed."⁴ There is a clear recognition, even a begrudging appreciation, for the guiding role that such individuals play in fostering order through draconian measures, extirpating evil to help stabilize the empire. Still, Sima

Qian pointedly (naming names) excluded a number of officials whose conduct he deemed devoid of socially or politically redeeming characteristics. Traits and actions that warranted disqualification included a penchant for savage oppression, dismembering people, sawing off heads, torturing to force confession, wanton killing, viperine cruelty or vulture-like ruthlessness, and extortion.[5]

While for most male rulers, standard histories employ rather gymnastic logic to mansplain the necessity of "cruel officials," female emperor Wu Zhao is held to different standards. Her "cruel officials" are never lauded as harsh guardians of order, but instead categorically depicted as callous purveyors of terror. Confucian histories frequently point to the bloodshed perpetrated by the female sovereign's "cruel officials" as evidence that Wu Zhao was a violent and unjust ruler (*baojun* 暴君), a usurper rather than a legitimate sovereign. Even Western historians like C. P. Fitzgerald, though he acknowledges that she later cast aside the system and "liquidated the torturers," opined that these "secret police" and their campaign of terror were "a dark stain upon the rule of Wu Chao."[6]

On the whole, recent scholars have been more measured in their assessment of Wu Zhao's "cruel officials": while never explicitly condoning the terror and violence that these men perpetrated, most argue that they played a significant and necessary role in buttressing her power by intimidating political opponents, keeping Li family kinsmen and upper echelon officials in a constant state of fear and uncertainty. Furthermore, in early and medieval China, reliance on violence and intimidation was no novelty. False accusations, forced confessions, and even the draconian punishment of clan extermination did not set Wu Zhao's henchmen apart; such practices were all—like the "cruel officials" who implemented them—long-standing traditions.

Tracking the pattern of "narrative condemnation" amid the "gender anarchy" of Wu Zhao's time, Rebecca Doran illustrates that centuries of Chinese history placed men who supported female leadership on the wrong side of the great binary and didactic narrative, casting "cruel officials" into the fetid cesspool at the base of history's ravine while ensconcing the so-called upright and principled court officials (who served male rulers and adhered to Confucian gendered norms) near the pinnacle of the mountain of virtue. Wu Zhao's "cruel officials" were disdainfully written into the script of standard and unofficial histories alike as men devoid of principle, set in the ignominious company of her sycophants and male favorites.[7] As Doran aptly points out, "The righteous official is actually the mouthpiece of the historian, driving home his judgments about politics, gender, and their intersection."[8] Though keenly aware of the nature of these Confucian sources, Doran still describes the notorious leader of Wu Zhao's "cruel officials," Lai Junchen, as the "extremely evil and corrupt official who served Empress Wu and supplied her with misinformation that led her to murder hundreds of innocent men."[9] While I certainly would not contend that Lai Junchen was actually a great guy, it is important to point out that he and his band of "cruel officials" were unfailingly assigned the part of villain or foil in Confucian annals, and also in *Court and Country*; after all, they belonged to a separate, parallel culture with an alternative set of values that were starkly different from, and had interests often antithetical to, the culturally conservative Confucian establishment—those tiresome arbiters of "the right side of history" in traditional China.

Wu Zhao almost never allowed "cruel officials" to become high ministers and wield power in court. Overall, her campaign of inquisition, imprisonment, and torture was top-heavy and narrow in scope, though several campaigns were launched against exiled Li princes in the south, directed almost exclusively at distinguished official families and imperial clansmen because of the direct political threat they posed. Indeed, Wu Zhao followed the hoary wisdom of the proverb "once the hares are caught, the hounds are boiled" (*tusi, goupeng* 兔死狗烹), often dispatching these men after they had fulfilled their function.

Court and Country spares few barbarous and gory details, providing numerous accounts of vicious acts perpetrated by Wu Zhao's murderous "teeth and horns," who intimidated the wealthy nobles and cowed influential ministers in the court. Indeed, with some gusto, Zhang Zhuo rolls up both his sleeves and pantlegs and, in the name of bringing to light the bad and the ugly, plunges into the orgiastic mire of bloodshed to provide ample stories and anecdotes of Wu Zhao's instrumental use of violence and terror. Below are more than a dozen accounts of the sadistic acts reportedly perpetrated by Wu Zhao's "cruel officials."

THE DAWN OF WU ZHAO'S "CRUEL OFFICIALS"

One event in 684—occurring just after Wu Zhao had deposed her son and began to preside over court as grand dowager-regent—is often cited as marking the beginning of her deployment of these "cruel officials" as her "teeth and horns," her secret police. Thereafter, informers played a pivotal role in Wu Zhao's reign of terror that began in 684, just days after she elevated her youngest son Ruizong to emperor. This incident is recorded in *Court and Country*:

> *When Zetian first deposed the Prince of Luling,*[10] *a dozen members of the Flying Cavalry were drinking together at a tavern in one of the wards. Someone said, "If I'd known earlier*

> that we'd be rewarded in such a paltry way for our work, I might as well have thrown my support behind the Prince of Luling." A person at the table rose and departed; entering the northern gate of the palace, he filed an accusation against them. Before the drinking party dispersed, they were seized by the Forest of Plumes imperial bodyguards. During the subsequent investigation, all told the truth. The accuser was promoted to fifth rank. The speaker was beheaded; others present for his seditious remarks who failed to report him were sentenced to death by strangulation. (Sup., 160)

After this event, all wishing to lodge secret accusation—even woodcutters and peasants—were given free post-horse transportation and an audience. While false allegations were not punished, information that proved true was richly rewarded. Secret informants from every quarter descended on the capital; the wealthy and influential waited in a state of tremulous fear. Undeniably, Wu Zhao's "cruel officials" were effective, expedient, and zealous in the prosecution of their duties; C. P. Fitzgerald observed that "the rapidity of action and efficiency of the secret police was surprising to an age in which such methods were largely unknown."[11]

A disproportionate number of the "cruel officials" given biographies in the *Old Tang History* come from Wu Zhao's regency and reign.[12] The most notorious among these henchmen (and the first two listed in the biography) were Lai Junchen and Zhou Xing. A number of anecdotes in *Court and Country*, like the one below, are calibrated to convey the malicious pride that these men took in their vocation:

> In the Zhou era, Vice Minister of Autumn[13] Zhou Xing was cruel and ruthless in his investigations and examinations. Outside the confines of law, he tormented and tortured—there was nothing that he wouldn't do! People of the time called Zhou the "Ox-headed Grannie," and the commonfolk, seething with resentment, slandered him. Zhou then placed a placard outside his gate, declaring, "Those arraigned all claim they have been falsely accused; yet once they are beheaded, they all shut up." (2.32)

In this excerpt, Zhou Xing is depicted as utterly remorseless; indeed, his less-than-affectionate nickname, "Ox-headed Grannie," evokes the ox-headed demons that populated the Buddhist underworld. He is clearly aware of the anger of the populace, but he responds to criticism defiantly, reminding all that it is he who gets the last word!

A complementary series of passages in *Court and Country* seek to demonstrate that Wu Zhao's "cruel officials" eliminated good, principled men. Take, for example, this account of Zhou Xing orchestrating the execution of Jiang Rong:

> In the Tang, Left Scribe[14] Jiang Rong was honest and frank, upright and straightforward. When Xu Jingye rebelled in Yangzhou, he was implicated and accused. Cruel officer Zhou

"CRUEL OFFICIALS"

Xing and others memorialized[15], urging that Jiang be executed. The petition was approved, and Jiang was led before the post station pavilion in the Eastern Market to be beheaded. Just before Jiang Rong was to be executed, he requested an audience with the emperor to plead his case.

Zhou Xing retorted, "How could a criminal like you be granted an audience?!"

Infuriated, Jiang Rong roared, "I'm an innocent man who has been framed and will be murdered. Even after I'm dead, I'll never release my hold on you." Shortly thereafter he was beheaded, but his body surged to its feet, staggering forward more than ten paces. The executioners pushed him down, but the body rose again. This happened three times, then finally the body lay still. Though his head had been severed, the fury in Jiang's eyes was unabated.

Not long thereafter, Zhou Xing was dead. (Sup., 155–56)

In addition to making for good storytelling, Jiang Rong's dramatic death and the unwavering, outraged gaze of his severed head no doubt helped inculcate a sense of indignation among readers. One of the official Tang histories also remarks on Jiang Rong's excellent reputation—and his death by beheading in the marketplace.[16] The passage's concluding note about Zhou Xing's death "[n]ot long thereafter" suggests that justice was ultimately served.

THE SAVAGE CRUELTY OF WU YIZONG

In the first two chapters, we saw Wu Yizong as an incompetent, cowardly general and as a cringing buffoon, abasing himself before his superior kin Wu Zhao. Here, we encounter a very different aspect of the man: the callous and violent henchman. The two passages below are set early in the Zhou dynasty, before Wu Yizong served as a general. He seems to have been a Censor, one of the "cruel officials" assigned to investigate cases and mete out brutal punishments:

In the Zhou era, Clerk Han Linggui, a fellow with no sense of shame or humiliation, had a face showing loyalty and magnanimity but a heart filled with ambitious malice. Han would slavishly greet all of the princes, dukes, and eminent men according to their rank and grade. He even called on those he had never met before, cloyingly seeking their favor and influence.

In the past, he was nominated to take the civil service examination by Lu Yuanfang. Official Wang Ju had returned early from mourning and sat supervising in the same examination hall as Lu Yuanfang. Feigning surprise, Han said, "How is that I've yet to see Fifth Wang?"[17] When Wang Ju descended the steps, Han affected deep sorrow, furrowing his brow in an aggrieved expression. He offered consolation, then departed. Lu Yuanfang and Wang Ju were old friends. Lu asked Han who Wang was; Han said he did not recognize him.

Later, his false displays were exposed, and an order came down that Han was to be punished by stick in the audience hall. From afar he saw Prince of Henei Wu Yizong, and called out, "Elder Brother, how is it that you're not coming to save me?" Yizong looked at him and said, "I don't know you." He then urged the man meting out punishment by stick to deal Wei some severe blows. Han Linggui died by the cudgel. (Sup., 160)

THE WORLD OF WU ZHAO

In the Zhou, when Turkish khan Mochuo breached Hengzhou and Dingzhou, by imperial order Ambassador of Marital Alliances Yang Qizhuang received third rank. He entered Xiongnu territory and fell into enemy hands. When he reached Zhaozhou, he encountered Duke of Xiang Duan Zan, who had been similarly captured. Duan called to Yang and asked if he wanted to try to escape. Yang was afraid and didn't dare leave, so subsequently Zan fled first and returned to Chinese territory. Zetian rewarded him and restored him to his former appointment. Shortly thereafter, Yang returned from enemy territory. By imperial decree, the emperor handed him over to Prince of Henei Wu Yizong for interrogation. Zhuang said, "In the past it was because of the support of others that my position reached third rank, but then I encountered adversity amidst swords and arrows. When I, Zhuang, escaped, I was pursued, but despite the blades and arrows, I managed to escape. Given this plight, I sincerely hope Your Excellency will show compassion."

By nature, Yizong was cruel and venomous. He sent a memorial claiming that as it was suspicious that Zhuang had initially hesitated to return, and he begged leave to execute him. Zetian issued an imperial decree consenting to this punishment. Yang Qizhuang was dragged south of Heaven's Ford Bridge in Luoyang, then bound and spread-eagled in the open space before the drumming platform. Wu Yizong ordered Duan Zan to be the first to fire arrows at him; thrice Duan shot his bow, and each arrow hit its mark. Next, Duan Jin fired a trio of arrows that all struck true. Then he ordered all of the officials to fire at once, so that the arrows riddling Qizhuang's body were dense as the quills of a hedgehog. And yet Qizhuang was still faintly breathing, his archer's thumb ring barely twitching. Yizong then drove a dagger into his chest, sundering his innards, then carved out his heart and cast it on the ground. The heart still beat and tremored a dozen times before finally stopping. Such was the toxic cruelty of Wu Yizong. (2.35–36)

In the first excerpt, tasked with adjudicating the case of the clerk Han Linggui, Wu Yizong summarily orders him beaten to death. Such episodes in *Court and Country* are calibrated to portray most of the men staffing Wu Zhao's court as either cringing sycophants or power-mongering sadists. With bemused contempt, Zhang Zhuo depicts the clumsy, failed efforts of Han Linggui to use *guanxi*—connections, relationships—the lubricious grease essential to navigating and networking in business, society, and politics. His conduct demonstrates the uglier aspects of a stratified society, where rank, title, and birth define a man's worth: those in inferior positions are often compelled to make a display of performative deference, scraping and fawning for all they are worth, while those in superior positions behave with contempt toward those beneath.

Though later in his career Wu Yizong fled from combat without engaging, he betrays not the slightest hint of empathy toward a former prisoner-of-war in the second passage; instead, he displays brutal ingenuity in devising an execution by arrows. Zhang Zhuo provides graphic detail of the man's evisceration and death.

"CRUEL OFFICIALS"

Ideally, in Confucian society, hierarchic relations between superior and inferior are mitigated by fraternal love, benevolence, and humaneness; such ideal relations assume the presence of filial piety to cohere the family, principled loyalty to buttress the state, and an abiding desire to maintain harmony within family and state. Human nature, however, often got in the way of this ideal.

GUO BA, THE SHIT-EATER

Another of Wu Zhao's "cruel officials," Censor Guo Ba, slaughtered more than 300 men in Songzhou, many of them exiles banished from the capital.[18] This brutality roused enduring loathing and outrage among their families and friends in the capital. Typical of the way that such men are represented, Guo is characterized as bloodthirsty and savage toward those beneath him and slavishly fawning toward those above him. *Extensive Records,* in one of the chapters on "Retribution," describes Guo's gory death: haunted and hounded by ghosts and apparitions of those he has wrongly implicated and killed, he finally plunges a knife into his stomach and expires. Shortly thereafter, Wu Zhao asked one of the court wags—the aforementioned "Toad Swimming against the Current," Zhang Yuanyi—what was transpiring outside the palace. Yuanyi answered, "Outside there are three felicities. Rains have ended the drought—felicity number one. The construction of the Central Bridge is complete, a boon to ten thousand future generations—felicity number two. And the common people all rejoice in the death of Guo Ba—felicity number three." The Celestial Empress chuckled, "Whoa, the people really detest Guo Ba!"[19]

In *Court and Country,* Zhang Zhuo lists Guo Ba among three despicable individuals who shamelessly ingratiate themselves with Wu Zhao's favorites to gain influence: one acts as a human mounting block for the female emperor's monk-lover Xue Huaiyi; another obsequiously holds a pisspot for Wu Zhao's handsome gigolo, Zhang Yizhi; and Guo Ba shamelessly tastes the shit of the ringleader of the "cruel officials," Lai Junchen:

> In the time of the Celestial Empress, Zhang Ji fawningly served Master Xue, stripping off his yellow scholar's turban and trailing after him. He prostrated himself on the ground beside Master Xue's horse, acting as a human dismounting stool. Vice Censor Guo Ba tasted Lai Junchen's shit. Song Zhiwen respectfully held Zhang Yizhi's pisspot. All of them tried to leverage servile toadying into status. Such men are truly an utter disgrace to the vaunted teachings of Confucianism. (5.124)

Extensive Records contains further evidence of Guo Ba's signature brand of toadying: "When Chief Censor Wei Yuanzhong was suffering from an illness,

Guo asked if he could have a taste of his shit. Yuanzhong would not permit it, but in the end Guo still tasted some and said, 'It's bitter! Soon you'll feel better.' Yuanzhong felt great loathing for his sycophantic manner."[20] In this passage he samples the stool of Wei Yuanzhong rather than Lai Junchen, suggesting that Guo Ba may have been a serial shit-eater.

In defense of Guo, such stool sampling was regarded as a medically sound form of diagnosis at the time. In the *History of the Liang Dynasty*, it is recorded that in 499 AD, shortly after an official named Yu Qianlou had taken a new post, he learned that his father was seriously ill. Being a filial son, he rushed home and sought a physician, who told him, "The prognosis can only be made by tasting the stool and testing whether it is sweet or bitter. If it is bitter, the prognosis is good." When his father, suffering from dysentery, spewed diarrhea, Yu had a taste (see Figure 4);[21] finding it to be sweet, he was filled with despair.[22] In the Sui dynasty, Tian Yi, fearing that his mother, who was suffering from violent dysentery, had been poisoned, tasted her posterior effluvia. Both men are honored in the dynastic histories as dutiful filial sons—enshrined in "Biographies of the Filial and Righteous."[23] However, Guo Ba sampled shit not out of a sense of filial piety, fearing for a parent's well-being, but out of a desire to curry favor with the powerful. In this sense, one might see Guo Ba's actions as a perversion of the noble tradition of filial stool sampling.

JI XU, A "CRUEL OFFICIAL" WHO BROUGHT ABOUT THE END OF THE "CRUEL OFFICIALS"

The passage below is an example of the clan eradications (*zhu* 誅) perpetrated by Wu Zhao's "cruel officials" to ferret out political enemies. Ji Xu, the instigator in this case, is counted among Wu Zhao's eleven "cruel officials" in the *Old Tang History*.[24] Zhang Zhuo begins the excerpt below with the story of Ji Xu's betrayal of his close friend Qi Lianyao to point out that Ji Xu, in addition to being a "cruel official" (and thus an integral part of the system of implication and entrapment), was a hypocrite:

> *By night, Zhou era Bright Hall Commandant Ji Xu shared a hostel with Investigating Censor Wang Zhu. Because of this intimacy, Wang Zhu told him that Qi Lianyao had two sons, Big Jue and Little Jue, explaining, "They are like a two-horned qilin. The yao* 耀 *character in Qi Lianyao's name contains the components guang* 光 *[vast, overspreading] and zhai* 翟 *[a homophone for empire]. It means, 'Presiding over the empire.'" The next day Ji Xu recorded this situation and handed it over to Lai Junchen. An imperial decree deputed Prince of Henei Wu Yizong to investigate. Wang Zhu and 41 others—and their entire clans—were executed, and their properties were confiscated.*

"CRUEL OFFICIALS"

Figure 4 A Qing dynasty painting of Yu Qianlou, a filial son who tastes his father's feces.

> *Later, when Lai Junchen was indicted for committing a crime, the Ministry of Justice sentenced him to death. Yet three days after the case was formally presented to the emperor, the verdict had not been formally approved. In court and country, people felt this was peculiar. When the emperor was in the Imperial Park, Ji Xu personally led her horse. The emperor asked about matters outside of the palace. Ji Xu reported, "Acting as Your Majesty's ears and eyes, I can inform you that beyond the palace walls people feel that it's strange that you have not made a final decision on Lai Junchen's case and put him to death."*
>
> *She answered, "Lai Junchen has rendered meritorious service for the state. I am taking this into consideration."*
>
> *Ji Xu memorialized: "Junchen's knot of adherents still have yet to reveal themselves. He slanders and implicates good and worthy men. In bribes and stolen goods, he has accumulated a mountain. Aggrieved ghosts of those wronged by Lai clog the roads. He is the foremost plunderer of the state! What regret is there in putting such a man to death!" The emperor then ratified the sentence of the Ministry of Justice and Lai Junchen was executed in the Western Market. Ji Xu's prestige grew, and he was appointed Vice Censor-in-Chief and granted a purple robe. Ji Xu thought that his further promotion to become a chief minister was due to his meritorious handling of the matter of Qi Lianyao. Later, he clashed with the Prince of Henei Wu Yizong and was demoted to Prefect of Wenzhou, where he died.*[25] *(2.33)*

Though Ji Xu ultimately convinced Wu Zhao to dispense with the leader of the secret police, Lai Junchen, Zhang Zhuo finds it repugnant that Ji Xu—an insider and favorite who worked with the "cruel officials" to implicate an intimate ally—should act as the voice of moral principle to condemn Lai. Once again, Wu Zhao's kinsman Wu Yizong was involved in the purge.

THE END OF WU ZHAO'S "CRUEL OFFICIALS": HOISTED ON THEIR OWN PETARDS![26]

William Nienhauser mentions a recurrent motif in the work of Sima Qian concerning "cruel officials" meeting with "early and unnatural deaths [...] at the hands of the harsh legal system they helped construct."[27] This motif of karmic comeuppance continued in Wu Zhao's time. One event marking the ascendancy of her "cruel officials" was an artisan's creation of a bronze "tattling box" where one could secretly lodge accusations and inform on seditious plots. Zhang Zhuo relates the story in *Court and Country*:

> *In the Tang, Yu Sixuan was a profound thinker who possessed remarkable ingenuity. When the emperor*[28] *wished to build a tattling box, she summoned all of the artisans, but found none of them were worthy of the task. Yu Sixuan crafted a box for her that fit all of her design requirements, and she soon put it to use. Shortly thereafter, someone filed a grievance against Sixuan, placing it in the complaint box. The accusation read: "When Xu Jingye rebelled in Yangzhou, Sixuan mounted blades on the chariot wheels for the charge against government troops. This weapon caused death and injury of countless soldiers." After an investigation,*

"CRUEL OFFICIALS"

Yu confessed to everything and was executed. This is precisely what is meant when one says, "Snared by his own device"! (Sup., 157)

Curiously, the craftsman Yu Sixuan had taught archery and charioteering to the leader of a rebellion against Wu Zhao when she first deposed Zhongzong and ruled as grand dowager-regent in 684. In a neat parable of karmic retribution, one of the first notes inserted into the metalsmith's box reported that its creator had cast weapons to furnish the rebels, a charge which led to the man being sentenced to death and sliced in half.[29]

A second instance of karmic comeuppance is offered in the account of two brothers from Luozhou who helped build one of the apparatuses of torment used by the "cruel officials." Official histories record that Gong Siye and Gong Siming were executed in the eighth month of the first year of Yongchang (689), just prior to Wu Zhao's inauguration of the Zhou dynasty. Despite their creating one of the punitive tools used by Wu Zhao's officials, it came to light that this duo had helped Xu Jingzhen, the brother of Xu Jingye, who had rebelled against the emperor in 684: [30]

In the Tang, Adjutant of Luozhou prefecture Gong Siye and Luozhou clerk Zhang Siming[31] *created a cangue six feet long, four feet wide, and five inches thick; it inclined slightly forward. No criminal could bear it. Later, Siming and Siye sent resources to help traitorous rebel Xu Zhen*[32] *escape northward to the Tujue Turks when he passed through Luozhou. The plot was exposed. Gong Siye and the others wore their own cangue. The common folk reveled in the irony.* (Sup., 156)

Much to the delight of the common folk, who lived in fear and loathing of the devious contraptions of torture devised by this group and their minions, the men who fashioned the cangue died manacled to their own creation.

An analogous case features Suo Yuanli, a Sogdian who, late in Wu Zhao's regency, rose to become one of her relentless investigating officials and also served as a general. This "cruel official" sometimes dressed as a wolf or a tiger when interrogating his victims; so horrific was the torment he inflicted that Suo could allegedly get a single individual to implicate thousands of others. He gained Wu Zhao's trust and confidence, earning gifts, rewards, and promotions. Reportedly, he went to extremes only equaled by Lai Junchen and Zhou Xing, killing several thousand people.[33] From the following passage in *Court and Country*, we know that—like the men in the previous passages—he also created implements of torture:

In the Tang, Suo Yuanli created an iron head-cage used to interrogate prisoners. Later, he was convicted for embezzlement and bribery but would not confess. One of the wardens said,

"Just go get His Excellency's iron head-cage." Suo Yuanli immediately confessed and was executed. (Sup., 157)

Again, the text stresses the poetic justice of a torturer subjected to the very instrument of sadistic torture he has contrived. Threatened with his own "iron head-cage," Suo confessed to embezzling money and accepting bribes. The *Comprehensive Mirror* records that he was killed in 691 to placate all of those agitated and horrified by his extreme brutality.[34]

Court and Country also contains an analogous episode featuring the two most prominent arch-villains among the female sovereign's violent henchmen, Lai Junchen and Zhou Xing:

> In the Tang, Vice Ministers of Justice Zhou Xing and Lai Junchen both were in charge of investigations. Lai Junchen separately suggested that the emperor order an interrogation of Zhou Xing. Zhou Xing was wholly unaware. Once when they were eating together, Lai Junchen said, "In the prison there are many people unwilling to confess their crimes. What can we do about it?" Zhou replied, "That's a cinch. All you need is a huge earthenware crock. Put charcoal on all sides to bring it to a boil, then order the criminal to go inside. He'd confess to anything!"
>
> Thereupon Lai Junchen ordered a huge earthenware crock be brought out and had a fire built around it. He rose and said to Zhou Xing, "Internally, there have been accusations lodged against you, old friend. Please get into this crock, elder brother." Trembling in terror, he kowtowed and confessed everything. Certain of death, Zhou Xing was banished to Lingnan. Among the banished there were countless people whose families Zhou had destroyed. He was killed by one of these enemies. In the Chronicles of Zuo it says, "When one frequently breaches propriety, it invariably recoils upon them." How true! (Sup., 156)

This famous episode birthed the proverb, "Please, fine gentleman, step into the crock" (*qing jun ru weng* 請君入甕), which has come to mean becoming ensnared in one's own trap.

A popular Chinese maxim today observes that, "Goodness is rewarded with goodness; evil is recompensed with evil." This is a modern evolution of the adage from the *Chronicles of Zuo* featured in Zhang Zhuo's anecdote, "when one frequently breaches propriety, it invariably recoils upon them."[35] Just retribution was a popular theme. A number of stories about the "cruel officials" in *Court and Country* end with these men's violent deaths and accompanying assertions that their brutal ends prompted outbursts of collective joy. One would assume that Zhang's readership found these conclusions satisfying.

"CRUEL OFFICIALS" IN THE AFTERMATH OF WU ZHAO'S ERA

An episode from *Court and Country* dating from after Wu Zhao's death readily illustrates that "cruel officials" were not an archetype unique to her reign:

"CRUEL OFFICIALS"

Luoyang Clerk Song Zhixun was the younger brother of Recorder in the Court of Imperial Sacrifices Song Zhiwen. He falsely implicated imperial son-in-law Wang Tongjiao,[36] which led to Wang's execution. In the beginning, Zhixun sycophantically attached himself to Zhang Yizhi and his brothers. He was appointed Granary Keeper of Yanzhou, then returned to the capital after the deaths of the Zhangs. Wang Tongjiao concealed him in a little shanty. Tongjiao was a fervent gentleman with a vehement sense of justice; furious that Traitor Wei and Wu Sansi had created turmoil in the state, he spoke of this to several intimate colleagues, gnashing his teeth. Surreptitiously, from behind a curtain, Zhixun overheard him. Hoping to gain the favor of Empress Wei, he sent his nephew Song Yun to submit a report accusing Wang. As one might expect, Wu Sansi and others were furious, and they proposed to emperor Zhongzong that Wang Tongjiao and his clique should be executed. As a result, Song Zhiwen and Song Zhixun both received fifth rank. Zhixun was made Vice Director of the Court of Imperial Entertainments, Song Zhiwen was named Vice Director of the Court of State Ceremonial, and Song Yun was named Chief Steward of the Palace Clothing Service. All of the realm resented them. All of the officials said, "The crimson gowns of Song Zhiwen and his lot are stained with the blood of Wang Tongjiao." After Traitor Wei was executed, Zhixun and the other Songs were banished to Lingnan.

Once a guest asked the Master Who Drifts then Rests, "What sort of people were the adherents of Lai Junchen?" He answered, "Once upon a time, deep in the mountains, the Lion King caught a jackal and was about to devour it when the cur-hearted creature said, 'Please let me present you two deer to ransom my hide.' The Lion King was delighted, and yet a full year later the promised deer still had yet to be delivered. The Lion King said, 'You've already killed your share of living things. Today it's your turn. Do you have any other clever schemes?' The jackal was silent, having no response. The Lion King then tore him asunder with his teeth. Junchen and his lot—how were they any different from these vile jackals?!"

(Sup., 162)

The villains in this piece are Empress Wei, here called "Traitor Wei," and Wu Zhao's nephew, Wu Sansi, both of whom dominated the court in the years immediately following Wu Zhao's deposal and death. Zhang Zhuo's point—drawn from the unfailingly schematic Confucian playbook—is that "gender anarchy" (to borrow Rebecca Doran's term) primarily begets three kinds of men: craven fawners, male favorites, and sadistic powermongers. The first was a pupal stage of the latter two, cozying up to them—seeking to borrow their influence and parlay it into career advancement. Presented as a righteous man filled with the requisite moral outrage, Wang Tongjiao is cast as the embodiment of proper literati masculinity, the Confucian foil to these other degraded and reprehensible categories of men. The "Lion King" represents Emperor Xuanzong—Wu Zhao's grandson—who is usually valorized (or, here, literally lionized) as one who restores the traditional Confucian moral order. The passage tacitly suggests that Xuanzong eliminated the evil of these "cruel officials." This suggestion is not accurate; Wu Zhao eliminated or banished the lot of her callous henchmen about halfway through her Zhou dynasty.

The next pair of accounts from *Court and Country* examine "cruel officials" Wang Xu and Li Quanjiao, two of the "Three Jackals" (sanchai 三豺) from early in Emperor Xuanzong's reign. In repugnant conduct and sadistic temperament, both rival the scoundrels from Wu Zhao's era:[37]

> *Palace Vice Censor Wang Xu searched his own household and other residences seeking women rumored to be sexy or attractive. Whenever a woman resisted in the slightest, he bound her netherparts with a rope and ordered strong men to strike them there with a bamboo rod. The agonizing pain was unbearable. He hung one woman upside-down with a stone pulling her hair. When she was held in custody, he offered her to Chang'an Commandant Fang Heng, who raped her. But even after three days the woman didn't comply. The woman said, "Since the Vice Censor has acted in such a manner, if your venomous behavior kills me, I'll most certainly bring a complaint before the authorities in the underworld. If you send me to the palace to be a maid or concubine, I will most certainly formally present my case explaining your conduct to the emperor. To the very end, I won't let this go." Ashamed and filled with dread, Xu released her.* (2.34)

> *In the Tang, Investigating Censor Li Quanjiao and others made a vocation of framing and entrapment, sadism and cruelty. In the Censorate, his nickname was the "Human-faced Raksha." Director of Palace Administration Wang Xu was called "Demon-faced Yaksha."*
> *When interrogating prisoners, they dragged the handle of the cangue forward; they called this "Dragging the Jackass Foal by the Bit." With the prisoner racked in the cangue, they would tie his head to a tree, calling it "Putting the Calf out to Pasture." When the cangue held both of the prisoner's hands aloft, bricks would be placed on top; this was called "Offering Fruit to the Immortals." When a prisoner would be stood upright atop a wooden pillar, his cangue would be yanked backward; this they called "The Jade Maiden Climbs the Ladder." When they were torturing Chenzhou Clerk Liao Fu and Transit Authorization Bureau Clerk Zhang Xing to get them to confess, both tormentors went through a series of prayers to entreat spirits, foxes, and forest sprites for the truth.[38] This pantomime they termed "Calling on a Crane to Act as a Phoenix" or "Proof the Snake has Become a Dragon."* (2.36)

In the first account, the complicity of other officials in Wang's depredations may be an indication that sharing in sexual depravity was not so uncommon in certain literati circles. Particularly noteworthy is the indomitable will of the woman who resists Wang Xu; despite days of torture, she remains sufficiently self-possessed to threaten to lodge a complaint on earth or in hell, before the emperor or the underworld judge Yama. Ultimately, her bold protestations and her evocation of names with far greater authority than his own leave Wang cowed, and he releases her.

In the second passage, the nicknames of Li and Wang, Rakshasa (*luocha* 罗刹) and Yaksha (*yecha* 夜叉), respectively, are terms lifted from Sanskrit that had become part of the Chinese vernacular by the seventh century—terms that suggest these men were viewed as hellspawn in human guise. The rakshasa is a "flesh-eating demon" capable of flight and possessing superhuman might; they were the ox-headed and horse-faced wardens of Buddhist hells, tasked with inflicting torture and torment upon those who end up there. Yaksha are "demonic ogres who devour infants and corpses of the dead."[39]

This insidious duo continued a tradition of "cruel officials" from Wu Zhao's era by using flowery language to gloss over the savage cruelty and suffering they inflicted with a veneer of aesthetics. It is curious that they would either bestialize—using metaphors that envisioned the interrogated as livestock or other creatures—or sacralize their victims, imagining them as supplicants to the divinities or "Jade Maidens." The pair of jackals, the "Black Jackal" (Wang) and the "White-browed Jackal" (Li), would even stage plays in which—in lieu of actual evidence to prove the guilt of alleged transgressors—their appeals to the spirit world would bring forth otherworldly spirits who confirmed the guilt of the accused.

CONCLUDING THOUGHTS: THE "ALTERNATIVE STATUS SYSTEM" OF "CRUEL OFFICIALS"

Scholar of French literature Alice Laborde argued that the Marquis de Sade—the man whose very name spawned the notion of sadism and still evokes graphic images of deviant cruelty and perversity without boundaries—was fundamentally misunderstood. While claiming that she had no desire to redeem the notorious Marquis, she sought instead to "destroy the myth" that had long defined him, complicating the cartoon of debauched excess and depraved cruelty by claiming that he was, in fact, a towering figure in French philosophy, aesthetics, and literature "as important as Diderot, Rousseau, Voltaire and Montesquieu." In his life, de Sade was, she contended, "really a family man, a loving husband and a loving father."[40]

Likewise, this conclusion is not an effort to redeem the "cruel officials" who acted as Wu Zhao's "teeth and horns"; rather, it is an attempt to better contextualize and understand their actions. I cannot go as far as Laborde and claim that Lai Junchen and Zhou Xing were misunderstood virtuous men of lofty character. I will, however, suggest that a degree or re-evaluation and reconsideration of these men is overdue.

Wielding the calligraphy brush that inscribed Chinese history with a possessive cultural centrism that reinforced their own self-interest and importance, Confucians celebrated court and literati culture and jealously disparaged other subcultures and status systems. We are forced to analyze their cultural representations of other groups: Buddhists are dismissed as "idle eaters," consuming state resources; those who engaged in hunting and falconry were written off as libertines and "wild-youth"; shamans and mystics are not infrequently represented as heretical practitioners of "evil cults"; and military men were often considered coarse and uncultured. Like these other groups, the "cruel officials" were consistently represented in an unfavorable fashion.

In his pioneering sociological work of the late 1950s, Albert Cohen delineated how delinquent working-class boys in post–World War II England, who failed at school and resultantly had low status, became frustrated and developed gangs as an alternative (deviant, from mainstream perspective) culture with a different set of values and norms, a subculture that challenged and inverted the values of mainstream society. Swearing, smoking, drinking, vandalism, daring, and toughness were valorized, determining hierarchy within gangs and their alternative status system.[41] In reimagining the role of "cruel officials," it may be useful to conceptualize them as participating in such an "alternative status system."

Court and Country contains a curious passage, set in 696, featuring Wu Zhao's "cruel officials" congregating for the Double Third Festival, a vernal holiday involving an outdoor picnic and orchid plucking:

> *Once, on the third day of the third month of 696, Lai Junchen gathered his clique together at Longmen. On a vertical stone they set up names of court officials who threatened them in order to determine who to accuse next. Then he ordered someone to throw rocks at them; whoever's name was knocked off first would be slandered. Throughout the summer, they targeted Li Zhaode's name placard, but always missed the target.* (Sup., 170–71)

While Lai and his band of "cruel officials" did not match wits and compose poetry couplets with elegant classical allusions on breezy pavilions like the court literati, they had their own distinctive brand of fun. Apparently, they often played this game, relying more on physical skill and accuracy than mental agility. Of course, Zhang Zhuo ensures that their errant throws are not without the usual didactic lesson: his point in this passage is that Heaven protected the placard of an upright and principled official—Li Zhaode—from the violent and arbitrary machinations of the "cruel officials."

4

Beyond court and capital: local officials

WU ZHAO'S ZHOU DYNASTY CONTAINED ROUGHLY 350 prefectures (*zhou* 州), presided over by Prefects, and 1500 districts (*xian* 縣), administered by magistrates.[1] Each prefecture was broken into three to six districts. "As late as 657," Denis Twitchett observes, "there were only 13,465 ranking officials to control a population perhaps in excess of 50,000,000."[2] With a population of 50 million people in the early Tang empire, the average magistrate was responsible for 60,000 people. The primary role of these local officials was to collect revenues—grain and cloth tax—and to coordinate corvée labor.[3] Prefects with appointments in and around the capital were often up-and-coming men on a fast track to promotions to higher-ranked positions in the imperial court. On the other hand, a court official guilty of offending the ruler or committing minor malfeasance might be punished with a demotion to become a local official in a remote district. As in any other culture, premodern or modern, some local administrators were conscientious, competent, and effective, while others were negligent, inept, and avaricious. While stories of both good and bad local officials appear in *Court and Country*, Zhang Zhuo was clearly partial to the more lurid stories of maladministration, power-mongering, and staggering incompetence.

JUDICIOUS PEI ZIYUN SOLVES THE CASE OF THE MISSING COWS

Known as the "father-and-mother official," the county magistrate was the lowest-level official who was part of the formal government bureaucracy. They were aided (or, at times, hindered) by an extensive sub-bureaucracy of clerks, village heads, local elders, wardens, bailiffs, strongarms, and runners. In addition to reporting to the Prefect, these magistrates were also responsible for levying grain and cloth taxes; managing floods and droughts; supervising construction and repair of dikes, roads, and bridges; adjudicating local disputes; and solving crimes. Thus, these local officials were also detectives. *Extensive Records* places the passage from *Court and Country* below in its chapters on "Brilliant Investigators" (*jingcha* 精察):[4]

> *In Xinxiang County of Weizhou*[5]*, magistrate Pei Ziyun was an excellent strategist. Wang Jing was conscripted to a border garrison, and he left six milch cows with his uncle Li Jin. Over the five years Li cared for them, the cows birthed thirty calves, each worth more than ten strings of cash. When Wang Jing returned from the border, two of the cows had died and only four remained. In addition, Li claimed Wang's cows hadn't birthed any of the calves, and so he didn't have to give any of them to Wang. Furious, Wang approached the county offices with a written grievance. Pei Ziyun ordered Wang locked in prison and instructed his subordinates to arrest "cow thief" Li Jin. Filled with anxiety and terror, Li reached the county offices and encountered magistrate Pei, who railed, "I've seized a cow thief who colluded with you to steal thirty head of cattle and hide them at your household. Call the other thief and we'll compare their testimonies." His underlings brought in Wang Jing with a cloth covering his head and stood him at the foot of the southern wall of the yamen courtyard. In trepidation, Li Jin spit out the truth: "All thirty of those cows were birthed by my nephew's cows!" The magistrate said, "If that's the way it is, then return all of his cows." Li Jin fell silent. Sizing up the circumstance, Pei pronounced, "Raising cows for five years is toilsome. You can keep several head of cattle, but give the remaining cows to Wang Jing." Throughout the county, all acknowledged Pei's brilliant investigation. (5.108)*

In the case above, magistrate Pei Ziyun cleverly employs his sleuthing skills to quickly resolve a dispute over thirty head of cattle. After speaking with the plaintiff, Wang Jing, he knows that Li Jin's farm has thirty extra head of cattle. He then concocts a story about Li's collusion with a thief as a scare tactic to get Li to confess the truth. Then, judiciously recognizing Li's cost in care and fodder over the five years, he awards several head of cattle to Li, and to Wang Jing rightly grants the remaining calves that Wang's cows had birthed over the preceding five years. Everyone went home content at the resolution and all in the county praised the judicious local magistrate.

YOUR REIGN OF TERROR IS OVER, LI HONG! THERE'S A NEW PREFECT IN TOWN

This story from *Court and Country* appears in the chapters on "Shameless Rogues" (*wulai* 無賴) in *Extensive Records*:[6]

> *Li Hong of Junyi County in Bianzhou*[7] *was vicious, perverse, shameless, violent, and utterly lacking in empathy. Sitting tall in the saddle of a powerful horse, he would cruise through shops and stores in different wards, intimidating vendors out of their grain, corvée labor, and cloth tax revenues, as well as shipping and docking taxes, extorting more than*

300 strings of cash. Overall, he forcibly extorted countless thousands from these merchants and never returned a copper. Alarmed and buffeted about by the unstinting peril, merchants and customers alike lived in dread of Li Hong's reign of terror. Shortly after Ren Zhengli was appointed as the Prefect of Bianzhou, he sent out his own men to seize Li Hong. Ren determined his punishment was sixty blows with a heavy stick; beneath the rod, Li Hong was beaten to death. Workers and merchants, customers and students alike raised toasts in mutual delight. Far and wide, everyone delighted in the demise of this odious local tyrant! (Sup., 161)

Li Hong, a member of the Tang imperial family, was the grandson of Tang founder Gaozu, and the son of Gaozu's fifteenth son, Li Feng. A powerful and imposing man, he held the noble title Duke of Dingxiang. Relying on pedigree and high-handed violence, he was a local terror in Bianzhou, a critical commercial artery along the Grand Canal, connecting north and south. One of the challenges faced by all local officials was learning to deal with the local elite. Often cooperation or collaboration was a necessary strategy, but not in this case. This "new-sheriff-in-town" story relates how a newly arrived prefect—not overawed in the least by Li Hong's prestige, physical prowess, or reputation—promptly eliminated the local hell-raiser, winning the respect and gratitude of the local population.

HUMORLESS LU YUQING AND HIS LESS-THAN-FILIAL SON

The preceding chapter on court officials examined the playful culture of humorous wordplay and literary one-upmanship in the court. Humor was, of course, not restricted to the court. One entry in *Court and Country* attests to this fact:

When Aide in the Department of State Affairs Lu Yuqing was demoted to Clerk of Luozhou, his son wrote a mocking verse:

Lu Yuqing: calligraphy brush can't do a thing, but he talks plenty tough.
Receives a case a day, but for a verdict ten days is not enough.

He placed the poem under Lu's cushion in the courtroom. When Lu Yuqing got hold of it and read it, he remarked, "This is definitely the work of that dog!" Subsequently, he had his son whipped. (2.46)

Local officials did not always take kindly to being lampooned, even if it came from their own flesh and blood. Lu Yuqing served as a Palace Censor and a low-level official in the Secretariat under Wu Zhao. He was, however, more than a dour father and a mediocre local official; he was a close friend of Chen Zi'ang, a celebrated poet of the early Tang who served as an official under Wu Zhao. He took his scholarship seriously, too: at one juncture, he closed the gates to his household and recited canonical texts for three years to internalize these works and their principles.[8] He seems to have held the position of Clerk in Luozhou at the tail-end of Wu Zhao's Zhou.[9]

LOCAL EXAMINATIONS: PUTTING A PREFECT IN HIS PLACE

This passage from *Court and Country*—also found in the "Mockery and Ridicule" chapters of *Extensive Records*[10]—features a blunt test-taker and member of the sub-bureaucracy who challenges the authority, and questions the mediocre talent, of a prefect:

> In the Zhou, Li Xiang, a man of Henei, was a chivalrous and straightforward fellow. At first, he was a District Defender in charge of Yanting County in Xinzhou. On the day candidates were sitting for the county examinations, the prefect asked if the test was fair or not. Li Xiang alone said it was unfair. The prefect said, "If it is unfair, why don't you, fine gentleman, pick up a brush and write a critique?" Li replied, "I request permission to write an assessment of Your Excellency." When he finished, he set down his brush, and read, "You are afraid of determining matters of importance, but good at dealing with trivia. Personally, you are opaque rather than transparent, yet you always suspect others of obfuscation. Furthermore, your own examination grades were mediocre or worse." The prefect fell silent and let the matter drop. (4.88–89)

Li Xiang skewers the prefect, who likely never sat for the examinations himself, offering a sound critique of the man's flawed character and limited capacity as an official.

Though only a relatively small proportion of officials in the early Tang were recruited through the developing examination system—it reached its full maturity in late imperial China—during Wu Zhao's time as empress, her regency, and her reign, these tests became an ever-more-viable path of social mobility. In addition to imperial exams, these tests were also periodically held under Wu Zhao on the prefectural level to identify and recruit talent.

BAD LOCAL OFFICIAL #1: A PREDATORY CLERK GETS A WELL-DESERVED BEATING

The following story from *Court and Country* suggests that Zhang Zhuo and his readers took a measure of delight in seeing bad officials get their comeuppance:

BEYOND COURT AND CAPITAL

In the Zhou, in Nanpi County of Cangzhou, when Clerk Guo Wujing was patrolling the countryside, he called on the wife of one of the countryfolk to sew and patch his clothing, then tried to rape her. Her husband arrived, bound Guo Wujing, and beat him a couple dozen times with a whip. Assistant Magistrate Li Zhe came along and rescued him from peril. Humiliated, Guo sought to conceal the real incident. He bowed and explained, "I can't take the pain," then sang out, "Ah, the agony! It's not that I, Jing, have been beaten. Oh, the agony!" (Sup., 177)

Clerks were part of the sub-bureaucracy, in theory helping the magistrate to administer the vast territory that he oversaw. While many were conscientious, others sought to take advantage of their positions of power, parlaying influence into profit or pleasure. Local official Guo Wujing attempted to take advantage of his station to sexually prey on women in his jurisdiction. His unconvincing and clumsy cover-up when another official arrived further marked him as a contemptible and reprehensible fellow.

A PAIR OF STINGY LOCAL OFFICIALS

Having internalized Confucian principles, the ideal literati–official was broad-minded and possessed a magnanimity of spirit. However, many local officials depicted in Zhang Zhuo's vignettes are petty, despicable men. One passage in *Court and Country* tells how, in the southeast of the empire, a parsimonious bachelor–official brutally whipped a slave for filching a pinch of salt:

Guangzhou Administrative Supervisor Liu Qing lived alone in a residence. Household items and foodstuffs were brought to his bedroom. When on one occasion a slave took a measure of salt for private use, Qing whipped her until she bled.[11] (1.14)

Elsewhere on the southern fringe of the empire, in modern-day northern Vietnam, Zhang exposes another miser:

The family household of Annam Superintendent Deng You, originally from Yunzhou,[12] *was immensely wealthy; he had 1000 male and female slaves. But he selfishly consumed all of the delectable food and drink, refusing to host banquets for guests. One day his grandson took one of his ducks for personal consumption. Claiming that the grandson had broken up the family estate, Deng had him whipped 20 times.* (1.15)

This tremendously rich but despicably selfish administrator whipped his own grandson for "breaking up the family estate," the miserly fellow's hyperbolic characterization of the grandson's unsanctioned appropriation of a single duck for personal use. Both of these men represent the antithesis of the ideal Confucian literati–official. Each of these cases represent officials meting out disproportioned punishments that betray their own failures as judicious administrators (and as human beings).

LIVING LARGE ON STATE MONEY

Censors were officials of the central government in Chang'an and Luoyang, but they were sent around the empire on tours of inspection to make sure that local officials were adhering to the laws of the realm. Censors were "charged with maintaining surveillance over the officialdom as a whole and submitting impeachments of wayward officials."[13] Of course, being on the dole, some officials treated these trips as vacation junkets and cheerfully squandered government coin on lavish feasts:

> *Yan Shengqi of Luozhou, serving as Temporary Vice Censor, was in Jiangnan on an inspection. He loved eating beef. In every prefecture and county he patrolled, many cattle were butchered and cooked. Wherever he went, he spent countless gold and silver on feasts large and small. Therefore, in Jiangnan Yan was known as the "Golden Ox Censor." (3.77–78)*

Though his tastes differed from those of Ren Zhengming or Chen Yuanguang (of which, more below), Golden Ox Censor Yan Shengqi similarly exploited his position. A one-man mobile banquet, Yan lived large on government coin and used his influence as a Censor to feast as he "surveilled" local officials.

BAD OFFICIAL #2: A THOUSAND-GOLD SON FOR A HARE

There is a time-honored proverb in traditional China: "Become an official and get rich" (*shengguan facai* 升官發財). Once men became officials, parlaying influence and power into wealth was an art form. They did not just rely on their government salaries; they devised different creative ways of making or extorting money from the people in their jurisdictions. The following passage features a local magistrate who takes advantage of the death of a village head within his jurisdiction in a novel fashion:

> *In Yingzhou prefecture, magistrate of Raoyang County*[14] *Dou Zhifan was greedy and corrupt. When one of the village heads in his jurisdiction died, he gathered the other heads and asked them each to contribute a string of cash to build a statue. Keeping all of these donations for himself, Dou said, "This village head had committed some wrongs and sins. I had to urgently rush the casting of the image." In the end, he appropriated 200,000 cash to have a five-and-a-half cun statue cast.*[15] *Such was the nature of his greed.*
>
> *Dou only had one son. While hunting hares, the young man loosed an eagle which spooked his horse. Brained by a mulberry branch, he was unhorsed and died. The commonfolk in*

the county delighted in this. Everyone said, "The life of that fellow's thousand-gold son exchanged for that of a hare!" (3.76)

On the pretext that he needs to do a rush-job to help the deceased in the afterlife, Dou Zhifan has a pathetically tiny commemorative statue cast, and then pockets the difference. The story ends, however, with the rascal getting his comeuppance when his son is killed in a hunting accident, occasioning a collective wave of schadenfreude from the people of Raoyang County. A "thousand-gold son" is a precious son, a treasure. There was a saying in traditional China, "A thousand gold son should not lean over the railing of a hall lest he fall!"[16] Seemingly, the local village leaders appreciated the grim symmetry: just as their return on more than 200 strings of cash was a pocket-sized commemorative image, so Dou's paltry recompense for his son's death was a hare (assuming the eagle caught it).

INEPT AND FOOLISH LOCAL OFFICIALS

Court and Country contains a number of stories about arrant and incompetent local officials, including the following:

> In the *Zhou*, an array of Tujue Turks twenty or thirty lines deep surrounded the walls of Dingzhou. Prefect Sun Chan'gao didn't dare go to the yamen hall to administer. Instead, when people came with tallies and documents needing his verification or authorization, he transacted all correspondence through a small window. The gates to the prefectural city and all of the administrative offices were all closed. When the Tujue rebels breached the ramparts, Sun concealed himself in a cabinet and ordered his servants, "Keep a tight grip on the key. When the rebels come, make sure it doesn't fall into their hands!"
>
> Once an idiot, headed to the capital in hopes of securing an official position, had his leather purse stolen by robbers. The man said, "These robbers stole my purse, but they can't get my possessions." Someone asked what he meant, and he answered, "The key's still on my belt. How are they going to open the lock?" Sun Chan'gao falls in the same category as this moron. (2.46–47)

In the first anecdote, the foolish local prefect Sun Chan'gao has such a distorted sense of reality when faced with a daunting enemy invader that he believes he might remain safe by hiding in a cabinet and telling an underling not to let the key fall into the hands of the Turks. Zhang Zhuo categorizes him as a hapless fool unfit for official duty; not only is he incapable of being an effective local bureaucrat, he quite literally does not understand the function of a bureau!

The local magistrate in a second passage is represented as the very antithesis of the Confucian gentleman:

> *In Quzhou prefecture, Longyou county magistrate Li Ningdao was narrow-minded and short-tempered. His elder sister's seven-year-old son often provoked and annoyed him; Li Ningdao would pursue his nephew, but could never catch him. Finally, he used a sweet pancake to entice the child then grabbed him; in the ensuing ruckus, he bit his nephew on the chest and back so that blood flowed. Hearing the commotion, his elder sister stormed in and saved the child.*
>
> *On another occasion, Li was riding his donkey along the street when the toe of the boot of a man riding a horse in the other direction brushed his knee. In a fury, he cursed and was about to beat the fellow. But the horseman rode off. Li pursued on muleback but couldn't catch him. Seething with rage, he grabbed a thorny jujube branch from the roadside and bit down on it so hard that his mouth bled.* (6.132–33)

The Confucian gentleman is a superior man, a *junzi* 君子, broad-minded, magnanimous of spirit, and even-tempered. Edward Slingerland defines the term in the following fashion: "Meaning literally son of a lord, *junzi* referred in Western Zhou times to a member of the warrior aristocracy. In Confucius's hands, it comes to refer to anyone capable of becoming a kind of moral aristocrat: an exemplar of ritually correct behavior, ethical courage, and noble sentiment—in short, a possessor of Goodness."[17] Li Ningdao is at the other end of the spectrum, a petty man (xiaoren 小人), an irascible buffoon who loses his equanimity, braying like the jackass he rides as he froths at children and passers-by at the slightest provocation.

THE LAWLESS FRONTIER

The Prince of Cao, Li Ming, was the fourteenth son of Tang Taizong.[18] When a power struggle developed late in Gaozong's reign between Wu Zhao and her son, Li Xian 李賢,[19] Li Ming was one of the young heir apparent's political allies. Wu Zhao ultimately outmaneuvered Li Xian, and the ill-starred heir apparent and his supporters like Li Ming were banished to a borderland outpost in modern-day Guizhou, to the south.[20] Though it would be a decade before Wu Zhao became emperor, this event marked the beginning of her effort to cull the Li clan. Some officials far from the capital, knowing that the banished prince and his allies had fallen from the Celestial Empress's favor, sought to prove their loyalty to her by eliminating her rivals. To avoid creating a divisive spectacle in the capital or in court, one way of disposing of enemies in traditional China was to sentence them to banishment, then have them killed along the route or hounded to death once they reached their destination in the malarial hinterlands.

There is a passage in *Court and Country* about the grim fate that the Prince of Cao suffered and the measure of revenge that his family gained:

BEYOND COURT AND CAPITAL

In the Zhou era, Qianzhou Garrison Supervisor-in-chief Xie You was vicious and insidious, cruel and venomous. During the rule of Zetian, when the Prince of Cao was exiled to Guizhou, Xie You intimidatingly said, "Zetian has requested that you commit suicide. I, Xie You, will personally respectfully supervise your comings and goings. There's no need to formally await an imperial order." Terrified, the Prince hung himself with a silken cord.

Later, Xie You was resting obliviously in the pavilion with a dozen servant girls and concubines when an assassin severed his head and carried it off. Years later, when the Prince of Cao's property was confiscated, those recording inventory found Xie You's head, with his name painted on the brow. It had been used as an unclean vessel. Only then did people realize that one of the Prince's sons had ordered the assassin to kill him. (2.35)

Zhang Zhuo is not simply relating an anecdote about death and retribution. In the Confucian narrative tradition, there are invariably good guys and bad guys. Given the characterization of Xie You as cruel and venomous, he is clearly the antagonist. The nameless killer who avenges Li Ming's death is part of a long tradition of righteous assassins stretching back a millennium.[21] Following the narrative logic of a Confucian morality play, the antagonist gets his just desserts: Xie You's head becomes an "unclean vessel" into which the aggrieved remnants of the fallen prince's family might defecate and urinate to vent their stifled rage.

WORSE LOCAL OFFICIALS: TAKING A POUND OF FLESH

As one Chinese proverb goes, "Heaven is high and the emperor is far away" (*tiangao huangdi yuan* 天高皇帝遠). Both the Tang empire and Wu Zhao's realm were massive. Though there was a huge, relatively efficient premodern bureaucracy, it was impossible for the emperor or the court to be aware of everything that transpired in the sprawling empire with a population of near to 100 million. Sometimes, especially in regions far from the capital, officials presided over their prefectures like avaricious tyrants ruling private satrapies. The worst of the bad local officials indulged every imaginable caprice; some literally got away with murder.

Court and Country tells of two men—a censor and a prefect in Shuzhou (modern-day Anhui), about 320 miles from Wu Zhao's capital, Luoyang—both with an addiction to consuming "human essence":

In the Zhou, Prefect of Shuzhou Zhang Huaisu was fond of drinking semen. Tang Bureau Director Ren Zhengming also had this illness. (Sup., 177)

From one of the Tang histories, we know that Ren Zhengming also served as a Vice Censor under Wu Zhao's son Ruizong after the Tang was restored. He was fond of throwing his weight around, using this position to impeach gentlemen and literati.²² Presumably, he used this influence to facilitate acquisition of "human essence" (*ren jing* 人精) as he moved around the empire. According to the principles of traditional Chinese medicine, semen, a distillation of male yang-energy, possessed curative properties; in conjunction with goshawk droppings, it has the capacity to heal external blemishes like moles and could be utilized as a topical, external salve for scalds and burns.²³ A text called *Cures for Fifty-two Ailments* (*Wushier bing fang* 五十二病方)—recovered in Mawangdui tomb No. 3 in Changsha, Hunan in 1973—indicates that bodily fluids have been used for medicinal purposes since at least the early Han dynasty.²⁴ A late sixteenth-century medical encyclopedia, the *Ben Cao Gang Mu*, warns that practitioners of the "evil arts [...] have sexual intercourse with young girls and drink the essence of these women" or they ingest their own sperm mixed with a woman's menstrual blood, wrongly believing they were combining ingredients to prepare a potion of longevity. Harshly denouncing this "extremely stupid" practice, Li Shizhen, the encyclopedia's author, remarks that licentious consumption of filth only serves to shorten one's lifespan!²⁵ It is unclear whether these two officials consumed sperm and other bodily fluids for medicinal purposes or for pleasure. Though the two examples in this excerpt do not reach the extreme of the cannibalism described below, these officials quite literally consumed the essence of the common people.

In another of Zhang Zhuo's anecdotes, a local official in faraway Lingnan goes much further than Zhang Huaisu and Ren Zhengming! Rashly and arbitrarily, Chen Yuanguang has an underling killed at a banquet; later, the man's dismembered body becomes a centerpiece at the feast:

> In the Zhou era, Lingnan leader Chen Yuanguang laid a feast. He ordered a sentinel to pour drinks for a toast. When the man balked, Chen became enraged, ordered the man dragged from the room, and had him killed.²⁶ Shortly, a well-done steamed dish was presented to feed the revelers. Later, as they were eating the dish, when the lid was lifted off a steaming plate the two hands of the sentinel were revealed. Appalled, the banqueters stuck their fingers down their throats and retched up gobbets of human flesh. (2.30)

Chen Yuanguang—the official who casually murders a subordinate—is not remembered as a murderous local tyrant. His family origins are complex: scholars are unclear, Hugh Clark points out, whether the Chen family were "assimilated indigenes" or "Han émigrés of long standing in the South." As a young man, Chen had served under his father in Gaozong's campaigns to "pacify" (a timeless cross-cultural euphemism and justification for imperial expansion) southern tribesmen. There are still local temples where he is honored as the "King who Settled Zhangzhou" (Kai-Zhang wang 開漳王).²⁷

BEYOND COURT AND CAPITAL

Another case involving anthropophagy among local officials appears in *Court and Country*:

> *During the Zhou era, in Hangzhou prefecture Lin'an Commandant*[28] *Xue Zhen enjoyed eating human flesh. When a moneylender and his servant went to Lin'an, they stayed in the official guest hostel, and got inebriated. Xue Zhen murdered them and sliced up their flesh, then fried them using quicksilver so that even the melted bones were softened and consumed. Later, Xue wished to devour the moneylender's wife, but the woman, aware of his intent, fled. When county authorities looked into the matter, they learned what had happened and reported to the prefecture. The prefect recorded the matter in a memorial, which was presented to the emperor. She issued an imperial decree to beat Xue to death with 100 strokes of a stick.* (2.29–30)

Sometimes in Wu Zhao's empire, the wheels of bureaucracy turned efficiently. The villainous Xue Zhen's misdeeds were reported to the Prefect of Hangzhou, who duly investigated and, in turn, memorialized Wu Zhao. She sentenced Xue Zhen to death. In this instance, justice was served.

These instances of cannibalism among officials hold fraught significance. Officials routinely extracted the fruits of the sweat and hard work of the common people through taxes and labor. In English, folks sometimes complain that the government, through excessive extraction of taxes, takes its "pound of flesh" from the working man, the everyman. In late seventh-century China, this metaphor seems to have occasionally become quite literal: corrupt government officials sometimes drained the semen and life's essence from the common people, or went even further—feasting on human marrow and flesh!

Zhang Zhuo was neither the first nor the last to incite outrage by cataloging the mind-blowing extent to which the mandarin class of government officials bled the common people. Long before his time, Yi Ya killed his infant son and cooked the head, presenting it to his master, Duke Huan of Qi, so that the latter might savor the delicacy.[29] Physician Chen Zangqi, a rough contemporary of Zhang Zhuo's, wrote a medicinal text claiming that human flesh could cure consumption and weakness.[30] In the chaos and carnage of the late Tang and early Five Dynasties era, rampaging generals and untrammeled military men ran riot, reveling in mayhem and killing; many developed a taste for human flesh.[31] Contemporary Nobel Prize–winning Chinese author Mo Yan's satirical *Republic of Wine* contains a scene where gluttonous, turn-of-the-millennium Communist party officials—exulting in a culture of rapacious excess and extravagant banquets—devour a baby boy at a feast.[32]

This exploitative anthropophagy by nobles and officials is clearly distinguished from "filial cannibalism" in traditional Confucian sources, in which children who cut pieces of their own flesh (often from thighs) to nourish sick and declining parents are often textually honored, upheld to posterity as paragons of virtue.³³ Key Ray Chong distinguishes between "survival cannibalism," born of necessity due to famine or natural disaster, and "learned cannibalism"; both Confucian filial cannibalism and the official banquets of human flesh, tucked into with gustatory zeal, fall into the latter category.³⁴

For Zhang Zhuo, these odious local gourmands—devouring the seed, essence, and life of the common people—are tacitly set in diametric opposition with celebrated models of imperial moderation like early Tang emperor Taizong. Famously, amid a drought and locust plague, Taizong stood before his court and, despite the urgent pleas of surrounding ministers standing by, seized and devoured a fistful of locusts, remarking that it was better that the locusts rend his bowels and innards than harm a single stalk of the peasantry's grain.³⁵ Jack Chen has capably demonstrated that, given the "semiotic echo" between locust (*huang* 蝗) and emperor (*huang* 皇), Taizong's acridophagic act of consuming the "imperial insect, the arthropodic double of the sovereign," marked him as a virtuous "true king," a model of disciplined self-moderation; this dramatic act might also be understood as a personal sacrifice, for the emperor was at once devouring the locusts and offering his body to the rapacious creatures for their consumption.³⁶

5

The common people

AMONG THE "FOUR PEOPLE" (*SIMIN* 四民), scholar–administrators, the literati, ranked highest (not surprising, as they were the architects of the hierarchy); peasants, who produced the food to sustain the empire, ranked next; artisans and craftsmen, who created clever and useful things, were third; and merchants, who moved and sold commodities, profiting off the labor of others, were last. However, this theoretical classification with deep Confucian roots had little bearing on social, economic, and political realities. *Court and Country* contains many accounts of the lives of common folk outside the ranks of the officialdom, offering curious glimpses of lives and livelihoods around the empire.

PEASANT-FARMERS

The hospitality of the common people

Chinese hospitality (*hao ke* 好客)—literally meaning "enjoying having guests" or treating guests well—knows no boundaries. This generosity is reflected in the following account from *Court and Country*:

> *Wei Hao, a county official, went out into the countryside and stopped at the home of villager Wang Xingzai. When he was resting there, he dreamed that a woman clad in black was leading a dozen or so children wearing yellow. All of them repeatedly kowtowed and asked him to spare their lives. Hao felt very unsettled about the matter and, upon waking, urged the Wang family to hurry up and prepare a meal. One of his travelling companions informed him, "Wang Xingzai's family is poor. They don't have the means to lay out fine delicacies— just a broody hen sheltering a nest of eggs; she's already been laying for more than ten days. Now, he's about to kill her!" Hao suddenly realized that the black-clad woman was none other than the black hen, then instructed Wang to let her go. That night Wei Hao had another dream in which the woman and children all thanked him and then departed.* (4.100)

In hosting an honored guest, families will go to extremes, taxing their paltry resources to put on a good face. Thus, when a county official and his attendants stopped by a Wang's homestead—a once-in-a-lifetime or once-in-a-generation occurrence for the family—they intended to pull out all the stops by killing their only hen so that they might lay a sumptuous feast, though doing so would mean losing the entire brood on which the hen was sitting. Fortunately, a timely dream during a siesta and the thoughtful advice of an attendant led the local official to stop the Wangs from killing the broody hen.

Folk wisdom

Most of the peasantry in seventh-century China was illiterate. However, some passages from *Court and Country* include proverbs that possess *Old Farmer's Almanac*-style folksy agrarian wisdom:

> A common proverb goes, "If you stuff a date up your nostril vent, keep the seeds hanging from the tall building and don't plant." Another saying went, "When the cicada's call summons locusts, there won't be much of a millet harvest." Another proverb held that "When spring rains fall on the first of the month, barren earth for 1000 li. When summer rains fall on the first of the month, leftover boats will float through the marketplace. When it rains on the first day of autumn, the panicle of the rice plant grows ears. When it rains of the first day of winter, magpies build their nests low to the ground."ᴬ (1.19)

One proverb mentions locusts—a periodic and cyclical scourge that could decimate harvests for years in succession. Another offers warning signs of coming floods and droughts. Presumably, these proverbs resulted from centuries of farmers' experience in monitoring the changing seasons and weather to better gauge the ideal time to plant and to harvest—hard-earned, hard-won lessons.

A second passage on folk wisdom from *Court and Country* also attests to the fragility of the agrarian cycle and the myriad hardships that peasants faced:

> When Jupiter is visible in the south, people and horses will be reduced to eating dirt. If it appears in the southeast, men will have to sell their wives and sons. But if it shows up in the southwest and west, people will pray for gruel and receive wine. (Sup., 174)

This passage indicates that, to some extent, the common folk used the appearance of planets and stars as a guide to predict an abundant harvest or, more often, to signal coming famine and dearth. In the worst of famines, folks were reduced to cannibalism or selling wives and children.

This final passage probably represents a regional folk superstition:

> When planting glutinous millet, snakes will come; if, however, one burns the horn and wool of a black ram on the planting area, the snakes will not dare emerge. (5.122)

THE COMMON PEOPLE

This is perhaps an apotropaic belief based on the similar sounds of "sheep/ram" (*yang* 羊) and auspicious (*xiang* 祥), which is sheep with an "omen"/"revelation" (*shi* 礻) radical. Folks still use the phrase "auspicious ram" to usher in the lunar Year of the Ram.

ARTISTS, ARTISANS, AND CRAFTSMEN[2]

The arts and crafts flourished during the Tang, stimulated by traffic along maritime and continental Silk Roads that brought endless shipments and caravans of goods, new ideas, and different peoples from India, Southeast Asia, Central Asia, and Asia Minor. Newly arrived goldsmiths, silversmiths, leatherworkers, and jewelers prompted existing craftsmen to hone their skills in order to compete, while the frenetic marketplaces and bazaars drove long-existing silk, porcelain, and pottery workshops to accelerate production and diversify their goods.

The eight accounts from *Court and Country* below feature artists, artisans, and craftsmen, including a transcendent painter, a masterful architect, woodworkers capable of creating automata, a deft bronzesmith, a skilled "ash calligrapher," and a craftsman with the mastery to create the gearwork for the prototype of a mechanical clock!

Zhang Sengyou, a famous painter who served Liang dynasty emperor Wudi (r. 502–549), lived 150 years before Zhang Zhuo. He is perhaps best known for a mural at a Buddhist temple featuring a number of lifelike dragons. He warned everyone that the creatures would animate if he painted the pupils. Legend has it that when he dotted the eyes of the dragons, they truly came to life, soaring and storming through the heavens! Only the dragons left without pupils remained on his painting.[3] This story from *Court and Country* also attests to the consummate skill and verisimilitude with which the master painter rendered his subjects:

> *Xingguo Temple in Runzhou prefecture was plagued by doves and pigeons in the rafters whose falling feces befouled and spattered the faces of Buddhist statuary. Zhang Sengyou then painted an eagle on the east wall and a kestrel on the west wall, both with their heads inclined upwards, looking toward the eaves. From that time onward, pigeons and doves no longer dared roost in the rafters of Xingguo Temple.* (Sup., 158)

Here artistry serves and preserves the sacred. Zhang's realistic depictions of birds of prey allegedly intimidated and drove away the pigeons and doves who had long befouled the Buddhist statuary in a temple with their droppings.

Another passage from *Court and Country* reveals a similar conviction that surpassingly ingenious craftsmanship possessed a divine or magical quality that animated the work. As the Turks raided the northeast in Wu Zhao's reign, they were stymied by a masterfully constructed bridge:

> *In Zhaozhou there is a stone bridge of extraordinary construction. Exquisitely cut stones and voussoirs fit so snugly it was as if they were pared down with a blade. To behold it was like looking at a crescent moon emerging from a cloud, like a long rainbow drinking from a brook. Above there were parapets, all wrought of stone. Uprights between the parapets were carved into stone lions. During the Longshuo era, a Koguryan spy stole two of the lions. Craftsmen were hired to restore the bridge, but none could imitate the original. In the Dazu era of the Celestial Empress, when the Tujue Qapaghan Khan sacked Zhaozhou and Dingzhou prefectures, the rebels wanted to head southward. However, when they reached the bridge, the horses all knelt on the ground and refused to advance. They saw an azure dragon lying on the bridge, aroused and writhing with alacrity and fury. The rebels then beat a hasty retreat. (5.119)*

The skill with which the bridge had been made could not be imitated. It tempted and overawed foreigners; a Koguryan stole an upright carved into a lion and Turkish horses, seeing the towering form of an azure dragon rising from the stone bridge—an animated extension of the majestic structure—genuflected before the kingly creature. Like the horse of Gu Zong, which balked at crossing the threshold of the gate of the audience hall for chief ministers because its master was unworthy (see Chapter 2), the Turkish horses possess heightened sensitivity for what the cosmos and nature deem appropriate. In this case, unlike their barbarian riders, the horses are duly awestruck by the power, culture, and civilization vested in the masterful architecture.

Another unique artisan mentioned in *Court and Country* warrants attention. The following passage describes a master of a peculiar form of calligraphy:

> *Talented artisan Zhang Chong excelled at writing calligraphy in ash to embellish bronze belt buckles and coin-sized ornamental studs. On these tiny palates, using fire, the raised lines of his fine "ash calligraphy" would become dragons, fish, birds, and beasts in all their intricate splendor, not lacking a single detail. (6.141)*

In a world where the paramount importance of official rank and family led to narrowly circumscribed sumptuary laws, Zhang Chong's mastery of ash calligraphy (*hui shu* 灰書)—a delicate form of pyrography—gave play to a distinctive individual style revealed in exquisitely rendered minutiae.

Court and Country also furnishes an impressive account of a prototypical mechanical clock that became an important ritual centerpiece in Wu Zhao's Divine Capital:

> *In the Ruyi era of Zetian, Haizhou sent an artisan to the court who created a vehicle with 12 zodiacal jacks. When the axle revolved to a position due south at high noon, a door opened*

*and a horse-headed jack would emerge. It revolved with perfect regularity, facing each of the four directions. He also crafted wood-burning stoves with inset iron trays to contain the fire; when they revolved, the fire wouldn't fall out.*⁴ (6.142)

The use of jackwork by the unnamed artisan sent to Luoyang by the prefect in coastal Haizhou (modern-day Jiangsu) suggests that the man's invention is an ornate time-keeping device; the 12 chronograms (*chen* 辰) correspond to 24-hour days set in two-hour blocks, and to the 12 creatures of the zodiac. Following the apparent position of the sun on the ecliptic, every two hours a jack—likely an animal head, for we know that at high noon a horse head emerged—would come out to mark the time, like the signature bird on a cuckoo clock. According to Joseph Needham, this chronometer from Wu Zhao's reign can be considered "the single ancestor" of the layered jack wheels found in the great astronomical clocks of later eras.⁵ Antonino Forte has identified both the jack-work and the wood-burning stoves with the rotating trays (he argues that these are a system of "braziers with Cardan suspension") as integral parts of the grand armillary sphere, a proto-mechanical clock built into a far larger architectural marvel: Wu Zhao's Bright Hall, a ritual complex containing Buddhist, Confucian, and Daoist elements that she used as an arena to mark a number of personal and political triumphs.⁶

Necessity was not always the mother of invention, however. Sometimes the best inspiration for innovation was a need to impress one's company with a clever wrinkle on a drinking game or a new-fangled tankard for imbibing! In the following quartet of passages, functional wooden automata like a Buddhist monk, a fish-catching otter, a bronze dove, and a courtesan all attest to impressive artisanal ingenuity:

Court architect Yang Wulian had an abundance of clever ideas. Once he carved a wooden Buddhist monk and placed an alms bowl in its hands and let it wander the Qinzhou market. The wooden mannequin was capable of walking and begging. When the bowl was full it would trigger a mechanism that would say, "Thank you for your donation!" Market-goers vied to get a look and, because people desired to hear the wooden monk speak, donators filled the bowl with several thousand cash per day. (6.142)

Prefect of Chenzhou Wang Ju carved a wooden otter that could catch fish; it would sink down in the water then pull them out by the head. The otter was submerged on a stone-weighted line, and moving bait that revolved would be placed in its jaws. When a fish took the bait, the trigger released and the jaws clamped down on the fish. The stone sinker fell off and the otter floated to the surface. (6.142–43)

Prince of Han Li Yuanjia⁷ had an elaborate bronze wine goblet. When filled with liquor, it stood straight upright on its pedestal; as it emptied, it would incline to one side. He also had a bronze dove fashioned. When rubbed on a felt carpet, it would call out, cooing just like a real dove. (6.142)

> *Yin Wenliang, a county leader in Luozhou prefecture, was an ingenious artisan who was fond of his liquor. He carved a wooden mannequin and attired it in coarse silk. At drinking banquets, it would always propose toasts with a sense of protocol and sequence. He also fashioned a courtesan capable of singing songs and playing the flute, all suited to the festal occasion. When someone failed to drink a penalty, a small wooden jack would refuse to pour them more spirits; whenever someone failed to finish a drink, the courtesan would sing and play bamboo pipes to hasten them along. No one really could fathom the divine ingenuity of these creations. (6.142)*

E. R. Truitt, in *Medieval Robots*, observes that such automata—which existed in medieval Europe as well as Tang China—took "many forms" and were "far more than delightful curiosities":

> Automata stood at the intersection of natural knowledge (including magic) and technology. [...] They performed a multitude of social and cultural functions: entertainment, instruction, prophecy, proxy, discipline, and surveillance. [...] They are mimetic objects that dramatize the structure of the cosmos and humankind's role in it.[8]

Yin Wenliang's wooden mannequins and courtesans were proxies that provided entertainment, as did Yang Wulian's begging Buddhist monk. The zodiacal jacks crafted by the nameless artisan from Haizhou were more impressive automata, cutting-edge science, part of the gearwork of what must have been one of the most sophisticated clocks in the world at the time.[9] Even the mimetic auto-otter promised both entertainment and function, while friction could prompt the robot-dove in Li Yuanjia's collection to generate song. The animal-headed jacks of the clock, the otter, and the doves also function to present a vision of the natural world and the cosmos flattering to the classes that could afford such costly wonders. The fact that these were not utilitarian marked them as precious and unique symbols of elite status. Perhaps Wu Zhao and the wealthy and powerful of the capitals sought to naturalize their status by virtue of their control over these approximations of/improvements upon the natural world. Control over the time, labor, and talent of these artisans provided this opportunity.

MERCHANTS: MANY ROUTES TO WEALTH

In theory, merchants were at the bottom of the social pyramid, beneath the scholar–officials, the peasants toiling in the fields, and the nimble-fingered artisans. They are often dismissed in the rhetoric of Confucian statecraft as selfish and avaricious parasites who produce nothing and grow fat on the labor and sweat of others. However, rhetoric belied reality: amid the bustling commerce of the cosmopolitan early Tang and under the dominion of Wu Zhao, a ruler whose family grew wealthy on the sale of timber, an abundance of caravan traffic flowed both ways along Silk Roads while argosies from India, Arabia, and Srivijaya poured into southeastern ports.

Long a nexus of commerce, Wu Zhao's capital Luoyang was situated near the northern terminus of the Grand Canal, the artery linking north and south China. Her "Divine Capital" was therefore much better situated than Chang'an as a nexus for the empire. Transport of grain from the south to Chang'an—a city of a million with great political and traditional prestige but situated at the center of a region of impoverished, overused soil—had long posed a difficult challenge.[10] In contrast, Luoyang, bisected by the Luo River, a major artery of commerce, had long been a hub of trade. The southern market alone contained 3000 shops representing 120 different occupations—apothecaries, goldsmiths, silversmiths, moneylenders, grocers, fishmongers, tea merchants, flat-cake hawkers, incense vendors, butchers, cosmetics peddlers, and haberdashers selling Central Asian garments.[11] Wu Zhao established new customs stations. One minister serving under the emperor gushed that, in the capital, "Sculls and boats of the empire all congregate, often more than ten thousand vessels filling the canals!" Of course, enterprise spilled beyond the metropole—the same fellow observed, "On the Huai River and in the Seas, day and night, there is a constant flow of commerce."[12] There are several records in *Court and Country* that show different paths to commercial wealth.

Merchant #1: Government official by day, wealthy silk magnate by night

The two examples from *Court and Country* below describe not merchants traveling along the Silk Road, but clever, homegrown examples of entrepreneurs who accumulated vast wealth by very different routes. Rather than showing tensions between profit-seeking merchants and purportedly virtuous mandarins administering the state, both examples reveal that men often straddled these two groups, moving fluidly between public and private sectors.

Merchant–official He Dayuan availed himself of a low-ranking office that placed him in charge of several post-horse stations in the northeastern prefecture, Dingzhou, taking advantage of the high volume of traffic:

> He Dayuan of Dingzhou was tremendously wealthy. He controlled three post-horse stations in the prefecture and set up stores and shops at each to do business with passing Sogdian/foreign merchants, amassing countless millions of cash. Because these Silk Road merchants often purchased silk, his family set up a factory with 500 looms. However, when He Dayuan

grew old, he lost his post; his household became poor and was nearly reduced to ruin. When He regained his former position, his family once again flourished. (3.75)

A constant flow of military men passed through Dingzhou en route to staffing border garrisons, bringing in their wake necessary merchants, both Chinese and foreign. Indeed, there were so many Central Asian or Sogdian merchants from the western oasis states that He Dayuan set up a huge silk workshop with 500 looms! There were a number of Sogdian colonies in the northeast, and this probably made it possible to directly transport finished silk goods westward, without heading south. The passage indicates that when He lost his official position, his businesses could no longer operate. Fortunately for the opportunistic merchant–official—a man who had a clear understanding of local, regional, national, and international commercial networks—he regained his position, and, along with it, his wealth. The hybrid Chinese–Central Asian culture of the early Tang exerted a huge impact on culture and style. As Chen BuYun characterizes it, "innovations in the textile industry"—like He Dayuan's immense workshop and its capacity for mass production and "foreign modes of adornment"—opened up novel, vital creative possibilities that informed a Tang chic. He Dayuan's privately owned workshop for twill damasks was larger than any of the competing state textile workshops in Chang'an, Luoyang, and other prefectural centers.[13] While official workshops produced clothing primarily for the court and imperial use, merchants like He Deyuan clearly had other trading partners, forming part of a growing textile industry that "supplied an increasing variety of patterned, dyed, printed, and embroidered fabrics for clothing."[14]

Merchant #2: All hail the shit king!

Chang'an, probably the largest city in the world in the seventh century, had a population of roughly one million. Unlike many civilizations, medieval China did not befoul rivers and waterways with human and animal waste; both were gathered and recycled for agriculture. Legally, the Tang Code imposed harsh penalties upon people who let waste run into sewers and streets. Basic sanitation—involving transportation of large volumes of human and animal waste along the broad thoroughfares between wards and out the gates (or by canal with barges) to the countryside where it might be recycled—presented a major logistic challenge. But merchants were up to challenge, for waste was a valuable commodity, used for fertilizer and even for medicine. As the quality of human waste, called "night-soil" because it was collected every evening, was "the function of the diet of urban residents," the excrement produced by the wealthy, who ate the most protein-rich foods, commanded the highest market price. The vital role of the merchant of human and animal waste—which linked "town and countryside in a great nutrient cycle and made [the Chinese] system of agriculture more sustainable than European practices"—cannot be overstated.[15] Indeed, "This is good shit!" was originally the catchphrase of a little-known hawker of excrement who collected his goods from wealthy homes in the wards proximate to the Western Market in Tang Chang'an.

During Gaozong's final years, an official suggested that the Two Sages could raise significant funds selling the rich manure from the well-fed chargers of the imperial stables! *Court and Country* records this proposal:

> *Vice Director of Imperial Manufactories Pei Feishu sent in a memorial to the emperor proposing to sell manure from imperial stables and pasturage, claiming that Gaozong could earn 200,000 strings of cash annually. Liu Rengui advised the emperor against it, saying, "I fear that future generations will say that the House of Tang were peddlers of horseshit." Subsequently, the memorial was laid to rest.*[16] (Sup., 172)

While this occupation may have been beneath the dignity of emperors and nobles, gentlemen and literati—as the passages from *Court and Country* above and below illustrate, literati considered scraping and gathering shit a "disgusting vocation"—waste removal, recycling, and repurposing offered lucrative economic opportunities:[17]

> *Wealthy magnate Luo Hui of Chang'an amassed a great fortune scraping manure off roads. This had been a family side occupation for many generations, and the household accumulated countless tens of thousands of cash. People called him the "Shit King" because the roads in his wake had all been scraped clean of manure and he had become wealthy. At Luo's invitation, court gentleman Lu Jingyang visited the household. All of the guesthouses and cottages on the estate were stunningly beautiful. On the interior, servants helped with grooming and washing, and he was given new silken clothes. The opulent household was replete with elegant folding screens, felt bed-mats, and a special kitchen for butchering and boiling livestock. Mouth agape, Jingyang asked Luo, "My host lives such an opulent life. Why not give up this disgusting vocation?" Hui answered, "Once I stopped gathering manure for a year or two. My slaves and servants started to die off; cows and horses dispersed and were lost. But once I resumed my former calling, the family path was gradually righted. It's not so much that I'm willing to gather manure [...] it's just my destiny."* (3.75)

The stories of merchants He Dayuan and Luo Hui both contain warnings that the lot of a merchant is a volatile one, with wild fluctuations. In each case, the merchant temporarily abandons the market he has cornered, rapidly plunging his wealthy family into fiscal freefall! Both men, however, are able to recover their hard-earned wealth by resuming their line of work, committing long hours to rebuild their dwindling fortunes. *Extensive Records* categorizes both of these sources in a chapter aptly titled "Making a Living" (*zhisheng* 治生).[18]

PERFORMERS: STREET ENTERTAINERS, ACROBATS, AND CHILD PRODIGIES

Zhang Zhuo sought to record all things bizarre and peculiar. One of the clear objectives in *Court and Country* is to shock and intrigue. Therefore, during his peregrinations around the empire, Zhang collected stories about individuals with odd talents.

Street performers and the lantern festival

Several of these individuals are street performers. The Janus-faced one-man band in the passage below is a memorable example:

> In Shouan[19] was a man—I don't know his family name or given name—who could play clappers with his elbows and the flute with his nose while singing a ditty. He could simultaneously laugh with one half of his face and weep with the other half. He had a black dog that understood human speech and would follow his instructions just as a human might. (6.144)

Street performers like this fellow might showcase their talents and earn money at events like the Buddhist Lantern Festival, a celebration set on the fifteenth day of the first lunar month (for more on this festival, see Chapter 9). Based on Dunhuang cave paintings and textual records, Qiang Ning describes the festival as featuring "female dancers performing under lamp trees" as

> streets and lanes filled with joyful people [...] in the capital and other prefectures. Friends come together and play drums, the noise of which goes up to the sky. [...] Entertainers and acrobats look grotesque and bizarre. The fantastic masks and unusual dresses make people laugh. [...] The colorful clothing and beautiful makeup dazzle passers-by. Horses and carts block the streets. Delicious food and good wine are on sale everywhere. Huge parties of music and dance are held in various places.[20]

The performer from Shou'an and his remarkable canine companion—whose repertoire presumably showcased a wide range of talents—would fit right in with this lively scene.

THE COMMON PEOPLE

The acrobatic pole acts of the daring Lius of Youzhou

China has a long and glorious history of acrobatics. Funerary art from the Han dynasty depicts tumblers, balancing acts, and other sorts of acrobatics—including pole-carriers with child acrobats performing at the top.[21] Celebrated Han emperor Wudi patronized acrobatic and gymnastic acts.[22] In Charles Benn's discussion of the many and variegated acrobatic acts that were popular in the Tang, he mentions pole acts as one of two sorts of "death-defying" performance—tightrope-walking being the other. Usually, an "anchorwoman [...] placed a tall, painted pole 70 to 100 feet long on her head. The shaft normally had a crossbar affixed to the top on which slim young girls performed acrobatic moves such as hanging by their chins or doing handstands and somersaults."[23]

Unlike the acts that Benn describes, the father, Liu Jiao, serves as an anchorman in the following description from *Court and Country*:

> Liu Jiao of Youzhou prefecture balanced a bamboo pole seventy feet tall atop his head. He could lift it up and let it down. He had twelve good-looking daughters who would sit in a seat or stand atop the pole. While the audience couldn't bear to watch, none of the girls showed the slightest hint of fear. Later, in the end, one of the girls fell to her death. (6.141)

The passage hints that these were often family acts, where skills were passed from one generation to the next; it also suggests that young children underwent countless hours of grueling training to perfect and hone athleticism, flexibility, and a performer's élan. The unfortunate fate of the girl falling from the pole serves as a grim reminder that death was not always defied in these performances. In *Extensive Records*, this passage is included in the chapters on "Remarkable Skills."[24]

Mao Jun's precocious son and a multitasking child prodigy

Occasionally, remarkably precocious children gained fame for possessing some special talent. In her studies on representations of childhood in early China, Anne Kinney has shown that in the Han dynasty, as Confucianism became the state orthodoxy, precocity in children progressively came to be defined by and associated with early mastery of classical and canonical texts.[25] The child described in the following passage from *Court and Country* is no exception:

> At the age of four, the son of Mao Jun of Bingzhou was summoned into the palace by Zetian to read and recognize characters. The child wrote the entire Thousand Character Primer from memory. Zetian gifted him scholar's robes then sent him back home. Folks all thought

the child was the incarnation of some forest sprite. After that, no one knew what became of him. (5.110)

Literary talent (*wen* 文) and mastery of the classics was held in the highest esteem in traditional China. The *Thousand Character Primer* mentioned in the passage above was comprised of 250 four-character lines and designed to inculcate Confucian values at an early age: one line reads, "In girls one admires chastity and purity; in boys, talent and goodness." Memorization of such texts was an important skill; it was not thought of as a rote mnemonic exercise, but as an admirable art for internalizing and wholly digesting a work's principles, so that they became second nature. As the child prodigy came from Wu Zhao's home prefecture, Bingzhou, the emperor was well disposed toward the youngster and gifted him scholar's robes, anticipating his bright future as a court minister.

Court and Country also contains an account of a "Divine Immortal Child":

When Yuan Jia was a young child, he was clever and extraordinary. While reciting classics and histories and counting sheep in a flock, he could simultaneously draw a circle with his left hand, a square with his right, and compose a forty-character poem which he would, with a calligraphy brush between his toes, write in eight lines of five characters. He could manage all six things at once! People of the time called him the "Divine Immortal Child."[26] (5.110)

This precocious lad took multitasking to the next level, simultaneously counting, reciting, drawing different shapes with each hand, mentally composing a poem, and writing his verses with his toes! Passers-by were no doubt delighted and awed by the youngster's scintillating combination of manual dexterity and nimble intellect.

GAMES AND GAMERS

The master of pitch-pot

Court and Country contains a short passage admiring poet–courtier Xue Shenhuo for his consummate skill at the game of pitch-pot (*touhu* 投壺):[27]

Xue Shenhuo was excellent at pitch-pot. Like a pouncing dragon or a striking falcon, he was always on target, never missing an arrow. Even when the pot was set behind his back and he tossed the arrow backwards over his shoulder, he would never miss: 100 throws, 100 on target! (6.143)

The origins of pitch-pot predate the Tang by more than a millennium: its target vessel has been discovered in tombs from the Warring States era and

THE COMMON PEOPLE

Figure 5   An ink rubbing of two men playing pitch pot (*touhu*).

the contest is mentioned in ancient texts like the *Chronicles of Zuo*.[28] The game seems to have had both more profound and more popular roots. There is evidence that it derived from early forms of divination.[29] Certainly, in its rudimentary incarnation, the game was far less elaborate. At a more popular level, the game, probably of military origin devised by bored off-duty archers, came to feature two men vying to pitch arrows into the open mouth of a vessel (see Figure 5).[30] There are certainly no mentions of behind-the-back or no-look, over-the-shoulder throws like those that Xue makes in *Court and Country*! However, it became an elite entertainment with ceremonial rules prescribed in the canonical *Book of Rites*. It remained popular in the Tang dynasty and was played on both popular and elite levels; by the Tang, "paintings regularly depict arrow-filled pots as part of the mise en scène of scholarly life."[31]

Following the ceremonial script for pitch-pot outlined in *Rites*, the host would begin by deprecating his inferior game set, making it sound as though the best he could offer was shoddy craftsmanship: "I have here these crooked arrows, and this pot with its skewed mouth; but we beg you to amuse yourself with them." In turn, the guest answered, with due politeness, "I have partaken, Sir, of your excellent drink and admirable viands; allow me to decline this further proposal for my pleasure." The host rejoins, "It is not worthwhile for you to decline these poor arrows and pot; let me earnestly beg you to try them." The art of what today's pop culture terms the "humblebrag" was a stylized form of etiquette by the Tang; a host plying his guest with the most elaborate meal and extravagant entertainments would dismiss the evening's laughably paltry fare and drab, unworthy amusements. Only after several rounds of this modulated dance of proposition and declination does the guest finally agree to play. Even then, only after an exchange of bows do host and guest adjourn to their respective mats. The "archery commandant," an official serving as the referee, sets up the large-bellied, thin-necked pot equidistant from the two competitors and a stand with eight arrows for host and guest to pitch. He goes over a complex set of rules. Zither music sets the ambience.

Finally, the game can begin! After each round, the archery commandant counts the arrows that each contestant has successfully thrown into the pot's mouth; he announces the results, and the vanquished drinks a forfeit.[32]

During the Sui and Tang dynasties, an anthem was composed for the occasion of an imperially hosted bout of pitch-pot.[33] The Tang imperial library even contained a one-chapter *Classic of Pitch-pot*.[34] Pitch-pot, known as *tuho* in the Korea and *toko* in Japan, spread through East Asia: Tang histories record that men in the Korean kingdom of Koguryo excelled at the game.[35]

Backgammon: for the love of the game

Deriving from the early Indian game *prasena* or the ancient Persian *nard*, a boardgame known as "two armies" (*shuanglu* 雙陸) or "double sixes" (*shuangliu* 雙六) was popular during the Tang.[36] It was a form of backgammon, based on the casting of dice. During the excavation of Tang tombs, a number of boards have been unearthed. Like pitch-pot, its origins and development are intertwined with divination. Potential fates and destinies in the game hinge on the roll of the dice. During the Tang, the game spread to Japan, where it is known as *suguroku*—double sixes. In a Japanese novel set shortly after the Tang, the game is part of high-stakes "political gambling to forecast a future event," the sex of the empress's unborn child, with the implicit possession of the empire hanging in the balance.[37]

There are several passages in official histories dating to the reigns of Wu Zhao and her son Zhongzong that indicate the game was enjoyed by the court and the imperial family. During the middle of her Zhou dynasty—when she still intended to pass the empire on to her Wu clan, and had ensconced her nephew Wu Sansi as her heir—Wu Zhao had a recurring dream about losing at backgammon. Respected minister Di Renjie explained that it was because she had misplaced her critical pieces (*zi* 子), her sons; if she were to restore these "pieces" to their rightful place, the imperial palace, he explained, the disturbing dream would cease. As a result, she recalled her son from exile and restored him as Crown Prince.[38]

Histories record that when Empress Wei—along with several other powerful women—dominated the court in the years immediately following the restoration of the Tang, she took Wu Zhao's nephew, Wu Sansi, as a lover. He moved freely in and out of the inner palace. Oblivious to the burgeoning cacophony of rumors about the liaison between his wife and his cousin, Emperor Zhongzong kept tallies while the two of them played backgammon.[39]

Shortly after Wu Zhao's time, the Chongqing region offered exquisite, locally-crafted backgammon pieces as tribute to the court, attesting to the ongoing popularity of the game among the elite.⁴⁰ Based in part upon a mid-Tang painting by Zhou Fang, Andrew Lo describes the game pieces as "tall, slender forms with rounded shoulders and slim necks [...] like bells or Chinese clothes-beaters."⁴¹ Later in imperial China's long history, one Ming emperor—feeling that the game was a frivolous pursuit distracting from necessary agriculture—made playing backgammon a crime punishable by the severance of one's hands!⁴²

This passage from *Court and Country* reflects one man's passion for the game and attachment to his game set:

> *In the Xianshou era, Pan Chan of Beizhou prefecture excelled at* shuanglu. *Every time he went abroad, he kept a gameboard close at hand. Once when he was asea, a storm blew up and wrecked the boat. With his right hand, Pan Chan clutched his board; in his left hand, he held the gaming table; and clenched in his mouth were the dice. After two days and a night, he reached shore. His hands were worn to the bone, but he held onto the* shuanglu *set; and the dice were still in his mouth.* (Sup., 158)

Pan Chan is a double winner, managing to survive a shipwreck and keep his set of backgammon pieces and dice intact!

OTHER VIGNETTES OF THE COMMON PEOPLE

Many of the anecdotes in *Court and Country* that deal with the common people do not fit neatly within the hierarchical structure described at the outset of this chapter; however, they reveal a good deal about Wu Zhao's multivarious empire in their very resistance to categorization.

A citizen's arrest in Huaizhou

This account from *Court and Country* tells of a citizen's arrest made by one Dong Xingcheng, a clever fellow from Huaizhou, in modern-day Henan:

> *In Henei County of Huaizhou prefecture, Dong Xingcheng was skilled in devising strategies to catch robbers. Once, a highwayman from Changdian in Heyang robbed a traveler of his mule and his leather bags. As the new day was dawning, he arrived in Huaizhou. When Xingcheng reached an intersection and saw the man, he said mockingly, "Stop, Thief! Dismount your donkey straightaway!" The man confessed to his crime and asked, "How did you know?" Xingcheng said, "You were riding quickly, and the donkey is lathered in sweat although the road isn't long. And when I saw you, you led the donkey further away. It is because of this that I know." Dong seized the thief and sent him to the county authorities. A short time later, the owner of the donkey arrived on foot; everything was exactly as Xingcheng had said.* (5.109)

It would seem that Dong was not an official, for when he captures the thief, he turns the man over to the county authorities. In addition, his name does not appear in either of the Tang dynastic histories. *Extensive Records* places this passage in its chapters on "Brilliant Investigators" (*jingcha* 精察).[43]

From day laborer to faith healer

Set late in Wu Zhao's reign, this story from *Court and Country* relates how a day laborer working at a Daoist abbey in the Southeast of the empire is visited in a dream state by a Daoist divinity who bestows upon him the power of healing:

> *In the Jiushi era, Yang Yuanliang of Xiangzhou*[44] *was twenty-odd years old; he was working as a hired laborer at the Wenshan Temple in Qianzhou.*[45] *In a dream, a celestial being said to him, "My votive hall is in ruins. If you repair it for me, I will endow you with the power to heal all sicknesses." When Yang awakened, he was delighted. When he tried to cure people, there was none who didn't get better. Li Zheng of Ganxian County*[46] *had a fist-sized swelling on his back. Yang used a knife to cut it off; in several days the site of the wound was level and Li Zhang had fully recovered. From his healing, Yang earned ten thousand cash a day. After he completed the construction of the divine being's hall, Yang gradually lost his efficacy as a healer.* (1.3)

It is interesting to note that while Zhang Zhuo often suggests that other faith healers are charlatans and rascals, the narrative here—though it does remark that the fellow exploits his newfound healing touch for profit—is straightforward and does not question the validity of the man's ability. This is perhaps because Yang was not allied with Wu Zhao, nor did he gather a militant band of followers and rebels.

Two rags-to-riches stories: lucky ducks and camels

From Cinderella (or Cinderella's older Chinese sister Ye Xian, who appears in Duan Chengshi's late Tang dynasty collectanea *Miscellaneous Morsels from Youyang* (*Youyang zazu*))[47] to the Arthurian knight Sir Gareth, from street urchin Aladdin to Horatio Alger's *Ragged Dick*, across cultures and epochs people seem to love wildly improbable rags-to-riches stories. In *Court and Country*, Zhang Zhuo fondly relates an anecdote about a lucky peasant in the Southland whose keen powers of observation while mucking out the duck pen led to wealth and office:

> *Chen Huaiqing, a man of Lingnan, raised a flock of more than a hundred ducks. Once he saw a glittering golden sheen on the duck shit he was digging up in their enclosure. He put the muck in a colander, ran water over it, and obtained 10 liang of gold.*[48] *Chen then closely*

THE COMMON PEOPLE

investigated the area where the ducks grazed at the base of the hill behind his house. He dug and discovered a vein of gold; after excavating he obtained twenty or thirty jin of gold.[49] *At the time, no one knew. Chen Huaiqing subsequently became incredibly wealthy and served as Prefect of Wuzhou.* (2.37)

A second account on Chen Huaiqing in *Court and Country* (see Chapter 10)—telling of his ability to develop an antidote to one of the more toxic flora in Lingnan—reveals that he was not just an ordinary peasant farmer.

In a similar account, Camel Zou, a seller of flat-cakes working in a residential ward in Chang'an—capital cities were built on a grid comprised of large, rectangular wards separated by wide thoroughfares—makes a fortuitous discovery under a troublesome rut in the brick road that often overturns his cart:

Camel Zou, a man of Chang'an, once was poor and pushed a small cart of steamed cakes to sell. Every time he passed the corner of Shengye Ward,[50] *some hidden bricks sticking up from the ground jostled and overturned the cart and the dirt fouled his cakes. Camel felt bitter about this, then used a pick to break through a dozen or so bricks. Beneath them was a porcelain jar with a five-bushel capacity. He opened it up to look. It was filled with gold, and he became tremendously wealthy. His son Zou Fang was close friends with Xiao Quan. A poet of the time wrote:*

Xiao Quan was the son of a side-horse;
Zou Fang was the son of a camel.
No need for principle and virtue to bind them in the end;
it only took money to make them mutual friends. (5.119–20)

A fellow who is stoop-backed from manual labor is sometimes known by the nickname "Camel"; the most famous example is the rickshaw-puller Camel Xiangzi (literally, Lucky Camel) in Republican-era (1912–1949) writer Lao She's eponymous novel.[51] Zhang Zhuo concludes the anecdote with a poem intimating that the profligate son of Camel Zou used his father's wealth to cultivate a friendship by drinking and carousing with a wealthy imperial in-law. Curiously, the term for the reserve horses for carriages or chariots, the extra side-horses, was also the term used for the husbands of imperial princesses (*fuma* 駙馬).

The three kindling gatherers of Shaozhou

When he went to Lingnan, Zhang Zhuo apparently took the court convention of bestowing unflattering nicknames with him:

> *In the Zhou, Clerk of Qujiang County in Shaozhou Zhu Suihou, his son-in-law Li Ti, and their retainer Erzhu Nine were all deficient in terms of graceful posture and visage. People of Guangzhou called them the "Three Kindling Gatherers." A local folk ditty went,*
>
>> *By imperial decree, we seek the kindling gatherers three*
>> *Beside the road Suihou walks first in line*
>> *Turns his head to Mr. Li he speaks,*
>> *And the echo brings Erzhu Nine.*
>
> *Sizing up Zhu Suihou, Zhang Zhuo dubbed him "Broth-Fouling Stunted Howlet."* (4.88)

When Zhang arrived in Shaozhou, locals already called the local clerk and his two companions the "Three Kindling Gatherers," probably because the unappealing trio were ugly and stooped like the laborers who carried firewood. Piling on, Zhang coined a nickname to further turn the hard-on-the-eyes clerk into a caricature. Lampooning government officials is a time-honored practice of the everyman in many cultures. After paying taxes of grain, cloth, and labor, mocking and parodying local officials is cathartic. In Zhang Zhuo's case, however, it comes across as gratuitous.

A cure lasting beyond the grave

The early Tang and Wu Zhao's time featured many remarkable physicians, perhaps the most famous among them Sun Simiao, the King of Medicine (Yaowang 藥王), whose prescriptions and formulas have been passed down for 1,300 years. Curiously, although he was a peer of Zhang Zhuo, there is not a single anecdote about this master physician in *Court and Country*. There is, however, an account of an unnamed doctor in Zhang Zhuo's work who improbably used a decoction of copper shavings and alcohol to mend a man's broken leg:

> *Cui Wu of Dingzhou fell off his horse and broke his leg. A doctor ordered him to drink copper shavings along with his wine. Subsequently, he completely recovered. More than a decade after his death, the family's burial site was changed. When his body was moved, people discovered that his tibia was sutured with copper shavings.* (1.4)

This passage on the healing of Cui Wu's broken leg from *Court and Country* is recorded in the great Ming medical encyclopedia, the *Ben Cao Gang Mu*, under a heading on the healing properties of red copper fragments.[52] As Zhang Zhuo's passage indicates, the cure was known during the Tang; the encyclopedia cites another physician, Chen Cangqi, a rough contemporary

THE COMMON PEOPLE

of Zhang Zhuo, who remarks upon the capacity of red copper fragments to "control harm caused by fractures and mend human bones and injuries of the six types of livestock. Ground to a fine [powder] and ingested with wine they directly enter the bones and the location of the injury."[53]

A Zhang Zhuo exposé: fake filial piety!

In Chapter 2, we saw that filial piety was a paramount Confucian virtue and an important measuring stick for quality of character. Becoming renowned for filial piety could lead to a family receiving recognition from the court, the state, and even the emperor! The Wangs of Hedong in the passage below were given an honorary banner of recognition by the court because Wang Sui's filiality was so great that an embracing aegis of harmony spread over the family:

> *In Hedong, the cats and dogs of filial son Wang Sui's family nursed each other's young. The prefectural and county authorities reported it to the court, and his family was bestowed with an honorary banner of recognition. In reality, the dogs and cats of the Wang family birthed their puppies and kittens at the same time. The litter of kittens were placed in the den with the bitch and the puppies were placed with the queen cat. There was really nothing extraordinary about it: the kittens grew used to nursing the bitch and the puppies became accustomed to nursing the queen. So far as trees with conjoined branches, melons growing from the same stalk, double-eared grain, or two stalks growing into the same ear/cluster of grain—some of these are natural oddities occurring in every kind of flora that are not all that uncommon. In some cases, they are fashioned by men. They are not worthy of being considered auspicious anomalies. (3.72)*

Instead of fighting, cats and dogs in this family of filial paragons raised each other's young. Great local prestige followed such occasions. To be included in dynastic annals among the filial exemplars would lead to enduring honor for a family, offering a potential path to local eminence or even office-holding. Except Zhang Zhuo, playing the Confucian skeptic and rationalist, isn't buying any of it. He claims to expose the Wang family—honored in Hedong for the filial tranquility that spread to the beasts of their household—as pious frauds. Indeed, not every performative expression of filial ardor was sincere.

In a second case, Zhang shows that a mourning son's expression of filial ardor, which won acclaim from local authorities, was little more than clumsy theater:

> *Every time filial son Guo Chun of Donghai*[54] *cried while mourning his mother, a huge flock of birds gathered. Local officials were sent to verify if it was true and set a banner at the gate of his household compound. Later, upon investigation it was discovered that every time the filial*

son wept, he would spread crumbled bread on the ground, causing flocking birds to contend to eat them. Thereafter, each time as soon as the birds heard Guo Chun start to cry, they all flocked around, vying for the crumbs. It was not prompted by their numinous response to Guo Chun's filiality. (3.71)

Like the cats and dogs in the prior story, the birds in this anecdote are conditioned by men to fabricate the appearance of nature responding to the magical power of filial love. Zhang Zhuo thus highlights two instances of carefully choreographed fake filial devotion from among the common people.[55]

6

Relationships: men, women, and family in the time of Wu Zhao

Why is there marriage in the Way of humanity? It is because among the great natural urges, there are none so great as those between male and female. The intercourse between male and female is the beginning of human relations; there is nothing as crucial as the bond between husband and wife.¹—*Comprehensive Discussions in White Tiger Hall*, first cent. AD

A NUMBER OF PASSAGES in *Court and Country* explore dimensions of relationships—between men and women, husbands and wives, masters and slaves, fathers and daughters, and even the impact that fetishes have upon relationships. Compiled by a court official and a talented literatus, Zhang Zhuo's work exudes, at times, a pungent androcentric Confucian fetor. Society in early and medieval China was, to quote Yang Lien-sheng, "predominantly patriarchal and patrilineal."² In general terms, men were conceptualized largely as creatures composed of *yang* energy—associated with the sun, light, an active nature, Heaven, and the public domain; women were understood to be wrought primarily of *yin*, linked to the moon, cold, darkness, passivity, Earth, and the inner, domestic sphere. But these are not discrete polar spheres. To an extent, there were "correlative," interdependent, and complementary aspects to *yin* and *yang*, inner (*nei* 內) and outer (*wai* 外), providing discursive space for a wider range of possibilities and opportunities in the construction of gender.³ Yenna Wu observes, "The patriarchal system that affirmed male supremacy actually provided [women] with openings for obtaining domestic power—especially if she were a principal wife of the gentry class."⁴ Similarly, Richard Guisso observes that, "If the *Five Classics* fostered the subordination of woman to man, they fostered even more the subordination of youth to age. Thus, in every age of Chinese history where Confucianism was exalted, the woman who survived, the woman who had age and the wisdom and experience that accompanied it, was revered, obeyed and respected [...] even if her son were an emperor."⁵ Wu Zhao availed herself of this discursive space to amplify her authority as grand dowager, a mother of state. Nonetheless, there were well-established cultural norms and expectations: In the "Domestic Rules" (*Neize* 內則) chapter of the early canonical *Book of Rites*, it is recorded that "men do not speak of the inner, women do not speak of the outer."[6]

The early Tang (618–690 and 705–712) and Wu Zhao's Zhou dynasty were extraordinary times when women exercised greater autonomy and influence. While women of earlier Chinese dynasties were largely sequestered in the inner, familial sphere, the far more visible Central Asian women were not immured in a domestic sphere, but lived a pastoral existence in hide yurts, grazing flocks. Ongoing Central Asian presence in North China continued to exert a powerful influence on gender roles. Impacted by this hybrid culture, women of the early Tang openly attended Buddhist temple-fairs and divorced husbands with greater facility.[7] One early Tang phenomenon, "wife-fearing" (*wei qi* 畏妻), prompted a proliferation of anecdotes about imperious shrews rounding on cowering husbands.[8] The vanity industry flourished, with myriad elaborate hairstyles, beauty marks, decorative mirrors, cosmetics, and elegant clothing.[9] The fashion industry was similarly robust: Chen BuYun terms the Tang an "empire of style" in which one's vestments served as "a site for contesting predetermined notions of status and gender."[10] Attired in tight-fitting Central Asian caftans, the bold, self-assured women of the period rode through the streets of Chang'an and Luoyang without veils, playing polo or tug-of-war.[11] The cult of chastity, a powerful Confucian force in later imperial China, lacked social and cultural currency in the Tang, prompting Gao Shiyu to observe, "woman's initiative [...] found expression outside of marriage in pre-marital and extra-marital sexual intercourse, which seems to have been quite common. The female almost always took the initiative and displayed great bravery."[12]

The passages from *Court and Country* in this chapter explore several facets of marriage and interpersonal relationships. Some anecdotes are interesting because, rather than representing women as paragons of virtue or caricatures of depravity, they show a greater degree of complexity: a woman who possesses both positive Confucian traits (loyalty, fidelity, chastity) and negative ones (extreme jealousy), or a woman who is on one hand a good filial daughter, and yet is, on the other hand, condemned for her lust, cupidity, and extravagance. Other accounts shed light upon male-male relationships, where the Confucian ideology of order inculcated a profound respect for hierarchy that demanded deference to the man of higher status. Thus, there are a number of examples where men of higher rank invite the wives or concubines of their inferiors into their households on thin pretexts, well aware that it is nigh impossible for those of lesser rank to refuse such requests. One passage exemplifies the aforementioned "wife-fearing" phenomena, detailing how a termagant browbeats her feckless husband. Several other accounts reveal just how vulnerable concubines, female slaves, and kept women were—and how few social and legal protections they had. Woman-on-woman violence, often linked to status, is a recurring element. Almost invariably, these stories end in the suicide or murder of these women. We also encounter several filial daughters—one who bails her family out of a crisis and another who serves as an improbable filial avenger. Finally, a couple of vignettes valorize staunchly loyal wives who choose disfigurement or death over contravention of Confucian principle. Such stories tend to survive, uncensored, passed from one era to the next.

THE DEATH OF A TALENTED SINGING GIRL

Court and Country includes the well-known story of Qiao Zhizhi and Jade Disc:

> *In the Zhou,[13] Rectifier of Omissions Qiao Zhizhi had a slave girl[14] named Jade Disc, who was breathtakingly alluring, a capable singer and dancer, cultured and literate. Because she was Zhizhi's favorite, he was unwilling to get married. On the pretext that he needed someone to teach his concubines how to do their hair and cosmetics, illegitimate Prince of Wei, Wu Chengsi, took her into his compound. Wu Chengsi made her his own concubine and did not return her to Qiao. Qiao Zhizhi wrote the "Lament of Green Pearl" and sent it to her. Its lyrics went,*
>
>> *Hearing novel sounds of music, Shi Chong of Golden Gorge,*
>> *With a ten-weight of shining pearls, purchased this beautiful woman.*
>> *In those days, you took pity on me and swore a troth;*
>> *In those times, my song and dance captured your passion.*
>> *But the doors to the inner chambers were left unlocked,*
>> *As My Lord enjoyed letting others behold my singing and dancing.*
>> *Ignoring boundaries of principle, an arrogant man of great prestige,*
>> *Relying on his influence, took me away by force.*
>> *Parting from My Lord, leaving him, is unbearable;*
>> *I bury my cosmetic-smeared face in my tear-stained sleeve,*
>> *In this lofty tower passing a hundred years of resentment since our separation.*
>> *For a stint with My Lord, my countenance and complexion are lost.*
>
> *After reading the poem, Jade Disc silently wept and didn't eat for three days. Then she jumped into a well and killed herself. When Chengsi had her corpse raised from the well, he discovered the poem tucked in the sash of her dress. In a towering rage, he deputed his army of implicaters and entrappers to levy an accusation against Qiao. Subsequently, Qiao Zhizhi*

was beheaded in the Southern Market.[15] *His household was destroyed, and their property was confiscated.*[16] (2.31)

Names of female slaves and concubines were pet names rather than personal names; Jade Disc, a name presumably bestowed by Qiao Zhizhi, literally objectified the beauty. High officials and men of noble rank could not marry slaves or concubines. Knowing that if he took a wife he would not be able to lavish as much attention and affection upon his favorite, Qiao Zhizhi remained unmarried. And yet, despite this affection and favor, Jade Disc clearly did not enjoy the protection or status of a wife. When guests came, she was trotted out—like a house courtesan—to perform her song and dance, to entertain.

Slave girls like Jade Disc were chattel, transferrable between wealthy and powerful men and families. Word of such talent and beauty traveled like gossip on the winds in Luoyang, quickly reaching the ears of covetous Wu Chengsi, Wu Zhao's nephew, a chief minister with tremendous social and political influence. On the pretext of needing someone to show his concubines the finer points of grooming and the application of make-up, he borrowed her with no intention of returning her to Qiao. In hierarchic premodern China, refusing such a request from an influential superior was socially and culturally very difficult.

The inset poem in the story—written by Qiao Zhizhi, an official in Wu Zhao's court—is written from the vantage of Green Pearl, a concubine of Shi Chong four centuries earlier, who had committed suicide after being seized by a powerful man in court. Assuming this feminine voice, Qiao nudges his favorite toward suicide. She complies by leaping into a well, a time-honored technique for women committing suicide in the inner quarters. Furious at being deprived of his new plaything, Wu Zhao's intemperate nephew Wu Chengsi—working with the "cruel officials" described in Chapter 3— implicated Qiao Zhizhi in short order, leading to his execution and the eradication of his household. "From today's standpoint," Rebecca Doran aptly points out, "Qiao Zhizhi and Wu Chengsi may both be condemned for treating [Jade Disc] as property whose death is meaningful only in terms of how it reflects upon their statuses." The focus of Zhang Zhuo's story, however, is not upon the victimization of Jade Disc. Doran further points out, "The various versions of this episode are united by their emphasis on Wu Chengsi's subversion of 'correct' hierarchy, and Qiao Zhizhi is constructed as a sympathetic figure because his rights are appropriated by an illegitimate power-holder."[17] In Zhang Zhuo's story, the pervasive iniquity, acquisitiveness, and vindictiveness of the Wus is at the crux of the narrative. Qiao Zhizhi's pain and his apt poetic allusion are the subplot. Although Graham Sanders points out the "poetic justice" in the fact that "Qiao's lethal poem surviv[es] to double back on him"; thus it prompts not only the suicide of Jade Disc, but the demise of its author as well.[18]

In one of the Tang histories, Qiao Zhizhi's otherwise brief and unremarkable biography records that "Zhizhi had a favorite female slave named Yaoniang who was beautiful and excellent at singing and dancing. She was seized by Wu Chengsi. Filled with resentment and regret, Zhizhi wrote 'Lament of Green Pearl' to express his feelings and secretly sent it to her. Overcome with indignation, she committed suicide. Infuriated, Wu Chengsi deputed the 'cruel officials' to frame and execute Zhizhi."[19]

Qiao intimates in his poem that he, like Shi Chong, was fond of having her show off her talents to others. While he lacked the courage to decline what he undoubtedly saw as a transparent ruse to seize his prize showpiece, he recognized the parallel between his loss and a famous episode from four centuries earlier and had the ingenuity to bribe a gatekeeper to smuggle his verse into Jade Disc's hands.

What is the nature of Jade Disc's "indignation"? Given Jade Disc's discerning intelligence and literary ability—she grasps at a glance Qiao's powerlessness to resist Wu Chengsi's seizure of her person, and she apprehends the meaning and intent of Qiao's verse—perhaps she is indignant because despite her intelligence, beauty, and skill, she has ended up as little more than a commodity and, in a performative display of loyalty and fidelity to a feckless man who has forsaken her, death is her only endgame.

CONDUCT UNBECOMING AN IMPERIAL PRINCE

Li Yuanying, the Prince of Teng, was the twenty-second son of Tang founder Gaozu. Gaozong once sent a letter scolding this Prince of Teng, his uncle, for his incorrigibly licentious and boorish conduct. In this letter, Gaozong admonishes Li Yuanying for requisitioning hounds and nets from people for unseasonable hunting, gambling with ne'er-do-wells, surrounding himself with loutish and sycophantic underlings, and using the common people for target practice (with his sling) and burying them in snow.[20] Using his status as an emperor's son in an overbearing fashion, the Prince of Teng imposed himself on all women within his orbit, gaining a reputation for relentless sexual depredations. In this story from *Court and Country*, the odious prince meets his match:

> The Prince of Teng was extremely lascivious. Among the beautiful wives of officials, there were none upon whom he had not preyed. Falsely saying that one of his concubines had called on them, he treated them in a most ungentlemanly manner. When Recordkeeper Cui Jian's

wife Zheng first arrived, the prince sent a summons. Knowing that if she went she would be despoiled by the prince, Cui didn't wish her to go, but he feared the prince's prestige. Zheng said, "In the past, the consort of Minhuai refused the coercive advances of an enemy barbarian. She is still upheld as a model of exalted purity. Who would have the audacity to engage in this sort of dastardly conduct?"

Subsequently, she entered the small pavilion outside the central gate where the prince awaited inside. When she entered, he wanted to rape her, but Zheng started screaming. His attendants said, "He's the prince."

Zheng answered, "How could a grand prince do this sort of thing—you must be a family servant." She took off a wooden clog and smashed the prince in the head, then scratched open his face. Hearing the commotion, the concubines came out and assisted Madame Zheng in returning home. The prince was humiliated and didn't attend to official matters for a ten-day xun*-week.*

Cui Jian nervously waited every day, not daring to leave the front gate. When the prince finally took his seat in the yamen to attend to official matters, Cui Jian approached him to apologize for his wife's mistake. But the prince was humiliated and retreated to his inner quarters and did not re-emerge to resume office for more than a month. Among the officials' wives who had previously been summoned in by the prince, none but felt humiliated. When their husbands inquired, there was nothing they could say.[21] (Sup., 175)

Here, the Prince of Teng ends up outwitted, shamed, and cudgeled in the head with a shoe by Mrs. Zheng, the spirited and resourceful wife of a low-ranking official. The prince's pretext for summoning the wife is a common one: the invitation ostensibly came from his concubines. Both husband and wife are well aware of the prince's designs. Overawed by the prestige and power of the imperial prince, however, the husband is afraid to refuse. Zheng's armor against ravagement is her knowledge of exemplary women of the past. She cites the case of Wang Huifeng, "the consort of Minhuai," the Crown Prince of Jin. When military officer Liu Yao seized Wang Huifeng to present her to his general, Qiao Shu, she defiantly proclaimed, "I am the daughter of a high minister and a consort of the Crown Prince. I will never be humiliated by the likes of you, a rebel barbarian!" She gets her wish of death before dishonor. Qiao Shu kills her, and she is immortalized in the "Biographies of Exemplary Women" in the *History of the Jin Dynasty*.[22] Alone with the ill-intentioned Prince of Teng, quick-witted Mrs. Zheng out-maneuvers him. Feigning ignorance of his identity while screaming to alert others, she claims to think that there is no way that her attacker could be the Prince of Teng because a highborn prince, schooled in Confucian values, would behave in a fashion guided by high-minded righteousness and virtue. Only a lowly reprobate cur would behave in such a despicable and hateful fashion! Seemingly disarmed and shamed by her impeccable Confucian logic, the Prince of Teng falters; his lust is further blunted when she bloodies his head with a sharp blow from a wooden clog.

Even after this brilliant display of defiance, her weak-willed husband goes to the Prince of Teng's household to apologize, but the prince, duly shamed, is too humiliated to show his face.

SELF-MUTILATION AS A TROTH OF CHASTITY: DON'T MESS WITH FANG XUANLING'S WIFE!

Ideal Confucian wives in the biographies of Tang women included in standard histories "show their dedication to the conjugal bond by maintaining chastity at all costs, even if this required them to resort to self-mutilation or suicide."[23] For example, a widow from Liang, pressed by the King to marry him, launched into a Confucian set piece (often a compulsory element to earn entry into the esteemed ranks of the exemplars):

> I have heard that a wife's duty is never to change once she has gone out to marry, so that she can maintain intact the principles of purity and fidelity. If I were now to forget the dead and rush toward the living, this would be infidelity, and if I were to see only honor and forget the humble, this would be impurity. If I were to disregard righteousness and follow profit, I would have nothing left with which to maintain my humanity.

At the conclusion of her speech, she lops off her nose, disfiguring her face so that she is unmarriable. Moved, the spurned King of Liang grants her the title "Exalted Conduct."[24] There was a strong and enduring cult of widow chastity, and the valorization of behaviors like those of this widow had long precedent: female pain and suffering to uphold Confucian principle was sometimes honored by commemorative arches or plaques for the family or even a spot in the "biographies of exemplary women" included in many dynastic histories.

Indeed, Madame Lu, the wife from the *Court and Country* passage below, received a cursory biography in the Song dynasty's *New Tang History*, indicating that she was counted among the female exemplars of the Tang in future eras:[25]

> *Madame Lu was the wife of Fang Xuanling. When Fang Xuanling was ailing, sick and nearing death, he instructed, "My illness is critical. You are still young and cannot live the rest of your days as a widow. It would be best if you took care of your future." Lu wept, entered the curtains of her boudoir, plucked out one of her eyes and presented it to Fang Xuanling to make it clear there would be no other in her life. After a while, Fang Xuanling recovered and treated her with respect and courtesy for the rest of his life. However, this Madame Lu also appears in* Records of Jealous Wives. *How could a woman be virtuous*

during her husband's ailing times, but jealous when he is flourishing? As a result of this I gained some insight. (Sup., 180)

Madame Lu's husband, Fang Xuanling (d. 648), served as a chief minister under Taizong, and died before Zhang Zhuo was born.[26] The story of the lovely wife of the convalescent, aging minister plucking out her eye as a troth of her sincerity, purity, and loyalty clearly had enduring resonance. What adds nuance and complexity to Madame Lu as a Confucian exemplar, however, is the addendum at the end of Zhang Zhuo's passage. In Confucian circles, wifely jealousy was considered most unbecoming.[27] There is an anecdote in *Extensive Records* that represents Fang Xuanling as an uxorious husband guilty of the "wife-fearing" that was widespread in the early Tang. When Emperor Taizong bestowed a beautiful concubine upon his chief minister, trepidatious Fang declined despite repeated offers, fearing to incur Madame Lu's displeasure. Taizong tried to have his empress intervene and persuade Madame Lu, but this failed. Even confronting the emperor himself, Madame Lu staunchly claimed that she preferred death and maintaining her jealousy to living with another woman under the roof of her household. When she was sent poisoned wine—refusing imperial largesse was not well tolerated—she drained it without a second thought and suffered no adverse effects. Taizong then remarked, "Even I'm afraid of seeing that woman again! How much more difficult it must be for Fang Xuanling to deal with her!"[28]

WE ALL HAVE OUR FETISHES, AFTER ALL!

Another passage from *Court and Country* provides a curious story featuring Zhu Qianyi, whom we have already encountered in several passages from Chapters 1 and 2. A pug-ugly social climber known by the mocking sobriquet "Table Maiden of the Court of Imperial Entertainments," Zhu briefly rose to a mid-ranking position by presenting auspicious dreams foretelling Wu Zhao's longevity. The following anecdote details how he rejected his voluptuous wife at home, preferring instead a begrimed and misshapen servant girl working in a winehouse:

> *Director of the Bureau of Military Appointments Zhu Qianyi was repulsive in appearance; his wife was beautiful and sensual. In the time of the Celestial Empress, he kept a servant girl with unkempt hair and a filthy face, a humpbacked creature with a distended stomach, in a winehouse outside the west gate of Zhiye Ward*[29] *in Luoyang. Throughout the entire world there were none so hideous as this woman. Yet Qianyi delighted in her to the point that he nearly forgot to sleep or eat. Thus, we can understand how in former ages men spoke of the unwavering love for Tumor-ridden Su and believe that it is not an empty story. In the*

world of men there is every imaginable peculiar sort of appetite and carnal desire. In the past, King Wen was addicted to eating pickled calamus.[30] The King of Chu loved eating pickled celery.[31] Qu Dao loved water caltrops.[32] Zeng Xi loved eating jujubes.[33] Liu Yong of the Song was addicted to eating scabs. His basic annals reads, "When Yong went to the Wuxing and was at Governor Meng Lingxiu's residence,[34] Meng Ling peeled off his socks, and a scab from his moxibustion[35] treatment peeled off and fell on the ground. Yong bent down, picked it up, and ate it!" Emperor Ming of Song was fond of stinkbugs marinated in honey; each sitting he would gulp down several sheng.[36] From this we can comprehend the proverb "chasing the stench across the sea"[37] and the story of "Lord Chen delighting in the ugly." So much strangeness! These examples all show the cravings and addictions of these men! (5.113)

Zhang Zhuo compares Zhu Qianyi's favorite, a hideous servant girl in a Luoyang tavern, to Tumor-Ridden Su, a peasant woman of grotesque appearance that King Min of Qi (r. 300–284 BC) encountered by the roadside. Impressed by her wisdom and oratory skills, he took her into the palace, where she rose to become Queen and was revered as a "female sage" based on her knowledge of principles of governance. Tumor-ridden Su is included in the chapters on "Accomplished Rhetoricians" (Biantong 辯通) in the Han work Biographies of Exemplary Women. Zhu Qianyi was no King Min of Qi; he was an official best known for his cupidity, his sycophancy, and his repulsive appearance. And the hunchbacked girl from the Zhiye winehouse was no Tumor-ridden Su. This off-target comparison was probably made for comic effect.

Perhaps more telling, Zhang Zhuo extracts from the example of Zhu Qianyi a larger insight about the fixations and compulsions that rule many men, often in defiance of logic and convention. To try to better contextualize and explain Zhu Qianyi's desire for the hunchbacked servant girl, Zhang Zhuo enumerates a number of celebrated figures from the past known for their intense cravings for certain foods; "In the world of men," he opines, "there is every imaginable sort of peculiar appetite and carnal desire." This insight holds significant implications for understanding medieval relationships. Individual compatibility was not an important criterion in negotiating marriages, which were social and political alliances that joined together families. Discussing marriage in his monograph *Women in Tang China*, Bret Hinsch remarks,

> Tang writers often referred to lofty sentiments when discussing marriage. Some emphasized the shared commitment of spouses to venerate the husband's ancestors, a duty so important that it made marriage a foundation of human relations. Other moralists stressed the importance of using righteousness (*yi*) to regulate the interactions of husband and wife, lest their relationship devolve into licentiousness.[38]

Zhang's account of Zhu suggests that there is something profoundly dissatisfying or lacking—or perhaps something anathema to desire itself—about such formal arrangements. Therefore, husbands, court officials, and wealthy men, moving far more freely in the outer, public domain than their wives, often sought to satisfy fixations or individual affinities outside the home.

"WHAT'S SO TRAGIC ABOUT SOCIAL MOBILITY?"

Marriages were not a matter of individual choice based on love, attraction, or personal preferences in Tang China. They were negotiations between two families. As the following story from *Court and Country* demonstrates, wealthy and powerful families could and did wield their influence to force matches:

> Senior Clerk of Jizhou Ji Mao wanted to take the daughter of Cui Jing, a lower-level administrator from Nangong County,[39] as the wife for his son, Xu. Initially, Cui Jing refused. Thereupon, Ji Mao took forceful measures to seek the betrothal and, fearful of disaster, Cui Jing assented. On the day chosen for the marriage, the official betrothal contract and the festooned flower carriage arrived at the gate of the Cui household to deliver the bride to the groom's household. Cui Jing's wife Madame Zheng, unaware of the betrothal, embraced her daughter and wept loudly, "Though we are a household of lowly status, we shan't take this Ji gentleman as an in-law!" Her daughter resolutely lay in bed, refusing to rise. The younger daughter, however, said to her mother, "Father is considering suicide as a path to extricate us from this urgent difficulty. Even if it meant being a concubine, it wouldn't be worth refusing, and there's certainly no shame to becoming a wife in a prestigious family! If my elder sister is unwilling, I'll happily take her place." She then got into the carriage and left. Ji Xu rose to become a chief minister, and everyone praised his spouse Madame Cui as a virtuous wife. However, Ji Xu later clashed with Wu Yizong and was demoted to a lesser official position in Wenzhou,[40] where he died. (3.57)

The story of Qiao Zhizhi earlier in this chapter made it clear that, in the status-and-hierarchy-conscious society of medieval China, resisting or refusing the advances of a wealthy and powerful individual could have dire consequences. This message is driven home again in the passage above: the social pressure that local powerbrokers, the Ji family, exert upon the Cuis to force the betrothal leaves the father of the bride Cui Jing pondering suicide. On the day of the wedding, when a flower carriage, a festively decorated palanquin, comes to pick up the girl, neither the unwillingly betrothed nor her mother, sequestered in the inner quarters, have any knowledge of the impending marriage; clearly, the women in the Cui household have no part in the decision-making. However, both mother and elder daughter steadfastly resist. The younger Cui daughter, cast in the story as the plucky pragmatist, saves her natal family and saves face for the Jis, as she essentially queries, "What's so tragic about social mobility?" and cheerfully takes her sister's place. The groom, Ji Xu, the "Willow-Gazing Camel," rose to become a chief minister under Wu Zhao. This anecdote, presented as a success story and delivered with a touch of levity, glosses over the forced betrothals and coerced marital arrangements that were more norm than exception.

A PREFECT'S WIFE LOYAL TO THE END

Wives of officials were often inner helpers, not merely controlling the family budget, educating the children, and keeping the home, but also advising and strategizing with their husbands on matters of local administration. In the *Analects* of Confucius, when paragon King Wu of the original Zhou dynasty reputedly claimed to "have ten capable ministers," he included in their number his mother and the spouse of dynastic founder King Wen, known as Wenmu 文母, Mother Wen.[41] Long before the Tang, Lady Ji of Lu, a widow of the late Spring and Autumn era (6th cent. BC), was depicted in *Biographies of Exemplary Women*; as Lisa Raphals notes, that depiction renders Lady Ji "as a woman of considerable expertise, who operates within (and appears to approve of) the gender codes of her society, but with no loss of acumen in expressing her views on both state and domestic affairs to her male relatives."[42] "The women closest to the ruler" (or, in this instance, the Prefect), Raphals contends, "were major agents of moral and intellectual influence," and "their intellectual abilities and specific knowledge [...] closely corresponded to those of their male counterparts—sages, ministers, and generals."[43]

The following passage from *Court and Country* upholds the wife of a prefect in the Northeast, Qin (we only know her family name), as a paragon of Confucian morality who champions principled and unswerving loyalty to the state. In making decisions, her husband unquestioningly follows her moral cues:

> *The wife of Gao Rui, the Prefect of Zhaozhou, was from the Qin family. When the Turkish Qapaghan Khan's rebels defeated the troops of Dingzhou and reached Zhaozhou, the elders and subordinates opened the gates to receive the enemy. Gao Rui had no other plot, so he and his wife lay down in bed, swallowed medicine, and feigned death. They were carried on the shoulders of Mochuo's subordinates to the Khan's quarters. After a while, Mochuo showed them his golden lion belt and his purple robes, proclaiming, "Surrender to me and become my official; if you don't surrender, you will die." Gao Rui looked at him wordlessly, then turned toward his wife Qin. Qin said, "You have received the favor of your country. Today is the day you compensate. If you receive a single rank from the enemy, how can this be honorable in the least?" They looked at each other and didn't speak another word. After two days, the rebels knew they would not submit and killed them.*[44] (Sup., 163–64)

This anecdote clearly illustrates that there were informal ways through which a woman could persuade or nudge her husband to follow a course of action, thereby wielding power and exerting influence. In the official Tang history written in the Song dynasty, Qin is given her own biography among the exemplary women.[45] Gao Rui, the husband, was a loyalist as well. When a subordinate recommended that he surrender to the Turks, he refused, remarking, "I am a Prefect of the Son of Heaven. To surrender without battle is an unconscionable crime!" Contrasting their staunch loyalism to other local officials who welcomed the Turks or abandoned their posts at the first sign of danger, Wu Zhao posthumously honored the couple.[46]

VULNERABILITY OF A KEPT WOMAN

The Yicheng Princess was the daughter of Wu Zhao's son, Zhongzong. Empress Wei was not her mother.[47] In this passage from the supplemental section of *Court and Country*, the Yicheng Princess is depicted as a savagely violent shrew who sends a rough bunch of eunuchs to cut off the facial features and genitalia of a rival:

> *Pei Xuan, the husband of the Yicheng Princess, kept a favorite outside. The princess sent eunuchs to seize her. They cut off her ears and nose, then peeled off her pudendal skin and plastered it on the husband's face. Then they cut off the husband's hair, then dragged him in public before the court, where all of the officials bore witness. Both husband and wife were demoted. The princess was reduced to Commandery Princess and the imperial-in-law was demoted in rank.*[48] (Sup., 177)

Such a public spectacle—in a culture where even today the proverb "the stench of family scandal is not to be aired outside" (*jia chou bu wai yang* 家醜不外揚) endures—was a disgrace to the imperial family. The imperial-in-law husband's career was damaged, and the imperial princess was demoted in nobility rank. She was recalled shortly thereafter. Yenna Wu has observed that such "anecdotes of a jealous wife's disfigurement of a beautiful rival may reflect a morbid fascination with a woman's cruelty to rivals of her own sex." These stories also degrade aristocratic men by "reducing their stature and dignity" and "satirize [these] men by contrasting them with stronger women."[49] What is lost in the narrative is the cruel fate that befalls the woman that Pei Xuan kept in the city, outside of the household. The narrative follows the aristocrats, while this nameless woman, mutilated and possibly dead, becomes an afterthought. The story is about the termagant-princess and her humiliated husband: Since this favorite was not a formal concubine of Pei's or part of the household, she would have been eminently vulnerable, with no legal status. Curiously, across many cultures, ear-cropping and rhinotomy, the severance of the nose, served as punishments for sexual transgression, often targeting women.[50]

EMPRESS WEI THROUGH A DIFFERENT LENS: A FILIAL DAUGHTER

Another passage in *Court and Country*, providing detail of the tribulations that the Wei family suffered when Wu Zhao banished them to Lingnan, offers a novel perspective on the oft-demonized Empress Wei:

> When Miss Wei suffered through Zetian's banishment of the Prince of Luling,[51] her father Wei Xuanzhen, his wife, his daughters, and others were all banished to Lingnan. Local chieftains from the Ning family forcibly seized his daughters. When they refused to submit, they then killed Wei Xuanzhen and his wife;[52] their seven daughters were all seized and taken away.
>
> When the Filial and Harmonious One[53] was restored to emperor and the empress [Wei] held sway, Guangzhou Commander-in-Chief Zhou Rengui marshalled soldiers, pursued the Ning clan back to the Southern Sea, butchering them to the point of eradication and plundering them. When Zhou Rengui returned to court, Empress Wei parted the curtains to offer thanks, and, because he had avenged her father, made him Prefect of Bingzhou. Later, when Missy Wei[54] rebelled, Zhou Rengui was considered to belong to her clique and was executed.[55] (Sup., 171)

Vilified in histories—written off as "Traitor Wei" and ensconced in the Confucian historiographical narrative as an anti-exemplar characterized by extravagance, avarice, and lust—Empress Wei is presented here from another vantage, recast as a filial daughter. C. P. Fitzgerald has remarked that empresses in the Han dynasty "played the role of the Trojan horse, introducing a crowd of ambitious relatives to the citadel of power, but themselves only providing the lure, and remaining the tool of their kin."[56] This is true to an extent in subsequent eras as well. When Zhongzong became emperor in 684, his strong-willed wife, Empress Wei, moved to have her father, Wei Xuanzhen, named a chief minister and her other Wei kinsmen advanced in rank.[57]

When some high-ranking court ministers steadfastly opposed the promotion, Zhongzong defiantly proclaimed, "If I wish to give the empire to Wei Xuanzhen, what is there to stop me? How much easier then to grant him the position of prime minister." Wu Zhao hastily intervened, removing him from the throne, and banishing him and his Wei in-laws. She installed her youngest son Ruizong on the throne and ruled as grand dowager-regent. Zhongzong and Empress Wei were banished to Fangzhou prefecture (modern-day Shiyan, in Hubei).⁵⁸ Wei Xuanzhen and other Wei kinsmen were banished to the distant south. Zhongzong's father-in-law Wei Xuanzhen died on the way to Qinzhou, on the Gulf of Tonkin.⁵⁹

As the passage above reveals, life in exile was hell for the extended Wei clan. A "Southern barbarian" chieftain and his brother made marriage offers to Wei Xuanzhen's widow Cui and some of the unmarried Wei women and, when their overture was spurned, butchered half a dozen Wei family members, including Cui and her four younger brothers, and seized several women.⁶⁰

In 706, shortly after his restoration, Zhongzong, spurred by his wife Empress Wei, ordered general Zhou Rengui to lead a campaign to avenge this generation-old wound. According to the *Comprehensive Mirror*, Zhou Rengui exacted a terrible revenge, driving the Liao into the sea with a punitive force of 20,000 soldiers, beheading the chieftain, and presenting the severed head at the tomb of the widow Cui. Deeply moved, Empress Wei, having avenged the death of a parent, bowed to pay formal respects to the victorious general from behind a curtain.⁶¹ It might thus be noted that, while Empress Wei may have been a "Trojan horse," she had her own agenda and was never simply "the tool of her kin."

Whatever Empress Wei's faults, it is clear that she was a filial daughter fiercely devoted to her father and to her natal family. Shortly before the campaign, she pushed Zhongzong to grant her father a posthumous princely title and other official titles. She even had a lesser rank bestowed upon her maternal uncles who had perished in Lingnan.⁶² Of course, Zhang Zhuo's inclusion of this vignette is not intended to illustrate Empress Wei's bloody filial devotion; rather, it is centered on the rise and fall of one of her martial henchmen, Zhou Rengui.

KARMIC RETRIBUTION IN THE SOUTHERN HINTERLANDS

On the south fringe of the Tang empire, as the flow of Chinese migration populated some of the arable lands and pushed aboriginal peoples to the mountainous and swampy margins, there were sporadic uprisings of the Liao people. Tang imperial expansion was an important initiative of the state, and military campaigns were mobilized to quash these insurrections. Women from these aboriginal peoples were war booty, spoils often kept by Tang or Zhou commanders.

Another passage in *Court and Country* relates to Zhou Rengui's campaign against these "southern barbarians." The story details the grim fate suffered by a Liao woman taken as a war captive:

RELATIONSHIPS

> *Hu Liang, an administrator of Huameng County in Guangzhou, accompanied general Zhu Rengui on a campaign against the Liao. Hu obtained the concubine of a Liao chieftain and came to favor her. After he returned to Huameng, when he went to the yamen to attend to business, his wife Madame He drove a white-hot nail into both of the new favorite's eyes. Shortly thereafter, the concubine hung herself. Later, when Madame He became pregnant, she birthed a snake whose eyes had no pupils. She asked a Chan master about it. He said, "Madame once heated iron and branded a woman's eyes. Birthing this blind snake is karmic retribution for Madame's venomous character. This snake is born of your branding! If you nurture it well, you can avoid disaster, otherwise catastrophe will befall you." Madame He took care of the snake for a year or two. As it couldn't see, she kept it in her clothing or tucked under her quilt. Unaware, one day Hu Liang shook the quilt and saw the snake. Shocked, he grabbed a knife and lopped it in half. Both of He's eyes immediately withered and she never again was able to see. It was too late for regrets!* (2.42–43)

This account shares a common denominator with the story of Qiao Zhizhi and Jade Disc: like Jade Disc, the female war captive ends up dead. Both women were pushed to commit suicide. As marginalized members of the larger, extended family, both women lacked societal or legal protection and were wholly reliant on the favor and protection of the patriarch of the household. Both quickly learned how unreliable and inconstant this favor could be. Faced with a more powerful man, Qiao Zhizhi failed to protect Jade Disc; similarly, in the absence of protector-household patriarch Hu Liang—who was part of a military expedition that had killed her family and loved ones[63]—the Liao concubine was left at the mercy of Hu's wife, who burned her eyes out with a searing nail.

This tale differs in that it contains an element of karmic retribution. For her cruelty, Madame He births an eyeless abomination, which, the Chan master explains, she is bound to protect. When she fails, she suffers karmic comeuppance and is promptly stricken with the same condition she inflicted upon the poor Liao woman.

7

Generals and military men

ONE OF THE FUNDAMENTAL BINARIES IN traditional China, sometimes complementary and sometimes oppositional, is that between the softer, cerebral *wen*—the civil literati pursuits of calligraphy, poetry, and classical learning that dominated court culture—and the more obdurate and rugged *wu*, the martial arts.[1] It was long recognized that for a state to flourish and succeed, both its civil and martial aspects had to be fostered and cultivated; the notion that "both civil and military must be utilized in tandem" (*wenwu bingyong* 文武並用) became an axiom of statecraft that frequently appeared in the histories.[2] Whereas in the Song and some later periods "the civil was venerated and the martial despised" (*zhongwen qingwu* 重文輕武), in the early Tang, with its Central Asian and steppe influence, there was more of a balance. Taizong, Wu Zhao's first husband, is generally depicted as a virile warrior–sovereign, hirsute and rugged, a master of archery and horsemanship (see Figure 6).[3] Many early Tang officers served in both civil and military capacities. This chapter examines Zhang Zhuo's depictions of military men in *Court and Country*, revealing the extent to which he championed the civil (*wen* 文) camp.

In late seventh-century East and Central Asia, a number of regional powers surrounded Tang/Zhou China: the greatest threats were the Turks to the north and northwest, the Khitan to the northeast, and the Tibetans to the southwest. To counter these threats, there were more than six hundred garrisons spread around the empire, many of them around the capitals and along the northern border.[4] As an official in Wu Zhao's court, Zhang Zhuo generally advocated following a policy of appeasement—cleaving to the Confucian stance that it is costly, bad policy, both politically and economically ill-advised, to vie with barbarians over desert hinterlands and uncultivable steppe. This policy dictated that it was prudent to nurture and protect the fertile, agrarian core and concede the rocky, inhospitable periphery. However, other generals and hawkish ministers advocated more aggressive military policy. During the Tang, this was a common debate in discussions of foreign policy: appeasement or confrontation? Diplomacy or military action?

Figure 6 A Ming dynasty painting of Emperor Taizong.

GENERALS AND MILITARY MEN

Zhang Zhuo was not a neutral bystander in this debate. He weighed in during a court debate in 702—late in Wu Zhao's reign—contending that it would be wiser to accommodate the Tibetans, placating them with silks, bows, and arrows, rather than confronting them in a frontier conflict that would drain state resources and cost lives.[5]

This ongoing court debate is a backdrop for a number of passages in *Court and Country* concerning the various ways in which military men and generals dealt with the threats posed by these powerful neighboring states. Other passages feature more general explorations of martial culture in the Tang.

NON-HAN GENERALS

Emperors in the early Tang and Wu Zhao presided over a large, multiethnic empire. Wu Zhao had a number of non-Chinese civil and military generals (*fanjiang* 番將), including Koguryan expat Quan Xiancheng; Li Duozuo, a Malgal (Mohe) leader; Shazha Zhongyi, a Turk; and Qibi Heli, a member of the Tiele, a steppe people also known as the "High Carts."[6] Mark Abramson, in his monograph on ethnicity in the Tang, notes that these leaders, often characterized as possessing heightened martiality and animality, served as "middlemen" and "cultural mediators."[7]

One of Wu Zhao's more effective non-Chinese generals was Blacktooth (Heichi 黑齒) Changzhi, a giant of a man from the Korean kingdom of Paekche, standing seven feet tall. Originally, Blacktooth led Paekche troops against an alliance between the Tang and Silla, and only several years after the fall of his kingdom did he finally surrender. He rose to become a general under Gaozong and Wu Zhao and played a central role in quashing a rebellion against her in 684, shortly after she deposed her son and took control of the state as dowager-regent. Just before Wu Zhao established her Zhou dynasty, Blacktooth ran afoul of her "cruel officials" and was hounded to death.

In 678, Blacktooth had been made vice commander of the Heyuan garrison as a promotion after leading a crack group of 500 "dare-to-die" troops on a nocturnal raid against a Tibetan encampment, scattering the enemy. In 680, he staved off another Tibetan raid and requested reinforcements from the court, arguing the strategic importance of Heyuan. The following year he defeated Tibetan troops led by their king. In the *Comprehensive Mirror*, it is recorded that "[d]uring the seven years Blacktooth served as general on the southwestern frontier, the Tibetans were petrified and dared not raid the borders."[8] He also served on the northern frontier, expertly using cavalry to defend against attacks from the Turks. In his decades as a frontier general, Blacktooth gained a reputation for generously sharing rewards with his rank-and-file men. He was following a long Eastern Eurasian tradition of such "patrimonial generosity," helping secure the loyalty and goodwill of soldiers.[9] However, the following anecdote from *Court and Country* does not show Blacktooth at his finest:

> When General Blacktooth Changzhi was ordered to protect/guard the Heyuan Army, the city walls were strictly monitored and precipitous. From who knows where, three wolves entered his encampment and wandered around the barracks of the leaders. Soldiers shot them with arrows and killed them. Loathing the creatures, Blacktooth had their bodies moved outside the city walls. Blacktooth memorialized the emperor requesting permission to launch an offensive against the Dangxiang of Sanqu. The emperor sent an imperial order assenting, but sent General Li Jinxing to replace him. One xun-week after Jinxing reached the troops, he became sick and died. (6.145)

Though the Dangxiang had submitted to Taizong back in 630, their loyalty was tenuous; like other southwestern peoples, they sought to survive by forming fluid alliances with the larger regional powers—the Tang and the Tibetans. In the passage, a half-century later, the Dangxiang were allied with the Tibetans.

Sent on a campaign against the Dangxiang people—perhaps forebears of the Qiang ethnic group in the southwestern highlands who spoke a Tibeto-Burman language—Blacktooth was garrisoned with his troops in the northeastern quarter of modern-day Qinghai province. He was troubled by the appearance of a trio of ill-omened wolves—animals that were a totem of many of the Turkish and steppe peoples the Tang and Zhou troops faced.

The general who replaced Blacktooth on the frontier, Li Jinxing, was also a non-Chinese general, a former Malgal chieftain. Composed of a collection of tribes known for their bellicose spirit—some allied with the Tang empire, some with the Korean kingdom of Koguryo, and some with the Turks—the semi-nomadic Malgal of Northeast Asia lived by a combination of agriculture and hunting.[10] Though Blacktooth would outlive his ill-fated replacement, it wasn't until a few years after his death that more than 10,000 Tibetans and the Dangxiang submitted to Zhou dominion and were settled in 10 prefectures.[11]

QAPAGHAN KHAN AND THE TUJUE TURKS, PART I: THE BALLAD OF YAN ZHIWEI

The Tujue Turks were the primary threat along the northern frontier of Wu Zhao's empire. After the Turks triumphed over regional rivals the Khitan

GENERALS AND MILITARY MEN

in 697, Wu Zhao bestowed a number of honorific titles upon Qapaghan, the khan of the Turks. Court official Yan Zhiwei was sent northward as an emissary of Wu Zhao to negotiate a marital alliance (*he qin* 和親) to help secure peace between Wu Zhao's Zhou and the powerful Turkish khan, Qapaghan (Mochuo). Imperial princesses were human bargaining chips in this common diplomatic practice.[12] This time, however, in a curious wrinkle, the khan requested an imperial prince to marry his daughter. In 698, Wu Zhao, ignoring protestations from ministers who maintained that there was no precedent for a man—a prince—to marry a "barbarian's daughter," sent her grandnephew Wu Yanxiu as a prospective groom. Qapaghan detained the youth, grumbling that Wu Zhao not only presented him substandard seeds and low-grade silk, but also offered inferior human products: a knockoff prince belonging to the Wu family instead of a true prince belonging to the House of Tang.[13] This clever rhetoric was geared toward creating rifts in Wu Zhao's court between her supporters and Tang loyalists. Recognizing tensions in the Chinese court, wily Qapaghan styled himself as a Tang restorationist.

Meanwhile, Yan Zhiwei gifted the Turkish emissaries silk and other presents, then groveled before the Turkish ruler; ultimately, he betrayed the Zhou and guided Turkish troops in their conquest of several prefectural capitals in the northeast of the empire. The Turkish khan designated Yan a lesser khan over these territories.

In this first passage from *Court and Country*, Yan Zhiwei, acting as an emissary of the Turkish khan after having betrayed Wu Zhao's Zhou, tries to convince a Zhou general to surrender the fortified prefectural capital of Zhaozhou:

> *In the Zhou, Minister of Spring*[14] *in the Department of State Affairs Yan Zhiwei was a petty and cowardly man of inferior talent. He was sent as an emissary to the northern barbarians. Qapaghan invested him as a khan. After the rebels entered Hengzhou and Dingzhou, Yan Zhiwei was sent in advance to Zhaozhou prefecture to enlist men and to pacify the people. General Chen Lingying was defending the western wall of the city. Zhiwei called to Lingying, "General Chen, how is it that you still haven't surrendered? If you wait until the khan's soldiers arrive before you surrender, you'll be scythed down and left without a grave." Lingying didn't respond. Zhiwei, standing at the base of the city walls, clasped his hands together, and sang a stamping song called "Anthem for Ten Thousand Years: Long Live the Khan." Lingying remarked, "Heading the Dept of State Affairs is one of the eight high positions of the state; the responsibilities with which one in this position is entrusted are not light. And yet you sing stomping songs for the barbarian rebels! Have you no shame?" But Zhiwei still sang on, "Sing out Ten Thousand Years, Ten Thousand Years! Long Live the Khan!" People of the time despised Yan.* (4.94)

Heedless of the general's efforts to shame him, Yan launches into a Turkish "stomping song," wishing his new master an infinitely long reign.[15] Zhang Zhuo's concluding remark, "people of the time despised Yan," reflects his own contempt for a man he views as a traitor who shamelessly ingratiated himself with his new master by praising Qapaghan's power and aping "barbarian" customs.

After Wu Zhao's armies captured Yan Zhiwei in late 698, he was bound and spread-eagled at Ford of Heaven Bridge; Wu Zhao led the court ministers to fire arrows at the traitor until his riddled body looked like a human porcupine. Three generations of his family members were also killed.[16] Zhang Zhuo's *Court and Country* vividly evokes both Yan Zhiwei's gruesome end and the piteous spectacle of youngsters from the Yan clan, completely innocent of any crime and oblivious to the fate that awaited them, cheerfully picking up fruit and pancakes cast by sympathetic gawkers as they marched toward the execution grounds:

> *From the Linde era onward, when people sang drinking songs, those who failed to drain their cup by song's end were assessed a "salt penalty." Later, after Yan Zhiwei joined the Tujue Turks and led rebels to destroy Zhaozhou and Dingzhou, he was captured and presented before the court. Zetian was enraged and commanded that he be dismembered in the Western Market. She ordered all of the officials to shoot arrows at his corpse. From seven paces, Prince of Henei Wu Yizong loosed three arrows and missed every time, reflecting his feckless and timorous character. Bristling with arrows, Zhiwei's corpse looked like a quill-covered hedgehog. After that, they chopped up and ground away his bones and flesh and eradicated his entire extended clan. Remote Yan relatives so distant they didn't even know each other were all decapitated. Little seven- and eight-year-old children of the Yan clan were carried on horseback to the Western Market. The common people, grieving their plight, threw them fruit and flatcakes. The children, thinking it a fun game, mutually vied to grab them. The Supervising Censor could not bear to harm them and memorialized the throne requesting their release. This marked the prophetic fulfillment of the "salt penalty." (1.11)*

Mentioned at the beginning of the excerpt, "salt penalty" (*zu yan* 族鹽), a popular drinking game among common folk from the 660s onward, was proximate to a homophone for "an execution of the Yan clan" (*zhu Yan* 誅閻), which led people of the time to claim that the name of the drinking game was a prophecy of the demise of the Yans.

This passage also explains and provides context for the nickname that court wag Zhang Yuanyi (see Chapter 2) bestowed upon Wu Yizong, "Great Bow with Short-flying Arrow": from twenty feet away, Wu Zhao's odious kinsman was incapable of hitting Yan Zhiwei. Archery is one of the six arts of a Confucian gentlemen—along with charioteering, rites, music, calligraphy, and mathematics.[17] Clearly, Wu Yizong fell short.

QAPAGHAN KHAN AND THE TUJUE TURKS, PART II: KILL THE MESSENGER!

Court and Country also includes an episode involving the Tujue Turks set five years after the end of Wu Zhao's reign. Qapaghan was still khan, but their confederation of tribes had splintered and some of them had submitted to the authority of the newly restored Tang. Zhang Rendan[18] proved himself a capable border defender against the Turks during the later years of Wu Zhao's Zhou dynasty; where he had been posted to defend the borders for several years, Zhang had built a trio of "garrisons to receive submission" north of the loop of the Yellow River and sustained an effective campaign against Qapaghan.[19] General Zhang had a long history of confronting Qapaghan, beginning with his resistance to the Turkish khan's invasion of the northeastern prefectures in 698 while serving under Wu Zhao as military supervisor of Youzhou. In his effort to stave off Qapaghan's incursion, he sustained an arrow wound to the hand; when Wu Zhao learned of this, she personally sent a physician and medicines.[20] The episode below occurred roughly a decade later:

> General Zhang Rendan loved killing. At that time, the Turks had surrendered and pledged allegiance to the Tang. Zhang then composed a public declaration cursing Qapaghan. In language and expression, it was extremely coarse. His declaration was carved into the flesh and sinew of the back of an emissary, tattooed with ink, and cauterized with fire until the man couldn't bear the agony and, day and night, howled in pain like the chirping of insects or trilling of birds. Later, the emissary was sent to Qapaghan. One of the Turks who recognized characters read the announcement off the man's skin. Piece by piece, the emissary's flesh was sliced off and he was killed. Deeply rankled, the Xiongnu did not dare surrender. (2.34)

Primarily engaged against Qapaghan for such an extended time, Zhang Rendan clearly felt an intense personal enmity toward the khan. Nor did he receive Turkish surrender gently; one is struck by how poorly *ren* 仁 (the *ren* of Rendan), "humanity," suits his given name. The act of the callous Tang general described in *Court and Country* alienated these recently surrendered subjects and prolonged the lingering border wars for almost another decade. Being an emissary moving between military camps was perilous: sadly, the sentiment that one should not "kill the messenger" had not reached the Tang borderlands in the early eighth century. The poor man suffers agonizing pain twice—at the hands of the Tang general and the Turkish khan—though the latter puts him out of his misery!

The term Xiongnu—initially referring to a powerful group of nomadic steppe people who loomed north of the central plains of China, launched repeated incursions, and emerged as a rival to the Han dynasty—is employed above by Zhang Zhuo as a generic term for "northern barbarians."

A FAILED CAMPAIGN AGAINST THE TIBETANS: A COURT MINISTER QUAVERS IN THE FIELD

While there was a clear division between civil and military in later periods like the Song, many early Tang men served in both a civil and a military capacity, "going out as generals, and serving within as court ministers" (*chujiang ruxiang* 出將入相). As we shall see in the following passages, not all court ministers were suited for military campaigns on the frontier, nor were all generals capable of fitting into roles as civil administrators.

Li Jingxuan was both a chief minister, heading the Secretariat, and a general, leading a frontier campaign against the Tibetans, who rose as a significant power in the southwest during the seventh century. As head of the Secretariat, Li consistently blocked every suggestion and memorial that veteran general Liu Rengui sent in from his frontier command in the southwest. Frustrated with Li Jingxuan's armchair proposals from the court and well aware of his inability to serve as a field general, Liu proposed that the Two Sages, Gaozong and Wu Zhao, designate Li Commander-in-Chief of the Tibetan campaign in 678. While the erstwhile court minister won an initial engagement, he suffered a crushing defeat in Qinghai in late autumn of that year.[21] This seems to be the battle to which Zhang Zhuo is referring in the passage below:

> In the Tang, Head of the Secretariat Li Jingxuan was made Commander-in-Chief to lead a punitive expedition against the Tibetans. When he reached Shudun City, he heard that Liu Xiangshu had been routed by the Tibetans. Without even strapping on his boots, he fled pell-mell. This shocked general Wang Gao, Vice Commander-in-Chief Cao Huaishun, and others, prompting them to retreat so abruptly that they left their wheat and rice behind as they fled. The grain they abandoned in their thousand-li wake lay more than a foot thick on the ground. At the time, a ditty circulated among the troops:
>
> > Yao River's Grandmother Li
> > And Shanzhou prefecture's Auntie Wang
> > See the enemy and flee—
> > And new bride Cao, too, got it all wrong. (4.89–90)

For his unspectacular failure and pell-mell retreat, Li—along with several other timorous military leaders on the campaign—was lampooned by his own soldiers. The fact that the coarse ditty of these battle-weary soldiers casts Li

GENERALS AND MILITARY MEN

Jingxuan as "Grandmother" and his two subordinates Wang Gao and Cao Huaishun[22] as "Auntie" and the "new bride," respectively, provides a glimpse of *wu* 武 (martial) masculinity in the early Tang. Engaging in the deep-rooted cross-cultural male tradition of denigration through effeminization, the rank-and-file men show their contempt for the failures of their commanding officers in a casual misogynistic ditty, othering them as women to indicate that they failed to live up to standards of martial masculinity.[23] In the case of "Grandmother Li" Jingxuan, the pointed criticism may relate to the sexagenarian's inability to transition from softer civil court life to rough life in the field.

ADMIRATION OF AGILITY AND STRENGTH IN MARTIAL CIRCLES

In *Extensive Records*, the passage below is contained in a chapter reserved for the "Intrepid and Brave" (*Xiaoyong* 驍勇).[24] Physical strength, manual dexterity, horsemanship, and prowess with weapons were measures of *wu* masculinity in the early Tang; these qualities were admired even by a literatus like Zhang Zhuo. The story below contains a pair of examples in which military men display consummate talent:

> General Xin Chengsi was light-footed and nimble. Once he took the saddle and crupper off of his horse, shed his armor, disrobed, and lay down. He ordered a man to mount his horse, level his lance, and charge. As his opponent advanced, Chengsi quickly rigged his horse's crupper and saddle, pulled on his clothes and strapped on his armor, mounted his horse and braced his spear. He pierced his opponent's horse, captured the man, and returned.
>
> On another occasion, Xin Chengsi had a horseracing contest with other generals and commanders. With one hand on the pommel of the saddle and his legs girding the horse, pressed down like a dragonfly, he rode upside-down for twenty li.
>
> When he and Pei Shaoye were surrounded by the Tibetans, he said, "Follow me and we can break free together."
>
> Pei was petrified and didn't dare.
>
> "Well, I'll give it a shot," Xin shrugged. With a solitary horse, clutching his lance, Xin charged forward, scattering Tibetan troops in his wake. Desiring to retrieve Pei Shaoye, he wheeled his horse and doubled back, but his mount was hit by an arrow. He leapt free of the falling horse, unhorsed one of the villains, and mounted the man's powerful steed—all without sustaining the slightest injury.
>
> When Pei Min was Superintendent of Youzhou, he went on a northern campaign with Sun Quan. They were surrounded by Xi villains. Standing atop his horse, he flourished his broad sword against a rain of arrows like shooting stars. Every arrow was cut in twain. The bandits didn't dare charge and seize them, and they fled like the wind. (6.140)

Here, *Court and Country* portrays General Xin Chengsi as a fearless leader, a remarkable horse rider, and a man possessing almost supernatural agility.

Pei Min is an indomitable warrior whose puissant presence strikes fear in the heart of the enemy. A certain flamboyance seems to have enhanced their deeds of derring-do: Xin's reckless upside-down equestrian skills and Pei Min's uncanny ability to deflect a hail of arrows with his lightning-quick blade both manifest not just skill, but panache.

This scene described probably dates from late in Gaozong's reign, during the joint rule of the Two Sages. The story of Xin Chengsi is certainly set before 684, when Pei Shaoye was implicated for involvement in an uprising against Wu Zhao and executed.[25] The second exemplar, Pei Min, was part of a campaign launched against the Xi in the northeast in 712.[26]

Prodigious strength was also admired in martial circles. Kam Louie classifies Guan Yu, from the Three Kingdoms era, as the paragon of martial arts, a "God of War" possessing "immovable self-control." Louie opines that from a Western vantage he might be imagined as "a combination of St. George and St. Peter, Robin Hood and Daniel Boone, El Cid and Ned Kelly, John Wayne and Arnold Schwarzenegger."[27] An imposing tower of fortitude with an impressive beard, Lord Guan's physical strength was awe-inspiring; according to later legend, he wielded a massive Green Dragon halberd that weighed over 100 pounds.[28]

Two passages from *Court and Country* below show that such rugged men were esteemed in Zhang Zhuo's time as well. The first features strongman Peng Botong:

> *Peng Botong of Hejian was eight chi tall.*[29] *Once, at the top of the stairs leading to the lecture hall, he pinned a pair of shoes under his arms and challenged any strong fellow to wrest them away. One fellow pulled so hard that he broke one of the shoes in half and tumbled backward; from the challenge's beginning to end, Botong's feet did not move an inch. On another occasion, Botong grabbed the back of a moving oxcart and started to drag it backward. He made it a couple of dozen steps, gouging two-foot-deep wagon ruts in the road, before the cart sundered and broke apart from the tension. Once while swimming in severe winds at Melonport—the kind of winds that swelled the sails of boats—Botong grabbed the stern hawser of a passing boat and pulled. The vessel couldn't move!*[30] (6.139)

After a pair of stalwart fellows fail to budge Peng an inch, he proves himself literally stronger than an ox, pulling an ox-drawn cart backward until it breaks. Given the reference to the "lecture hall," Peng clearly ran in circles of both literati and military men, though there are no records that he served in an official capacity.

The father of Han Wan 韩琬, author of *Records from the Censor's Terrace* (*Yushitai ji* 御史台記), a mid-Tang work, once shared a meal with Peng, who regaled the elder Han with tales of his might. When Han was not duly

GENERALS AND MILITARY MEN

impressed, Peng lifted his heavy low supper table with one hand and raised Han's table, fully laden with food and drink vessels, with the other hand, then carried both out into the courtyard without a drop of liquor spilling or a single dish sloshing. On another occasion, Peng challenged Song Lingwen and two other strongmen to remove the pillow from under his head as he was lying on a couch. Each of the three men tried to yank the pillow free individually, but all failed. Peng must have been using some sort of qigong to hold the pillow fast. Then, as a crowd gathered, perching on walls and rooftops to gain a view, all three men pulled together to wrest the pillow free. Even when the frame of the couch cracked and crashed to the ground, Peng did not allow the pillow to move an inch. The awestruck audience broadcast the spectacle and Peng's celebrity grew in the greater Chang'an metropolitan area.[31]

From the Tang histories, we know that the aforementioned Song Lingwen, the protagonist in the second account below, was a military officer during the later years of Gaozong's reign. He was sent as a commandant-emissary to attend the funerary gathering for the Tibetan ruler in 679.[32] A macho man with few equals (Peng Botong was one), Song killed a temperamental bull in a Buddhist monastery and lifted a stone pillar in the imperial academy!

> Song Lingwen possessed god-like strength. In Chanding Temple,[33] a man was gored by a bull; no one dared approach the creature, so they built an enclosure to contain it. Lingwen felt it strange that everyone should be so fearful, stripped off his hempen clothes, and entered the pen bare-chested. The bull lowered his horns and charged. Lingwen grabbed the brute by the horns and wrenched him over so violently that the bull's neck was broken, and he died.
>
> On another occasion, he pinched a pestle with his five fingers and wrote a forty-character poem on the wall. Another time, when he was a student at the imperial academy, he lifted up one of the pillars in the lecture hall and placed a classmate's robes beneath the pillar, refusing to move it until his classmate agreed to host a drinking banquet.
>
> Song Lingwen had three sons. The eldest, Song Zhiwen, was praised for his literary prowess. The middle son, Song Zhisun, excelled in calligraphy. The youngest, Song Zhiti, was brave and strong. When Song Zhiti was slandered, he was exiled to Zhuchi County on the fringes of the empire.[34] At this time, bandits sacked Huanzhou and Zhiti was made a military commander and ordered to stop them. After levying a small crack force of eight stalwart men, Zhiti, who stood nearly eight chi tall and was clad in layered armor, shouted, "Thieving Liao! One move and you're dead!" All 700 Liao rebels were promptly cut down and routed. (6.139)

It is curious that, like Peng Botong, Song Lingwen had a civil aspect and was at ease in literati circles. The *Old Tang History* mentions that, in the 670s, Song was a "well known scholar–gentleman" who kept the company of poetic master Lu Zhaolin and honored master physician Sun Simiao as a teacher.[35] The passage in *Court and Country* tells us that Song Lingwen was a student at the imperial academy; his son, Song Zhiwen, was one of the most talented poetic and literary masters of Wu Zhao's era. Lingwen also evidently passed on his martial prowess to his thirdborn, Song Zhiti. Clearly, the Song family was versed in both the civil and military arts.

Both Peng Botong and Song Lingwen come across as rather vain, but each possesses an impish streak of mischief—broken furniture and vehicles are left strewn in the wake of their feats of strength, and unfortunate classmates end up footing the bill for drinking banquets!

WHEN WU TRIES TO BE WEN: A MILITARY MAN'S FAILED EFFORTS IN THE CIVIL SPHERE

Timothy Barrett has observed that in *Court and Country*, Zhang Zhuo ridicules "the general Quan Longxiang for his incompetent pretensions to poetic ability." Later, in an anthology of anecdotes about Tang poetry written in the Song period, Quan receives the dubious distinction of being "duly ensconced in the penultimate fascicle [...] as the worst poet of the Tang."[36]

Indeed, sometimes the civil and martial spheres—with their distinct visions of masculinity—were not compatible. We have previously examined a song that expressed the contempt of soldiers for Li Jingxuan; military men viewed Li as an effete member of the literati, poorly suited to the military, a man of *wen* incapable of meeting the demands of *wu* culture. In the following lengthy passage from *Court and Country*, the circumstance is reversed when Quan Longxiang, a career general, is assigned to several prefectural positions in civil administration:

> In the Tang, General of the Left Quan Longxiang, narrow-minded and ill-tempered by disposition, boasted that he could compose poetry. During the Tongtian era, he was made Prefect of Cangzhou. He composed a poem and showed it to the prefectural officials:
>
>> From afar looking at the city walls of Cangzhou
>> Poplars and willows cluster lusher and thicker
>> In the center, gather a group of hardy men
>> Seated hoisting horns of wine and cups of liquor
>
> The officials all thanked him, saying, "Your Excellency truly possesses remarkable talent." Longxiang said, "I'm unworthy of such praise. I merely availed myself of a little rhyme." He also recited "Expressing my Bosom Feelings on an Autumn Day":
>
>> Beneath the eaves fly seven hundred,
>> A powerful snow-white in the rear garden hung.

GENERALS AND MILITARY MEN

Surfeited reclining in my room,
As on the privy mound gather wild beetles of dung.

His adjutants had no idea what he was talking about and asked him to explain. Longxiang replied, "The kestrels flying beneath the eaves are worth seven hundred cash. Washed robes hanging in the rear garden to dry are white as snow. When I'm full after a meal, I lie down in my room. And in the swampy moisture of the shit and piss of the family privy, clusters of dung beetles gather." All who spoke of the poem mocked him.

When the crown prince held a banquet and courtiers composed a verse for the summer day, he wrote,

> *Pure white the formidable frost*
> *Brilliant red the luminous moon.*

The crown prince took up his writing brush and wrote his appraisal: "Talented Longxiang, gentleman of Qinzhou: Your luminous moon shines brightest at dawn and the formidable frost comes out in the summer! In this sort of poem, one merely avails oneself of an easy rhyme."

Because of the matter of Zhang Yizhi, Quan was demoted and sent to Mount Rong as a Garrison Commandant. Upon returning to the capital in the Shenlong era, he presented to the emperor a poem that read,

> *For some little matter I was sent to Mount Rong.*
> *Today to the Eastern Capital I return from this distant border*
> *Your Majesty has issued an edict summoning me forth,*
> *To serve as Imperial Insignia Guard by formal order*

He also composed the poem "Happy Rain," which read,

> *Going out in the gloom there is no rain;*
> *the light comes forth, no clouds to be seen.*
> *The sunlight glows a radiant red,*
> *The ground is covered with ribbon of fecund steam.*

When Quan was appointed Prefect of Yingzhou,[37] New Year's had just passed. Several couriers from the capital arrived bearing a missive from the emperor that read, "The changing of the year brings many feelings. Respect and consider this in others." Misinterpreting the letter, he then summoned all of the officials and people to gather, announcing that by imperial proclamation the ruler had inaugurated a new era, "the first year of Abundant Feelings." He took the missive and passed it on to his subordinates. The entire crowd brayed with laughter. Longxiang overheard the laughter but remained puzzled that no writ of amnesty had come.[38]

Vying over territorial claims, two counties within his prefecture, Gaoyang and Boye, made a plea to Longxiang and submitted records. Longxiang then rendered a decision that read, "Two counties have competing territorial claims. This is not a matter for the prefect to decide." Everyone who spoke of the matter scoffed. "Since it is a matter involving the two counties, might as well let the county authorities administer it. Turn this matter over to the county authorities, as instructed by Quan Longxiang."

His clerk said, "Lately, when senior officials make decisions, none of them sign their family names."

Longxiang replied, "I can't explain the actions of others. If I don't sign my family name, how do people know which family this wandering donkey belongs to?"

Longxiang had no knowledge of taboo days, and once asked the office clerk, "What is a taboo day?" The clerk responded, "On the anniversary of a parent's death, one requests leave and sits alone in one's residence, not going out." When the day arrived, Longxiang took leave of office and was sitting quietly at his residence when a black dog suddenly entered his home. In a towering fury, Longxiang said, "You've disrupted my day of mourning!" He then wrote out a document to change his day of mourning to the following day. All who discussed the matter laughed at him. (4.95–96)

With elegance and casual arrogance befitting a career literatus, Zhang Zhuo takes no small delight in relating the ex-general's bumbling missteps in his vain efforts to fit into literati culture, even on a provincial level far from the metropole. When Quan keeps imperial company in the capital, his boorishness—as Zhang tells it—becomes even more transparent.

In a *wen* culture where aesthetic flair was a social currency, episode after episode in the lengthy passage above reveals the general's coarseness and utter lack of refinement. When he first takes the position of Prefect of Cangzhou (a bit south of Beijing in modern-day Hebei), he recites a poem for a gathering of the local gentlemen. While Quan's lyrics are hackneyed and off in meter and rhyme, none of the men have the temerity to correct the newly arrived superior with military credentials. Emboldened by what he mistakes for a triumphant entry into the literary world, Quan thereafter rarely misses an opportunity to flaunt his poetic mastery. His poems are vulgar, and he misses basic cues: when the Crown Prince asks for a verse to evoke the summer season, Quan begins, "Pure white the severe frost." Not only does his verse fail to match the occasion but it also lacks any classical references. Instead, like the dung beetles he describes clustered atop a dung-heap, vulgar expressions congregate in his poetry. His reputation even reached imperial circles. On another occasion a few years after Wu Zhao's death, when the erstwhile general joined court scholars on an outing that involved poetry recitation, Emperor Zhongzong mockingly called him "Scholar Quan."[39]

It wasn't solely his singular lack of poetic talent; Quan Longxiang also displayed comic ineptitude in his effort to perform routine administrative duties in the civil sphere. Not particularly literate, he misreads the language of an imperial writ, mistaking the emperor's pronouncement that "The changing of the year brings an abundance of feelings" for a formal declaration changing the reign era to "Abundant Feelings"—a ridiculous gaffe given the context, as this would clearly be an absurd reign name. Moreover, Quan compounds his mistake by announcing this momentous change to congregated local officials, who bray with laughter. Alas, even then he is none the wiser.

As Prefect, when two counties under his authority engaged in a territorial dispute approach him and request that he render a decision, he absurdly dismisses the case. This shows that he grasps neither the purview of his duties nor the basic hierarchic structure of local administration. As the senior official in the prefecture, he casually refers to himself as a "wandering donkey" in front of an underling, without regard for self-presentation or the gravitas of his position.

The final example in Zhang Zhuo's string of anecdotes calibrated to show Quan's ignorance features the general's utter lack of understanding of taboo days (*jiri* 忌日)—designated days marking a parent's (usually a father's) death spent seated in quiet, filial reflection. After a clerk explains the fundamentals of such a day of ritual abstinence, Quan undertakes the taboo day, only to be interrupted by an untimely canine intruder. With no understanding of the time-honored rules governing ritual, he naively thinks that he can have a "do-over" and switch his taboo day to the following day.

The passage also indicates that Quan Longxiang was implicated for his ties to Zhang Yizhi—one of Wu Zhao's influential favorites killed in the coup that re-enthroned the Li family and restored the Tang—and banished to distant Mount Rong in Lingnan. His connections to the offending Zhang brothers were apparently not that close, for he was soon recalled to the court and made a member of the imperial bodyguards.

WHILING AWAY THE IDLE HOURS

Salvaged from *Miscellaneous Morsels from Youyang*, a late Tang collection of anomalies, this tidbit appears in the supplemental section of *Court and Country*:[40]

> *During the illegitimate Zhou dynasty, Guard Supervisor of Tengzhou Yuan Sizhong, son of Yuan Ping, was capable of balancing a chopstick on the tip of a knife and then swiping it at a fly and pinning it down by its rear leg. He would never miss.* (Sup., 154)

Not every moment in the military was filled with martial drills, routine guard duty, construction of fortifications, agricultural labor to plant and harvest crops to sustain the garrison, and combat against the "four barbarians."

Even today, there are numerous Reddit posts about things "to keep you from becoming bored to death" in the army.[41] There were staggeringly dull hours, filled with dirty jokes and ribald songs, old war stories, nostalgic recollections of hometowns, wistful thoughts of family left behind, games and sports, or the tireless cultivation of obscure skills—like Yuan Sizhong's novel mode of insect immobilization![42]

8

The frontier and beyond: foreigners and others during Wu Zhao's reign

IN THE SIMPLEST TERMS, A TRADITIONAL Chinese worldview contrasted a civil, agrarian interior with a barbaric, steppe/nomadic outside. Whatever the category, various binary oppositions—cooked versus raw foods, silken garments as opposed to coarse felt—functioned to construct the civility and refinement of the center in opposition to the progressive wildness and savagery of the periphery. In one of the earliest texts, *The Book of History*, there is a description of concentric circles radiating outward from the innermost nucleus of the "Imperial Domain" to the benighted far-off reaches, peopled with banished criminals and barbarians.[1] The notion of the Four Barbarians (*Siyi* 四夷) representing the cardinal directions also originates in the *Book of History*. It is explicitly articulated in the *Record of Rites* (*Li ji* 禮記), where these so-called savages from different quadrants are labeled: "The Yi of the east, the Di of the north, the Rong of the west, and the Man of the south."[2] In theory, these barbarians paid tribute to the Chinese court and saw themselves as political and cultural inferiors. Robert Marks has remarked on the "heroic tinge" of the Chinese-Confucian narrative arc of history and literature in which the Chinese, as the "font of culture," "spread the benefits of their high civilization to less advanced peoples, bringing them within the fold."[3] More often than not, stories about cultural Others in Zhang Zhuo's *Court and Country* fit this paradigm.

To complicate matters of ethnicity, the imperial Li clan, the Tang rulers, were not Han Chinese; their lineage—though they claimed to belong to the aristocratic Longxi Lis and descend from the Daoist sage Laozi—can be traced to the Türkic Xianbei, a people connected to the steppe. This background created tensions between them and the "few dozen old Han clans" rooted in northern China who had for centuries "dominated high society and formed a quasi-aristocracy."[4] Though the ruling family had "barbarian" blood, it "made enormous efforts to present itself as a bona fide Han [Chinese] house."[5]

The early Tang featured a hybrid culture, blending Chinese and Central Asian elements. To cite one example, "barbarian dress" (*hufu* 胡服)—caftans, wide-brimmed veiled hats, shoes with upturned toes—and dances held an exotic appeal. "Fascination with foreign dress," BuYun Chen observes, "was linked to the popularity of equestrian outings and sports, as well as foreign music, dance, and goods that were all readily consumed by the Tang court"; however, acrid "barbarian" felt was contemptuously contrasted with elegant, sleek Chinese silk.[6] Zhang Zhuo was aware of these conflicted sensibilities, of the curiosity and fascination that surrounded "barbarian clothing." *Court and Country* includes a passage that mentions chief minister Zhangsun Wuji using black fleece to fashion a felt hat early in Gaozong's reign. Admired by one and all, the distinctive chapeau came to be known as the "The Black Fleece Cap of the Duke of Zhao," after his nobility title (1.10).[7]

In practice, diplomacy was complex. Wang Zhenping views the Tang as a time of multipolarity and "complex external relations" when a number of rival "countries" in East, Central, and Northeast Asia vied for regional supremacy. At this juncture, "The lord-vassal relationship between the Tang and its neighbors was largely nominal."[8] Depending upon shifting power dynamics, the stance of the Chinese center fluctuated from a policy of appeasement to one of imperial aggression. When neighboring states were strong, early Tang rulers and Wu Zhao often offered titles, agricultural implements, and marital alliances to placate them. Occasionally, powerful khans like the Turks' Qapaghan united loose confederations of tribes; styling themselves predatory, nomadic raider-kings of the steppe, such khans likened the Chinese to their flocks, resources to be herded and culled when the need arrived.

In the famous novel *Journey to the West*, when Buddhist pilgrim Xuanzang—having set out from the capital Chang'an bound for India to fetch Buddhist scriptures—reaches the western frontier of the Tang empire, he encounters a hunter. The man informs the trepidatious monk, "On the east side of this mountain lies the land of our Tang. On the west side lies the land of the Tartars. The wolves and tigers there are not subject to my jurisdiction. I have no right to cross the border. You must carry on alone."[9] In late seventh-century China, however, there were rarely clear-cut boundaries between the Tang realm or Wu Zhao's Zhou empire and the territories claimed by surrounding peoples.

The previous chapter, "Generals and Military Men," established that, in the early Tang and during Wu Zhao's reign, there were a number of formidable peoples who at times formed confederations or states that rivaled Tang and Zhou China in might. Late in the joint reign of the Two Sages, the Tibetans waxed in power. During Wu Zhao's reign, both the Khitan and the Turks rose and controlled huge dominions along the northern borders.

THE FRONTIER AND BEYOND

Though there were serious tensions, Wu Zhao's cosmopolitan capital, Luoyang, reflected her inclusive approach to governing the multiethnic and diverse empire of her day. For non-Chinese peoples on the periphery of the empire, her tolerant governance held great appeal. In a number of cases of borderland diplomacy, she provided grain and agricultural implements to peoples of the periphery. During the first years of her Zhou dynasty, more than a million non-Chinese people submitted and were resettled within her borders—Turks to the northwest, Tibetans to the west, and 200,000 households of Man people to the southwest.[10] In Wu Zhao's words, her empire extended "East as far as the Korean peninsula, south to the nation of Zhenla, west to Persia (modern Iran), and north to the lands of the Khitan, the Mohe, and the Turks—these may be called 'submitted non-Chinese peoples.' That which lies beyond these boundaries may be called the 'distant lands.'"[11] In reality, these imagined boundaries were in constant flux; smaller groups and peoples had alliances both with the Chinese empire and with neighboring dominions like the Tibetans or the Turks, doing whatever it took to survive.

This chapter initially examines passages from *Court and Country* that explore the role that these so-called barbarians played in diplomacy and politics. In such passages, Zhang Zhuo frequently follows the well-established tendency in Chinese rhetoric to animalize or bestialize the cultural Other. Thereafter, the chapter unpacks a number of anecdotes from *Court and Country* concerning the lives and customs of various peoples of the periphery, including a brief but ferocious military uprising of the Khitan, the sad fate of a young Koguryan girl taken as a prisoner of war, the religious practices of Sogdians, and the marital traditions in countries of Southeast Asia beyond the borders of the Tang or Zhou.

OMINOUS SIGNS: RUMBLINGS ON THE FRONTIER, TROUBLE IN THE CENTER

The following three passages from *Court and Country* all attest to frontier threats during Wu Zhao's co-reign as one of the Two Sages, her regency, and her reign as emperor. The first uses this spate of border threats to critique the Two Sages' efforts to stage a grand celebratory rite. The second links the series of encroachments and invasions to an ill-omened comet. The third is a short passage from late in Wu Zhao's reign as emperor.

The first passage enumerates frontier threats late in Gaozong's reign. During this time, the Two Sages were considering an encore performance of the sacrosanct *feng* and *shan* sacrifice at Mount Song, the Central Marchmount. With powerful religiopolitical overtones, the *feng* and *shan* were the rarest and most solemn of all rites of state; only seven rulers in all of Chinese history staged these grand ceremonies.¹² From one of the five marchmounts, the emperor would—as part of a massive procession of court, military, and foreign embassies—broadcast the harmony between Heaven and Earth that marked a halcyon age. The Two Sages held them at Mount Tai in 666.¹³ Wu Zhao held them again in 696. Between these performances, in the late 670s and early 680s, the Two Sages planned to hold them again:

> *In the Diaolu era, when the Great Emperor wished to perform the feng sacrifice on the Central Peak, dependent Tujue Turks rebelled, so he halted the proceedings. Later, when he again wished to perform the feng sacrifice, the Tibetans entered the borders and the rite was cancelled. In the Yongchun era, when he yet again took the imperial carriage to go to the peak of Mount Song, a folk ditty circulated:*
>
> > *How tall great Mount Song! Ah, how lofty and sublime!*
> > *Don't fear never reaching the peak, just fear never making the climb.*
> > *Thrice horses and troops are mustered and levied,*
> > *Clamoring and fighting rages on the side roads so heavy!*
>
> *When the imperial procession reached the base of the Central Peak, the Great Emperor became ill. After failing to improve, he returned to the palace and perished.* (1.9)

In this excerpt, Zhang Zhuo offers neither a casual observation nor a neutral commentary. He mentions each of the three occasions on which the Two Sages attempted to perform the *feng* and *shan*. Every time, their plans were scuttled: the first time, in 679, submitted Turks rebelled;¹⁴ the second time, Tibetans plundered border settlements in the southwest;¹⁵ and the third and final time, Gaozong fell ill at the base of the mountain.¹⁶ In short, Zhang depicts an empire on the brink: vassal peoples in the borderlands are rebelling, barbarians encroach, and the imperial body—always a metaphor for the state and its well-being—is ailing! The inclusion of the ditty serves to suggest that the commonfolk, too, recognized that this performative rite of tranquility was ill-suited to the turbulent times.

Coupled with bad harvests, the spate of crises in the late 670s and early 680s precipitated a financial crisis, wild inflation of rice prices, and mass migrations as peasant-farmers fled from these dangers, abandoning their plots of land.¹⁷ A second passage from *Court and Country* indicates that a portentous comet anticipated not only these domestic crises but also a wider range of border threats:

> *In the Yifeng era, a comet emerged in the east and traversed half the sky. It lasted more than thirty days, then disappeared. After this, the Tibetans rose up, the Xiongnu rebelled,*

THE FRONTIER AND BEYOND

Xu Jingye fomented chaos, Bai Tieyu rose in revolt, and there was turmoil in Bozhou and Yuzhou.[18] *Khitan leaders Sun Wanrong and Li Jinzhong seized Liangzhou and routed Yingzhou garrison. The Tujue Turks laid ruin to Zhaozhou and Dingzhou prefectures. Ma Renjie, Zhang Xuanyu, Wang Xiaojie, and others lost more than a million troops. For more than thirty years, wars and uprisings continued without cease.* (1.18–19)

Looming on the borders of the fragile Chinese empire were Tibetans, Turks, and Khitan, and within the empire, the Jihu people (examined in this chapter below), led by Bai Tieyu, rebelled. Zhang Zhuo's representation of the comet is in keeping with enviropolitical convictions concerning "the mutual resonance of Heaven and Earth" (mentioned in Chapter 2)—the idea that cosmic, meteorological, and natural phenomena were reflections of, and projections bearing on, the state of the realm of men.[19] In the *Doctrine of the Mean* (*Zhong Yong* 中庸), Confucius remarks that sage kings of antiquity grasped "the transformative and regenerative processes of Heaven and Earth," and thus patterned their governance upon the movements of the cosmos and the seasonal rhythm of nature.[20] From this and other sources, Joseph Needham reasonably observes that, in early China, human laws—poetically and metaphorically derived from elemental and cosmic processes—"were thought of as mirroring certain desirable qualities seen in non-human Nature."[21] The *Huainanzi*, a second-century BC work, states that if a ruler improperly carried out the ordinances of winter in the spring, "floods would create ruin; there would be rain, frost, and great hailstones. The first-sown seeds would not sprout."[22] In the Han dynasty, Confucian scholar–statesman Dong Zhongshu (179–104 BC) helped develop and systematize the idea of the "mutual responsiveness of Heaven and Earth."[23] Contemporary scholar Wang Yuquan frames the principle in the following terms:

> Evil done by a ruler finds its reflection in natural phenomena. Thus, any anomalous happenings in nature, such as eclipses of the sun and moon, and any calamities, such as floods droughts, earthquakes, locusts, were construed as signs of warnings by heaven toward the misbehavior or misgovernment of the ruler of man.[24]

Environmental historian Mark Elvin coined the term "moral meteorology" to describe this notion that "seasonal or unseasonal, appropriate or excessive" weather and climate accorded with virtuous or improper conduct of the ruler.[25] By the seventh century, this idea of cosmopolitical consonance had become an axiom of statecraft, a staple element in court discourse and historical narrative.

Therefore, in early and medieval Chinese history and literature, the mention of an earthquake, a flood, or a comet was rarely just a passing or incidental remark. Like a plague of locusts, an incursion of "barbarians" is an ill-omened event—reflecting that the realm of men and the natural world are out of kilter. Zhang's causal connection between the comet and the spate of barbarian incursions is a suggestion that Heaven above, responding to disequilibrium in the human world, manifested the ill-omened comet. In *Court and Country* and in other official sources, Wu Zhao's regency and reign are often depicted as decades of unremitting chaos and warfare. To no small extent, Zhang is offering a gendered commentary and judgment: when a woman occupies a male position like the imperial throne, it is a contravention of nature and of the natural harmonious rhythm of the cosmos. In such a topsy-turvy realm, where Confucian ethical conventions are unheeded, the boundaries between inner and outer have broken down, and "barbarians" encroach upon the territory of the Central Kingdom with impunity.

Another passage from *Court and Country* also explores the relationship between "barbarian" invasions and extraordinary meteorological phenomena:

> *On the first day of the ninth month of the second year of the Chang'an era, there was a total eclipse of the sun and rebels led by Tujue ruler Qapaghan reached Bingzhou. On the night of the fifteenth, there was a total eclipse of the moon and the rebels fully retreated.* (1.19)

Late in Wu Zhao's reign, in the autumn of 703, a total eclipse of the sun occurred on the date of the new moon; this indicated that the female *yin* element was completely overwhelming the male *yang* element and occupying its rightful place, turning the Chinese normative order upside down. Emboldened by this omen and perhaps supposing that it betokened disharmony within, the Turkish khan Qapaghan occupied Bingzhou, the Northern Capital of the female sovereign's empire. However, when a total eclipse of the moon occurred a fortnight later, perhaps understanding the ascendant *yang* as a harbinger that Wu Zhao's reign would soon end and thus return things to "normal," the Turks retreated to their homeland.

ANIMALIZING THE BARBARIANS: TURKISH MACAQUES AND SPARROWS

After a half century under Tang dominion, the Turks were united by a new, powerful khan from the royal Ashina line, who emerged to galvanize scattered rebel groups and formerly submitted tribes late in the joint reign of the Two Sages. By 690, when Wu Zhao inaugurated her Zhou dynasty, the Turks had already established a substantial empire in modern-day Mongolia; looming to the north, they frequently and successfully raided northern prefectures.[26]

Two passages in *Court and Country* on the Turks and the Khitan from this period reflect a Tang and Chinese centrist tendency toward ethnic othering:

THE FRONTIER AND BEYOND

bestializing and attributing animality to non-Chinese "barbarians." In his study on this topic, Marc Abramson observes, "The stereotype of the ethnic Other as animalistic, ranging from bestial humans to figures who were figuratively or literally animals, is the most frequently encountered image of non-Han in explicitly ethnic discourse in the Tang."[27]

In the first passage, ominous flocks of sand grouse in the desert and steppe of the borderlands anticipate the coming of the Turks:

From the later Diaolu era on, massive formations of millions of a dove-sized birds the color of crows or magpies flew everywhere, sounding like the whoosh of the winds. People of the time called them "sand grouse." They were also called "Tujue sparrows," because when they came, the Tujue Turks would inevitably follow, without exception. (1.19)

In the second, Li Liangbi, through a "scholarly" dissection of a Khitan leader's name, attempts to convince a fellow border official that resistance to these beast-men from the northland is futile:

In the Zhou, Right Reminder Li Liangbi often boasted of his eloquence and loved discussing profound principles. He begged leave to lead an embassy to the northern barbarians to persuade the Ilterish Khan. The Xiongnu covered a wooden platter with shit to feed him and held a naked blade to Liangbi. Terrified, he wolfed down the entire platter, after which he was released and allowed to return. People ridiculed him, mocking, "Li the Reminder—he's able to pick up that which the Tujue leave behind." He was demoted to become a local head in Zhenyuan county.[28] When his term of service was complete, he returned to Yingzhou prefecture and met with He Axiao, an emissary sent by Khitan rebel leader Sun Wanrong to annex Qiangzhou, Yingzhou, Jizhou, and Beizhou. To Deer City head Li Huaibi, Liangbi remarked, "The Sun in Sun Wanrong's name means descendant of the Hu barbarians—that is to say, a macaque; he will be difficult to hold back. The Wan in his name has a grass radical on top—that is to say, capable of hiding in the grass." He persuaded Huaibi to surrender to He Axiao; as a result, the Khitan emissary granted Huaibi the position of fifth-ranked general. When He Axiao was defeated, Li Huaibi, Li Liangbi, and their sons were decapitated by Prince of Henei Wu Yizong. (4.94)

Li Liangbi notes that the Khitan leader's Sun 孫 surname—a homophone for simian *sun* 猻, with the beast radical (犭) added—effectively made the man a macaque (*mihou* 獼猴). Not only that, the grass radical in one part of the Khitan leader's given name, the Chinese official argues, shows the barbarian's capacity to conceal himself in the steppe grass, evoking the image of a predator lying in wait.

Li held the office of Reminder (*shiyi* 拾遺), which is composed of two characters: *shi* 拾, to pick up, and *yi* 遺, to leave behind, to forget. The role of this remonstrance official was to remind the emperor and court of oversights—to pick up on omissions or mistakes.²⁹ This account mocks craven Li Liangbi. The humor is found in the way that his title is redeployed to indicate that he is still filling his office in a manner of speaking: the Reminder is picking up (*shi*) that which the Tujue left behind (*yi*)—that is, their shit. Zhang Zhuo depicts him as an incapable diplomat, a coward, and a traitor, though he does not question Li's utilization of the rhetoric of animality to scare a fellow official. In *Extensive Records*, this passage is placed in the chapters on the "Despicable and Contemptible" (*chibi* 嗤鄙).³⁰

THE KHITAN UPRISING OF 696–697

In the Tang, the Khitan were a nomadic, proto-Mongolian people of Xianbei origins, known for their archery and horsemanship; they occupied territories north and northeast of the Chinese heartland. During Wu Zhao's reign, the Khitan—who had been a vassal people in the northeast since late in Taizong's reign, settling in the northeast of the Tang empire with a degree of autonomy—rebelled, spurred by a callous local official who mistreated them during a famine. Under the leadership of Li Jinzhong and Sun Wanrong, both of whom had served as officials in the Tang and Zhou, they rose to become a regional threat. Wu Zhao entered into a brief, costly, and ill-advised alliance with the Turkish khan Qapaghan, who helped her quash this uprising. Though the rise of the Khitan was short-lived, the passages from *Court and Country* below confirm that their uprising inflicted tremendous damage upon Wu Zhao's hard-pressed military.³¹

The passage below examines the capture of Li Jiegu, a Khitan general who later served in Wu Zhao's Zhou military, and provides a terse account of Li's subsequent career:

> In the time of the Tang Celestial Empress, General Li Jiegu, a Khitan, excelled in throwing the lasso. On the occasion that Li Jinzhong defeated the Zhou armies, generals Ma Renjie and Zhang Xuanyu managed to ensnare the Khitan general. Whether roebuck or deer, fox or rabbit, Li Jiegu could intercept them with his horse and snare them with his lasso—not one in a hundred could slip his noose. In saddle his skill with bow and arrow, with spear and lance, matched that of a flying immortal. Cherishing his talent, the Heavenly Empress chose not to execute him, instead employing him as a general. However, he proved acquisitive of wealth and lascivious, so he was demoted and sent to the mouth of Tanzhou Bridge as a Protector General. Infuriated, in a towering rage, he died. (6.138–39)

This is one of many examples of how defeated non-Han generals came to fight for China. For Wu Zhao's troops, Li Jiegu's capture was one of the few high points in the bloody battle of Yellow Roebuck Gorge. The campaigns launched against the Khitan in 696 and 697 were "two of the bloodiest

THE FRONTIER AND BEYOND

in Tang history."[32] In the first and worst of the catastrophic engagements between the Zhou troops and the Khitan, a battle fought in the autumn of 696, Wu Zhao's massive army of 200,000 troops (under joint command of 28 generals) was utterly routed; bodies filled Yellow Roebuck Gorge.[33]

A second selection from *Court and Country* contains one of the prophetic folk ditties we have seen in earlier chapters; the song began to circulate in the Ruyi era (692), three or four years before the conflict:

> *From the Ruyi era of the Zhou onward, people started singing the "Yellow Roebuck" ditty. Its lyrics went,*
>
> > *Yellow roebuck, yellow roebuck, in the tall grass it hides;*
> > *The arrow from the recurved bow pierces it in the side.*
>
> *Not long thereafter, the Qidan rose up and rebelled, killing Commander-in-Chief Zhao Wenhui and overrunning and destroying Yingzhou Garrison. During the course of the conflict, generals Cao Renjie, Zhang Xuanyu, Ma Renjie, and Wang Xiaojie—leading a total of a million troops—were defeated by the Qidan rebels in Yellow Roebuck Gorge. The troops were completely routed, without a single survivor. This event represented the fulfillment of the Yellow Roebuck ditty.* (1.9)

The song's use of the "yellow roebuck" concealed in the grass can be understood as another example of attributing animality to the cultural Other. The account's claim that there were no survivors is not entirely accurate, for, as we have just seen, some of the generals did manage to capture Khitan leader Li Jiegu.

A third passage shows that even eminent court ministers like Li Zhaode were involved with these disputes on the periphery—indicating that court and frontier were more closely linked than one might imagine:

> *In the Tang, power and influence was concentrated in the person of Vice Minister of Phoenix Hall*[34] *Li Zhaode. He promulgated an imperial order reading, "Henceforth, if one publicly confesses to a crime, the punishment shall be corvée labor. If you acknowledge a crime in private, then the punishment shall be exile. If more than 100 days elapse and you do not confess, you will be punished according to the full extent of the law." Prior to this, Li Zhaode had received bribes and property from Sun Wanrong and had sent a memorial to make him third rank. Later Sun Wanrong had occupied Yingzhou prefecture and rebelled. Their plot fell through and was exposed. Despite several amnesties and acts of imperial grace, because 100 days had elapsed and Li did not confess to the crime, he received the punishment for accepting bribes according to law: death by strangulation.* (Sup., 156)

Prior to Sun Wanrong's emergence as a Khitan leader in the rebellion, Li had received bribes from the future rebel. As a chief minister, he had set forth an imperial order dictating that "*If more than 100 days elapse and you do not confess, you will be punished according to the full extent of the law.*" When his involvement with the rebel leader was exposed, Li was caught in his own snare. Li left behind a complex, checkered legacy. He was revered by Confucian historians for challenging the "cruel officials" and for trying to persuade Wu Zhao to hand power back to the Li family. However, he is also known for monopolizing power to the point that "he was loathed by all in court and country." The tenor of Zhang Zhuo's passage suggests that Li Zhaode got his just desserts for his abuses of power. After more than two years as a chief minister, he was exiled to a lesser position in the Southland, then recalled.[35] He was executed in 697 along with the notorious "cruel official" Lai Junchen, a man with whom he had clashed on numerous occasions.[36]

The fourth account from Zhang Zhuo describes the spring 697 death and defeat of Zhou general Wang Xiaojie, who had a long career as a frontier defender against the Tibetans:

> *Thoroughly routed, four hundred thousand troops led by Wang Xiaojie retreated. They were driven to the brink of a steep cliff. Gradually, they were forced backward, and one row of soldiers after another plunged down the slope into a chasm ten thousand zhang deep. Corpses were piled level to the rim of the cliff. Countless horses and soldiers were lost, none to ever return home.* (Sup., 170)

The intrepid general led a vanguard force in pursuit of the retreating Khitan along the edge of the same gorge; the Khitan doubled back with reinforcements, driving the general and thousands of troops over the edge.[37]

A fifth and final account, a little fragment in *Court and Country*, attests to the demoralization of the Khitan when the Turkish khan Qapaghan, having allied with Wu Zhao, destroyed their new city:

> *When the Khitan rebels learned that the Tujue Turks destroyed the new fortified city of their commander Sun Wanrong, the throngs of rebels all lost their spirits and dispersed.*[38] (Sup., 171).

Several centuries later, after the Tang fell, the Khitan established the Liao dynasty, a huge state with dominion over much of northeast Asia.

KOGURYANS: THE BALLAD OF JADE WHITE

Richard Guisso remarks that in the early Tang "the Korea question formed one of the focal points" of foreign affairs: the effort to equal the northeastern extent of the empire reached by celebrated Han ruler Wudi (r. 141–86 BC), a benchmark of dynastic greatness, "was either the greatest folly or the greatest triumph" for Taizong and the Two Sages.[39] With the fall of the fortified city of Pyong'yang in 668, following a number of grueling campaigns, the armies of Wu Zhao and Gaozong conquered the kingdom of Koguryo, which included the northern half of the Korean peninsula and a sizable chunk of Northeast Asia. Pushing the eastern reach of the Chinese empire to an extent that rivaled the territory of Han Wudi, the Two Sages set up the Andong protectorate to administer this territory. Taken as slaves and captives, tens of thousands of Koguryan expatriates were incorporated into the Tang and, later, Wu Zhao's Zhou.[40] Edward Schafer has observed that, in the early Tang, "girls of the states of Koguryo and Silla [...] were in great demand as personal maids, concubines, and entertainers in rich houses."[41]

This anecdote from *Court and Country*, set roughly a decade[42] after the fall of the Korean kingdom, reveals that Koguryan expatriates—foreigners within the Tang realm bound by culture and language—tried to stick together:

> *When Secretarial Drafter Guo Zhengyi helped conquer Pyong'yang, he obtained a Koguryan slave girl named Jade White who was extraordinarily sensual and voluptuous. He ordered that she be given exclusive responsibility over the warehouse where all his property was stored. Each evening she and she alone would boil the water for his porridge. Jade White poisoned the porridge and offered it to him. Upon eating it, Zhengyi anxiously cried, "The slave girl drugged me!" He took a decoction of opium and licorice to dispel the effects of the poison, and after quite a while the pain stopped. They searched for the slave girl but couldn't find her—in addition, a dozen or so gold and silver vessels went missing. The events were recorded in a memorial sent to the emperor. Gaozong decreed that a search be conducted in Chang'an and Wannian to arrest her. When the search proved unsuccessful, the bailiffs were beaten until their backs were a bloody pulp. Yet after three days of searching as frantically as water roiling in a ding-tripod, they failed to find her.*
>
> *Head bailiff Wei Chang devised a plan. Finding three young, good-looking family servants of Guo Zhengyi, he paraded them as criminals out on the streets with cloth sacks covering their heads. Later, the bailiffs seized four city guardsmen, asking them who, in the past ten days, had inquired about Guo Zhengyi's home. One guardsman said, "A surrendered Koguryan expatriate left a letter with a groom from Guo's household." The letter was still there. Upon examination it read, "In Jincheng Ward*[43] *there is an empty house." The "bad guy" grabbers searched all of the empty houses in Jincheng Ward and found one of the gates to be tightly secured. When they broke the lock and smashed open the gate, they discovered the servant girl Jade White and the Koguryan inside. Upon investigation, the groom and the submitted Koguryan expatriate had concealed the slave girl there. By imperial order, all three were executed in the Eastern Market.* (5.108–09)

This passage indicates that Tang troops took foreign women as the spoils of war—not surprising. While the intended point of the story is to emphasize bailiff Wei Chang's admirable investigative prowess in bringing the foreign criminals to justice, the story also offers unintended insight into the cultural struggles and estrangement of Koguryan expatriates lacking a homeland to which they might return.[44] Jade White sought an ally in a fellow Koguryan, a groom close to her own age with whom she shared a common linguistic and cultural background.

The conquest of the northern Korean peninsula proved short-lived. Even prior to Gaozong's death, the united kingdom of Silla gained control over this territory; the Tang forces moved the seat of their protectorate to another city a good distance west of the Yalu River, which even today serves as the boundary between North Korea and China.[45]

SOGDIANS IN THE CHINESE CAPITAL AND ON THE FRONTIER

Best known for their prodigious ability as traders and middlemen along the Silk Roads, the Sogdians had, by the early Tang, long-established and widespread networks of communities throughout China.[46] They spoke an Eastern Iranic language and their homeland was in Transoxiana, part of modern-day Tajikistan, southern Uzbekistan, and northern Afghanistan.[47] Physically, Sogdians were distinguished in China by high, aquiline noses, deep-set eyes, curly hair, and beards.[48] Culturally, they were recognized for whirling dances, distinctive tight-sleeved caftans, and Zoroastrianism.[49] More than mere transporters of commodities, Sogdians were purveyors of culture—artisans, translators, entertainers, and stockbreeders. While their primary religion in the early Tang was Zoroastrianism, Sogdian texts, art, and architecture from the period project the same cultural pluralism as the people—revealing a bricolage of Buddhism, Manicheism, Nestorian Christianity, and Hinduism.

Court and Country contains several passages on Sogdians, referred to as *hu* 胡. *Hu* can be a slippery term. Victor Xiong observes that *hu* is "a term loosely used in sources to refer to northern and western barbarians. In the Tang, it generally referred to Central and Western Asians."[50] Edward Schafer remarks that, "In T'ang times, persons and goods from many foreign countries were styled *hu*. In ancient times, this epithet had been applied mostly to China's Northern neighbors, but in medieval times, including T'ang, it applied chiefly to Westerners, and especially to Iranians, though sometimes also to Indians, Arabs, and Romans."[51] In a similar vein, Al Dien argues that often *hu* specifically referred to Sogdians: "Iranians in Transoxiana, more commonly called Sogdia, were called *hu* in Chinese, a word perhaps etymologically related to the word for beard."[52] *Hu* 胡 meaning Sogdian/Western barbarian is a

THE FRONTIER AND BEYOND

Figure 7   A Tang dynasty porcelain camel and groom.

homophone for *hu* 鬍, beard. Most Tang depictions, like this "three-colored porcelain" (*sancai* 三彩) representation of a Sogdian groom and camel (see Figure 7), show Sogdian men as bearded.[53] The designation *hu* thus fashioned Sogdians as hirsute and animalistic, barbarian Others.

Examining "Chinese stereotypes" of, and "popular attitudes" toward, "Western barbarians" like the Sogdians, Edward Schafer opines that the "same young poets who languished over a pretty Iranian waitress in the metropolitan wineshops" guffawed at puppet shows featuring Westerners as drunkards with prominent noses and lots of facial hair. Famed late Tang poet Bo Juyi waxed rhapsodic about tireless Sogdian girls whirling like falling snowflakes:

> Girls of the Sogdian whirl! Girls of the Sogdian whirl! [...]
> Like whirling snow so graceful, revolving in the opulent dance!
> Whirling to the left, turning to the right, not knowing weariness;
> A thousand circuits, ten thousand revolutions, time without end!
> Among all things known to mankind, there is nothing comparable![54]

Here, the female Other is exoticized and sexualized for her whirling dances and unrestrained sensuality. Meanwhile, the male Sogdian/*hu*—though his mercantile prowess might be admired—was often lampooned for intemperance and animality; the "Bacchic motif" of the inebriated Sogdian had a stock place in Tang music and culture.[55] Representative of these respective gendered characterizations, two of the songs the Tang court incorporated into its musical repertoire were the "Sogdian Whirl" and "The Drunken Sogdians."[56]

In the following pair of passages, Zhang Zhuo depicts Sogdian communities practicing religious ceremonies that he finds peculiar and disturbing:

> In Lide Ward[57] of Luoyang and in the ward to the west of the South Market there was a Zoroastrian temple where merchant Sogdians annually worshipped fire spirits. They cooked pigs and goats; reveled to the accompaniment of the pipa lute, drums, and flute; sang inebriated songs; and danced drunken dances. After sprinkling libations to the spirits, a priest would be chosen to preside over the next ceremony and all those participating in the festival would give him offerings of cash. The priest would take a blade as sharp as frost and snow, capable of splitting a feather on its keen edge, and impale his stomach so the tip stuck out his back. He then twisted the handle back and forth so that the inserted blade cut into the intestines and stomach, spraying blood all over the place. After the time it takes to eat a meal, the priest spurted water out of his mouth and uttered incantations, then fully recovered. This is one of the conjuring arts of the western barbarians.[58] (3.64–65)

> At the Zoroastrian shrine in Liangzhou[59] on the day of prayer, the priest stuck a long iron nail into his forehead; it was so long that the end poked out of his armpit. He emerged from the doorway of the shrine, his body light as a feather, and covered the several hundred li distance in no time. When he reached the site of the Western Zoroastrian temple, he danced in front of the deity, then withdrew. Upon his return to the old shrine in Liangzhou, he pulled out the nail and there was no sign of injury. After ten-odd days of repose, he fully recovered. No one knows how he was able to do this.[60] (3.65)

The ceremonial self-mutilation featured in both passages is not part of orthodox Zoroastrianism. It may be a ritualistic death commemoration of legendary Prince Siavash, a Persian–Iranian culture hero, that was a part of festivals and mourning rites. Despite prohibitions in Zoroastrianism against such self-harm, facial lacerations, severing noses, and impalement were important ceremonial components in Sogdians' funerary rites.[61] Alternatively, these practices may represent what Pénélope Riboud calls the "Altaic legacy," reflecting the religious syncretism of the Sogdians and their close cultural ties to the Turks.[62] Riboud also plausibly suggests that, to a degree, the descriptions of Zoroastrian rites in the works of Zhang Zhuo and other Chinese observers may reflect "confusion [...] as to the nature of rituals performed."[63] In Zhang Zhuo's case, rather than confusion, a better explanation might be his penchant for shock value, for the sensational and the macabre. Written in the early Tang, the *History of the Sui Dynasty* mentions that Northern Zhou and Northern Qi rulers tried to follow some Zoroastrian practices, ceremonies too

THE FRONTIER AND BEYOND

"licentious and depraved to be recorded."[64] Both of these passages in *Court and Country* are clearly preoccupied with representing the practices of the barbarian Other as frenzied, macabre, and violent.

There is another, very different sort of passage about a Sogdian in *Court and Country*. Chapter 1 featured a passage from Zhang Zhuo's work that mentions how a master of playing the four-stringed lute from the western borderlands, a Sogdian named Luo Hei, had been taken into the inner palace of early Tang emperor Taizong to teach music to the ruler's concubines. The point in that passage was that the musician had been castrated, as was proper, for it was a contravention of decency for an ungelded male to make an ingress upon the inner quarters. Though the episode predates his birth, Zhang Zhuo includes another account of this same Luo Hei (here, Luo Heihei):

> *In the time of Taizong, an embassy from the Western nations presented a Sogdian who excelled in playing the pipa. When he played the song, even the strings were twice as thick. Displeased that the barbarians surpassed the Chinese, the emperor ordered a grand banquet with lots of wine laid, then had the Sogdian musician play the song while Luo Heihei listened, concealed behind a curtain. Taizong remarked to the members of the embassy from the Western nations, "Now listen as one of my palace girls plays that tune." He passed the thick-stringed pipa lute under the curtain to Luo Heihei, who played the song without missing a single note. Informed that it was a mere palace girl who had played the song with such perfection, the ambassadors sighed in admiration, and departed. When the Western nations learned of this, more than ten states submitted to the Tang!* (5.113)

The strings of the non-Chinese maestro's instrument were different, and his consummate skill was unrivaled. Taizong, in this instance, is represented as a master of cultural diplomacy. He outsmarts the ambassadors of the Western barbarians by creating the illusion that the people of Tang China had already mastered a prized Sogdian cultural art. Overawed, the ambassadors returned, telling everyone that even palace girls had a flawless grasp on their most refined musical skills. To the Western barbarians, who clearly held musical talent in the highest regard, this redounded thunderously to the power of the Tang, indeed so much so that a dozen oasis states along the Silk Road reportedly submitted to Tang authority—a tidy parable of Chinese mastery.

THE JIHU

The following passage from *Court and Country* features Bai Tieyu, a member of a small, internally pacified "barbarian" tribe known as the Jihu or the "Mountain Barbarians of the West" (*Shanhu* 山胡). During the Tang, where the Yellow River flows north to south, the Jihu people lived along both banks in modern-day Shaanxi and across the river in Shanxi. There are several different theories on the origins of the Jihu. Some scholars conjecture that they were descended from a southern branch of the Xiongnu, while others claim they were indigenous, an "autochthonous, self-formed nationality."[65]

The most famous leader of the Jihu was Liu Sahe (b. 345), a Buddhist miracle worker and a human dowsing rod capable of mystically discovering Buddhist stupas and relics. He circulated a short sutra in the Jihu language and spread distinctive religious practices. In almost all Chinese records of the Jihu, their leaders come from two families: the Liu family and the Bai family. The Jihu were known as a fierce and bellicose group; between the fourth and seventh centuries, they would rebel against the political center every few generations, usually galvanized under a Liu 劉 or Bai 白 leader. In the final years of ailing Gaozong's reign, amid a litany of other crises—crop failure, famine, comets, incursions by the Turks and Tibetans—Bai Tieyu drew on Jihu Buddhist traditions of discovering Buddhist relics and light faith healing. Ultimately, styling himself a radiant Buddhist king on the cusp of the apocalypse, he led his people in a failed armed rebellion.[66] Zhang Zhuo recounts the story:

> *Bai Tieyu was a Jihu from Yanzhou. He followed a sinister path and beguiled the masses. Formerly, deep in the mountains, he buried a golden bronze image beneath a cypress tree. When, after several years, grass had grown over it, he deceived the countryfolk, saying, "Last night, as I passed the foot of the mountain, I saw Buddha light." He laid out a huge vegetarian feast and divined an auspicious day to unearth the Saintly Buddha. When the time came, he gathered several hundred people and ordered them to dig in a location where the statue was not hidden. Therefore, they did not find it.*
>
> *He then exhorted them with the words, "Fine folks, if you do not offer donations with absolute sincerity, the Buddha cannot be seen." Because of this, men and women vied to contribute more than one million cash. They dug again at the site where Bai Tieyu had buried the statue and obtained the golden bronze image. The country folk believed it to be a Saint, and far and near they transmitted word of the wondrous discovery, so that there were none who did not wish to see it. Bai Tieyu then circulated rumor that those who looked upon the Saintly Buddha would have all of their maladies cured. Neighbors from hundreds of li away—old and young, gentlemen and ladies alike—went there. Bai Tieyu then took silken gauze of violet, purple, red, and yellow and wrapped it around the statue in several tens of layers. For a donation, those who gathered to see the image could strip away one layer. Only once a thousand swathes were removed was the statue revealed. Such a fraud continued for a year or two, as more and more countryfolk took refuge and submitted. In the end, Bai Tieyu staged a rebellion, assumed the title Luminous King, set up administrative offices, and killed senior subalterns, causing turmoil for several years. General Cheng Wuting was ordered to decapitate him. (3.73)*

Whereas the Jihu saw Bai Tieyu as a Buddhist savior and a hero—the second coming of Liu Sahe, whose rise occasioned an ethnic revival—from a Tang centrist perspective, he was a rabble-rouser who incited a rebellion less than 200 miles from the capital, Chang'an! Adhering to this perspective, *Court and Country* depicts Bai as a charismatic snake-oil salesman perpetrating a hoax. Building on the success of his fraud and fundraising and taking advantage of instability, the Jihu rebel fomented chaos until a Tang general quashed the movement. Consistent with this characterization, the account of Bai Tieyu in *Extensive Records* is relegated to the chapter on "Perpetrators of Hoaxes and Deceivers" (*guizha* 詭詐).[67]

THE SOUTHLAND

In the Tang literati imagination, the south was an exotic, malarial hinterland filled with curious, sensual, subtropical aboriginal peoples—dangerous, though not as threatening or martial as the Turks, Khitan, and Tibetans to the north and west. From this Sinocentric vantage, these southern barbarians were more primitive and less civil, their lives less regulated by ritual, their bodies tattooed, their teeth blackened, their hair unbound or sheared.[68] Cautioning about taking such accounts at face value, Erica Brindley has remarked on how, in traditional Chinese characterizations of southerners, "rhetoric, fantasy, misinformation, or error" may "reflect false or incomplete assumptions about the alien other."[69] Though the following passages are still colored by the "literati prism" that tends to casually exoticize the Other and embellish upon "strange" customs and practices,[70] Zhang Zhuo, having spent significant time in Lingnan, was better informed than most. About a decade after Wu Zhao's deposal and death, early in the reign of her grandson Xuanzong, Zhang was accused of administrative malfeasance and sentenced to death. His death sentence was commuted, and he was banished to Lingnan, where he remained for a number of years.

In the early Tang, southward migrations of agrarian settlers—under the military and administrative aegis of the political center—marked a continuation of Chinese imperial encroachment that dated back to the Han dynasty. "The Han Chinese war against the native peoples [of the south] was also a war against their environment, for the point of removing the non-Chinese peoples and settling Han on their lands was to transform the region into farms," Robert Marks observes, noting that Chinese settlers first learned from indigenous locals then honed techniques of wet-rice cultivation.[71] Control over the Southland during the early Tang and Wu Zhao's Zhou was tenuous; the region remained a wild and often lawless borderland.

Below is a sequence of four accounts from *Court and Country*, moving progressively further from the metropoles of Chang'an and Luoyang. The first involves the burial practices of the Man of the Wuxi region in modern-day southwestern Hunan,[72] with a rugged terrain of mountains and gorges, shot through with rivers, and set 200 miles south of the more civilized Yangzi River Valley. Man 蠻 (Liao 獠 is also used in Tang histories)—as mentioned above—is a generic Chinese term for southern aborigines or barbarians. Reflecting the tendency to bestialize the cultural Other, the character contains the radical for worm or insect (虫)! The second and third anecdotes feature, respectively, culinary and medicinal/funerary rites from Lingnan, the large region south of the Nanling peaks which includes modern-day Guangdong, Guangxi, and Annam in northern Vietnam. The final excerpt examines the marital customs in Champa, a kingdom in Southeast Asia where a female sovereign, Jayadevi, reigned contemporaneously with Wu Zhao.[73]

The first passage describes the distinct burial practices of the fierce and bellicose kingdom of Ba, a southerly realm in the Yangzi River Valley and gorges with roots in the Warring States era:

> *When a parent of the Man of the Five Rivers in the Wuxi region dies, the body is placed on a pavilion outside their village for three years before the burial. Family and relatives beat drums and sing along the road, then drink, banquet, dance, and stage plays for more than a month. The children of the deceased spare no expense to have a grand coffin fashioned, then select a site halfway up the sheer mountain slopes and carve a niche in the cliff for the burial. The coffin is suspended from the mountainside, its lofty height representing the extreme filiality of the offspring. But after the body is encoffined and installed, no further sacrifices or offerings are made for the rest of the descendants' lives. After performing these funerary rites for the first time, people don't eat salt for three years.* (2.40)

Even today, along the cliff faces in eastern Sichuan and in Hubei and Hunan, the remnants of some of these enduring burials are still visible, attesting to this regional custom.[74] Although the Man people may have been non-Sinitic, Zhang Zhuo recognizes that the core of this custom contains a germ of filial piety—the endeavor to revere one's deceased parents—even if the surrounding rituals were not familiar to Chinese funerary practices.

The next two passages are set in Lingnan, a region on the southern periphery of the Tang empire in modern-day Guangdong, Guangxi, and northern Vietnam:[75]

> *In Lingnan, the Liao people like "honey chirpers." When writhing newborn mice are pink and hairless, with their eyes still sealed, they are stuffed with honey, pinned to a plate, and laid out on the table, wriggling around and crying. When people pince them with bamboo chopsticks and chew on them, they make a chirping sound—hence the name "honey chirpers."* (2.41)

> *According to customs in Lingnan, when a member of the family is ill, people will first sacrifice a rooster or a goose to the spirits in order to cultivate blessings. If the sick person still doesn't recover, they will sacrifice a pig or a dog in order to pray for them. If they still don't recover, a great sacrifice of an ox, a pig, and a sheep is made to entreat the spirits. If the person still does*

THE FRONTIER AND BEYOND

not recover, the family assumes that their death is fated and no further prayers or sacrifices are made. Once a person dies, the family beats drums and clangs bells in their ancestral hall until the funeral concludes. When the sick person first dies, everyone congregates around the body, wailing and crying. (5.114–15)

In the first passage, Zhang Zhuo describes an exotic local dish in this remote hinterland—live, naked, newborn mice, stuffed with honey; the graphic imagery conjured in the description of this dish no doubt spurred him to include this passage in his collection. Edward Schafer speculates that this dish was "an aboriginal custom adopted by Chinese settlers."[76] In the second passage, reflecting shamanic practices popular in the region, an escalating series of animal sacrifices are used to cure a family member of a serious sickness or disease. While human and animal sacrifice had been part of burials in ancient and early China, by the seventh century, figurines and elaborate pictorial representations had long since replaced flesh-and-blood victims. The drums and bells that are part of the Lingnan funerary custom described seem to have been an integral part of funerary and burial practices in southeastern China; sets of drums and bells have been found in numerous burial sites in the region.[77] The noisy send-off for the soul of the deceased—with the wailing of mourners and the clanging of bells and drums—was a ceremonial practice shared with the Tang.

In the following, final passage, Zhang Zhuo primarily describes marital customs of Champa, a kingdom that rose in the seventh century in southern Vietnam and Cambodia. He also includes information on sartorial customs (or lack thereof) and hunting practices:

The country Champa is 500 li south of Huanzhou. According to their customs, when guests come, they lay a table serving betel nuts, dragon-brain fragrance,[78] mussels, and crabs. As their alcohol provokes lasciviousness, they usually only drink it with their wives in their own homes. Thus, when there is an honored guest and alcohol is served, the wife avoids them and vacates the premises. The people do not like others to see the sexual relations between husband and wife; in this respect, their customs are like those of China. People of this country do not wear clothes and laugh at those who do. They use neither salt nor iron implements. They use a crossbow that shoots bamboo arrows to hunt snakes and birds. (2.40)

Some details in Zhang's account conflicts with later accounts from the Tang histories: for instance, while Zhang contends that the people of Champa wear no clothing, the Tang histories record that they followed practices similar to those of the Cham kingdom of Lâm Ấp (192–629 AD) that fell in the early Tang, wearing a certain sort of cotton cloth. In the Tang histories, Champa had more than thirty cities, practiced elephant warfare, had a religion that commingled Buddhism and animistic spirits, and sought to dispel miasmal ethers with animal sacrifices.[79]

9

Religion and the supernatural world

HOWARD WECHSLER HAS REMARKED THAT, BY the early Tang, rulers "drew upon the newer legitimating values of Buddhism and Taoism in order to expand the conventional body of philosophico-religious legitimation that had previously been centered on Confucianism."[1] David McMullen seconds this sense of the Tang as a cosmopolitan, multidenominational era, remarking that "the transcendental faiths of Buddhism and Daoism also exerted claims on the emperor's commitment, time and resources."[2] On elite and popular levels, numerous cults developed around eminent Buddhist and Daoist figures in the pluralistic and multiethnic realm of seventh-century China.

Though Buddhism, Daoism, and Confucianism were collectively known as the "three teachings" (*sanjiao* 三教) in the Tang, an ideological rivalry existed between them. In the period—excepting clergy, monks, and adepts—a person did not identify as a Daoist, a Buddhist, or a Confucian the same way someone in contemporary times might consider themselves a Democrat or a Republican. On a folk level, these "three teachings" were intermingled and jumbled; on an elite, textual and scriptural level, they were differentiated.[3] Even literati and ministers might be "workday Confucians and weekend Daoists,"[4] escaping from the structured rigidity and tribulations of official life by wandering the hills, drinking wine on an open pavilion, writing free-flowing calligraphy, waxing poetic in inebriated company, or practicing Daoist breathing techniques to relax and prolong life. These same individuals might retreat to a Buddhist temple for prayer or hold a Buddhist mass for a deceased parent. Nonetheless, when wielding their calligraphy brushes in discursive combat, Confucian court officials—Zhang Zhuo was no exception—sometimes cast Daoists as charlatans and frequently skewered Buddhism as a wasteful and extravagant foreign religion. On the whole, Zhang Zhuo's attitude toward Daoism is much more open-minded and less skeptical than his biased perspective toward Buddhism.

A number of anecdotes in *Court and Country* reveal that Zhang Zhuo was not a stone-cold Confucian rationalist, impervious to folk superstitions and popular beliefs. Many accounts—not necessarily skeptical or dubious in tone—provide interesting insights into the practices of diviners, shamans, achillomancers, and interpreters of dreams. Other stories and snippets offer curious and distinctive glances into beliefs about the supernatural.

DAOISTS

In the first anecdote below, Zhang Zhuo represents Wu Zhao as a credulous septuagenarian ruler who placed her faith in the costly, ineffective decoctions of Daoist Hu Chao, a huckster peddling snake oil to the doddering and gullible sovereign:

> *In the Shengli era, monk Hu Chao of Hongzhou[5] left his home and became a recluse on White Crane Mountain and studied the Way. When he possessed some slight magical powers, he claimed that he was several hundred years old. Zetian ordered him to decoct a potion of longevity. Overall, it cost countless tens of thousands of cash and took three years. Hu Chao personally presented the potion at Sanyang Palace. Zetian swallowed it, taking it to be a divine and marvelous concoction that would make her as long-lived as Pengzu.[6] She changed the reign era to Jiushi in 700 and released Hu Chao from service to return to the mountains, rewarding him lavishly. Three years after she drank the decoction, Zetian passed away.* (5.116)

Like many rulers, Wu Zhao looked to Daoism. Zhang's representations of his dual targets—the easily deceived, extravagant female emperor and the guileful fraud of a Daoist—both validate the moral authority and centrality of Confucianism.

Wu Zhao's relationship with Daoism was conflicted. Daoism was the teaching most amenable to female power: celebrating the latent potency of the female water element, proclaiming the power vested in the mother, and urging a would-be Daoist ruler to adhere to "the role of the female."[7] However, Daoism was also the official state orthodoxy of the Tang dynasty, for her Li in-laws claimed founding Daoist sage Laozi (or Li Er 李耳) as a blood ancestor, linking him closely with Tang legitimation.[8] Thus, Daoism was difficult to reconcile with her own imperial aspirations. Indeed, at times during her regency and reign, Wu Zhao favored Buddhism and allowed subordinates to persecute Daoists.

Late in her reign, however—weary after a half-century of wrangling in court and having already decided to hand the empire back to her sons in the Li family—she began, like many senescent Chinese rulers before and after

RELIGION AND THE SUPERNATURAL WORLD

her, to seek recipes for longevity or immortality. These fell largely under the purview of Daoist medicine, and she sought counsel of men like Hu Chao. When Wu Zhao summoned him to the palace, Hu Chao was already widely known as a Daoist thaumaturge in the Southeast—destroying an evil camphor tree, miraculously revealing a cache of relics, and living to a venerable age. He also assisted Wu Zhao in a sacred Daoist rite of expiation called "tossing the dragons" (*tou long* 投龍) on Mount Song.[9] In casting Hu Chao as a simple charlatan, Zhang Zhuo thus gives short shrift to Hu's impressive resume as a ceremonial master and a miracle worker.

Another passage on Daoism from *Court and Country* relates the discovery of cryptic stone inscriptions carved by fifth-century Daoist master Kou Qianzhi on Mount Song, not far from Wu Zhao's Divine Capital, Luoyang:[10]

> *Celestial Master Kou Qianzhi attained the Dao in the later Wei. He often carved inscriptions into stones and concealed them on Mount Song. In the beginning of the Shangyuan era, while gathering medicinal herbs, a person from Gaocheng County in Luozhou prefecture discovered one and presented it to County Head Fan Wen, who, in turn, told the prefectural authorities, who reported to the emperor. Emperor Gaozong issued a proclamation that the inscribed stone would be stored in the Palace Treasury.*
>
> *There were many cryptic and abstruse inscriptions on the stone, including, in brief, "The sons of wood will take charge of the realm"; "Stop-halberds Dragon"; "The Li dynasty will represent; its ancestors shan't be moved"; "The Central Tripod will manifest the true face"; and "a foundation for ten million years."*
>
> *"The sons of wood will take charge of the realm" is a reference to the Tang dynastic family receiving the mandate. "Stop-halberds Dragon" means that the Grand Dowager will preside over the court—the characters "stop" and "halberd" are a rebus for Wu; Wu is the clan of the Celestial Empress. "The Li dynasty will represent; its ancestors shan't be moved" meant that Zhongzong would bring about a restoration of the Tang, a renewal of Heaven and Earth. In "The Central Tripod will manifest the true face," "Manifest" was the taboo name of Zhongzong and "True" was part of Ruizong's posthumous temple name. Is this not unbelievable? The "foundation" in "Foundation for ten million years" is the personal name of Xuanzong. "Ten million years" means that the dynasty will endure forever.*
>
> *When Zhongzong ascended to emperor, Fan Wen's son Fan Qinben presented a book of Celestial Master Kou's stone inscriptions. The emperor ordered that it be edited for inclusion in the dynastic records.*[11] (5.118)

According to Zhang Zhuo, these enigmatic snippets, discovered late in Gaozong's reign, foretold both Wu Zhao's ascendancy and the eventual restoration of the Tang dynasty. Other sources, including Dunhuang documents, corroborate Zhang Zhuo's claim as to the timing of this discovery.[12]

Many of Kou's cryptic fragments contain rebuses. For instance, "wood" (*mu* 木) and "son" (*zi* 子) are components of Li 李 (木 + 子 = 李), the surname of the imperial family that ruled the Tang; the Daoist master's remark that the "sons of wood will take charge of the realm" is thus a prognostication that the Li family would govern the empire. In the second rebus, the combination of "stop" (*zhi* 止) and "halberds" (*ge* 戈) form the character Wu 武 (止 + 戈 = 武)—Wu Zhao's surname, which, as Zhang Zhuo points out, can be understood as a prophecy of her future emperorship. This, Zhang Zhuo contends, shows that Kou Qianzhi predicted both the rule of the Li family that established the Tang and the ascendancy of the female emperor several hundred years in advance.

Zhang Zhuo goes on to explain that the other fragments from Kou Qianzhi anticipated the Tang restoration after Wu Zhao's deposal. For instance, in Kou's concise assertion that "The Central Tripod will manifest the true face," Zhang discovers evidence for the return of the Tang. Of course, interpreting this passage after the restoration has come to pass, Zhang has the advantage of hindsight. The tripod is a vessel that symbolized imperial authority. The character for manifest (*xian* 顯) is the same as that of Emperor Zhongzong's given name. The posthumous temple name of Zhongzong's younger brother and successor, Ruizong, Great Sage True August Sovereign (Dasheng zhen Huangdi 大聖真皇帝), included the character "true" (*zhen* 真), part of Kou's "true face."[13] Emperor Xuanzong's given name was Li Longji 李隆基. The second character in his given name, *ji* 基, meaning "foundation," was part of the Daoist master's prophetic inscription, "foundation for ten million years," which Zhang interprets to mean that the restored Tang will last for a long time.

A third anecdote on Daoists from *Court and Country* recounts an event from early in the storied career of celebrated miracle worker Ye Fashan, a third-generation descendant of Daoist masters. Ye lived for more than a century, consulting with four Tang emperors and Wu Zhao before reputedly ascending to become an immortal:[14]

> *Daoist Master Ye Fashan of Lingkong Monastery*[15] *would utter an incantation over his sword, then, with all his might, plunge the blade into the stomach of a sick person. Across the abdomen of the patient, he would place peach and willow branches; when he thrust the sword, the willow and peach branches would break, but internally the patient would remain unharmed. He also used twin swords to cut a woman in half. Blood was all over the ground; the family wept aloud. But when the Daoist put the two halves together, spurted water out of his mouth, and uttered an incantation, the woman fully recovered in no time.* (3.64)

This passage describes the rather violent somatic ceremonial elements and the interesting components involved in Ye's healing spell. This Great Offering ritual (*Dajiao* 大醮), performed to exorcise demons, may have been inspired by Vedic or Iranian fire rites (indeed, it shares certain elements with the Sogdian Zoroastrian rites in Chapter 8). Other sources show that when Ye publicly performed this ceremony, dozens of people—collectively bewitched by demons—leaped into the flames, but emerged unscathed and purged of the evil spirits that had possessed them.[16] Zhang Zhuo's account reveals no evidence of skepticism.

A half century later, Wu Zhao's son Zhongzong invited Ye Fashan into a palace chapel where Buddhist monks and Daoist adepts were debating which teaching was greater and more profound. Even after Ye ate a huge measure of walnuts, the Buddhists would not admit defeat. Therefore, the Daoist master picked up a white-hot overturned bowl with his bare hands and was about to place it on the head of a venerable Buddhist monk. Swearing at Ye and covering his head with his kasaya, the Buddhist monk scuttled off in defeat, prompting the emperor to clap his hands and erupt in peals of laughter (3.66–67).

A final passage features Ming Chongyan, a Daoist mystic whom the Two Sages hosted in their court late in Gaozong's reign:

> *Ming Chongyan possessed mystical divinatory powers. The Great Emperor*[17] *tested him by fashioning an underground chamber, where he had courtesans play music. He summoned Ming Chongyan and, when the mystic entered, Gaozong said, "I often hear such mysterious strains of music issuing from this ground. Can you tell me if it is auspicious?" Ming replied that it was indeed auspicious and pinned two peach charms on the ground above the hidden chamber. Suddenly there was silence. Gaozong laughed and summoned forth the courtesans. The girls said that they had seen two open-mouthed dragon's heads above and had been too terrified to continue. Gaozong was delighted.* (3.65)

With supernatural foresight, Ming deploys magical amulets to expose the emperor's elaborate efforts to trick him. Again, there is no indication that Zhang Zhuo questioned the veracity of the account. The peachwood talismans that Ming used were thought to be especially potent, with apotropaic powers.[18]

Several other passages in *Court and Country* attest to Ming Chongyan's extraordinary healing prowess and magical powers. When the wife of Liu Jing, an official in Sichuan, was suffering from a strange ailment that no one else could diagnose, Ming examined her and then announced that only a dragon's liver could cure her illness. He had Liu Jing put up a cooking pot, then drew several talismans that a wind carried up to the heavens. A dragon then descended and entered the cooking pot; the Daoist wizard cut out its liver. When it was prepared, Liu Jing's wife consumed it. Shortly thereafter, she recovered from her illness (3.65)! In another passage, at the height of summer, Gaozong had a yearning for snow and iced loquats and longans. In a blink of an eye, Ming Chongyan—not only a Daoist mystic but a fourth-ranked Grand Master of Remonstrance in the court of the Two Sages—improbably produced the snow and iced fruits! When the astounded emperor asked how he pulled it off, the Daoist answered, *"First I went to Lingnan to pick the fruit, then I headed off to Shady Mountains[19] to fetch the snow."* On another occasion, Gaozong had a hankering for melon in the fourth lunar month. Ming Chongyan asked him 100 cash, then disappeared. In an instant, he returned bearing a huge melon, which he said he had purchased from an old farmer tending a melon patch near Mount Kou. The incredulous sovereign then ordered subordinates to fetch the peasant and bring him to the palace. When he arrived, the melon farmer confirmed that Ming had purchased the melon for 100 cash! The magician had made the seventy-mile round trip in the blink of an eye (3.65–66).

Ming Chongyan was also a physiognomist. When the Two Sages questioned the Daoist magician about their children, he remarked that while their younger sons were graced with noble countenances, the visage of the Crown Prince revealed his lack of fitness for the throne. Shortly thereafter, Ming Chongyan was murdered. In the ensuing investigation, driven by Wu Zhao, a servant with whom the Crown Prince had an affair confessed that the Crown Prince had plotted the Daoist's murder. Later, hundreds of suits of black armor were discovered concealed in the Crown Prince's palace, evidence that many in court took to mean that he was plotting to usurp the throne. The Crown Prince was removed and eventually exiled to Sichuan, where he was quietly murdered several years later, shortly after his father's death.[20]

Another story in *Court and Country* offers an alternative account of Ming's death. One night when the Daoist mystic was seated alone in a meditation hall, Ming was pierced through the heart with a sword. Though the emperor ordered an urgent search immediately, no trace of the wrongdoers was found. Because of his reputation as a demon exorcist and ghostbuster, some people felt that he had been murdered by a demon. Zhang Zhuo concludes by quoting Confucius—*"The study of strange doctrines is injurious indeed!"*[21]—then remarking *"How true!"* (3.66). This explanation potentially suggests Zhang's conviction that Ming Chongyan brought about his own untimely end by plumbing the depths of the occult. Alternatively, if—as some apparently suspected when the mystic was murdered—the perpetrator was a demon rather than the Crown Prince, then Wu Zhao wrongly accused and killed the young man. Perhaps this is what Zhang Zhuo wishes to intimate.

BUDDHISTS

Wu Zhao was an ardent supporter of Buddhism. Remarking on her relationship with the Buddhist religion, French curator–historian René Grousset commented that "this wild woman turned out to be one of the most zealous protectors of the faith of Śākyamuni."[22] Zhang Zhuo, however, tended to denigrate Buddhism and Buddhist monks, casting both the faith and the faithful in a negative light. For instance, he depicted Xue Huaiyi, a Buddhist architect and abbot as well as a general, as little more than a male favorite and a scoundrel (see Chapters 1 and 3). Another passage in *Court and Country* recounts the conflagration that burned to the ground the unfinished sky-piercing Buddhist hall that Huaiyi had been charged with building (5.115–16).[23] Likewise, Jihu leader Bai Tieyu, who styled himself a faith healer and led a Buddhist uprising, Zhang represented as the perpetrator of an elaborate hoax (see Chapter 8). However, when the actions of Buddhists did not conflict with the dynastic interests of the Li family with whom Zhang's career ambitions were closely bound, he did not judge them in such a harsh manner.

In this first of five passages about Buddhists and Buddhism selected from *Court and Country*, Zhang introduces Master Ding, a quirky eccentric with whom Zhang is personally acquainted:

> *Divine Master Ding refused to tonsure his hair and wolfed bushels of bean paste down without a care. Whenever he went begging door to door, he wore whatever he was given, whether coarse cloth and raggedy clothing or fine brocades and elegant gauzy silks. Once, when he was listening to Master Li Zhen lecture, he asked, "Are the myriad things unchanging?" Li Zhen answered, "They are unchanging." Ding then said, "If you, Buddhist monk, claim they are unchanging, then why does the lofty precipice become a gorge and the deep abyss become a peak? Why do the dead live again and why do the living then perish? The myriad things are intertwined and the six paths of reincarnation revolve. How can this be called stable?"*
>
> *Li Zhen acknowledged, "Okay, the myriad things are not unchanging."*
>
> *Ding rebutted, "If they are not unchanging, why don't we call heaven earth and call earth heaven? Why not call the moon a star and call stars the moon? How can you claim they are not unchanging?"*
>
> *Zhen was left with no response.*
>
> *When Zhang Wencheng*[24] *met Ding, he remarked, "From what I observe, your conduct is like that of a bodhisattva."*
>
> *Ding answered, "A bodhisattva neither delights in gain, nor takes sorrow in loss. When struck, he does not grow angry; when cursed, he does not get irritated. This is the conduct of a bodhisattva. I, Ding, take delight when my begging yields something and feel sorrow when I get nothing. When someone strikes me, I get angry; when someone curses me, I grow irritated. Looking at it from this vantage, I'm far from a bodhisattva."* (6.131–32)

Master Ding questions Buddhist teachings on the changeability of the physical world and willingly acknowledges his own inability to attain the Buddhist ideal of overcoming one's emotions.

A second passage also focuses on this peculiar figure. Here, he is introduced to Wu Zhao by her daughter, the Taiping Princess, not because he was a Buddhist monk, but because of his capacious stomach:

> *In the era of Zetian, there was a man known as Master Ding heralding from Boye county in Yingzhou prefecture, who had a most peculiar talent. The Taiping Princess presented him to Zetian, who tested him. He raised a silver vessel filled with three dou of liquor and drained it in a single draught. The Taiping Princess also said, "He can eat a prodigious quantity of bean paste." Then she ordered a silver tureen filled with one dou of bean paste. Using a ladle, Master Ding finished it all in a trice. Zetian wished to confer upon him official rank, but Ding said, "I'd prefer to leave home and become an ascetic." Thereupon, Wu Zetian granted that his head be shaved. Later, when Wu Zhao was emperor, Master Ding said, "Maitreya put his hair up in a coil, the bodhisattva Guanyin left hair on his precious head. If I cultivate my conduct, why must I take the tonsure?" Subsequently, he let his hair grow. Wu Zetian ordered Zhang Qian[25] to punish him with 100 blows, but did not restrict his movements or vocation. After the punishment, there were neither wounds nor scars. None of the people of the time could fathom it. (3.66)*

Divine Master Ding's most striking talent was his voluminous ability to eat and drink, consuming thirty pints of liquor or ten pounds of bean paste at a sitting! Wu Zhao—carrying on a long tradition of retaining men with strange and unusual talents—wished to offer him a position, but Ding declined her offer and, citing Buddhist deities who had kept their hair, refused her request that he take the tonsure. This earned Master Ding a beating, though the redoubtable if unorthodox monk was left unscathed.

A third passage offers an account of the transformative power of the Buddhist faith:

> *In Shadymount County of Yuezhou prefecture there was a wise Chan Master. In his monastery there was a pool. He often redeemed living creatures and released them into its waters. However, a three-foot alligator often ate the pool's fish, which troubled the Chan master. He caught the gator and had it moved to the pool in front of a Temple of King Yu.[26] However, that night the gator returned to the Chan monastery. The Chan Master scolded, "If you don't eat my fish, you can stay here." Thenceforth, when the crocodile came out of the water to shit, there was only pure muck in his feces and so sign of fish. Whenever the Chan Master went to the pool, he called the alligator and it would emerge and come out onto the ground in front of him. Over several decades, it gradually grew to be seven or eight feet long. After the Chan master passed away, the alligator was never seen again. (Sup., 154)*

In the remote South, a pious abbot of a Chan monastery—Chan (known in Japan as Zen) was a sect of meditative Buddhism—adhered to the practice of "compassionate release of living beings" (*fangsheng* 放生). He would "redeem" fish and turtles from local markets and release them in a pool at

RELIGION AND THE SUPERNATURAL WORLD

his temple, where, as monks ate a vegetarian diet, these watery tribes would be spared. When the abbot discovered an alligator—a creature related to the dragon[27]—eating fish from the pond where these creatures were released, he scolded the creature, prompting it to change its nature and abstain from eating fish.

In another excerpt from *Court and Country*, Zhao Xuanjing from greater Luoyang finds himself with a magical wand of healing following an encounter with a mysterious Buddhist monk in the liminal space between near-death and the afterlife:

> *During the Ruyi era, Zhao Xuanjing of Luozhou died of illness but then revived five days later. He said, "I saw a Buddhist monk who offered me a stick of wood a little more than a foot long. The monk told me, 'If you encounter someone who is sick, simply touch them with this wand and they will instantly be cured.'" Awakening, Xuanjing found a wand a little more than a foot long, exactly like the one the monk had offered. He tried to use it to cure illnesses, and as soon as he touched a sick person with the wand, their condition immediately improved. Soon from every doorway and courtyard hundreds of people gathered before his gate to seek help. Concerned that he was inciting the masses, Censor Ma Zhiji took him into custody. The sick then thronged the gates of the Censorate.*
>
> *Zetian learned of this and summoned Zhao into the palace, where one of the female attendants had fallen ill. As soon as Xuanjing touched her with the wand, the sick woman instantly recovered. Zetian then released him, giving him the duty of going among the common people and healing the sick. Within several months he accumulated seven hundred strings of cash. After that, the wand slowly lost its efficacy and people stopped seeking him out.* (1.3)

In this passage we see—in Censor Ma's arrest of the man—the state's fear that popular religion could inflame and confuse the masses. The state sanctioned official Buddhism and Daoism, registering and to some degree controlling monks and monasteries. Popular religion was less regulated; when local tutelary deities or cults became too powerful, they were branded "licentious cults" (*yinci* 淫祠) or "heterodox teachings" (*xiejiao* 邪教) and suppressed, or else they were coopted. Thus, hearing wind of the fellow's burgeoning fame as a healer, Wu Zhao summoned him to the palace where the wand once again showed its miraculous power. As emperor, Wu Zhao determined that—unlike Bai Tieyu in the previous chapter—Zhao Xuanjing was using his power in a more-or-less constructive and non-threatening fashion that did not undermine the stability of the state; she therefore allowed him to continue his practice, amassing a small fortune in the process, until his wand ran out of charges.

The last passage features a mysterious woman from the northeastern part of the empire whose body is tattooed with Buddhist temples and Buddhas:

> *In the Jinglong era of the Tang, a woman from Yingzhou prefecture was presented to court. Faint outlines of Buddhist temples and all of the Buddhas were visible on her body. The Surveillance Commissioner[28] who presented her was awarded fifth rank. The woman remained in the Palace Chapel. After the death of Traitor Wei, her whereabouts were unknown.* (5.115)

The woman was presented in the court as human tribute a few years after Wu Zhao's death. She was kept in the palace chapel, within the precincts of the inner sanctum of the imperial palace, before disappearing after a coup in 710.[29]

Wu Zhao's celebration of the Buddhist Lantern Festival goes awry!

In Chapter 5, the Buddhist Lantern Festival—held on the 14th, 15th, and 16th of the first lunar month—is mentioned as an important seasonal festival that punctuated the lives of the common people. This open festival broke down barriers between men and women, between rich and poor. Drawing on Japanese Monk Ennin's accounts from the late Tang, modern historian Kenneth Chen describes this holiday:

> The city portals ordinarily closed between eight at night and four in the morning, with travel restricted. [...] At the time of the festival, however, these portals remained open all night by imperial order, and the streets were illuminated by thousands of torches carried by people roaming the streets around the city. Even the emperor would go out and view the procession of torches and lanterns, and he often permitted the inhabitants of the capitals to take a vacation from their usual duties to participate.[30]

In conjunction with one of her alleged male favorites, Xue Huaiyi, Wu Zhao hosted the Lantern Festival in late 694, a grand event featuring Buddhist miracles and vegetarian feasts.[31] Zhang Zhuo records its dramatic unraveling in *Court and Country*:

> *In the first year of the Verification of Sagehood reign era of the Zhou dynasty, Master Xue, surnamed Huaiyi, constructed a Hall of Merit of 1000 chi to the north of the Bright Hall. Inside was a great statue 900 chi in height. Its nose was like a 1000-hu boat and could contain twenty or thirty people seated together. It was made with inserted hemp and lacquered.[32] On the fifteenth day of the first month,[33] the Pancavarsika began at the audience hall. The ground was excavated five zhang deep, and silk was unraveled to make palaces and halls, terraces and pavilions. Bamboos were bent to form the womb, stretching out to form a canopy of supports. Buddhist statues were also fashioned of precious, obdurate metals, and raised from the pit. It was falsely claimed that they had emerged from the earth. Master Xue*

RELIGION AND THE SUPERNATURAL WORLD

also bled an ox and drew the head of the Buddha, some 200 chi *in height. It was deceitfully said that blood from Master Xue's knee had been used to render the image. Observers of these Buddhist miracles filled the city walls, as men and women thronged. Master Xue took cartloads of money from within the palace and threw it to them. In the ensuing chaos, people trampled one another. There was more than one death among the elderly and children. On the sixteenth, the blood-drawn Buddha image was stretched out to the south of Heaven's Ford Bridge, and a vegetarian feast was laid. On the second watch that evening, a fire broke out at the Hall of Merit and spread to the Bright Hall. The soaring blaze mounted to the Heavens. By night, Luoyang was as bright as day. His hall was not yet half completed, but was already more than 70* chi *tall. The fire also spread to consume the Gold and Silver Workshop warehouses.*[34] *Iron melted and flowed like liquid, pooling on flat ground more than a foot deep. People who didn't know and mistakenly entered were then scorched to a crisp. The ritual hall was burnt to ashes, so that not even one* chi *of wood remained. When dawn arrived, then a feast was laid once again. But a violent wind suddenly rose up and tore the 200* chi *Buddha image into hundreds of shreds.*[35] (5.115–16)

Overseeing the Lantern Festival, Wu Zhao ritually opened her arms to embrace the throngs. She styled herself the host of hosts, the king of kings, emceeing a marvelous show. Surrounded by a pageant of colored silk, the common people of Luoyang rubbed elbows with the mighty as they filled their bellies with vegetarian delicacies. Entertained by the frenzied tumult precipitated by scattered cash, their spirits buoyed by the spectacle of Buddhas rising from the earth, these people felt that they had a proprietary stake in the social order. They were allowed into the inner sanctum, the Palatine City!

However, things went terribly awry. A multitude of torches amid this chaotic festal scene of bacchanal celebration staged around wood and stone architecture made fires a legitimate danger.[36] The occasion devolved into a fiery disaster that burned down Wu Zhao's ritual center and, according to Zhang Zhuo, led to a number of deaths. This is not the entire passage. Zhang Zhuo appends a personal commentary at the end:

Master Who Drifts then Rests remarked, "When Liang Wudi offered himself up at Tongtai Temple, all the court officials emptied the treasuries in order to ransom him. That night there was suddenly lightning and thunder, a thick darkness of wind and rain. The temple's pagoda and Buddhist halls were completely destroyed. How is it possible that this incomprehensible event could be the original intent of the Maitreya Buddha?" (5.116)

The point of this observation—which concerns inclement weather destroying a pagoda and Buddhist halls when Liang Wudi hosted a similar festival a century and a half earlier—appears to be that when unworthy rulers like Wudi or Wu Zhao stage theatrical Buddhist rites, just Heaven visits ruinous disaster.

A few decades before the Tang, a Confucian court official, chastising Sui emperor Wendi and urging that this open, free-wheeling Buddhist holiday be banned, warned of the dire corrupting and deleterious moral influence of this event that allowed the sexes to commingle amid such vertiginous festal din.[37] In the aftermath of the fire, a Confucian court minister—his logic anticipating Zhang Zhuo's—warned that Wu Zhao must respond appropriately to Heaven's fiery censure and cancel the rest of the festival.[38] The "Treatise on Rites and Ceremonies" in the *Old Tang History* corroborates the fact that on the occasion of the fire, "[d]espite the fact there were no clouds, thunder rose in the northwest."[39] This guttural growl from above, foreshadowing the conflagration that destroyed Wu Zhao's Buddhist ritual center, was understood to reflect Heaven's disapprobation.

Court and Country also provides a description of the Lantern Festival in Chang'an two decades later under Wu Zhao's son, Ruizong:

> *Emperor Ruizong, on the evenings of the fifteenth and sixteenth of the first lunar month of the second year of Xiantian, had a two-hundred-foot lantern wheel constructed outside the gate of Peace and Prosperity in the capital. It was covered with silk and adorned in gold and jade; 50,000 lamps burned, cluster together so that it seemed like a flowering tree. Made up with halcyon and fragrant rouge, a thousand silk-clad palace ladies were in attendance. A single floral headdress or mantle was worth 10,000 cash; to outfit each of these women cost 300,000 cash. 1000 of the most beautiful girls from Chang'an and Wannian counties had been selected for the occasion, all with identical coiffures, decked out in matching garments and hair clasps. For three days and nights, they performed stomping songs at the foot of the lantern wheel. Never before had such a zenith of revelry been reached.*[40] (3.69)

This description of the visual and audible festal spectacle provides a sense of an imperially sponsored holiday entertainment that, in the dead of the harsh Chang'an winter, might add color and excitement to the lives of the common people. While Zhang Zhuo is very critical of Wu Zhao's Buddhist extravagance and excess, there is a curious lack of critical voice in this commentary on Ruizong's celebration of the Lantern Festival.

YIN–YANG MASTERS, PHYSIOGNOMISTS, ACHILLOMANCERS, AND PIPA DIVINERS

Because Zhang Zhuo was far more interested in racy or bizarre stories and anomalies than in orthodox and routine religious practices, *Court and Country* contains a number of stories about curious popular and folk practices that do not fit neatly under the purview of the "three teachings": Confucianism, Buddhism, and Daoism. While Paul Kroll has remarked upon "the gradually diminishing place in refined culture of mantic arts" in medieval China,[41]

RELIGION AND THE SUPERNATURAL WORLD

Zhang Zhuo's work indicates that, on both popular and elite levels, there was a rich and widespread interest in a diverse range of divinatory practices.

Robert Campany observes that, in an uncertain and chaotic world, divination provides a sense of control and reduces anxiety "by moving across a cosmic, ontological, and epistemological boundary, bringing information into human space where it can be used to advantage."[42] People sought guidance from diviners to make sense of the fluctuations and perils they encountered. There were numerous techniques used to divine the future in medieval China: assessing the ebb and flow of *yin* and *yang* ethers; scrutinizing physiognomy; analyzing cryptic verses or riddles (a skill which Daoist master Kou Qianzhi, above, possessed); reading cracks in tortoise shells; drawing yarrow stalks; interpreting dreams; or prognosticating based on the strains of one's *pipa* lute.

The account below draws upon Zhang Zhuo's personal experience with *yin–yang* divination. This kind of divination examines variations in the flow or fluctuation of *yin* and *yang* ethers and changes in the five elements as a basis for predicting future events. Different manuals existed as guides to facilitate these prognostications. Zhang was familiar with *yin–yang* manuals and his family consulted *yin–yang* diviners. In *Court and Country*, he locates correspondences between two seemingly routine events on his family estate—his own excavation of a pit as a young child and the death of a mulberry tree—and *yin–yang* divinatory predictions, one from a manual and one from a diviner:

> *In the Yonghui era,*[43] *when Zhang Zhuo's family was building a horse stable and mangers, to its due north he excavated a hole more than ten feet deep. The* Book of Yin and Yang *said that when a child digs a hole in the earth it was a sign someone would fall into a well and die. Zhang Zhuo had a servant named Yong Jin who was digging a well when the earth collapsed and killed him.*
>
> *Zhang Zhuo's family had a mulberry tree that was 40 or 50 feet tall near their estate. Without reason, it withered and died. Soon thereafter, his grandfather perished. Later a clever* yin *and* yang *master said, "After the great tree withers, the sons invariably will be left alone." This confirms the omen.* (6.145)

In both cases, the passages emphasize that the prophecies proved accurate, suggesting that Zhang found *yin–yang* divination to be a credible practice.

Indeed, with the advantage of hindsight, Zhang Zhuo himself plays the role of *yin–yang* diviner in a brief, subsequent passage, characterizing the final months of Wu Zhao's rule as a gloomy, overcast time when the realm was eclipsed by *yin* (female, dark) ethers:

> *Beginning in the tenth month of the fourth year of Chang'an, under* yin *gloom rain and snow fell; for more than 100 days, the stars were obscured. Then, in the first month of the new lunar year, Zhang Yizhi, Zhang Changzong, and others were killed. Zetian was deposed.* (1.20)

Zhang Zhuo implies that the realm brightened with the coup that killed the Zhangs and deposed Wu Zhao.

Physiognomy, prognostication based on facial features and expressions, was also a long-established divination practice. One of the Tang histories contains the story of celebrated physiognomist Yuan Tiangang visiting Wu Zhao's household and seeing her when she was a mere toddler:

> When Wu Zetian was still in a swaddling quilt, physiognomist Yuan Tiangang came to her home to examine the family's features and tell fortunes. At the time, Wu Zetian's wet nurse held her, clad in boy's clothing. Tiangang pronounced, "This young gentleman has a divine countenance, one that is difficult to fathom. Let me see him walk." Wu Zetian then walked in front of him, and, at Yuan's request, raised her eyes. Stunned, Tiangang exclaimed, "This boy has the pupils of a dragon and the neck of a phoenix—presages of supreme honor!"[44]

Physiognomy evidently augured better for Wu Zhao than *yin–yang* divination!

Another vignette from *Court and Country* shows that there were already guides and manuals on physiognomy by the seventh century:

> In the Zhou, Madame Zhao, beautiful concubine of Court Gentleman Pei Gui, once went to diviner Zhang Jingzang to prognosticate her future. Zhang said, "Madame, your eyes are elongated and your gaze unrestrained. According to manuals of physiognomy, such swine-like eyes reflect lasciviousness. Your Ladyship's pupils have four whites; five men have their eyes on your residence. In the end, you may be banished for adultery. Be heedful!"
>
> Madame Zhao laughed and departed. Later, as predicted, she entered into an adulterous liaison and was cast out of the Zhao household. (1.1)

Zhang Zhuo may have included this account as further evidence that Wu Zhao's Zhou era was fraught with gender anarchy, citing anecdotal evidence of "lascivious" Madame Zhao, a woman predisposed to contravene Confucian norms—her bestial nature betrayed by her "swine-like eyes."

This was not Zhang Jingzang's only prognostication recorded in *Court and Country*. In the passage below, he demonstrates that, in addition to his skill at physiognomy, he possesses a facility with prognostic verses (*yao* 謠):

> In the Tang, when Duke of Ying Xu Ji initially divined a burial date and site, a prognostic ballad circulated that went, "When the vermillion sparrow sings harmoniously, sons and grandsons will flourish and prosper." Zhang Jingzang heard this and secretly told someone, "The prognostication was wrong. The so-called vermilion sparrow is grieving and lamenting because its coffin will be reduced to ash." Later, the Duke of Ying's grandson Jingye rebelled in Yangzhou and his brother Li Jingzhen admitted, "When Jingye was born, a turtle was found while digging in the rushes. People said it was a sign of great future eminence.[45] The

RELIGION AND THE SUPERNATURAL WORLD

Duke of Ying ordered that it should be kept secret and never spoken of, as it symbolized a great rebellion." Wu Zetian was furious. At her behest, the Duke of Ying's coffin was exhumed and chopped to splinters; his body was burned. This was the fulfillment of Jingzang's prediction of "ash."[46] (Sup., 165–66)

Li Ji had risen to become a successful general. The conquest of Koguryo in North Korea was the culminating moment of his long and storied military career—he had served under Tang founder Gaozu, Taizong, and Gaozong. He died shortly thereafter. Around the time of his death, a prophetic ditty circulated that many understood as a prediction of the ascending eminence of the descendants of this triumphant general. Drawing on his powers of prognostication, Zhang Jingzang—a quarter century before he studied the physiognomy of Madame Zhao—anticipated that this particular verse missed the target; he made a separate prediction, which, unfortunately for Li Ji's scions, was on target. The general's grandson, Li Jingye, led a rebellion against Wu Zhao when she took control of the court as Grand Dowager in 684. After it was quashed, this entire branch of the Li family was eradicated, and their family name changed to Xu.[47] Moreover, when Wu Zhao learned that the once-revered general had kept a prediction of his grandson's prospective ascendancy quiet, she exhumed and burned his coffin!

Court and Country also provides examples of one of the most ancient forms of divination in China: achillomancy, a form of prognostication using yarrow stalks. Diviners referenced oracles defined by the hexagrams in the *Book of Changes* based upon the count of yarrow wands. According to Zhang Zhuo, occultist Zu Zhenjian practiced this form of divination late in the joint rule of the Two Sages:

In the Xianheng era, Zu Zhenjian of Zhaozhou mastered the occult arts. He could cut the rope of a water-filled earthenware crock suspended from the joists of a building, and the vessel would not fall. Once, he placed an earthenware crock of water in a tightly sealed empty room with a sword on top, its blade up. After a while, out of curiosity, someone opened the door and discovered the crock full of blood and Zu dismembered in five pieces. The person ran to get help and returned to discover Zu, the crock, and the sword all back to normal. In the coldest part of winter, a rice mortar was frozen to the ground; with an incantation, he pulled it loose. Selling divinatory prognostications in Xindu,[48] *he could make 100 strings of cash a day. He said he employed the method used by Han dynasty mystic Zhuang Junping! Later, someone accused him of wrongdoing. As he was bound and dragged to the marketplace to be beheaded, his face and complexion remained unchanged, showing neither fear nor dread. When brush and paper arrived for him to write his last will, he received them unflustered.* (3.64)

In addition to other mystical powers, this anecdote contends that Zu employed the same methods as Daoist diviner Zhuang Junping, who had lived back in the Western Han; Zhaung was a master of yarrow divination, following the technique based on the *Book of Changes*.[49]

A second passage involving achillomancy features Du Jingquan, who was a strong voice of remonstrance unafraid of confronting Wu Zhao. In 694, when she plucked an unseasonable autumnal pear blossom, other ministers sought to curry favor by praising its auspiciousness. Du alone opined, "Now, though most vegetation has withered and fallen, this branch has flowered. *Yin* and *yang* are out of kilter and the fault lies with us ministers!"[50] Wu Zhao demoted this outspoken minister on several occasions. Du survived his demotion to Zhenzhou (Chongqing), but a few years later, having been reappointed Minister of Justice, he committed a further offense—allegedly leaking state secrets—and was demoted to be prefect of Wu Zhao's home prefecture of Bingzhou to the north. He became ill and died along the route.[51] This account from *Court and Country* provides some details of the circumstances leading up to his death:

> *Du Jingquan of Xindu was originally known as Yuanfang. During the Chuigong era, he changed his name to Jingquan. Unyielding and straightforward, serious and upright, he passed the civil service exam to become a presented scholar. Later he was promoted to chief minister and member of the Simurgh Terrace.*[52] *At this time, Royal Secretary Li Zhaode had been imprisoned because of his resolute directness. In court, Jingquan argued that Li was public-minded and incorruptible, upright and direct. Taking his words as an affront to her face, Wu Zhao was furious and demoted Jingquan to Prefect of Zhenzhou. When he was initially assigned to Zhenzhou,*[53] *he encountered an excellent achillomancer along the route, who said that Jingquan would again reach third rank and be appointed chief minister, yet would not don the long purple gown. At the end of that summer, wearing the lesser purple robes of a military official, he passed away.*[54] (1.1–2)

The cryptic pronouncements of the achillomancer proved prophetic; though Du would once again reach the third rank, he would never again wear the long purple gown of a chief minister.

Another passage in *Court and Country* describes the inauspicious appearance of a shooting star on the eve of Du's embarkment to Bingzhou:

> *When Minister of Justice Du Jingquan was demoted to Prefect of Bingzhou, he was slated to travel to his appointment by post-horse relay. That night, a large, dipper-shaped shooting star descended in front of his courtyard but disappeared when it reached the earth. When Jingquan reached the border of Qi County in Bingzhou, he died. The group of local officials who came to greet him mourned his passing. On the return trip, they used the food they had brought to banquet him as sacrificial offerings.* (6.145)

The dire prognostic utterance of the achillomancer and the ill-omened falling star both anticipated the demise of unfortunate Du Jingquan. This final

RELIGION AND THE SUPERNATURAL WORLD

passage also shows that, in instances not involving Wu Zhao, Zhang Zhuo was not necessarily skeptical of omens.

The practice of oneiromancy, divination based on dreams, also has a long history in China. In his study on dreams in early and medieval China, Robert Campany notes that dreams are not directly interpreted; rather, they serve as representations, simulacra, or symbols that have tangible correlatives or counterparts in the real world. By the Tang, "dreambooks," guides to aid in these interpretations, were an established resource. According to such sources, a dream of ascending skyward presaged the birth of a noble child, while the disappearance of the sun and moon was highly inauspicious.[55] There were also specialists, diviners who interpreted dreams, oneiromancers able to connect the dots, linking the dreamscape to the quotidian world. Campany goes on to observe that "a great many dream interpretations centered on wordplay, [...] substituting homophones for the words for things seen in dreams."[56]

This sort of dream interpretation has already been mentioned in Chapter 2—in the passage from *Court and Country* where chief minister Di Renjie deciphers Wu Zhao's dream of a parrot—although the substitution of homophone is only part of the interpretation in that case. The following account from *Court and Country* also features dream divination:

> *When he came of age, the son of official Chen Anping took the examination. Chen invited local diviner Immortal Medicine Li over to his household to find out how his son had fared. With the diviner staying over that night, Chen Anping's son dreamt that he was raising silkworms in the eleventh month. Immortal Medicine Li prognosticated and pronounced, "Raising silkworms in the eleventh month means 'winter silk.' Thus, Your Lordship will definitely be appointed to the eastern offices." Several days later, as predicted, he received an appointment to the Eastern Capital's offices.* (3.60)

The oneiromancer—identifying the homophony between the "winter silk" (*dongsi* 冬絲) of the eleventh-month silkworms that appeared in the dream and the "eastern offices" (*dongsi* 東司) where ministers were staffed in the Eastern Capital, Luoyang—correctly interpreted the son's dream as an intimation of the future success of a promising examination candidate.

Two additional passages from *Court and Country*—both featuring Zhang Zhuo's personal encounters—provide a glimpse into another form of divination utilizing a *pipa* lute. In the initial passage, Zhang—referring to himself by his nom de plume, Master Who Drifts then Rests—accomplishes in a single day what a bevy of local witches, shamans, Buddhist monks, and Daoist adepts cannot:

> *When the Master Who Drifts then Rests was a local official in Changping County of Dezhou,[57] there was a massive drought. Local authorities called for all of the local witches, shamans, and Daoist and Buddhist monks to pray for rain, but, after more than 20 days,*

the drought continued. The Master Who Drifts then Rests then pushed over the idol of an earthen dragon, and that very night rain fell.

There are no physicians in the Yangzi and Huai River valleys; rather, people believe in ghosts and demons, and, when they are sick, they make sacrificial offerings to them. Once when passing through this Jiangnan region with another official named Guo, the Master Who Drifts then Rests stopped in Hongzhou for several days and heard from the locals talk of an old diviner, Grannie He, who excelled in prognosticating with her pipa. When they went to investigate, the gate to Grannie He's residence was crowded with men and women. The path was clotted with gifts of food for Grannie, who simply sat with a cheerful air and a lofty expression. Guo then paid his respects and offered her strings of cash, asking about his family's future official rank and status. Strumming her pipa, in a warm voice Grannie He said, "You, sir, have an air of wealth and nobility. This year you will obtain first rank; next year, second rank; the following year, third rank; and the year after that, fourth rank." Guo responded, "Grannie He, you have it all wrong! The lower the number, the higher the rank; the higher the number the lower the rank." The diviner said, "This year you will lose one rank, next year you will lose two ranks, the year after you will lose three ranks, the following year you will lose four ranks, and in the end, after five or six years, you'll have no rank at all." Guo cursed her loudly and stormed off! (3.63)

Zhang Zhuo succeeds, the first section of the passage suggests, due to his contempt for heterodox folk superstitions: as soon as he topples the local earthen idol of the Dragon King, timely rains fall. By contrast, the practitioner of lute divination in the second part of this same passage, Grannie He, is presented as a theatrical fraud, a yokel with no conception of how court rank works; thinking that ninth rank is higher than first, she errantly congratulates a customer on his future demotions![58] Grannie He's dulcet tones and complaisant air may deceive locals in Jiangnan, but Zhang Zhuo and his traveling companion quickly expose her.

Plying her trade in a ward in the capital, the female lute diviner in the passage below is clearly much more sophisticated than Grannie He:

In the Chongren Ward, Grannie Lai strummed the pipa and offered divination. All of the purple and vermilion-clad elites and nobles clustered around her gate. Master Who Drifts then Rests once went to observe her and saw an imposing purple-clad general, girded with a jade-belt, offering her finely embroidered silk and requesting that she divine his future. Burning incense and closing her eyes, Grannie Lai strummed her pipa and sang, "May the spirits from the east announce the eastern quadrant, the spirits from the west announce the western quadrant, the spirits from the south announce the southern quadrant, the spirits from the north announce the northern quadrant, the spirits from above announce the upper quadrant, and the spirits from below announce the lower quadrant." With utmost ceremony and respect, the general explained his circumstances in some detail and asked what was necessary to anticipate the future in order to avoid uncertainties. Subsequently, the general fell under her control and acted in accord with her wishes. (3.64)

Instead of easily impressed Jiangnan locals, Grannie Lai's clientele are nobles, court ministers, and generals from Chang'an. Chongren Ward, where she plied her trade, is located to the immediate east of the Imperial City. Civil service examination candidates were housed in this bustling quarter;[59] anxious about their results, they no doubt sought Grannie Lai's services. The fact that the esteemed general fell under her sway suggests that her prognostications proved accurate and helpful. Stephen Kory points out that this account leaves the reader "with a positive impression. Perhaps Zhang approves of Granny Lai's abilities to scrutinize and resolve doubts because he really thought they were marvelous, or perhaps it is because of the company she kept."[60] For Zhang Zhuo, Grannie Lai's highborn and high-ranking clients clearly helped lend veracity and authority to her mystical and magical capabilities.

DUPLICITOUS SORCERERS AND FALSE FAITH HEALERS

There is a rich if inglorious history of tricksters and perpetrators of hoaxes availing themselves of folk superstitions to become cultic leaders or to gain the confidence of credulous rulers and thus gain access to circles of power. Referring to the following passage from *Court and Country*, contemporary scholar Luo Manling counts Li Cide among the "religious frauds" (*zongjiao pianzi* 宗教騙子) in Zhang Zhuo's text, placing him in the company of Dragon-son Liu (see below) and the Buddhist monk Huifan:[61]

> *In the Dazu era, bewitcher and deceiver Li Cide claimed he could design amulets and draw hexes. Zetian installed him in a position in the inner palace. He claimed that he could spread beans on the ground that became soldiers and horses, and draw lines on the ground that became streams and rivers. Colluding with an official with whom he was close, he sharpened bamboo into spears, used bundles of quilting as armor, and fomented an uprising at third watch*[62] *in the inner palace. In the confusion, twelve or thirteen female palace attendants were killed. Forest of Plumes*[63] *General Yang Xuanji heard the ruckus and shouts and ordered his soldiers to hack down the gate and enter. They killed Li Cide and several dozen young eunuchs. Ah, such a pity! Li Cide's wicked spellcasting helped him rise to become a retainer of the mighty, and his wicked spellcasting led to his funeral!* (3.66)

In *Extensive Records*, this story is placed in the category of *huanshu* 幻術—a broad category that encompasses the arts of sorcery, conjury, illusion, or deception.[64] The story of Li Cide is also intended to make manifest Wu Zhao's abysmal judgment in bringing a reckless and unprincipled sorcerer into the inner palace; it is an indictment of the ruler and the era over which she presided. In the passage, Zhang Zhuo exposes the conjuror as a fraud who works with a collaborator to recruit and dress young eunuchs as soldiers and fashion weapons and armor inside the palace, ultimately staging a coup. Faced with imperial bodyguards, these "supernatural" forces summoned by Li Cide were promptly subdued.

As with Li Cide, Zhang Zhuo explicitly characterizes Dragon-son Liu as a fraud:

> *In the time of Emperor Gaozong, Dragon-son Liu used beguiling words to confuse the masses. He fashioned the head of a golden dragon and concealed it in his sleeve. A length of sheep's intestine filled with honey water was fastened and wrapped around it. Whenever a crowed would gather, he would take out his dragon's head and claim, "If you drink the water disgorged by this divine dragon, all your maladies can be cured." Thereupon, he would twist the sheep's intestine, causing water to spurt from the dragon's mouth, and then give it to the people to drink. Deceived throngs all said that their illnesses had improved and contributed offerings of cash beyond reckoning. Thereafter Liu conspired to rebel, fleeing when the plot was discovered. After a long search to arrest him, Liu was captured. He was beheaded in the marketplace along with a dozen or so of his adherents.* (3.71)

This account contends that Dragon-son Liu rigged a sheep's intestine in his sleeve to spurt supposedly magical healing nectar from the mouth of a metal dragon, a gimmick that gained him a wide base of followers and copious wealth. *Extensive Records* places him in the chapter on "Perpetrators of Hoaxes and Deceivers."[65] The *New Tang History* tersely records that in the fifth lunar month of 681, Dragon-son Liu staged a short-lived rebellion in Changzhou. It was quashed; he was killed.[66] In literati sources and state histories, the common people are always depicted as easily led astray by the beguiling words of hoaxsters and frauds—false faith healers taking advantage of the credulity of peasant-farmers, with their belief in popular religion and the supernatural, to make profit and stir up trouble. The willingness of people to place their confidence and faith in men like Dragon-son Liu suggests that he was attuned to local beliefs and circumstances and offered locals something that the state did not. As noted above, Zhang Zhuo tends to relegate such individuals, who the state deemed rebels, to the category of dangerous and duplicitous charlatans, whereas he is far more likely to find credible the monks, healers, miracle workers, and magicians who worked with the literati and the powerful.

FURTHER OMENS OF THE DEMISE OF XU JINGYE

In the section on divination above, we have seen that physiognomist and prognosticator Zhang Jingzang foretold the demise of Xu Jingye, the grandson of great early Tang general Li Ji who rebelled against Wu Zhao in 684 after she seized control of the court as grand dowager. *Court and Country* contains several additional passages containing prophecies that indicate that this Yangzhou Rebellion of 684 was destined for failure:

> *When Xu Jingye raised soldiers, a great star puffed up like a great bamboo basket. After three nights it disappeared. Soon, Jingye was defeated.* (6.145)

> *Mingtang Recorder*[67] *Luo Binwang's composition "The Imperial Capital" contains the lines "Rapidly, braving the winds, I sprout wings and soar. Yet in an instant, I am lost in the waves, abandoned in the mucky sands." Luo Binwang joined Xu Jingye when he raised an army in Yangzhou. When the army was routed, he leapt into a river and drowned. In his verse, he prophesied his own demise!* (1.11)

Like the shooting star that served as a harbinger of the death of Du Jingquan (described earlier), a nova, an exploding star lighting up brilliantly before fading to darkness, in the initial passage serves as both metaphor and prophecy, foretelling the abrupt end of Xu Jingye's ill-fated uprising.

The second passage involves one of Xu Jingye's co-conspirators, poet–official Luo Binwang. In 684, the rebels at Yangzhou, a commercial node along the Yangzi, took an oath to "expunge the she-demon scourge" (*qing yao nie* 清妖孽).[68] Luo Binwang, one of the "Four Paragons" of early Tang poetry, was one of Xu Jingye's most ardent backers and a fierce rhetorical critic of Wu Zhao. He wrote a biting polemic damning Wu Zhao and questioning her legitimacy:

> Miss Wu, who has falsely usurped authority to run the court, is by nature cold and unyielding, by birth lowly and obscure. [...] Innately jealous, her moth-like eyebrows allow other women no quarter. All embroidered sleeves and artful slander, her vulpine glamour beguiled the ruler. Beneath her pheasant's plumage, the former Empress Wang was trampled. This musky doe once plunged my true Sovereign into rutting frenzy, vying with his own father. Her heart is half viper and half chameleon. Her disposition is that of a ravenous jackal or wolf. [...] She is hated by men and spirits alike! Neither Heaven nor Earth can stand her![69]

Luo Binwang's graphic animal imagery paints Wu Zhao as bestial and cold-blooded, an odious creature with utter contempt for human ethics. Despite these oaths and rhetoric, the rebellion failed to drum up widespread support and was summarily routed by imperial armies. A verse from one of Luo's poems, "The Imperial Capital," written years before the rebellion, describes wild, high-soaring ambitions that end with a plunge into the mire; Zhang Zhuo points out that these lines serve as a prophetic mirror to Luo's death, since the thwarted rebel flung himself into a river as the failed uprising was crushed.

MORE STRANGE TALES FROM THE SUPERNATURAL REALM

Zhang Zhuo did not shy away from stories of the supernatural and bizarre, in which shock value was often an important component. Featuring a mysterious pair of white hares, the passage from *Court and Country* below also appears in a chapter on "Curios" (*Qiwan* 器玩) in *Extensive Records*:[70]

> In the Qianfeng era of the Tang, a man in the wilderlands to the east of Zhenzhou[71] saw two white rabbits and captured them. Suddenly they entered the ground, disappearing without a trace. He dug in the place where they vanished, and, after excavating about three feet of earth, found a pair of finely crafted bronze swords wrought in antiquity. At the time, it was local elder Zhang Zu's family that learned of this incident. (Sup., 159)

White animals like the pair of hares in this passage were considered to be auspicious in early and medieval China, often taken as signs of virtue or longevity.[72] Well into the Tang, pelts of white hares were presented to Tang emperors.[73]

For Wu Zhao, white hares seem to have been more problematic. Jealous of the influence of Li Xiaoyi—a general who helped Wu Zhao quash the Yangzhou uprising in 684 and nephew of the founding Tang emperor—Wu Zhao's nephew Wu Chengsi slandered the man. In 687, Wu Chengsi claimed that Li Xiaoyi had boasted, "My name contains the loping hare,[74] a creature of the moon. I have been chosen by Heaven." Whether the purported boast was truly reported or fabricated, the unfortunate general was exiled and killed as a result. For Wu Zhao, having not yet formally ascended the throne, the lunar hare—who in lore assisted Moon Goddess Chang'e in her preparation of an elixir of immortality—suggested evidence of Heaven's sanction for a potentially dangerous imperial contender.[75] Subsequently, she ordered the eradication of all hares in the empire. One troublemaker, after a neighbor had rejected his plea for a melon, reported that he had spotted a white hare in the neighbor's melon field. The county official sent subordinates to search for the creature and trampled the field flat.[76] Clearly, Wu Zhao saw the hare as a powerful and ominous creature.

Another account relates the macabre demise of Zhou Yunyuan, who rather suddenly rose to become one of Wu Zhao's chief ministers at the height of her Zhou dynasty late in 694:

> In the time of Wu Zetian, after court concluded, Vice Secretary Zhou Yunyuan entered the inner pavilion.[77] The Taiping Princess summoned a doctor, who entered through Guangzheng Gate. The physician saw a demon toting Zhou Yunyuan's head, trailed by two other demons carrying wooden staves, exiting through the Jingyun Gate.[78] The physician informed the

RELIGION AND THE SUPERNATURAL WORLD

> *Taiping Princess, who memorialized the emperor. The emperor ordered that the case be presented to the officials for further deliberation and investigation. Nothing was awry with Zhou Yunyuan during the meeting, and, after finishing a meal, he returned home. In the afternoon he went to the privy. An attendant felt it peculiar that Yunyuan remained in the outhouse for so long and entered to check on him. Yunyuan had fallen and slumped forward, face down in the privy. His eyes stared straight forward, but he was speechless; a strand of drool hung down from his mouth. An attendant reported this to the emperor, who asked the doctor, "How long does he have?"*
>
> *The doctor replied, "At the longest, three days; at the soonest, one." The emperor used a silken quilt to cover him and had him transported back to his residence on a wooden pallet-bed. He died in the middle of the night. Wu Zetian wrote a monody to lament his passing.* (1.3)

While the supernatural story of a trio of demons infiltrating the palace and possessing Zhou Yunyuan is sensational, Wu Zhao's gentle solicitude toward her official is perhaps even more striking. Zhang Zhuo does not question the veracity of the tale. In another curious detail from the story, Wu Zhao's own daughter, the Taiping Princess, sent a memorial to her mother to alert her of this unusual matter. Zhou Yunyuan death so soon after his elevation was clearly a blow to Wu Zhao, who honored Zhou by personally writing a verse to mark his passing.[79]

Sometimes vignettes of the supernatural in *Court and Country* serve as cautionary tales. For instance, it is clearly prudent to heed the admonitions of a spirit medium:

> *In the Zhou, Minister of Rites Zhang Xiwang moved from his old residence and was building a new one. During construction, spirit medium Feng Yi saw him and remarked, "Beneath your new great hall there is the pronate corpse of a third-rank Jin dynasty general. His spirit is enraged. Sir, it would be wise to avoid him." Wang laughed and said, "From my youth to the present I've never heard of this sort of thing. There's no need for you, Sir, to speak of it." A little more than a month later, Feng Yi entered to witness the spirit notching an arrow to a bowstring and following behind Zhang. As Zhang began to ascend the steps, the ghost pulled back the bowstring and shot the arrow between Zhang's arm and shoulder. Xiwang felt his back ache and reached his hand up to press the spot. That same day he died.*[80] (2.38)

Ghosts and demons are often animated by grievances that they have suffered, remaining restless and resentful until those wrongs have been rectified. When cautioned by one attuned to the supernatural realm that his actions are infuriating the corpse spirit of a long-dead general buried on the site he is refurbishing, Zhang Xiwang ignores the warning, only to have the aggrieved spirit fell him with a phantasmal arrow!

In another curious, supernatural offering from *Court and Country*, Zhou Zigong, an official in Wu Zhao's court, experiences a near-death encounter with deceased Tang emperor Gaozong in the netherworld:

> *In the court the Celestial Empress, Vice Minister of Revenue Zhou Zigong died a sudden death. In the afterlife he saw the Great Emperor*[81] *seated in his throne with Pei Ziyi standing in attendance at his side. Zigong prostrated himself and paid obeisance. The emperor asked who he was. Pei Ziyi answered, "I brought Zhou Zigong here." The emperor responded, "I called for Xu Ziru. How is it that Zigong has wrongly come before me?" The emperor then dismissed him. Zigong revived and asked his family, "Is Vice Minister Xu still okay?" At the time, Vice Minister of State Xu Ziru was already sick; that night he died. When Zetian heard this, she sent riders on post-horse relay to Bingzhou to inquire after Pei Ziyi, at that time an Administrative Assistant. He was fine. (6.143)*

The imagined afterlife bore a close resemblance to the known mundane world. The netherworld was just as bureaucratic as the living world: deceased emperors were naturally surrounded by a coterie of ministers. When they needed counsel, these rulers in the next life would not hesitate to call on capable advisors. Fortunately for Zhou Zigong, the netherworld Gaozong had intended to summon another man into service and not him, and he was sent back to the world of the living. When he revived, it turned out that Xu Ziru, the official Gaozong had sought to summon into service in the next life, had perished in his stead.[82] When Zhou told Wu Zhao that he had seen Pei Ziyi, another living official, in the netherworld, Wu Zhao sent riders to check on the man's well-being, only to discover that he was unharmed.

A number of additional mysterious and supernatural events are recorded in *Court and Country*. When burying a parent or selecting a site for a family tomb, choosing an auspicious locale was vital. Families would hire geomancers and diviners to find the ideal burial site. In this brief anecdote, it is made clear that mortals are not supposed to encroach upon the numinous and powerful subterranean realm of dragons:

> *Former Vice Censor Wang Jingrong came from Pingshu in Yingzhou prefecture. He planned to move his father's coffin to Luozhou. Along the entry path to the new tomb, workers excavated the entry to a dragon grotto that was about the size of a great earthenware jar. Wang Jingrong looked down at it. Smoke-like ethers rose from the hole and spurted into Wang's eyes. Shortly thereafter, he lost his vision. A xun-week later he suddenly perished. (5.126)*

Here, accidental exposure of the underground entry to a dragon cavern leads to disastrous consequences that proved the Wang family burial was not meant for such sacred grounds. In a recent Chinese novel, Fang Qi's *Elegy of a River*

RELIGION AND THE SUPERNATURAL WORLD

Shaman, a pair of geomancers, masters of *fengshui*, wind and water, seek the site of a similar dragon grotto (*long ku* 龍窟) in a remote and rugged borderland:

> Meanwhile, the geomancers [...] stood in the cold, eyes animated with fervent excitement, gasping in delight as their tattered robes flapped in the biting wind. At long last they had located the site where the Immortal Tiger Lord had descended from the White Tiger Star to the mortal world in the tiger hour, of the tiger day, of the tiger month, in the Year of the Tiger! [...] From the ancient misty ethers enveloping the Mountain of the Supreme Ancestor, the dragon seekers had followed the geomantic emanations over countless ridges, hunting for this mountain-engirded site. Now, having reached the site that radiated such powerful numinous energy, sensing its momentous importance, to confirm their hypothesis they took out their geomantic compass to measure its azimuth in respect to the constellations and the Five Elements. With their celestial and terrestrial compasses they tabulated the precise meridian of the location of this site. [...]
>
> The mountain air was pregnant with the potent numinous ethers radiating from the subterranean cavern! If an unworthy corpse were buried on the site, the stone guardian tigers crouching on the mountain-slope, protecting the grotto beneath for countless eons, would exhume the body with their fearsome claws and cast it away.
>
> [One awestruck geomancer said], "While this is a burial site befitting an emperor, it emanates a murderous air. It may bring military success to the offspring of the man buried herein, but future generations of the family will be ravaged by war and suffer profoundly in a world awash in blood!"[83]

These fictional geomancers knew what Wang Jingrong learned too late: with the rare exception perhaps of a great and indomitable emperor, a dragon cavern is no site for a mortal burial.

Two more passages from *Court and Country* center on wounds and ailments with supernatural elements:

> *Yuezhou military adjutant Liu Chong was suddenly stricken by an unbearable wound on his head; the intolerable pain caused him to groan. That night, he summoned a magician to take a look at his malady. The man said, "There's a lady in a green dress beneath your windowsill. If you speak to her, she won't respond. Get rid of her immediately!" Liu Chong looked beneath the sill of his window and discovered a green-glazed porcelain figurine of an extremely comely singing girl. He smashed it to smithereens in an iron mortar and burned the remainder. Subsequently, his wound improved.* (6.144–45)

> *Gao Yi of the Bohai*[84] *was incredibly wealthy. One day he was suddenly stricken by an illness that lasted for more than a month and then he peacefully passed away. His chest remained warm, however, and after several days he revived, claiming that a man in white clothing, blind in one eye, had accused him of killing his wife and children, and had taken*

him to court in the underworld. Gao Yi told the underworld authorities, "I don't even know this old guy." The underworld judge said, "Your fate, sir, has not yet run its course. You may return to the world of the living." Subsequently, they figured out it was the family's blind white rooster. Gao ordered a servant to shoot it with an arrow. Thereafter, the creature's bewitchment was broken. (4.99)

In each case, a man's illness is connected to a bewitchment or curse. In the first, it is a porcelain figurine that causes the illness: in *Extensive Records*, this passage is included in the chapters on "wicked spirits" (*jingguai* 精怪), spectral forces bent on haunting and bringing harm and misfortune to humans.[85] In the latter, it is discovered that a blind white rooster from the family barnyard, filled with malice and harboring a grievance because his hens and chicks had been slaughtered, had complained to the underworld, where checks and balances, registers keeping positive and negative karma for the living, are kept. Fortunately for both individuals, the respective sources of their illness are identified and destroyed. In the latter account, one is left to wonder whether Gao Yi enjoyed his chicken soup!

10

Flora, fauna, and the natural world

IN THE EARLY TANG AND DURING Wu Zhao's Zhou dynasty, the empire was vast, encompassing a range of climates, from the great central river valleys, the Yellow and the Yangzi, to the taiga, steppe, and desert along the northern borders, to rugged, sky-piercing mountains in the west and southwest, to the swamps and jungles of the distant southland. Concomitant to this panoramic range of environs, there was staggering biodiversity. There were, as environmental historian Robert Marks frames it, "numerous ecological niches where people could, and did, exploit the environment to sustain and reproduce themselves and their cultures." Environment, to a degree, conditioned and dictated terms for human settlement; people, over time, altered the environment and sculpted the landscape.[1] Edward Schafer remarks, "Even before Tang times, the ancient pines of the mountains of Shandong had been reduced to carbon, and now the busy brushes of the vast Tang bureaucracy were rapidly bringing baldness to the Taihang Mountains between Shanxi and Hebei."[2] The larger picture of the tension between environment and development was, according to Mark Elvin, "one of Han Chinese expansion up to natural limits—coasts, steppes, deserts, mountains, and jungles."[3]

Like virtually every premodern culture, in medieval China, the interaction between man and nature contains a built-in paradox: on a religious and spiritual plane, mountains and rivers were objects of veneration; on a utilitarian level, they afforded transportation and offered sources of food, resources, medicine, and irrigation. An eighth-century Tang scholar–official echoed one of the classics: "Mountains, swamps, forests, and salt are the treasures of the nation."[4] In the Tang, notions of the conservation and preservation of nature connected to Buddhism and Daoism sometimes influenced human behaviors. Tombs and temples were protected from hunting and harvest.[5]

Ongoing warfare with steppe peoples (and the occasional occupation of the North by different groups of these peoples) prompted sustained instability in the Yellow River Valley during the centuries of division that followed the demise of the Han dynasty. In simplest terms, as Robert Marks frames it, "antagonism between nomadic pastoralists and agriculturalists" led to the deforestation and depopulation of the North and progressive colonization of the South.⁶ In conjunction with the pronounced climatic cooling in the sixth century, which accelerated and exacerbated long-term processes of progressive deforestation and soil exhaustion, this tumult in the North led to mass southbound migrations.

The Sui dynasty conquest and reunification in the late sixth century and their engineering of the Grand Canal helped link together long-divided North and South China. To consolidate the empire and facilitate commerce, the early Tang continued to develop networks of canals and roads.⁷ Despite the reunified empire, the demographic shifts continued in the seventh century as peasant-farmers abandoned the arid Yellow River Valley, heading ever further south beyond the already-populated Yangzi River Valley, slashing and burning forests and terracing mountainscapes to open up new fields in these lush, fertile territories.⁸ This longer-term process was well underway when Zhang Zhuo was compiling his collection of anecdotes. During Wu Zhao's regency and reign, officials warned of the increasing instances of farmers abandoning their unproductive land to migrate southward.⁹ This ongoing demographic shift stimulated exposures to and encounters with a new range of flora and fauna.

Zhang Zhuo was remarkably well positioned to chronicle such phenomena in this vast empire. He was born in the Northeast, in modern-day Hebei. During his half-century career, he served in both capitals, Chang'an and Luoyang, in several posts in modern-day Henan, and out west along the Silk Road. Later on, he was banished to faraway austral Lingnan. The passages and annotations below represent but a partial investigation of the flora, fauna, and larger environmental transformations in the early Tang and Wu Zhao's Zhou dynasty as witnessed and described in *Court and Country*.

BESTIARY

Tigers

In China, the tiger, rather than the lion, was the king of beasts. The pattern of stripes on the creature's formidable brow is thought to resemble the character for "king" (*wang* 王). Despite, or perhaps because of this, there is a long record in Chinese history, literature, and art of adversarial relations between man and the king of beasts. Edward Schafer remarks that "Chinese literature from the earliest times is full of tiger stories—man-eating tigers, weretigers, symbolic tigers, anti-tiger spells, tiger hunts. [...] [T]igers ruled the mountains of China as dragons lorded it over the lakes and seas."¹⁰ Today,

FLORA, FAUNA, AND THE NATURAL WORLD

every man, woman, and child in China knows of the famous tiger hunter, Wu Song, celebrated in classical novels, operas, and movies for bravely and foolishly crossing Jingyang Ridge while deeply inebriated and killing a fierce, man-devouring tiger with his bare hands.[11] There are numerous artistic and literary depictions of Wu Song pummeling the tiger to death.

In the greater Yangzi River Valley, the tiger was a revered, totemic object of worship.[12] In the Tang, sacrifices were performed to tigers and cats to acknowledge them for killing, respectively, the wild boars that ravaged the fields and the rats that pilfered precious grain.[13] The white tiger was the symbol of the West. In the *New Tang History*, there is a record of a tiger entering a ward in the capital, Chang'an, followed by the ominous remark, "The tiger is the emblem of the west. It is imposing and fierce, devouring its prey. It is a harbinger of killing and death."[14] Tang physicians treated tiger bites with a wash of molten iron to cauterize the wound, stop bleeding, and prevent infection.[15]

In the impressive bestiary contained within *Court and Country*, there are four accounts of tigers:

> *Duke of Dingxiang Li Hong, the son of the Prince of Guo,*[16] *was seven feet tall. When he was hunting, he encountered a tiger. Engaged in combat, Li Hong stumbled and fell. As he lay supine, the tiger sat on top of him. One of Hong's servants passed by riding a horse. The tiger pounced and tore off the saddle from beneath the servant. Hong rose, drew his bow, shot the tiger in the shoulder, and killed it. Neither Hong nor the servant were harmed in the least.* (6.139–40)

> *In the time of the Celestial Empress, Prince of Cheng Li Qianli*[17] *brought a tiger into the palace to raise. It injured a palace girl. Subsequently, he ordered the tiger to be starved for several days, and it died. The Celestial Empress then ordered that the tiger be interred and erected a pagoda above the burial site. Its construction took 1000 men. A stele was raised, calling it "Tiger Pagoda." It still stands today.* (2.45)

> *In the time of the Celestial Empress, there were a number of violent tiger attacks on the margins of Wulong County in Fuzhou Prefecture. There was a creature much like a tiger but massive. One midday the beast pursued a tiger right into one family's homestead. It tore the tiger to death with its teeth but didn't eat its flesh. Thereafter, there were no longer tigers in Wulong County. The creature's presence was recorded in a memorial. According to the text* Illustrations of Auspicious Omens, *the creature is a qiu'er* 酋耳 *beast, which doesn't eat living things but kills tigers that engage in violent attacks.* (2.45)

> *When Chuan Huangzhong was made leader of Zhuji County in Yuezhou prefecture, one of his underlings became greatly inebriated and wandered through the mountains at night, falling asleep on the edge of a precipice. Suddenly a tiger approached and sniffed him. When the tiger's whiskers entered the drunkard's nostrils, the man sneezed violently. The noise startled the tiger, who leapt back in terror, fell off the cliff, and shattered its back. The fellow was able to bring back the tiger.* (2.45)

In each of these accounts, a tiger is killed. In the first, a menacing tiger is shot on a hunting expedition by Li Hong. Through no skill of his own, the reprobate imperial scion (see Chapter 4) survived a near-death experience. In the second anecdote, when an effort to domesticate a tiger fails, the creature is inadvertently starved to death. On this occasion, Wu Zhao, perhaps considering the death of a kingly tiger within palace walls to be an inauspicious event, orders an elaborate burial and the erection of a pagoda on the site to placate the tiger's spirit. Zhang Zhuo may also intend to emphasize Wu Zhao's poor leadership—she allows chaos within the palace walls as the tiger runs rampant—and wasteful extravagance, using a large labor force and resources based on superstition after the beast dies. The third passage features a *qiu'er* beast, a mythological, white tigrine creature with black markings and a long tail (see Figure 8), that ushers in an era of great peace by killing man-eating tigers and leopards, thus preventing them from devouring human quarry.[18] Sometimes fortune favors the inebriated and foolish: set in the southeastern hills, the final passage features a wastrel whose sneeze startles the ill-starred tiger, causing the beast to fall backward off a precipice and meet its doom. Combining this last account with the story of the famous tiger-killer Wu Song, one reaches the conclusion that, prior to heading into the mountain wilderness to engage a tiger in unarmed combat, the best defense is copious consumption of alcohol!

Elephants

The largest land mammals, elephants were sacrosanct and widely revered in early and medieval Asia, multivalent symbols of strength, auspiciousness, wisdom, peace, and prosperity.[19] Elephants were a well-known presence in seventh-century China. Widely represented in Buddhist art and literature of the time, the elephant was a symbol of Buddhist power associated with the Buddha's miraculous conception.[20]

While elephants once inhabited the Yellow River Valley in China, by the Tang dynasty a "protracted war" with humans had driven them far south.[21] Elephant trunk, fatty and crisp, was considered a regional delicacy in the Southland.[22] Many tributary embassies from Southeast Asia gifted elephants to China in the late seventh century.[23] When Wu Zhao was empress, an emissary to the court of the Two Sages reported that when the tusks of a four-tusked elephant from their state were cleansed, the residual wash-water could heal sickness and cure disease.[24] As emperor, Wu Zhao set up six palace corrals where not only horses, but camels and huge elephants were stabled.[25]

A passage about an elephant in *Court and Country* reads like a fable:

Figure 8 A Qing dynasty woodblock print of a qiu'er beast.

> *In Huarong County²⁶ during the Shangyuan era, an elephant entered the central courtyard of a farmhouse and lay down. In its foot there was a thorn. A man removed it. The elephant bowed its head to indicate that its benefactor should mount its back, then carried him into the deep mountains. As an offering of reward, the elephant used its trunk to gouge up the earth and reveal several dozen ivory tusks. (5.123)*

From Aesop's "Androcles and the Lion" to "The Mouse and the Elephant," one type of cross-cultural fable features a human or smaller creature that is able to take advantage of its relatively diminutive size to aid a larger beast. In these tales of unexpected reciprocity, the larger creature is invariably indebted, and desires to do the smaller creature a good turn. Zhang Zhuo's passage reflects more than a passing familiarity with this universal motif. In this case, the elephant improbably leads his benefactor to an elephant graveyard, a treasure trove of ivory.

Gibbons

Edward Schafer contends that the term *xingxing* 猩猩, which now designates the gorilla, formerly indicated the Chinese gibbon,²⁷ the loquacious and bibulous anthropoid in the passage from *Court and Country* below:

> *The gibbons living in the Fengxi Stream area of Wuping County of Annam had a regal bearing, understood the language of men, and possessed a knowledge of past events. Because they had a weakness for liquor, they could be lured into cages and bound with wooden clogs until several hundred were confined together. When people wanted to eat them, the crowd of gibbons would push forward the fattest among them. They would all send off the chosen gibbon, shedding tears in parting. Once, a gibbon was offered to the mayor of Fengxi. The mayor asked what sort of creature it was. From inside the cage, the gibbon responded, "Just lowly old me and a jar of wine." The mayor laughed and took a liking to the creature. He brought it into his household as a pet. The creature could speak and hold conversations better than most men. (6.135)*

The gibbons of Wuping County in Annam were well known. Pei Yan, a chief minister from the time of the Two Sages who later ran afoul of Wu Zhao, once wrote an "Inscription on Gibbons," citing an earlier text that mentions Wuping as a site known for these creatures with simian forms and human-like faces, possessed of the capacity to speak the language of men. Sogdians reportedly favored the blood of these creatures as a fabric dye. Apparently, when one would ask the gibbon how much blood it was willing to give, the creature would answer "two pints (*sheng* 升)." If that proved inadequate, the gibbon could be whipped and beaten into offering far more. The passage also indicates that the gibbons were, to their lasting detriment, fond of liquor.²⁸

FLORA, FAUNA, AND THE NATURAL WORLD

Cattle

In the northwestern region of the empire, land was allotted for keeping cattle, but not elsewhere.[29] People of the South utilized water buffalo to harrow and plow rice paddies; people of the North harnessed yellow (*Bos taurus*) and black (*Bos longifrons*) cattle to plow their fields and to draw carts.[30] There are several odd excerpts on cattle in *Court and Country*:

> In the Ruyi era, to the south of the Luo River there was a three-legged cow. (Sup., 178)

> In the Xiantian era, a man from south of the Luo River led an ox, rushing about. In the hollow of its foreleg grew a human hand, more than a foot long. The man wandered through the wards of Luoyang, begging. (5.120)

One wonders why both of these mutant yellow cows were found within 20 miles of each other, in a region of the Central Plain known for agriculture rather than grazing. Something in the waters of the Luo River? In any event, Zhang Zhuo has little interest in the toiling, steadfast, and dependable oxen; he is drawn to anomalies.

Foxes

> "When a fox is fifty years old, it can transform itself into a woman. When it is one hundred, it becomes a beautiful woman or a shaman; some become men and have sex with women. They can know events from more than 1000 *li* away and are good at witchcraft, beguiling people and making them lose their senses. When they are 1000 years old, they can commune with the heavens and become heavenly foxes."[31]
>
> —attributed to Guo Pu, early fourth century

Dwelling on the margins of human habitation, foxes have long fascinated peoples of all cultures. Often, they are imagined as clever tricksters. Foxes, fox spirits (*huli jing* 狐狸精), and foxlore in general feature prominently in premodern China. Xiaofei Kang, who has devoted a great deal of energy to the study of these creatures with "quasi-human intelligence," observes that "Fox spirits fascinated the Tang people. [...] They were widely worshipped in village homes and enjoyed food offerings. Interactions between humans and fox spirits were also extensively recorded by Tang literati in the *zhiguai* [accounts of anomalies] collections, which have preserved a wealth of fox tales." The shape-shifting fox "haunted and bewitched people, causing sickness and death, but it also had celestial connections, provided divine help to people, and inspired genuine love in some mortals." Thus, foxes were both "worshipped as deities and exorcised as demons."[32]

In essence, the fox was a bewitching creature, an often haunting, unnerving, and ominous presence. Only rarely were they unambiguously evil. Not surprisingly, there are a number of passages in *Court and Country* in which these disturbing vulpine interlopers make their mysterious presence felt. The first passage attests to the popularity of a fox cult among the common people:

> From the beginning of the Tang, many commonfolk worshipped fox deities. In their bedchambers, people offered sacrifices to foxes to beg them to bestow favor, presenting them the same food and drink that people consume. They often worship multiple fox divinities. At the time, a proverb went, "Without the bewitchments of foxes you can't have a village."[33] (Sup., 167)

The Tang marked a zenith in the popularity of fox tales and fox worship.[34] The common folk worshipped foxes and presented them offerings.

In a second passage, a shape-shifting fox haunts a scholar–official:

> Instructor in the Directorate of Education Zhang Jian heralded from the Goushi region of Henan.[35] Once, he went to lecture on Selections of Refined Literature to rural scholars. A wild fox assumed his guise, lectured on a passage from the text, then left. Shortly thereafter, when Zhang Jian arrived, his disciples inquired about it. Zhang, feeling this to be strange, opined, "Whoever was here before must have been a wild fox." Afterwards, he returned home to find his younger sister reeling silk. She said, "Elder brother, your food is already cold. Why have you come home so late?" Zhang Jian sat down and waited a long while for her to serve the meal, and, when it didn't arrive, he upbraided his sister. She responded, "I never saw you return, Elder Brother. This is definitely the work of a wild fox. If you see it, kill it right away." The next day when Zhang returned, his younger sister was reeling silk. She said, "Just now that demon-spirit was out behind the house!" Zhang Jian then grabbed a cudgel and, seeing his younger sister returning from the privy, smashed her. His sister called out, "It's me!" But Zhang Jian didn't believe her and beat her to death. Returning, he questioned the silk-reeler, who transformed into a wild fox and fled. (Sup., 167)

Gruesomely befuddled, Zhang Jian beats his sister to death after confusing her for the vexatious vixen. The fox in this account plays what Rania Huntington terms the dark role of a "doppelgänger" that "incite[s] family members to slay one another."[36]

In another passage, a spectral troop of pillaging foxes appears at the mansion of the Zhang brothers, Wu Zhao's favorites during the later years of her Zhou dynasty (see Chapter 1):

> Just before the fall of Zhang Yizhi, while his mother Wei Azang was seated in her residence, a family member reported that a huge procession of carriages and horses was passing the gate. Thinking it was someone from the imperial palace, she went outside the residence to welcome

them, *but there was no one there. Several dozen wild foxes breached the wall and carried off earthenware vats of stored food. In less than a week, the Zhangs met with disaster.* (6.143)

Given Zhang Zhuo's consistent portrayal of the Zhang brothers and their kin as emblems of vice, greed, extravagance, sexual impropriety, and the inversion of Confucian norms and virtues, it is evident that, for the author of *Court and Country*, this portentous appearance of the foxes presages doom for the Zhangs.

A final passage about foxes is similar:

In the Shenlong era, Minister of Revenue Li Chengjia couldn't read and was illiterate. When he became Chief Censor and jointly senior administrator of Luozhou prefecture, he called his administrative assistants "dogs" and cursed the Censors as "jackasses." His might shook the court. In the Western Capital when Li completed a residential hall in his new mansion, people in the ward saw countless foxes. Shortly thereafter, the entire building collapsed, its tiles and timbers jackstrawed together. The bamboo writing brush of the supervising official splintered. He took another brush, which also ruptured. Several days later, Li was demoted to Vice Commander of Tengzhou[37] *and sent away, where he died.* (6.143–44)

For Li Chengjia—a powerful minister at the end of Wu Zhao's reign and in the first years of the restored Tang whom Zhang Zhuo represents as intemperate and illiterate—foxes served once again as a sign of a richly-deserved impending misfortune, demolition, and death.

Cats

"Cats catch mice and other small animals. They are raised everywhere. They may be different colors, yellow, black, white, and multicolored. They have the body of a leopard cat and the face of a tiger. Their fur is soft, their teeth are sharp. [...] They draw plans on the ground to forecast the whereabouts of their prey. Depending on whether it is the beginning or the end of the month, they eat the head or the tail of the mouse. In all these regards they are like tigers."[38]
—Li Shizhen, *from a Ming encyclopedia of medicine and natural history*

Earlier in this chapter, it was noted that, in the Tang, joint sacrifices were performed in honor of kingly tigers and their smaller cousins, cats, who dutifully guarded precious granaries from rats. A short late Tang essay entitled "Discourse on Cats and Tigers" intimates a taxonomic correspondence, a family resemblance, between the creatures. But cats were more than dutiful creatures, protecting life-sustaining rice and millet for human masters; they were believed to possess a demonic power.[39] This black magic, Rebecca

Doran illustrates, was "thoroughly female," connected to poison and demonic possession.[40] There were Buddhist incantations to dispel the power of cat demons.[41] *Court and Country* contains the remark that

> in the Daye era of the Sui dynasty, matters involving the cat demon arose. Families began to raise cats to avoid bewitchments. There were many divine and numinous occurrences that spurred mutual false accusations, leading to the deaths of several thousand in the capital and surrounding prefectures and counties.[42] (1.18/1.26 fn.50)

Fraught with wild accusations of dark magic and possession, this cat demon scare—just a decade or so prior to Wu Zhao's birth—spread into a deadly epidemic of fear.

In the ominous light of the passage above, we are perhaps better able to comprehend Wu Zhao's alarm at hearing the dying oath of vengeance uttered by her palace rival, Pure Consort Xiao (discussed in Chapter 1): in the next life, Xiao claimed, she would be born a cat and Wu Zhao a mouse, powerless to resist as the predator descended to claw open her throat. This unsettling event in the late 650s prompted Wu Zhao, then Gaozong's empress, to ban cats from the palace. A passage from *Court and Country* translated in Chapter 1 demonstrates that Wu Zhao attempted to restore felines as emperor in the 690s, hosting a symbolic performance before her court where a cat and a parrot peacefully shared a cage—a disastrous effort that ended with the cat killing its cagemate.

Another anecdote in *Court and Country* also intimates the feline's otherworldly power:

> When Xue Jichang was serving as a Clerk in Jingzhou, he dreamt that a cat was lying on the threshold of the hall, its head facing toward the outside. He asked diviner Zhang You about it, who observed, "The cat represents claws and fangs [of military force]. It is lying on the threshold of the hall. There will be a matter dealing with the outer regions. Your Excellency will certainly obtain a military position." In less than a xun-week, Xue was appointed Commander-in-Chief of Guizhou and Commissioner for Suppressing Rebellion in Lingnan.[43] (3.60)

A diviner interprets the portentous dream of Xue Jichang, in which the presence of a guardian cat suggests his imminent promotion to serve as a martial officer. Among his other positions under Wu Zhao, Xue Jichang served as a Censor, before being demoted.[44]

Felines were also consumed as food, and there were a variety of medicinal uses for the various parts of the cat.[45] Cat meat was thought to be sweet, sour, and warm.[46] The manner in which the cat is eaten in the following passage from *Court and Country* is, we can hope, atypical:

FLORA, FAUNA, AND THE NATURAL WORLD

> *In the Zhenguan era, Peng Ta and Gao Zan of Hengzhou vied in competitions of audacity. At a banquet, Peng Ta seized a live suckling pig and with his teeth tore gobbets of flesh from its head all the way down to its neck, before releasing the creature, still living, to stagger off. Not do be outdone, Gao Zan grabbed a live cat and started to devour it, tail-end first. While the creature was caterwauling and howling without cease, he ate ever forward, even devouring its intestines and stomach. At that, Peng Ta had to submit and admit defeat. (6.140)*

Rivaling the Zhang brothers' "Bitter Anguish" (see Chapter One), this alarming vignette, set during Wu Zhao's younger years and before Zhang Zhuo's birth, features a rival contest in animal cruelty. One local reprobate bests his crony—who takes bites out of a squealing piglet headfirst—by devouring a living cat, commencing at its tail-end! There is no moral to be found in this story, only Zhang Zhuo's delight to shock and appall.

Rabbits

Rabbits, like rodents and other vermin, devoured grains and vegetables to the extent that it jeopardized the livelihood of peasant-farmers. The passage from *Court and Country* below is set late in the joint reign of Gaozong and Wu Zhao, when all manner of disruptions threatened the natural order. Comets traversed the heavens, uprisings undermined domestic tranquility, and multiple border incursions disturbed the peace (see Chapter 8):

> *In the Yongchun era, in Lanzhou and Shengzhou there were sudden infestations of rabbits, clusters of millions who completely devoured all the sprouts and shoots. When the infestation ended, the rabbits disappeared without a trace. No one knew where they had gone. Bizarre!*[47] (Sup., 166)

Zhang Zhuo adds an air of mystery—providing the sense that these sprout-devouring lapines were a projection of heaven's disapproval of the uxorious Tang emperor and his ascendant spouse. Heaven above, it is intimated, was revoking its sanction and mandate. This Mandate of Heaven was an important political concept in dynastic China that had long since become part of political discourse and commentary. The core idea is as follows: when a ruler was virtuous and committed to the well-being of the common people, Heaven and the ancestors rewarded the ruling family with bountiful harvests and greater peace. On the other hand, a selfish, profligate sovereign who conscripted the people to build extravagant palaces without heeding the natural cycles of planting and harvest would be punished by Heaven; his or her mandate to rule would be revoked.[48] Natural disasters like rabbit infestations were Heaven's punitive vehicle. Readers of Zhang Zhuo would have been well aware his point was not simply that an unfortunate and damaging lapine plague occurred in the early 680s. This was pointed didactic commentary in which Zhang amplifies his narrative authority by tacitly aligning himself with a censorious natural world.

AVIARY

Court and Country is inhabited by a veritable aviary ranging from barnyard fowl to exotic mynahs, from elegant hummingbird-sized birds that serve as living hair ornaments to albino magpies.

The first two passages below record the transformation of hens into roosters during Wu Zhao's regency:

> *From the Chuigong era on, all of the prefectures presented hens that had turned into roosters. These signs corroborated the rise of Zetian.*[49] (6.143)
>
> *Beginning in the Wenming era, people from prefectures around the realm presented hens that had changed—or half-changed—into roosters. This was a sign that Wu Zetian had taken the rightful position of the emperor.* (4.99)

Once Wu Zhao removed Zhongzong from the throne and presided over the court as grand dowager-regent in 684, conventional omens like droughts, floods, and famine (long utilized in critical rhetoric and remonstrance) were no longer adequate to convey the sense of outrage that the Confucian court felt at her burgeoning authority. Therefore, to make manifest Heaven's disapproval, they resorted to more rhetorically striking imagery like gender-confused fowl.

One of the earliest classics, the *Book of History*, written more than a millennium before Wu Zhao's time, cautions, "When the hen crows to welcome the dawn, the family is doomed."[50] To show that Wu Zhao was a corrupt usurper seeking to destroy the legitimate House of Tang, Zhang Zhuo availed himself of such accounts and rumors in *Court and Country*. This set a precedent for later official historians, who also recorded that, once Wu Zhao took control of the court in 684, "throughout the empire in every prefecture hens changed into roosters, or half-changed."[51] Zhang's message is abundantly clear: a woman in a position of paramount power was an abomination of natural and human order. Zhang intimates that the transformed hens are perversions of nature that mimic Wu Zhao's deviation from human norms, her unnatural occupation of a male imperial throne.[52]

A third passage features a tender-hearted, low-level official who buys a goose to save it from the dinner table:

> *In the Jiushi reign era, there was a clerk in Yuezhou named Zu; his given name is not known. In the morning as he set out, he saw someone carrying a goose, heading for the market. Time*

FLORA, FAUNA, AND THE NATURAL WORLD

and again, the goose looked up at Zu and honked. He then ransomed the goose with some cash and brought it to a Buddhist temple to be released as a "longevity goose." In the end, however, the goose was unwilling to enter the temple and followed after Zu. As he passed through the clustered wards and crowded markets of the city, the goose followed close on his heels. So Zu kept and raised the creature. Aide Zhang Xi saw it with his own eyes and spoke of it. (4.100)

Clerk Zu brought the goose to a Buddhist temple, where, as monks practiced only a vegetarian diet, animals would be saved. Fish and turtles would swim blithely in a "pond for compassionate release of living creatures" (*fangsheng chi* 放生池) within the temple precincts; fowl and other creatures within the confines were likewise protected from the slaughterer's knife. Desiring to gain merit, Wu Zhao, an enthusiastic patron and sponsor of the Buddhist faith, placed a prohibition on the butchering of animals in 692, shortly after she became emperor.[53] In mid-Tang scholar–official Liu Su's 劉餗 *Splendid Stories of the Sui and Tang* (*Sui-Tang jiahua* 隋唐嘉話)—a collection akin to *Court and Country*—there is a story of Wu Zhao's daughter, the Taiping Princess, "ransoming the watery tribes" and using the rescued creatures to stock a "pond for compassionate release of living creatures" on her grand estate.[54] In this story from *Court and Country*, though, the loyal goose, a sensitive and gracious creature, eschewed the Buddhist safe haven and insisted on following Clerk Zu back to his home.

A pair of crested mynahs from Lingnan is the focus of another passage. These birds were reportedly capable not only of mimicking human speech, but of comprehension and intelligent response:

In the time of the Celestial Empress, when Left Adjutant of the Metropolitan Guard Liu Jingyang was sent to Lingnan, he obtained a pair of crested mynahs, one male and one female, capable of speaking the language of men. When he arrived at the capital, he presented the male mynah to the emperor but kept the female himself. Upset, the male mynah refused to eat. Zetian asked, "Why are you out of sorts?" The mynah told her that he was depressed because the emissary had kept his mate, and that now he sorely missed her. Zetian thereupon summoned Liu Jingyang and asked, "Minister, for what reason did you conceal one bird and not present it to me?" Jingyang kowtowed and admitted his fault, then presented her with the female mynah. Zetian forgave his transgression. (4.100)

Five-colored parrots and mynahs were often presented at the Tang and Zhou courts as tribute items from Southeast Asian countries.[55] Sometimes officials like Liu Jingyang, returning from assignments in the remote Southland, also gifted rulers exotic birds.

Another passage provides an account of delightful and colorful diminutive birds that were widely beloved in the Jiannan Circuit, an administrative region seated in Chengdu, but extending much further south:

> *In the Jiannan Circuit there is a five-colored bird the size of a fingernail with a crest like a phoenix that eats the flowers of the tong-oil tree. When tong-oil trees flower, they appear; when the blossoms fall, they disappear to who knows where. Common folk call them "tong-oil flower birds." They are extremely docile and tractable. They will land on a lady's ornamental hairpin and remain perched there for the duration of a meal. People love these tiny birds and no one harms them. (Sup., 168)*

Unlike many creatures of the Southland, these delicate birds were harmless. The passage offers a rare instance of harmonious coexistence between man and nature.

By contrast, the next passage features the relentless pursuit of an albino magpie by Zhang Changqi, one of the brothers of Wu Zhao's notorious male favorites:

> *Ruzhou Prefect Zhang Changqi was the younger brother of Zhang Yizhi. Relying on his brother's favor, he adopted a supercilious air, behaving in a cruel and violent fashion toward lesser officials. When someone in Liang County[56] said, "A white magpie has been spotted," Changqi ordered Revenue Manager Yang Chuyu to catch it. Under Yang, subordinates released seventy sparrow hawks from cages after spreading sticky wax on their talons. In the forest they saw the white magpie, followed by a throng of ordinary magpies. When the flock saw them, the magpies burst forth in flight, dispersing. Only the white one remained. One of the kestrels swooped down and seized the magpie, but it was not harmed in the least. Yang's men caged it and presented it to Changqi, who laughed and said, "You, Sir, just redeemed your life with this magpie." Yang Chuyu kowtowed and said, "Heaven above has allowed me to survive! Otherwise, even if I had to throw myself into a river or fling myself into the ocean, I wouldn't have dared face Your Excellency!" He then bowed and departed. (4.99)*

White birds, because they sometimes magnetized a flock of lesser birds, were often understood as auspicious signs of a virtuous ruler.[57] Because of this correspondence, Zhang Changqi likely sought to capture the magpie and present it to Wu Zhao. In addition to manifesting the Zhangs' overbearing treatment of subordinates and casual appropriation of human resources, this passage reveals something of the techniques of falconry used to capture prey alive.

More often than not, in seventh-century China—as in the rest of the medieval world—interaction between man and beast was oppositional and exploitative. Zhang Zhuo and subsequent chroniclers singled out Wu Zhao and the powerful group of women who succeeded her in the early eighth century—particularly her daughter the Taiping Princess, her granddaughter the Anle Princess, and her daughter-in-law Empress Wei—weaving these "transgressive women," as Rebecca Doran terms them, into a wider narrative of wasteful extravagance, self-indulgent excess, and rapacious "conspicuous consumption" of the natural world.[58]

FLORA, FAUNA, AND THE NATURAL WORLD

For instance, *Court and Country* contains a description of the Anle Princess's polychrome feathered skirt made with the plumage of 100 different avian species. Seeing this remarkable rainbow raiment, *"all of the officials and the common people copied her. In search of exotic birds and unusual animals, they scoured through the mountains and disturbed the valleys. They swept the ground until nothing was left, to the point that their nets and traps had trapped and killed a countless number of creatures"* (3.70–71).[59] The imagined ideal Confucian male ruler followed principles of moderation and virtue in utilizing the bounty of nature; he was a sage-king, establishing a harmonious rapport with the natural environment and the larger cosmos, and thereby serving as a model for the rest of the empire. In stark contrast, these women and their male favorites (especially in the unfavorable light in which Zhang Zhuo portrays them) are acquisitive anti-exemplars whose unsustainable hubris spawned widespread rapacity that led to ecological disaster! Cultural and religious tensions existed between the Buddhist prohibitions against killing animals and the social and economic demand for feathered and furred creatures to enhance fashion and supplement the usual culinary fare.[60]

Wild birds like crows, mynahs, and parrots were captured, domesticated, and trained in medieval China. The following passage features a local official who supervised the market in Chang'an; this fellow trained a red-billed chough—a bird in the crow family—to beg for coins and bring them back to him:

> *In the Tang, a man named Wei Ling was an assistant official in charge of monitoring the Western Market. He raised a red-billed chough that would beg for money amidst crowds. When people offered it a coin, the bird would pinch the cash in his beak and carry it back to Wei Ling. In a single day, it could gather several hundred coins. People of the time called it "Assistant Wei's crow."* (Sup., 167–68)

Wei Ling's nimble-beaked partner could garner 10,000 cash a year! Though in rhetoric and poetry crows were ignoble and pedestrian birds, often set in contrast to the regal red-capped crane or phoenix, some resourceful folks could harness the capacities of clever, raucous corvines.

The "bird of 100 tongues" (*baishe* 百舌) described in this final passage may be a reference to the mockingbird, given its capacity for imitating songs:[61]

> *From the time it arrives warbling in spring through the summer, the "Bird of 100 Tongues" eats only earthworms. It comes when the freeze ends in the first month of spring and leaves when the earthworms hibernate deeper in the ground. This shows the mutual responsiveness of different creatures.* (Sup., 168)

This last account is a thoughtful, if brief, rumination about creatures attuned to the natural world. This bird appears when spring brings worms to the surface and departs again when first frosts harden the earth in late fall. In addition, we learn the practical recipe that, for sores resulting from malignant worm and bug bites, a mixture of vinegar and soil from the nest of the "bird of 100 tongues" could be plastered on the injury.[62]

WATERY TRIBES

Nine chapters in Li Fang's *Extensive Records* are devoted to "Watery Tribes" (*Shuizu* 水族), a term which ranges from natural to supernatural, encompassing fish and turtles, otters and water dragons, water monsters and aquatic shape-shifters alike.[63] Fish are considered a lesser incarnation of a dragon.[64] Each of the passages from *Court and Country* below is included in this later compendium. As these passages are bunched together in Zhang Zhuo's fourth chapter, one might assume that he shared a similar conception of taxonomy.[65] To an extent, these passages reflect Zhang Zhuo's beliefs and understandings about interactions between humans and the natural environment. The first two passages reflect the mundane world; the latter two stray into the supernatural realm.

One passage describes the sporadic appearance of seemingly limitless fish in a particular river:

> *Originating in Tibet, a river flowed through Fengzhou.*[66] *Even in summer its waters were cold as snow and ice. From time to time, tiny fish, just an inch or two long, filled the water, thick as congee. People caught the fish then boiled and ate them. Even when millions of households caught them, the supply of these tiny fish was endless. No one knew where they came from.* (4.101)

Essential to this passage is the belief that "even when millions of households caught them, the supply of these tiny fish was endless"; author and people alike assumed that nature's bounty was inexhaustible and that there were no grave ecological consequences for rapacious consumption.

A second passage indicates that, in the Sichuan region, people learned to domesticate and train otters to help catch fish:

> *In the precincts of Tongchuan,*[67] *many otters live by the riverside; all of them have human masters who raise and feed them. When otters enter their holes and a pheasant feather is stuck in the ground in front of them, they don't dare come out. But as soon as the feather is removed, they promptly emerge. When otters catch fish, they bring them up on the bank and their masters snatch them away. Only when they catch a good number of fish are the otters released from service and allowed to eat fish themselves. Once the otters eat their fill, the owners beat a stick to drive them back into their burrows, then stick the pheasant feather in front so that, once again, the otters dare not emerge.* (4.101)

FLORA, FAUNA, AND THE NATURAL WORLD

Following the logic of this taxonomy, otters—fond of their watery habitat in the rivers and streams of Sichuan—belonged to the "Watery Tribes." This passage also provides insight into how people interacted with, sought to master, or partnered with creatures in medieval China.

Another account relates the discovery of peculiar mud guppies or loaches during the excavation of a well in Hangzhou:

> *Digging a well on his estate in Fuyang County in Hangzhou Prefecture, Han Xun discovered several dozen strange fish at a depth of only five or six feet when the earth became slightly moist.* (4.102)

One is left to wonder whether Han Xun had unearthed a mudskipper, a mud puppy, or some other creature.

Stranger creatures putatively dwelled beneath the water's surface, such as a subspecies of water dragon (*jiao* 蛟) known as the "white special" (*baite* 白特):

> *Someone saw a young servant washing a horse in the Luo River. Soon thereafter he saw a bright, glittering white creature like a silken belt wrap itself around the young groom's neck several times. The lad fell into the water and died. These creatures are found in rivers, bays, and ponds. Everyone says that people who die cleansing themselves or washing their horses are dragged under by giant softshell turtles, but this is not the case. This creature is called "white special" and it is prudent to be on guard. They fall under the category of jiao-water dragons.* (4.101)

This account shows that stories grew from inexplicable events that occurred around rivers and watering holes, and that creatures of the watery deep stirred a powerful degree of fear and awe.

In a final passage, a mystical Buddhist monk in Shandong—a being somewhere between a were-fish and the tutelary god of the copious watery tribes in the local river—is snagged by a local fisherman:

> *The waters of Myriad Acres Slope in Qizhou*[68] *contain every variety of fish and turtle from the watery tribes. In the Xianheng era, a Buddhist monk suddenly appeared, holding a bowl and begging for alms. The village elders collected him an offering of vegetable dishes. When the monk finished eating, he departed. Shortly, a fisherman caught a fish six or seven feet long in his net, its silky scales patterned like graven, burnished armor, like a brocade weaving or an imperial insignia. This was a most exceptional fish! The fisherman wanted to present it to the soldiers stationed at the prefectural barracks, but when he reached town, the fish had died. The villagers all cut up and divided the fish. In its stomach they discovered the vegetarian food they had offered to the monk. Although the villagers laid a vegetarian feast to expiate their sins and send off its soul, the watery tribes disappeared from Myriad Acres Slope. So it is to this day.* (4.101–02)

When the shining fish caught in Qizhou was gutted, the contents of its stomach proved to be the same vegetarian fare that townsfolk had recently fed the mysterious monk! Killing the monk–fish placed the village in the toils of evil karma: the river's bounty immediately dried up!

SNAKES

There are a number of passages about snakes in *Court and Country*:

In the Eastern Sea there is a place called Snakemound. There, the treacherous ground is saturated with moisture. Throngs of snakes inhabit this place, but no men. Some snakes have human heads and serpents' bodies. (5.121)

There is a green snake that lives in the redstone caverns of Mount Guzhu.[69] *It can grow to more than three feet but is thin as one's pinkie finger. It likes to coil in tree-tops, and to the eye looks like a leather belt tangled in the boughs and the leaves. It has neither fangs nor venom, and when it sees people, it soars off into the sky.* (5.121)

In Lingnan there is an "avenging snake." When people encounter it, the snake will pursue them, following along for three or five li. If a person kills one of these snakes, then a hundred will band together to exact revenge. The only way to avoid their vengeance is to protect oneself with centipedes.[70] (5.121)

Quanzhou and Jianzhou send python gallbladder bile gathered on the fifth day of the fifth lunar month to the court as tribute. At this time of year, the gallbladder separates into two parts that are five or six feet apart. The snake's head and tail are bound together and elevated, while a stick is set beneath its belly to help hold down the python and allow the two parts of the gallbladder to come together. Then, with a knife a man performs a surgery to obtain the gallbladder. After that, the wound is sutured and medicine is plastered. The snake is released. If the same snake is captured again, people release it right away after they see the scar.[71] (Sup., 167)

Geographically, not one of this quartet of ophidian anecdotes is set in the Yellow River Valley or the Central Plains. The initial account above takes place on a fanciful island in the Eastern Sea populated by snakes and nagas—yet another example of the penchant of Zhang Zhuo and other literati to fashion exotic and fantastical realms for the Other in these accounts of anomalies. The second features a timid, tree-dwelling snake in the southeast that possesses the power of flight; this is probably the paradise tree snake, one of the five species of *Chrysopelea*, the flying or gliding snakes still present in southern China and Southeast Asia today. The third tells of an aggressive snake from Lingnan which, like most creatures Zhang Zhuo mentions from this jungle-and-swamp-bound region, is threatening and potentially deadly.

FLORA, FAUNA, AND THE NATURAL WORLD

The curious final passage—set along the southeast coast—explains the technique by which python bile, an important medicinal drug, is gathered without killing the snake. Python bile was a local tribute item sent to the court from this region. Physicians used the gallbladder for a wide range of maladies, from leprosy to dysentery to hemorrhages. The gall bladder of the python changed its location within the body at different times of the month and year. To obtain this valuable commodity, "professional python farmers" in some of the southernmost counties of the empire raised the snakes and "got a steady supply of the precious bile from their serpentine livestock."[72] Python gall bladder was reputed to cure a wide range of childhood illnesses, swellings, piles, and several diseases caused by worms and bugs.[73]

LANDSCAPES, TREES, AND SPRINGS

The character Kuafu comes from the ancient *Classic of Mountains and Seas* (*Shanhaijing* 山海經), a text cataloging how myths were carved into the Chinese landscape, which dates from a millennia before the time of Wu Zhao and Zhang Zhuo. Anne Birrell, an expert on Chinese lore who translated the work, renders Kuafu as "Boast Father," describing him in the following manner:

> A demigod, given divine descent from the soil deity Sovereign Earth, and located in the mythogeographic south and east. His attributes are yellow snakes in his ears and hands. His myth relates to how he competed against the light of the sun in a race to the place where the sun sets, but died of thirst on the way.[74]

In *Mountains and Seas*, Kuafu dies beside a mountain in the middle of the northern wilderlands. Zhang Zhou offers an updated rendition of this myth in *Court and Country*:

> *In the eastern part of Chenzhou prefecture there are three mountains, each several thousand zhang tall and sticking up like a leg of a cooking tripod. According to ancient legend, when Boast Father raced against the sun, he stopped at this site to cook a meal. These three mountains are the stones he used to build the legs of his cooking pot.* (5.119)

Apparently, while Kuafu may have died of thirst, he did not die of hunger. Three mountains on the borders of Hunan and Guizhou form the tripod from which the god–giant hung his cooking pot to cook his rice while taking a break from his ill-fated pursuit of the solar orb.

Another of Zhang Zhuo's passages tells of terrestrial displacement; a flying slope near Mount Hua, between Chang'an and Luoyang, suddenly relocated just a year or two prior to Wu Zhao's accession to emperor:

> On a clear day in the Yongchang era, the western slope to the south of Fushuidian in Taizhou prefecture flew four or five li and dropped directly down on the Red River.[75] The cultivated mulberry trees and rows of wheat on the slope's farmland remained unchanged. (5.119)

Though this unusual movement did not damage the mulberry and wheat, this account might be construed as a criticism of Wu Zhao, an indication that the Five Elements were bizarrely out of kilter.

Just a few years prior to this peculiar event, not far from Chang'an, a 200-foot peak suddenly jutted from the ground in the midst of a torrential storm. Reportedly, hidden drums sounded from the mountain's heart and a pearl-disgorging yellow dragon swam in a pool on its slopes. Feeling this to be highly auspicious, Wu Zhao dubbed the peak "Mount Felicity." While some ministers vied to offer congratulations, others cast it as a calamity. One minister admonished,

> Your Majesty, a female ruler, improperly has occupied a male position, which has inverted and altered the hard and soft, therefore the earth's emanations are obstructed and separated. This mountain born of the sudden convulsion of earth represents a calamity. Your Majesty may take this as 'Mount Felicity,' but Your Subject feels there is nothing to celebrate. To respond properly to Heaven's censure, it is suitable that you lead the quiet life of a widow and cultivate virtue, otherwise I fear further disasters will befall us.

In cursory fashion, she dismissed this warning that as a female ruler her authority was, by its very nature, an affront to larger cosmic principles and Heaven's will, and summarily exiled the man to the swampy, disease-ridden Southland.[76] Although Zhang Zhuo does not overtly use the anecdote of a flying slope to criticize Wu Zhao (its ungainly flight took place just prior to the female emperor's inauguration of the Zhou dynasty), his depiction of a massive clump of the female Earth element soaring through male Heaven suggests tacit disapproval.

Another passage in *Court and Country* indicates that maple trees in the Yangzi River region had an animate and numinous quality:

> Amidst the southern mountains around the Yangzi River there are maple men. They are born at the foot of maple trees with a shape resembling that of humans and grow to three or four feet in size. During nocturnal thunderstorms, they grow to the size of trees; but when people see them, the maple men shrink back to their original size. Once, a man left a bamboo hat on

the head of a maple man, returning the following day to discover the hat hanging from the top of the tree. In times of drought when people wished for rain, they would perform a ceremony, pegging strips of bamboo that were wound round the head of the maple man, and it would rain immediately. People cut down maple men to make diviner's boards, believing that this wood possessed a numinous quality. Maple men come into being when maples grow on land where jujubes grow. (Sup., 166)

Zhang Zhuo's account relates that, because of its innate mystical potency, the wood of these peculiar maples could be used to fashion *shipan* 式盤, mantic astrolabes or diviner's boards. This passage is not unique in attesting to the strange power of these trees. Written two centuries later, Liu Xun's 劉恂 *Records of Strange Things in Guangdong and Guangxi* (Lingbiao luyi 嶺表錄異) also suggests that these maples could grow at an astonishing rate and that their knotted wood possessed a mystical potency:

Amidst the Southern Peaks grow many maple trees. Quite a few of the older trees developed tumescent burls. After violent thunder and torrential rain, these excrescences suddenly grow three feet overnight! Southerners call them "maple men." A shaman of Yue[77] said, "If you obtain them, you can carve spirits and demons. Because they are extraordinary, they possess numinous efficacy."[78]

The name "maple men" suggests that, like ginseng root or mandrake, the tendrils and burls of these trees assumed a humanoid form.[79] The suitability of the wood for contacting otherworldly spirits and the rapidity of the growth of the "maple men"—apparently nurtured by storms and violent rains—attests to its numinous essence.

One final passage tells of a Spring of the Jealous Woman, connected to the younger sister of a minister from the Spring and Autumn era:[80]

In Bingzhou, on the border between Shi'ai County and Shouyang County,[81] *there is a Spring of the Jealous Woman. Beside it there is a votive temple to her spirit. The water was crystal clear and thousands of feet deep. Those offering sacrifices threw in coins and sheep bones, which all could see on the bottom. According to folk legend, the Jealous Girl was the younger sister of Jie Zhitui who had competed with her elder brother. Within one hundred li from the spring, no one is allowed to light fires on the day of the Cold Food Festival; until today this remains the case. When women wearing festive costumes of resplendent red pass through the mountains to pick coral lilies and lily bulbs, they are invariably alarmed by thunder and lightning, wind and hail.* (6.135)

The man mentioned in this anecdote, Jie Zhitui, faithfully served Double Ears (Chong'er 重耳; Duke Wen of Jin) during years of struggle and wandering, but in the corrupt administration after the restoration of his liege, he entered the forests and mountains near Bingzhou to become a recluse rather than serving in office.[82] After multiple failed attempts to recall Jie Zhitui to service, frustrated Double Ears finally decided to burn the mountains and forests to the ground and smoke him out. Jie Zhitui was burned to death. According to legend, the locals honoring Jie Zhitui made this a taboo day when fire was forbidden, or, alternatively, the regretful Double Ears then forbade the lighting of fires on this day—the fifth day of the third lunar month. Eventually, this date evolved into the Cold Food Festival, a holiday to venerate one's ancestors, though no fire could be lit for food preparation.[83]

The *Old Tang History* records that a local official in Bingzhou, learning that the Two Sages were planning to visit the region, remarked that he was worried because those traveling the road near the shrine dedicated to the Jealous Girl while decked out in gay apparel inevitably met with the calamity of wind and thunder. He ordered a massive crew of thirty thousand to clear a new road for the prospective imperial progress. Urging Gaozong to issue an abrupt countermand, Di Renjie, who had held an appointment in Bingzhou and was familiar with the region, remarked that the deities of wind and rain would invariably place the grand cortege of the Son of Heaven, the imperial sovereign, under their aegis; thus, the Jealous Girl (outranked by these greater divinities) would cause no damage and the construction of the road was unnecessary.[84] The road project was shelved. This episode helped solidify Di Renjie's reputation as a Confucian rationalist, one unswayed by folk superstitions.

The nature of the sibling rivalry between the Jealous Girl and her elder brother Jie Zhitui is not clear from this anecdote. This story of a spring in the woman emperor's home prefecture may also be understood, once again, as an oblique criticism of Wu Zhao, as well as a commentary on the tempestuous and volatile temperament of women. The character for jealousy (*du* 妒) contains the radical for woman (*nü* 女), indicating that this trait was inherent in the female character. Curiously, a much later folk iteration of the story from the early Qing has Jie Zhitui return from his wanderings with Double Ears only to have his jealous wife, fearful that he has been unfaithful, leash herself to him, literally binding him to her with a silken cord, unwilling to let him free for an instant. Humiliated, as the fire kindled by Double Ears closes in, Jie lights a fire of his own, and he and his jealous wife are immolated together.[85]

Stories like these from *Court and Country*, illustrating how history and culture are etched into the landscape, augmented Zhang Zhuo's reputation as a raconteur who had crisscrossed the empire collecting tales strange and wonderful.

FLORA, FAUNA, AND THE NATURAL WORLD

NATURAL TOXINS AND CURES

By the early Tang, drugs manufactured from animal parts and plant products had long since been compiled in vast pharmacopeias. People were also well aware of a wide variety of natural toxins. Some of this hard-won knowledge, a passage in *Court and Country* relates, came from the painstaking observation of animal behavior:

> *Medical books say that when a tiger is struck by a poison arrow, it eats green-black mud; when a wild pig is struck by a poison arrow, it uproots bellflowers[86] with its snout and eats them; when a pheasant is wounded by a hawk, it uses glutinous foxglove[87] leaves as a poultice to paste over the injury. Also, alumite can harm rats. Zhang Zhuo[88] once tried it. When rats are poisoned with alumite, they stagger as if drunk, unable to recognize humans. But if they drink muddy water, they can recover instantly. Birds and beasts, insects and reptiles, all know how to detoxify—let humans learn from them!*
>
> *For a silkworm sting, use wing casings of a beetle to bind it; for a horse bite, daub on ashes from the thongs at the end of a whip. They mutually counteract each other. For a spider bite, use ground realgar[89] to bind it. And when one ruptures a tendon but must carry on, one wrings the juice from the roots of* inula japonica, *aligns the ruptured ends of tendon, smears the juice on, then seal it. The tendon will then be connected as before. When slaves in Sichuan fled, a number ruptured their tendons. Using this method to carry on, not one in a hundred were lost.* (1.5)

Watching the behavior of injured or poisoned animals sometimes led to discoveries. If even animals possess an innate awareness of the curative capacity of poultices and plasters, the instinct to utilize natural detoxicants, then mankind also can avail themselves of the healing powers of plants and animals. After drawing upon his personal experience of using alumite to incapacitate rats, Zhang enumerates different ways in which flora and insects might be employed to detoxify or heal.

Another account in *Court and Country*—containing further evidence that Lingnan and the southern hinterlands were rife with every conceivable poison and peril—refers to Chen Huaiqing (whom we encountered in the Chapter 5 as fortune's favored), a man who discovered a vein of gold after noticing the golden sheen in the shit of his flock of ducks:

> *In the customs of Lingnan, many kinds of toxins were made. A slave would be ordered to eat poisonous heartbreak grass, then would be buried in the ground. Anyone who ate the fungi that grew from his stomach would immediately die. Anyone who ate the fungi that grew from the hands, feet, and forehead would die the same day; if anyone ate fungi that grew in the immediate proximity of the body, they would die within several days; slightly further away, they would die in a month or two; and even those who ate more distant fungi would die within one to three years. Only a recipe made by Chen Huaiqing's family could cure this. If someone*

> *smeared this toxin [heartbreak grass] on the end of a horsewhip, a simple touch was enough to poison a man; one who so much as tasted it was certain to die.* (1.4)

Clearly, Chen Huaiqing was no mere lucky simpleton: he and his family devised a cure for those poisoned by ultra-toxic heartbreak grass (*Gelsemium elegans*), apparently a well-guarded secret recipe. Zhang Zhuo does not relate the ingredients. The essay "On Poison," in Wang Chong's *Lunheng*, a Han dynasty text, contends that toxic heartbreak grass is to flora what vipers and adders are to fauna.[90]

In another passage, Zhang Zhuo cites another courtier who served in the early eighth century, Zhao Yanxi, as the source of wisdom on using moxibustion—cauterizing using burned moxa (mugwort)—on the site of a snakebite as antivenom:

> *Zhao Yanxi said, "If one is bitten by a venomous snake, cauterize the site with moxa paste immediately. If this is done, the person can recover; otherwise, the person will die. For snakebites, continually utilize moxibustion until all of the poison is drawn out. Only then can the treatment stop."* (1.5)

Curiously, this was anything but a new prescription: records on silk unearthed from a Han dynasty tomb indicate that moxa cauterization was used on snake bites in the second-century BC.[91] Though no physician, Zhang Zhuo and other literati were familiar with many medicines, pharmacopeias, and folk remedies. Many of the passages in *Court and Country* that delineate the dangers of the natural world also provide measures that men might take to counteract or avoid such poisons and hazards.

FAUNA AND FLORA OF LINGNAN, THE SOUTHERN BORDERLANDS, AND BEYOND

Lingnan, in the southeast of the Tang empire, the region south of the Nanling Mountains, was considered a remote and abysmal, malarial hinterland, full of noxious ethers. For literati–officials acclimated to the metropoles of Chang'an and Luoyang, banishment or appointment to an office situated in these pestilential and savage fringes represented an unbearable exile from the height of civilization to a sweltering miasma of swamp-bound barbarism.[92]

Capable of sustaining double or triple cropping of rice if paddies could be formed, the lush region is known for its cornucopia of oranges, limes, tangerines, kumquats, lychees, longans, bananas, and pomelos. Different palm trees in these austral climes yielded coconuts, bananas, dates, palm flour, and the betel nut—a stimulant with medicinal properties.[93] Palms offered food, fuel, fiber for ropes, and lumber for shelter.

FLORA, FAUNA, AND THE NATURAL WORLD

The following five passages from *Court and Country* all reinforce the widely shared notion that the southerly regions were a poisonous zone filled with every imaginable lethal fauna and flora—whether voracious packs of diminutive but carnivorous turtles, swarms of disease-carrying insects, toxic grasses, venomous snakes, or pterodactyl-sized aggressive birds.

This initial passage shows that, once you move south of the Yangzi River Valley, even in the territory north of the Nanling Mountains, the lands were fraught with hazard!

> *South of the Yellow River and north of the Southern Peaks there were invisible multitudes of flying insects that emitted a strange sound like the chirping and twittering of birds. People caught in the middle of the infestation of these noisy insects suffered from dysentery, with bloody discharge in their excrement. Neither physicians nor medicines could cure this malady. Beyond salvation, the afflicted would die within a xun-week. (Sup., 158)*

A second passage issues a dire warning about the wee turtles of Lingnan:

> *An abundance of small bright red turtles the size of a ladle inhabit the waters of Luozhou and Bianzhou prefectures in Lingnan. Any creature entering their waters—whether bird, beast, or water buffalo—is dragged to a deep pool, drained of its blood, and perishes. Some say that water dragons pull these unfortunate creatures to their watery demise; they don't know that it is, in fact, swarms of these tiny turtles. (Sup., 168)*

A third entry offers another warning about the extreme toxicity of heartbreak grass, but also mentions a cure and intimates the lessons clever folks can derive from the drinking habits of serpent eagles and rhinos:

> *Anyone who eats heartbreak grass will immediately die. In sites where heartbreak grass grows there are also white-flowering wisteria that can cure the toxins of heartbreak grass. When rhinoceroses come to a place where the serpent eagle drinks, they won't immerse their horns in the water because any creature that drinks the water will invariably perish. This is because serpent eagles eat poisonous snakes. (1.5)*

In another passage, Zhang Zhuo alerts his readers of the peril posed by an aggressive pit viper in these austral climes:

> *There is a venomous snake in the Wuxi region of Qian,[94] black with an upturned nose. It lies coiled in the grass, its fangs curved backward.[95] When a person walks past at a distance of several paces, it launches itself straight as an arrow and, almost as soon as it sinks its lethal fangs in, the person dies. If it bites one's hand, one must immediately sever the hand; if it bites one's foot, one must immediately sever the foot. Otherwise, the whole body will swell and go septic. The snake is called the Halys pit viper. There is also a yellow-throated*

snake[96] that is fond of living around human dwellings. It is not poisonous and is harmless to humans but excels in eating venomous snakes. After it has eaten to satiety, it hangs its head downward. As it rests, its drool forms a small tumulus-shaped mound on the ground below, which transforms into sand lice. People bitten by these sand lice become sick. On its brow are characters reading "Great King"; other kinds of snake revere it as the lord-elder of serpents. It often eats pit vipers. (5.121–22)

The final account from *Court and Country* in this subsection describes the clever means by which the King of Champa, a Southeast Asian state in modern-day northern Laos and southern Cambodia, rid the region of an alpine-dwelling, man-eating bird the size of a dragon:

Halfway up the slope of Champa's Mount Gelang, 10000 zhang tall, is a cavern. Formerly it was home to the "Bird of the Waves," a giant kite-like avian the size of a camel that snatched up men who passed by the foot of the mountain in its mighty talons and devoured them. The commonfolk came to dread the creature. The King of Champa inserted two swords inside huge slabs of beef and ordered his soldiers to wear them as hats. The birds swooped down, seized the meat-hats, devoured them, then perished. The species has not been seen since. (Sup., 168)

Every one of these passages on Lingnan titillated Zhang Zhuo's audience with the vicarious dangers and horrors of these exotic hinterlands to the south.

Afternote

COURT AND COUNTRY—COMPRISED OF STORIES AND anecdotes that Zhang Zhuo saw, heard, and collected over the tortuous course of his half-century career—is usually classified as "brush notes" (*biji* 筆記) or "small stories" (*xiaoshuo* 小說). Zhang's work includes a number of "accounts of anomalies" (*zhiguai* 志怪) and "miscellaneous records" (*zalu* 雜錄).[1] Antonino Forte remarks that such "tales of little importance" (as he renders *xiaoshuo*) were "somewhat looked down upon by professional historians" who considered them "irrelevant or unworthy of inclusion in an official history."[2] Of *Court and Country*, Song chronicler Hong Mai offers the following contemptuous assessment: "All of the events that he has recorded are scattered fragments and trifling remnants. Moreover, in most cases he has taken creative liberties."[3] Furthermore, as the Introduction has shown, Zhang's text is problematic and manifestly corrupt. So what, then, is the value of these translations, these shards of thought, these bits and pieces of a mercurial chronicler's peculiar collection of fragments and anecdotes?

First off, these translations are made of bits and pieces of information that Zhang Zhuo gleaned and gathered. They are accounts of events that a man living in late seventh and early eighth century China heard or personally witnessed. Standard histories of the Tang dynasty (the two Tang histories and the *Comprehensive Mirror*) are all written after a lapse of two or three centuries following Wu Zhao's death; *Court and Country* features vignettes compiled by a widely traveled and opinionated man who served in her court and was acquainted with a large cast of characters inhabiting her era.

Second, *Court and Country* amplifies not only our understanding of social and cultural history, but our grasp of the routine machinations of the court and bureaucracy. Anecdotes and "small stories," as Xiaofei Tian frames them, "disrupt the flow of the grand historical narrative and expose the real workaday lives 'behind' such narratives."[4] Ellen Cong Zhang contends that unofficial sources of miscellaneous notes—works akin to Zhang Zhuo's—from the Song dynasty have "proven invaluable to our understanding of many aspects of Song political, social, and cultural history."[5] In a similar vein, Anna Shields asserts that "anecdotal texts can, with careful contextualization, give us a finer-grained picture of Tang cultural activity."[6] Luo Manling's examination of "historical miscellanies" from the Tang includes Zhang Zhuo's *Court and Country*. This sort of work, she argues, made "possible a special kind of cultural memory construction in that writers piece together anecdotes to create a composite, multi-faceted picture of the past"—a "mosaic memory" that became a vital part of a "communal discourse," a shared, collective memory. These anecdotes are snippets of "private knowledge born of the social network of gossip," "snapshots portraying vivid details of a bygone social and political life, revealing diverse and even contradictory points of view."[7] When interwoven with the known wider background of military and political events from official histories, *Court and Country* helps provide this sort of mosaic, offering revealing glimpses into individual lives, into quirks and personalities that help complicate and add significant nuance to our understanding of larger events.

Finally, the sweeping breadth of *Court and Country*—moving from the political center to the margins of empire, outward from towns and villages to the steppe, forests, and jungles, from the world of men to the natural world and beyond, to the realm of spirits—offers a fresh, panoramic vantage on medieval China. While many of these stories are designed to show the culture of corruption, ugliness, and favoritism of Wu Zhao's regency (684–690) and reign as emperor (690–705)—to bring to light the wolfish violence of her "cruel officials" and expose the tensions between fawning sycophants and righteous voices of remonstrance in her court—the text moves well beyond the female sovereign's inner palace and contentious court. This work often takes common people and low-ranking officials as subjects, featuring humorous anecdotes, strange accounts of the supernatural, and tales of karmic retribution, thereby providing glimpses into the human, natural, and supernatural worlds of medieval China.

As its title suggests, *Court and Country* topically ranges from the court to local villages and wilderlands. While standard histories are largely limited to major political and military endeavors of state, *Court and Country* sheds light on the lives of men and women in cities, prefectures, and counties throughout the empire, presenting remarkable and peculiar events that punctuated those everyday lives. Zhang Zhuo's stories examine the foibles of local officials, the generosity of peasant-farmers, the bad behavior of aristocrats, the arcane arts of diviners, the arrogance of local despots, the remarkable dexterity and physical prowess of soldiers, the curative or toxic properties of unusual animals and plants, and the customs of peoples dwelling beyond the borders. Breathing a much-needed folk vitality into medieval China, this collection of miscellany provides vivid depictions of people largely erased from standard histories: lute-strumming diviners, Sogdian priests, false prophets, ingenious craftsmen, clever and arrant local officials, oily-mouthed sycophants, glib humorists, and a bevy of sinister and benevolent spirits.

Carrie Reed compared another "hodge-podge" from later in the Tang dynasty, Duan Chengshi's *Miscellaneous Morsels of Youyang*, to a "sumptuous stew" best appreciated if one recognizes the "richness and complexity" of all its ingredients blended together. Reed describes the volume as "a running chronicle of the multi-faceted world (literary and material, human and otherworldly)" that at once captures the tension and strikes a balance between the familiar and the strange, the inexplicable and the mundane.[8] Zhang Zhuo's earlier work, though not as wide-ranging or nuanced (it has less than half as many entries), shares these qualities. Contemporary scholar Ma Xueqin opines that the "brush notes" and "small stories" gathered in *Court and Country* record "both the great affairs of Wu Zetian's court and folk anecdotes from around the realm. This is precious material quintessential to any study of early Tang history."[9] Taken as a whole, *Court and Country* offers a lively and novel perspective from the empire of Wu Zhao that will not only amuse and shock readers, but also prompt them to recalibrate much of what they think they know about medieval China.

Dislocated from her native country, a Koguryan slave girl, a captive of war, plots to poison her master and plans a desperate escape with a fellow expatriate. Traces of gold discovered in the muck deposited by a flock of ducks lead a southern family to shocking and unexpected wealth. Court ministers match wits trying to devise comic nicknames to disparage colleagues. In the remote south, the enraged wife of a local administrator blinds her husband's new, non-Chinese concubine, only to meet a macabre and karmic justice. In isolation, such stories are perhaps merely oddities; collectively, however, the two hundred anecdotes from *Court and Country* translated here offer a sampling of the aromas, flavors, colors, and textures that compose the rich pottage that is the tumultuous world of Wu Zhao.

Appendix: People and Places

NAMES

Anle Princess 安樂公主
Bai (Bo) Juyi 白居易
Bai Tieyu 白鐵余
Ban Zhao 班昭 (Lady of Handsome Fairness Ban 班婕妤)
Bi Gan 比干
Boast Father 夸父/誇父
Bole 伯樂 (Sun Yang 孫陽)
Cai Heng 蔡衡
Cao Huaishun 曹懷舜
Chang'E 嫦娥
Chen Anping 陳安平
Chen Cangqi 陳藏器
Chen Huaiqing 陳懷卿
Chen Lingying 陳令英
Chen Ximin 陳希閔
Chen Yuanguang 陳元光
Chen Zangqi 陳藏器
Chen Ziang 陳子昂
Cheng Wuting 程務挺
Cheng Xingmou 程行謀
Chuan Huangzhong 傅黃中
Confucius 孔子
Cui Hun 崔渾
Cui Jian 崔簡
Cui Rizhi 崔日知
Cui Shi 崔湜
Cui Wu 崔務
Cui Xuansheng 崔玄升
Deng You 鄧祐

Di Renjie 狄仁傑
Dong Xingcheng 董行成
Dong Yan 董偃
Dongfang Zha 東方虬
Dou Zhifan 竇知範
Double Ears (Duke Wen of Jin) 重耳, 晉文公
Dragon-son Liu 劉籠子
Du Jingquan 杜景佺 (Du Yuanfang 元方)
Duan Jin 段瑾
Duan Zan 段瓚
Duke Mu of Qin 秦穆公
Empress Wang 王后
Empress Wei 韋后 (Traitor Wei 逆韋, Commoner Wei 韋庶人, Miss Wei 韋氏, Missy Wei 阿韋)
Erzhu Jiu 爾朱九
Fan Wen 樊文
Fan Qinben 樊欽賁
Fang Xuanling 房玄齡
Feng Yi 馮毅
Feng Zidu 馮子都
Fu Yue 傅說
Gao Rui 高睿
Gao Yi 高嶷
Gao Zan 高瓚
Gong Siye 弓嗣業
Grannie He 何婆
Grannie Lai 阿來
Gu Zong 顧琮
Guanyin 觀音
Guo Ba 郭霸
Guo Chun 郭純
Guo Wujing 郭務靜
Guo Zhengyi 郭正一
Han Linggui 韓令珪
Han Xun 韓珣
He Axiao 何阿小
He Qiao 和嶠
He Ruojin 賀若瑾
Heichi Changzhi 黑齒常之
Helan Minzhi 賀蘭敏之
Hu Chao 胡超

APPENDIX

Huifan 慧範
Hu Liang 胡亮
Hu Yuanli 胡元禮
Ilterish Khan (Ashina Gumalu) 骨篤祿
Immortal Medicine Li 李仙藥
Jade Disc 碧玉
Jade White 玉素
Jealous Girl 妬女
Ji Mao 吉懋
Ji Xi 吉晢
Ji Xianzhi 紀先知
Ji Xu 吉頊
Jiang Chen 江琛
Jiang Chong 江充
Jiang Rong 江融
Jie Zhitui 介之推
Jingle County Princess 靜樂縣主
Kong Luqiu 孔魯丘
Kou Qianzhi 寇謙之
Lao Ai 嫪毐
Laozi 老子 (Li Er 李耳)
Li Chengjia 李承嘉
Li Chongfu 李重福
Li Chongjun 李重俊
Li Cide 李慈德
Li Fang 李方
Li Feng 李鳳
Li Hong 李宏
Li Huaibi 李懷璧
Li Ji 李勣 (Xu Ji 徐勣)
Li Jiegu 李楷固
Li Jin 李進
Li Jingxuan 李敬玄
Li Jinxing 李謹行
Li Jingye (Xu Jingye) 李敬業 (徐)
Li Jingzhen 李敬貞
Li Jinzhong 李盡忠
Li Liangbi 李良弼
Li Longfan 李隆範
Li Longji 李隆基
Li Ming 李明

APPENDIX

Li Ningdao 李凝道
Li Rizhi 李日知
Li Ruoxu 李若虛
Li Qianli 李千里
Li Quanjiao 李全交
Li Ti 李逖
Li Xiang 李詳
Li Xiaoyi 李孝逸
Li Yuanjia 李元嘉
Li Yuanying (Prince of Teng) 李元嬰 (滕王)
Li Zhaode 李昭德
Li Zhe 李愀
Li Zhen 利貞
Li Zheng 里正
Liang Xuzhou 梁虛州
Liu Chong 柳崇
Liu Jiao 劉交
Liu Jing 劉靜
Liu Jingyang 劉景陽
Liu Qing 柳慶
Liu Rengui 劉仁軌
Liu Sahe 劉薩訶
Liu Shangshu 劉尚書
Liu Yao 劉曜
Lu Jingyang 陸景旸
Lu Renjie 逯仁傑
Lu Xian 盧獻
Lu Xun 魯迅
Liu Yong 劉邕/雍
Lu Yuanfang 陸元方
Lu Yuqing 陸餘慶
Lu Shide 婁師德
Lü Zhiwei 閭知微
Luo Binwang 駱賓王
Luo Hei(hei) 羅黑（黑）
Luo Hui 羅會
Luo Wuzheng 駱務整
Ma Jipu 馬吉甫
Ma Renjie 麻仁節
Ma Xiantong 馬仙童
Ma Zhiji 馬知己

APPENDIX

Madame Lu 盧夫人
Madame Zhao 趙氏
Mao Jun 毛俊
Master Ding 鼎師
Meng Lingxiu 孟靈休
Ming Chongyan 明崇儼
Minhuai (Crown Prince of Jin) 愍懷太子
Mrs. Zheng 鄭氏
Ning family 寧氏
Pan Chan 潘彥
Pei Guang 裴光
Pei Gui 裴珪
Pei Min 裴旻
Pei Shaoye 裴紹業
Pei Xuan 裴巽
Pei Ziyi 裴子儀
Pei Ziyun 裴子雲
Peng Botong 彭博通
Peng Ta 彭闥
Peng Xianjue 彭先覺
Pengzu 彭祖
Pure Consort Xiao 蕭淑妃
Qapaghan 默啜, Khan of the Tujue Turks
Qi Lianyao 綦連耀
Qian Weidao 騫味道
Qiao Shu 喬屬
Qiao Zhizhi 喬知之
Qibi Heli 契苾何力
Quan Longxiang 權龍襄
Ren Zhengli 任正理
Ren Zhengming 任正名
Sakyamuni 釋迦
Shazha Zhongyi 沙吒忠義
Shen Quanjiao 沈全交
Shen Yue 沈約
Shen Zirong 沈子榮
Shi Chong 石崇
Song Lingwen 宋令文
Song Yun 宋雲
Song Zhiwen 宋之問
Song Zhixun 宋之遜

Song Zhiti 宋之悌
Su Gui 蘇瓌
Su Ting 蘇頲
Su Weidao
Su Zheng 蘇征
Sun Chan'gao 孫彥高
Sun Quan 孫佺
Sun Rongshi 孙容师
Sun Simiao 孫思邈
Sun Wanrong 孫萬榮
Suo Yuanli 索元禮
Taiping Princess 太平公主
Tang Boruo 唐波若
Tao Zongyi 陶宗儀
Tenth Lady 十娘
Tian Yi 田翼
Tumor-riddled Su 宿瘤
Wang Fangqing
Wang Gao 王杲
Wang Huifeng 王惠風
Wang Jing 王敬
Wang Jingrong 王景融
Wang Jishan 王及善
Wang Ju 王勮
Wang Ju 王琚
Wang Qiuli 王求禮
Wang Sui 王燧
Wang Tongjiao 王同皎
Wang Xiaojie 王孝傑
Wang Xingzai 王幸在
Wang Xu 王旭
Wang Zhiyin 王誌愔
Wang Zhu 王助
Wei Azang 韋阿藏
Wei Chang 魏昶
Wei Hao 衛鎬
Wei Ling 魏伶
Wei Xuanzhen 韋玄貞
Wei Yuanzhong 魏元忠
Wei Zhigu 魏知古
Wu Chengsi 武承嗣

APPENDIX

Wu Ding 武丁
Wu Sansi 武三思
Wu Shikai 武士開
Wu Shihuo 武士彟
Wu Song 武松
Wu Xiwu 武栖梧
Wu Yizong 武懿宗
Xiao Quan 蕭佺
Xie You 謝祐
Xin Chengsi 辛承嗣
Xu (Li) Jingye 徐敬業
Xu (Li) Jingzhen 徐敬真
Xu Yougong 徐有功
Xu Ziru 許子儒
Xue Huaiyi 薛懷義
Xue Jichang 薛季昶
Xue Shenhuo 薛眘惑
Xue Zhen 薛震
Yan (Zhuang) Junping 閻 (莊) 君平
Yan Shengqi 嚴升期
Yan Zhiwei 閻知微
Yang Chuyu 楊楚玉
Yang Qizhuang 楊齊莊
Yang Xuanji 楊玄基
Yang Yuanliang 楊元亮
Yang Wulian 楊務廉
Yao Chong 姚崇
Ye Fashan 葉法善
Yi Shentong 尹神童
Yicheng Princess 宜城公主
Yin Wenliang 殷文亮
Yong Jin 永進
Yu Dingguo 于定國
Yu Qianlou 庾黔婁
Yu Sixuan 魚思咺
Yuan Banqian 員半千
Yuan Bensong 元本竦
Yuan Jia 元嘉
Yuan Sizhong 袁思中
Yuan Tiangang 袁天綱
Yuan Zhihong 袁智弘

Zeng Xi 曾晳
Zengzi 曾子
Zhang Changling 張昌齡
Zhang Changqi 張昌期
Zhang Changyi 張昌儀
Zhang Changzong 張昌宗
Zhang Chong 張崇
Zhang Chujin 張楚金
Zhang Huaisu 張懷肅
Zhang Jian 張薦 (Zhang Zhuo's grandson)
Zhang Jian 張簡
Zhang Jingzang 張璟藏
Zhang Qian 張潛
Zhang Rentan 張仁亶
Zhang Ruzi 長孺子
Zhang Sengyou 僧繇
Zhang Shiqi 張食其
Zhang Shizhi 張釋之
Zhang Sigong 張思恭
Zhang Siming 張嗣明
Zhang Tinggui 張廷圭
Zhang Xi 張錫
Zhang Yizhi 張易之
Zhang You 張猷
Zhang Yuanyi 張元一
Zhang Xiwang 張希望
Zhang Xuanyu 張玄遇
Zhang Zhuo 張鷟 (Zhang Wencheng 張文成); Master Who Drifts then Rests 浮休子
Zhang Zu 張祖
Zhangsun Wuji 長孫無忌
Zhao Kuo 趙廓
Zhao Luwen 趙履溫
Zhao Wenhui 趙文翙
Zhao Xuanjing 趙玄景
Zhao Yanxi 趙延禧
Zheng Yin 鄭愔
Zhou Rengui 周仁軌
Zhou Yunyuan 周允元
Zhou Zigong 周子恭
Zhu Qianyi 朱前疑

APPENDIX

Zhu Qinming 祝欽明
Zhu Suihou 朱隨侯
Zhuangzi 莊子
Zong Chuke 宗楚客
Zou Luotuo (Camel Zou) 鄒駱駝
Zu Zhenxian 祖珍儉
Zuo Fen 左芬

Non-Han Ethnic Groups
Dangxiang 党項
Hu 胡
Jihu 稽胡 (Shanhu 山胡)
Liao 獠
Man 蠻
Mohe (Malgal) 靺鞨
Qiang 羌
Qibi 契苾
Qidan (Khitan) 契丹
Sogdian 胡
Tiele (High Carts) 鐵勒
Tufan (Tibetans) 吐蕃
Tujue (Turks) 突厥
Xi 奚
Xiongnu 匈奴
Zhuang 壯

Places
Annam 安南
Ba 巴
Balhae 渤海
Beizhou 貝州
Bianzhou 汴州
Bianzhou 辯州
Bingzhou 并州
Bohai Commandery 渤海郡
Boye 博野 (a county in Yingzhou)
Bozhou 博州
Cangzhou 滄州
Champa 真臘
Chang'an 長安
Changdian 長店 (in Heyang)

APPENDIX

Changping County 昌平縣 (in Dezhou)
Changzhou 常州
Chenzhou 辰州
Chenzhou 郴州
Chuzhou 處州
Dazhou 達州
Dezhou 德州
Dingxiang 定襄公
Dingzhou 定州
Divine Capital 神都 (Luoyang)
Donghai 東海
Duanzhou 端州
Eastern Sea 東海
Fangzhou 房州
Fengzhou 峰州
Fuping 富平
Fuyang County 富陽縣
Fuzhou 涪州
Gan County 贛縣 (in Qianzhou)
Gansu 甘肅
Gaocheng County 郜城 (in Luozhou)
Gaoyao Country 高要縣
Gongzhou 龔州
Goushi 緱氏
Guangzheng Gate 光政門
Guangxi 廣西
Guangzhou 廣州
Haizhou 海州
Hangzhou 杭州
Hebei 河北
Hedong 河東
Hejian 河間
Henan 河南
Henei 河內
Hengzhou 恒州
Hexi 河西
Heyang 河陽
Hongzhou 洪州
Hunan 湖南
Huzhou 湖州
Huaizhou 懷州

APPENDIX

Huameng County (in Guangzhou) 化蒙縣
Huangshan 黃山
Huanzhou 驩州
Huarong County 華容縣
Jiangnan 江南
Jiannan 劍南
Jiangnan 江南
Jianzhou 建州
Ji'nan 濟南
Jingcheng Ward (Chang'an) 金城坊
Jingyang Ridge 景陽岡
Jingyun Gate 景運門
Jingzhou 邢州
Jizhou 冀州
Junyi County (Bianzhou) 浚儀
Koguryo 高麗
Lake Tai 太湖
Lâm Ấp 林邑
Lantian 藍田
Lanzhou 嵐州
Liangzhou 梁州
Liang County 梁縣
Lin'an 臨安
Lingnan 嶺南
Liuzhou 柳州
Longyou County 龍遊縣
Luo River 洛
Luoyang 洛陽 （also Divine Capital）
Luozhou 洛州
Luozhou 羅州
Luze 陸澤
Maitreya 彌勒
Mawangdui 馬王堆
Melonport 瓜埠
Mount Felicity 慶山
Mount Gelang 葛浪山
Mount Guzhu 顧渚山
Mount Hua 華山
Mount Song 嵩山
Mount Tai 泰山
Nanchang 南昌

APPENDIX

Nangong County 南宮縣
Nanling Peaks 南嶺
Nanpi County (in Cangzhou) 南皮縣
Ningzhou 寧州
Pakeche 百濟
Pingshu 平舒
Pyong'yang 平壤
Qi county 祈縣 (Bingzhou)
Qian(fu) 黔府 (Qianzhou Garrison), Guizhou region
Qianzhou 虔州
Quanzhou 泉州
Qiangzhou 滄
Qinzhou 沁州
Qinzhou 秦州
Qu Jiang 曲江
Quzhou 衢州
Raoyang County (in Yingzhou 1) 饒陽縣
Rongshan 容山
Runzhou 潤州
Ruzhou 汝州
Sanqu 三曲
Sanyang Palace 三陽宮
Shady Mountains 陰山
Shadymount County 山陰縣 (in Yuezhou)
Shandong 山東
Shanxi 山西
Shanzhou 鄯州
Shaozhou 韶州
She County 歙縣
Shengwu Ward 勝業坊
Shengzhou 勝州
Shi'ai County 石艾縣
Shouan 壽安
Shouyang County 壽陽縣
Shudun 樹墩
Shu 蜀 (Sichuan)
Shuzhou 舒州
Sichuan 四川
Silla 新羅
Sishui 汜水
Sizhou 思州

APPENDIX

Songzhou 宋州
South Sea 南海
Taihang Mountains 太行山
Taizhou 太州
Tengzhou 滕州
Tongchuan 通川
Tongzhou 同州
Wannian County 萬年縣
Weizhou 衛州
Wenzhou 溫州
White Crane Mountain 白鶴山
Wulong County 武龍縣
Wuxi 五溪
Wuxing 吳興
Wuping 武平縣
Wuzhou 梧州
Xiangle County 襄樂縣
Xiangzhou 襄州
Xindu 信都 (seat of Jizhou prefecture)
Xinxiang County 新鄉縣
Yangzi River 長江; 揚子江
Yellow River 黃河
Yellow Roebuck 黃獐
Yanzhou 延州
Yanzhou 兗州 (near Jining in Shandong)
Yizhou 易州
Yingzhou 1 瀛州
Yingzhou 營州
Youzhou 幽州
Yue 越
Yuezhou 越州
Yunzhou 韻州
Yuzhang 豫章
Yuzhou 豫州
Zhangzhou 漳州
Zhaozhou 趙州
Zhenzhou 溱州
Zhenzhou 鎮州
Zhiye Ward 殖業坊
Zhuchi County 朱鳶縣
Zhuji County (in Yuezhou) 諸暨縣

Notes

TABLES

1 Also see Hiraoka Takeo, *Todai no koyomi* [The Tang Calendar] (Shanghai: Shanghai guji, 1990); Paul Kroll, "The True Dates of the Reigns and Reign Periods of T'ang," *Tang Studies* 2 (1984): 25–30; Rothschild, "An Inquiry into Reign Era Changes Under Wu Zhao, China's Only Female Emperor," *Early Medieval China* 12 (2006); A. C. Moule, *The Rulers of China, 221 BC to AD 1949* (New York: Praeger, 1957), 54–59. Some translations of reign eras are lifted from Kroll.

WEIGHTS AND MEASURES

1 Denis Twitchett and John Fairbank, (eds.), *Cambridge History of China, Vol. 3: Sui and Tang China, 589–906, Part I* (Cambridge: Cambridge University Press, 1979), xx; Twitchett, *Financial Administration under the T'ang Dynasty*, second ed. (Cambridge: Cambridge University Press, 1970), xiii; Hu Ji 胡戟, "Tangdai duliang heng yu mouli zhidu" 唐代度量衡與畝里制度, *Xibei daxue xuebao* (1980.4): 34–41; Peng Xinwei, *A Monetary History of China*, Vol.1, Edward Kaplan trans. (Bellingham: Western Washington University, 1993), 246–48; BuYun Chen, *Empire of Style: Silk and Fashion in Tang China* (Seattle: University of Washington Press, 2019), 124.

INTRODUCTION

1 Herman Melville, *The Confidence-Man: His Masquerade*, eds. Harrison Hayford, Hershel Parker, and G. Thomas Tanselle (Evanston and Chicago: Northwestern University Press and The Newberry Library, 1984), 70.
2 Whenever possible, I use posthumous honorary names (*yihao* 謚號) for emperors rather than given names. In this instance, Wu Zhao's husband is called Gaozong rather than Li Zhi; her sons, Zhongzong and Ruizong, not Li Xian and Li Dan; her grandson, Xuanzong, not Li Longji. See the list of "Dynasties and Rulers" at the beginning of this volume.
3 The following two sections on Zhang Zhuo's life, official career, and literary background help constitute a composite biography based on a number of primary and secondary sources. There is a brief biography and introduction provided in Zhao Shouyan's 趙守儼 collated and annotated *Sui-Tang jiahua Chaoye qianzai* 隋唐嘉華朝野僉載 (Beijing: Zhonghua, 1997), "Editor's Notes," 3–5. Zhang Zhuo does not have an independent biography in the two Tang histories. He is

relegated to a sub-heading in the biography of his grandson, Zhang Jian, a late Tang official; these accounts contain a terse description of his life and career: Ouyang Xiu 歐陽修, *Xin Tang shu* 新唐書 [New Tang History] (Beijing: Zhonghua, 1997; hereafter *XTS*), 161.4979–80 and Liu Xu 劉昫, *Jiu Tang shu* 舊唐書 [Old Tang History], (Beijing: Zhonghua, 1997; hereafter *JTS*), 149.4023–24. Further background is found in Liu Su's 劉肅 late Tang *Da Tang Xinyu* 大唐新語 [New Words from the Great Tang], in *Tang-Song shiliao biji congkan* 唐宋史料筆記叢刊 (Beijing: Zhonghua, 1997; hereafter *DTXY*), 8.128–29. Attesting to Zhang Zhuo's late career presence in the south, a late Tang work, Mo Xiufu's 莫休夫 *Record of the Customs and Geography of Guilin* (Guilin fengtu ji 桂林風土記), includes a biographical paragraph on Zhang, his works, and his examination accomplishments; Mo IS likely a pseudonym. There is also the early Southern Song *Continued Jottings of Rongzhai* (Rongzhai xubi 容齋續筆), written by Hong Mai 洪邁 (1123–1202), a harsh critic of Zhang Zhuo who seeks to denigrate his examination credentials; Rongzhai is Hong Mai's pen name. Xu Song's 徐松 (1781–1848) Qing dynasty *Study of Records of Examination Candidates in the Tang* (Tang dengke jikao 唐登科記考) also contains a listing of some of Zhang's examination records.

Most modern scholarship tends to treat Zhang Zhuo as a literary figure rather than a popular historian and historical actor shaped by his time; this work seeks to remedy that. Historians have, of course, long cited *Court and Country* and Zhang's other works, for they provide a valuable supplement to the official record left by state histories. Perhaps the most extensive Western writings on Zhang Zhuo come from Howard Levy's work on Zhang's racy debut novel, which is discussed below in detail. Other useful secondary sources on Zhang Zhuo include Tony Qian, "Classical Learning and the Law: Erudition as Persuasion in the *Dragon Sinews, Phoenix Marrows Judgments* of Zhang Zhuo," *Tang Studies* 35.1 (2017): 20–50; Yao Ping, "Historicizing Great Bliss: Erotica in Tang China (618–907)," *Journal of the History of Sexuality* 22.2 (2013): 207–229; Rong Zhaozu 容肇祖, "Tang Zhang Zhuo shiji kao" 唐張鷟事跡考, *Lingnan xuebao* 嶺南學報 6.4 (1941): 129–39; Guo Dianchen 郭殿忱, "Shenzhou tangxian Zhang Zhuo ji qi 'Yong yan' shi kaoshi" 深州唐賢張鷟及其'咏燕'詩考釋, *Hengshui xueyuan xuebao* 衡水學院學報 17.3 (2015): 68–70; Han Ting 韓婷 and Zhang jinxi 張金銑, "Zhang Zhuo ji qi Chaoye qianzai kaoshi" 張鷟及其朝野僉載考釋, *Hefei gongye daxue xuebao* 合肥工業大學學報 30.2 (2016): 73–79. Neither of these lists of primary and secondary scholarship on Zhang Zhuo is intended to be complete.

To my knowledge, no Chinese or Western scholar has written a comprehensive historiography of Zhang Zhuo. Such an endeavor is beyond the parameters of this annotated translation, but these lists of some of the seminal primary and secondary sources on Zhang may prove helpful as a thumbnail historiography. Lots of the best sources on Zhang's life and career come from his own brush, like *Court and Country* and the scores of his memorials and other writings contained in chapters 172 to 174 of the *Quan Tangwen* 全唐文 [Complete Anthology of Tang Prose], (Beijing: Zhonghua, 1996; hereafter *QTW*). Though this source is referenced several times in this book, the *Complete Anthology* remains one of the most extensive repositories—one almost unexplored in Western language—of Zhang Zhuo's writings.

4 From the "Circumscribed Will" (*Keyi* 刻意) section of the Outer Chapters (*Waipian* 外篇) of Zhuangzi. Compare to Burton Watson trans., *The Complete Works of Zhuangzi* (New York: Columbia University Press, 2013), 120, where this passage 其生若浮, 其死若休 is rendered "His life is a floating, his death a rest."

5 *Chaoye qianzai* 朝野僉載 [Collected Records of Court and Country], Zhang Zhuo, collated and annotated by Zhao Shouyan, in *Sui-Tang jiahua Chaoye qianzai* (Beijing:

NOTES

Zhonghua, 1997), 3.61. Hereafter all citations from this source will be placed in parenthesis, giving chapter and page number, at the end of the passage. For example, this passage comes for Chapter 3, p. 61, hence the notation (3.61) following the text above.

6 Other sources question Zhang Zhuo's status as a peerless valedictorian: Hong Mai and Xu Song's *Deng keji kao*, claimed that he ranked 29th on one of the exams. See below.

7 Duan Chengshi 段成式, *Youyang zazu* 酉陽雜俎 [Miscellaneous Morsels from the Youyang Region] (Shenyang: Wanjuan Publishing, 2020; hereafter *YYZZ*), 12.122. The timing of this failed marriage is problematic. We know that Zhang's colleague, Wei Zhigu, who was presumably a peer, was born in 646 and died in 715 (*JTS* 98.3064). Given Wei Zhigu's birth date, one would assume that, as peers, Zhang and he would have sought marriage at roughly the same age. Based on an autobiographical passage from *Court and Country* set during the Yonghui era (650–656; translated in Chapter 9), and on the fact that the latest dated passage in Zhang's work comes from 721, Ma Xueqin 馬雪芹, in "Zhang Zhuo shengping jingli ji shengzu nian kaoshi" 張鷟生平經歷生卒年考釋, *Hebei daxue xuebao* 河北大學學報 24.3 (2001), 63–64, has reconstructed the timeline of Zhang Zhuo's life, arguing that he was born in 648 and died in 722. Only following this logic could the two have been rival suitors.

8 In *Court and Country*, the site of this office is Yangxian, but I can find no Tang county with this name. There was a Yangxian established in the Western Han, but it was abolished in the Eastern Han. The translation above follows Li Fang's 李方 early Song-era *Extensive Records of the Taiping Era* (Taiping guangji 太平廣記; hereafter *Extensive Records*) (Beijing: Zhonghua, 1996), 171.1257, which records this same passage but lists the location of Zhang Zhuo's office as Heyang. Heyang County was part of Mengzhou prefecture.

9 *Quan Tangshi* 全唐詩 [Complete Anthology of Tang Poetry; hereafter *QTS*], compiled by Peng Dingqiu 彭定求 (Beijing: Zhonghua shuju, 1995), 45.553. Also see, *DTXY* 8.128. Xu Song (*Dengkeji*, Chapter 4), suggests "Cry of the Swallows" was written in 706, when Zhang passed a pair of exams (see below), matching the pair of swallows.

10 *XTS* 150.3768; 161.4979; Wang Pu 王溥, *Tang huiyao* 唐會要 [Essential institutions of the Tang] (Beijing: Zhonghua, 1998; hereafter *THY*), 75.1356.

11 *DTXY* 8.129; modified based on a similar account in *JTS* 149.4024.

12 See Chapter 9.

13 *THY* 76.1387.

14 Hong Mai, *Rongzhai xubi*, ch. 12.

15 Chapter 9 examines other passages featuring dream divination, or oneiromancy.

16 *XTS* 38.1257. This contradicts *Court and Country*'s assertion that this was a fifth-ranked position.

17 This passage is incomplete and corrupted in *Court and Country*. I have followed the version of the story presented in *TPGJ* 137.986.

18 *JTS* 7.157.

19 Charles Hucker, *A Dictionary of Official Titles in Imperial China* (Stanford, CA: Stanford University Press, 1985), 302.

20 The "nine palaces" (*jiugong* 九宮) form of astrological divination uses the stars of the Dipper and/or the corresponding numbers of the magic square to predict the future;

see Ho Peng Yoke, *Chinese Mathematical Astrology: Reaching Out for the Stars* (London: Routledge, 2003), 19–30.
21 His birth year, month, day, and hour.
22 *JTS* 149.4023.
23 *XTS* 161.4979.
24 Zhang Zhuo, *Dwelling of a Playful Goddess: China's First Novelette*, trans. and commentary by Howard Levy (Japan: Dai Nippon Insatsu Tokyo, 1965), 65–66.
25 Qian, "Classical Learning and the Law," 43–48.
26 For more on this locust plague and the debate it sparked in Xuanzong's court, see Rothschild, "Sovereignty, Virtue and Crisis Management: Prime Minister Yao Chong's Proactive Handling of the Locust Plague of 715–16," *Journal of Environmental History* 17.4 (2012): 783–812.
27 *QTW* 172.1749. This memorial has been translated in Esther Sunkyung Klein, "The History of the Historian: Perspectives on the Authorial Roles of Sima Qian," (Princeton University Ph.D. diss., 2010), 242–43. I have used her translations here.
28 *Guilin fengtu ji*, https://ctext.org/wiki.pl?if=gb&chapter=376333 (accessed 5 July 2021).
29 Ibid.
30 *JTS* 149.4023.
31 Ibid. Levy, *Dwelling of a Playful Goddess*, remarks that this nickname may be due to "the superior quality of the bronze used in coining money" (65).
32 *XTS* 161.4979–80.
33 Levy has translated this work. See Zhang Zhuo, *Dwelling of a Playful Goddess: China's First Novelette*.
34 Yao Ping, "Historicizing Great Bliss," 208.
35 Rong Zhaozu, "Tang Zhang Zhuo shiji kao," argues that the novel—chock-full of autobiographical elements—was written by young Zhang in Xiangle County (131–32).
36 Levy, *Dwelling of a Playful Goddess*, 8.
37 Ibid., Part I, 1.
38 Ibid., 75–99, "Chapter VI: The Influence on Japanese Literature." Curiously, in several of these later Japanese iterations of the story, the "Scholar Zhang" figure is depicted as a dashing sensualist who finds a jade-like empress, revealed at the end to be Wu Zhao, alluring and superior to all other women. In return, she finds the handsome young scholar irresistible. They manage to sleep together in a dream-like state, though pressures from court and state ultimately keep them apart.
39 Qian, "Classical Learning and the Law," 48.
40 Ibid., 21.
41 Ibid., 21, fn.2, from *Rongzhai suibi*.
42 Ibid., 26.
43 Jack Chen, "Introduction," in *Idle Talk: Gossip and Anecdotes in Traditional China*, eds. Jack Chen and David Schaberg (Berkeley: University of California Press, 2012), 4.
44 Ellen Cong Zhang, "'To Be Erudite in Miscellaneous Knowledge': A Study of Song (960–1279) Biji Writing," *Asia Major* 25.2 (2012): 45.
45 Graham Sanders, "I Read They Said He Sang What He Wrote: Orality, Writing, and Gossip in Tang Poetry Anecdotes," in *Idle Talk*, 89–90. Sanders discusses the rather weighty "status" of the anecdote as a form of transmitted knowledge in Tang China.

NOTES

46 Anna Shields, "Gossip, Anecdote, and Literary History: Representations of the Yuanhe Era in Tang Anecdote Collections," in *Idle Talk: Gossip and Anecdotes in Traditional China*, 108. Shields examines compilers of late Tang collections, but her observation can be applied to Zhang Zhuo.
47 Robert Campany, *Strange Writing: Anomaly Accounts in Early Medieval China* (Albany: SUNY Press, 1996), 125.
48 *XTS* 58.1425. Tuo Tuo's 脫脫 compiled *History of the Song Dynasty* (Song shi 宋史) (Beijing: Zhonghua, 1997), 203.5111 records *Court and Country* as having 20 chapters and three additional supplementary chapters.
49 Li Fang's 500-chapter *Extensive Records*—which contains a large number of the stories that cite *Court and Country* as their source—is topically organized, with separate sections on immortals, female divinities, extraordinary Buddhist monks, karmic retribution, prophecies and their fulfillment, tolerant and measured officials, cruel officials, brilliant investigators, perpetrators of hoaxes and deceivers, divination, music, remarkable talents, ghosts, demons, tombs, inscriptions, and numerous subcategories of flora and fauna (four entire chapters are devoted to snakes!). In this book, I have provided this categorization when translated passages from *Court and Country* were lifted from *Extensive Records*.
50 Levy, *Dwelling of a Playful Goddess*, Part II, 66.
51 This introduction of Wu Zhao is intended only as a thumbnail biography to provide context for this book. It draws on a number of biographies of Wu Zhao that I have written, including *Wu Zhao, China's Only Woman Emperor* (New York: Pearson Longman, 2008); "Wu Zhao," in *The Berkshire Encyclopedia of Chinese Biography* (Great Barrington, MA: Berkshire Publishing, 2014), 571–84; "Wu Zetian," in *Routledge Encyclopedia of Chinese History* (Abingdon, UK: Routledge, 2017), 673–74; and "Empress Wu" in John Makeham, Chief Consultant, *China: The World's Oldest Living Civilization* (Lane Cove, AU: Global Book Publishing, 2008), 212–15. Throughout this book, I use as her name her self-styled designation, Wu Zhao, assumed in 689. For her assumption of the name Zhao, see Sima Guang, *Zizhi tongjian* 資治通鑒 [Comprehensive Mirror for the Advancement of Governance] (Beijing: Zhonghua, 1995; hereafter *ZZTJ*) 204.6463; and *XTS* 76.3481.
52 Lewis, *China's Cosmopolitan Empire: The Tang Dynasty* (Cambridge: Belknap Press of Harvard, 2009), 214.
53 *ZZTJ* 195.6134–35.
54 *ZZTJ* 201.6343.
55 See Rothschild, *Emperor Wu Zhao and Her Pantheon of Devis, Divinities, and Dynastic Mothers* (New York: Columbia University Press, 2015), Chapter 3, "First Ladies of Sericulture: Wu Zhao and Leizu," 60–74.
56 See Bret Hinsch, "Textiles and Female Virtue in Early Imperial Chinese Historical Writings," *Nan nü* 5.2 (2003), "Paired Virtues: Plowing and Weaving," 185–91.
57 *ZZTJ* 201.6344–47; also see Howard Wechsler, *Offerings of Jade and Silk: Ritual and Symbol in the Legitimization of the T'ang* (New Haven: Yale University Press, 1985), 184–88.
58 *JTS* 6.116, *XTS* 4.82.
59 *ZZTJ* 203.6421.
60 *XTS* 76.3480, *JTS* 24.925, *ZZTJ* 204.6454. Eugene Yuejin Wang, in *Shaping the Lotus Sutra: Buddhist Visual Culture in Medieval China* (Seattle: University of Washington Press, 2005), recognizes this staged event as "part of an elaborately planned process of legitimation" (144) in Wu Zhao's protracted campaign for emperorship.

NOTES

61. For more on the Axis of the Sky (*Tianshu* 天樞), see Rothschild, "Severing Grandma's Phallus: A Gendered Re-examination of the Raising and Razing of Female Emperor Wu Zhao's Axis of the Sky," *Journal of Left History* 21.2 (2018): 51–72.
62. *ZZTJ* 207.6558.
63. *JTS* 6.133.
64. See Charles Stone, translation and critical annotation, *The Fountainhead of Chinese Erotica: The Lord of Perfect Satisfaction* (Honolulu: University of Hawaii Press, 2003).
65. See Li Ruzhen, *Destinies of Flowers in the Mirror*, trans. Lin Tai-yi (Berkeley: University of California Press, 1965).
66. *XTS* 76.3496.
67. *ZZTJ* 205.6478.
68. Hu Ji, *Wu Zetian benzhuan* (Xi'an: Shaanxi Shifan daxue chubanshe, 1998), 154; c.f. *THY* 84.1550–51.
69. David McMullen, "The Real Judge Dee: Ti Ren-chieh and the T'ang Restoration of 705," *Asia Major* 6.1 (1993): 75. Of course, McMullen points out that, despite this lofty armature, "official historians themselves represented the interests of a small and self-perpetuating minority in the serving bureaucracy."

CHAPTER 1

1. *JTS* 6.115.
2. *XTS* 76.3474.
3. *ZZTJ* 200.6494; *XTS* 76.3474.
4. *ZZTJ* 205.6484 sets the event in 692.
5. See Chapter 2 for a dream Wu Zhao had about a parrot where this same homophone is pivotal in the interpretation.
6. Erik Zürcher, "Foreword," in Tiziana Lippiello, *Auspicious Omens and Miracles in Ancient China: Han, Three Dynasties, and Six Kingdoms* (Nettetal: Steyler Verlag, 2001), 11.
7. Lippiello, *Auspicious Omens and Miracles in Ancient China*, 20–21.
8. Ibid., 122–49.
9. Sarah Schneewind, *A Tale of Two Melons: Emperor and Subject in Ming China* (Indianapolis: Hackett Publishing, 2006), xx.
10. *JTS* 58.2316–17.
11. This dream—which seems rather straightforward—does not conform to any of the oneiric categories that Robert Campany delineates in *The Chinese Dreamscape, 300 BCE–800AD* (Cambridge: Harvard Asia Center, 2020): contact by external spirits, responses to valorized action (for instance, a filial son dreaming where he might find grain), wandering of souls, response to body stimuli, manifestation of inner struggle, manifestation of inner imbalance, or the result of mental activity (33–52). Zhu Qianyi's dream does fit one category in Wang Fu's 王符 (90–165) Eastern Han work, *Discourses of a Recluse* (*Qianfulun* 潛夫論): "dreams that are literal and direct" (Campany, 54).
12. Campany, *The Chinese Dreamscape*, 115–16; c.f. *Nan Qi shu* 南齊書 [History of the Southern Qi Dynasty], ed. Xiao Zixian (Beijing: Zhonghua, 1997), 18.353–54. This list includes young Emperor Wu's dreams of a brilliant feathered peacock cloak. Based on the homophonous proximity of "peacock" (*que* 雀) and nobility rank (*jue* 爵), the interpreter explains this auspicious dream augured future rank.

NOTES

13 This section about the tally may be a bit confused, as elsewhere in the text Zhang Zhuo tells us that Wu Zhao used tallies resembling the Xuanwu (a serpent engirding a turtle) rather than the fish tally used in the Tang. See Figures 2 and 3.
14 A similar account of these events can be found in *ZZTJ* 206.6517–18. "Ten thousand years" (*Wansui* 萬歲) is generally understood as "Long live the emperor!"
15 Chris Roberts, *Heavy Words Lightly Thrown: The Reason Behind the Rhyme* (New York: Gotham Books, 2006), 13.
16 In speaking, Wu Zhao here uses Zhen 朕, the Royal We.
17 Charles Benn, *Daily Life in Traditional China: The Tang Dynasty* (Westport, CT: Greenwood Press, 2002), 127, and larger subsection on "Preservation," 126–28.
18 *ZZTJ* 203.6441 indicates that this memorial was filed in 686. See also Antonino Forte, *Political Propaganda and Ideology in China at the End of the Seventh Century* (Kyoto: Italian School of East Asian Studies, 2005), 150–56 for a full translation of Xue Huaiyi's biography in *JTS* 183.4741–43. Also see Forte, *Mingtang and Buddhist Utopias in the History of the Astronomical Clock* (Rome: Istituto Italiano per il Medio ed Estremo Oriente; Paris: École Française D'Extrême Oriente, 1988), 215–17.
19 *JTS* 183.4741; translation from Forte, *Political Propaganda and Ideology*, 151.
20 Stone trans., *Lord of Perfect Satisfaction*, 139.
21 Lin Yutang, *Wu Zetian zhuan* (Xi'an: Shaanxi shifan daxue chubanshe, 2005), chapter 42, 179–80.
22 Dora Shu-fang Dien, *Empress Wu Zetian in Fiction and in History: Female Defiance in Confucian China* (New York: Nova Science Publishers Inc, 2003), 49.
23 Rebecca Doran, "Insatiable Women and Transgressive Authority: Constructions of Gender and Power in Early Tang China" (PhD diss., Harvard, 2011), 385.
24 Richard Guisso, *Wu Ts'e-t'ien and the Politics of Legitimation in T'ang China* (Bellingham, WA: Center for Asian Studies, Western Washington University, 1978), 88.
25 Lu Simian 呂思勉, *Sui-Tang-Wudai shi* 隋唐五代史 (Shanghai: Shanghai guji, 1984), 160. C. P. Fitzgerald, *The Empress Wu* (Melbourne, 1955), 163–79, titles the tenth chapter of his biography "Ascendancy of the Favorites." Fitzgerald vividly depicts her court during her final years: "Conscious of her own immense prestige and her unchallenged authority she was now content to enjoy her Indian summer in the company of her young and gay favorites, and in the seclusion of her summer palaces."
26 Hu Ji, *Wu Zetian benzhuan*, 171. Hu Ji titles Chapter 24 of his biography "Excessive Trust and Fondness of the Two Zhangs" (Chongxin er Zhang 寵信二張), 171–77. Giovanni Vitiello, *The Libertine's Friend: Homosexuality and Masculinity in Late Imperial China* (Chicago: University of Chicago Press, 2011), 221 fn. 124, notes that "external favorite" (*waichong* 外寵) was sometimes used as a synonym for "male favorite" (*nanchong*).
27 Huang Guangren, *Nü huang Wu Zhao* (Xi'an: Shaanxi luyou chubanshe, 2000), 167.
28 Luoyang.
29 See Jonathan Skaff, *Sui-Tang China and Its Turko-Mongol Neighbors* (Oxford, UK: Oxford University Press, 2012), 100.
30 See Marc Abramson, *Ethnic Identity in Tang China* (Philadelphia: University of Pennsylvania Press, 2008).
31 Leslie Wallace, "Wild Youths and Fallen Officials: Falconry and Moral Opprobrium in Early Medieval China," in *Behaving Badly in Early and Medieval China,* eds. Rothschild and Wallace (Honolulu: University of Hawai'i Press, 2017), 124.

NOTES

32. Rebecca Doran, *Transgressive Typologies: Constructions of Gender and Power in Early Tang China* (Cambridge, MA: Harvard University Asia Center, 2016), 162–63, also analyzes and partially translates this passage.
33. A county that is part of metropolitan Chang'an, which indicates this event occurred between 701 and 705, after Wu Zhao moved from Luoyang back to Chang'an.
34. For more on the tattling box, which Wu Zhao set up in 686 as grand dowager, see *ZZTJ* 203.6437–38; Rothschild, *Wu Zhao: China's Only Woman Emperor*, 126–27; Qiang Fang, "Hot Potatoes: Chinese Complaint Systems from Early Times to the Late Qing (1898)," *Journal of Asian Studies* 68.4 (2009): 1111–13.
35. *ZZTJ* 207.6580–81. For a good account of the latter days of the Zhangs, see Guisso, *Wu Tse-t'ien and the Politics of Legitimation*, 153–54.
36. Doran uses "Gender Anarchy" as a chapter title in *Transgressive Typologies*, 188–226. For a brief account of this turbulent period, see *ZZTJ*, chapters 207–209. Also see Guisso, "The reigns of empress Wu, Chung-tsung and Jui-tsung," *Cambridge History of China*, Vol. 3: Sui and T'ang China, eds. Denis Twitchett and John Fairbank (Cambridge, UK: Cambridge University Press, 1979), 321–29.
37. I have not translated the entire quote at the end of this passage.
38. Rothschild, *Wu Zhao, China's Only Woman Emperor*, 101–02.
39. For more on Wu Zhao's utilization of family members to buttress her political authority, see Rothschild, "Rhetoric, Ritual, and Support Constituencies," 240–51.
40. *ZZTJ* 204.6468.
41. *ZZTJ* 204.6474–76.
42. *ZZTJ* 205.6488.
43. *XTS* 115.4212; *ZZTJ* 206.6526. See Chapter 2 for Di Renjie's interpretation of Wu Zhao's dream about a parrot with broken wings at this same critical juncture.
44. He was a low-ranking bureau official responsible for state ritual and sacrificial regulations.
45. North of Baoding in modern-day Hebei.
46. A mid-ranking position charged with maintaining pasturage and equipping horses in the imperial stables.
47. For the briefest sketch of this endemic cultural history of corruption, see Qiang Fang and Xiaobing Li, "Introduction: Who is to Blame: Party, State, or Society?" in *Corruption and Anti-Corruption in Modern China*, eds. Qiang and Li (London: Lexington Books, 2019), xii–xiv.
48. See Rothschild, *Emperor Wu Zhao and Her Pantheon of Devis, Divinities, and Dynastic Mothers*, 157–66; Rothschild, "Wu Zhao's Remarkable Aviary," *Southeast Review of Asian Studies* 27 (2005): 77–78.
49. "Auntie Lai" was a nickname for Lai Junchen, the leader of the "cruel officials" in Wu Zhao's time; see Chapter 3.
50. Benn, *Daily Life in Traditional China*, 27–28; J. K. Rideout, "The Rise of Eunuchs During the T'ang Dynasty, Part I," *Asia Major* (New Series) 1 (1949–50), 53–72; Rideout, "The Rise of Eunuchs During the T'ang Dynasty, Part II," *Asia Major* (New Series) 3 (1952), 42–58.
51. Rideout, "The Rise of Eunuchs During the T'ang Dynasty, Part I," 53–54.
52. *JTS* 92.2971.
53. *XTS* 4.91.
54. *ZZTJ* 204.6468.
55. *XTS* 109.4102–03.

NOTES

56 See translation of *SJ* 85.2511–13, "Biography of Lu Buwei," in Sima Qian, *Historical Records*, trans. Raymond Dawson (New York: Oxford University Press, 1994), 6–9.
57 Prince of Qiao 譙王 Li Chongfu was the second son of Emperor Zhongzong (a grandson of Wu Zhao) who, egged on by Zheng Yin, returned from exile after his father's death in 710 and attempted to seize the throne; he failed to escape and leapt into a canal, committing suicide. See *JTS* 86.2835–37; *XTS* 81.3594.
58 Doran, *Transgressive Typologies*, 95 fn. 93.
59 "Commoner Wei" (Wei shuren 韋庶人) is the derisive epithet for Zhongzong's spouse Empress Wei, given after she was allegedly party to poisoning her husband in 710.
60 Doran, *Transgressive Typologies*, also translates this passage on p. 202.
61 Ibid., 202 fn.49, c.f. *Han shu* 漢書 [History of the Han Dynasty], Ban Gu and Ban Biao (Beijing: Zhonghua, 1997), 65.2853–57. For more on Feng Zidu, who took up with Huo Guang's wife after the general's death, also see Bret Hinsch, *Passions of the Cut Sleeve: The Male Homosexual Tradition in China* (Berkeley: University of California Press, 1992), 49–50. For more on Dong Yan, see Bao Shanben, "Liu Piao, the Grand Princess," in *Biographical Dictionary of Chinese Women, Antiquity through the Sui* (1600 BCE–618 CE), Chief Eds. Lily Xiao Hong Lee and A. D. Stefanowska (London: Routledge, 2015), 166–68.
62 *JTS* 51.2175; *XTS* 76.3488 (for Shangguan Wan'er); *ZZTJ* 210.6677 (for Taiping Princess).
63 Doran, *Transgressive Typologies*, 202.
64 Ibid., 189.
65 *JTS* 190.4995–96. This short biography of Zhang Changling also mentions that at Helan Minzhi's behest he was brought in through the Northern Gate into the inner palace, presumably to ghostwrite works like the stele inscription mentioned below, but was dismissed shortly thereafter. The *Feng* Sacrifice of 666 is discussed in more detail in Chapter 7. This stele must have been one of Zhang's final compositions; he died that same year.
66 Rothschild, *Wu Zhao: China's Only Woman Emperor*, 56–57; Wang Shuanghuai and Zhao Wenrun, *Wu Zetian pingzhuan* (Xi'an: Sanqin, 1993), 72–73; *XTS* 206.5836; *JTS* 183.4728.
67 Doran, *Transgressive Typologies*, 215–16.
68 Doran (*Transgressive Typologies*, 215) has translated this passage.
69 *XTS* 104.4014–15.
70 Doran, *Transgressive Typologies*, 156.
71 Ibid. For additional examples of this narrative of the excess and luxury enjoyed by female power-holders that appear in *Court and Country*, see Doran, *Transgressive Typologies*, Chapters 4 and 5.
72 Though she does not translate the passage, Doran also refers to this elaborate incense burner commissioned by the Anle Princess (*Transgressive Typologies*, 171–72).
73 Ping Yao, "Tang Women in the Transformation of Buddhist Filiality," in *Gendering Chinese Religion: Subject, Identity, and Body*, eds. Jinhua Jia, Xiaofei Kang, and Ping Yao (Albany: SUNY Press, 2014), 27–28.
74 *XTS* 76.3486–87; *ZZTJ* 209.6641–42.
75 Shangguan Wan'er, who had already worked closely with Wu Zhao, was taken into her son Zhongzong's inner palace as a third-ranked concubine, a Lady of Bright Countenance (*Zhaorong* 昭容).

NOTES

76 Shangguan Wan'er's grandfather, Shangguan Yi (d. 664), was a chief minister under Gaozong (and Wu Zhao). He was charged in a plot to depose Wu Zhao in 664 and executed along with most of the extended clan. The family properties were confiscated. Curiously, his granddaughter, infant Shangguan Wan'er, was spared this purge and made a palace slave. See Rothschild, Wu Zhao: *China's Only Woman Emperor,* 52–53; Guisso, *Politics of Legitimation,* 19–20; *ZZTJ* 201.6342.

77 Wilt Idema and Beata Grant, *The Red Brush: Writing Women of Imperial China* (Cambridge, MA: Harvard University Asia Center, 2004), 17–42, contains commentary on and analysis of Ban Zhao's remarkable career, in addition to translations of her poetry, several memorials that she wrote to the emperor, and the seven-chapter *Lessons for Women.*

78 For more on Zuo Fen, see Idema and Grant, *The Red Brush,* 43–48, and Lily Xiao Hong Lee, "Zuo Fen," in *Biographical Dictionary of Chinese Women, Antiquity through the Sui* (1600 BCE–618 CE), Chief Eds. Lily Xiao Hong Lee and A. D. Stefanowska (London: Routledge, 2015), 393–95. There are translations of a number of her rhapsodies and poems expressing her sadness at separation from her natal family.

79 For a translation of Shangguan Wan'er's biography in the *Old Tang History* (*JTS* 51.2175–76) and a much more detailed account of her political and literary career, see Rothschild, "'Her Influence Great, Her Merit Beyond Measure': A Translation and Initial Investigation of the Epitaph of Shangguan Wan'er," *Studies in Chinese Religion* 1.2 (2015): 131–48.

CHAPTER 2

1 Guisso, *Politics of Legitimation,* 28.
2 Du You's 杜佑 mid-Tang *Tongdian* 通典 [Comprehensive Manual of Institutions] (Beijing: Zhonghua, 1996; hereafter *TD*), 15.363–64.
3 Guisso, *Politics of Legitimation,* "The Examination System and the Bureaucracy," 89–103.
4 Archaic name for the Minister of State adopted by Wu Zhao.
5 A *xun* 旬-week is ten-day week composed of days corresponding with the ten heavenly stems (*tiangan* 天干). See Adam Smith, "The Chinese Sexagenary Cycle and Ritual Foundations of the Calendar," in *Calendars and Years II: Astronomy and Time in the Ancient and Medieval World,* ed. John Steele (Oxford: Oxbow Books, 2010), 1–37.
6 Records on Gu Zong are sparse. He became a chief minister in the fifth month of 701 (*JTS* 6.130: *XTS* 4.102). He died in 702 (*XTS* 4.103). It is not clear why he was such a singularly unworthy candidate.
7 Chen, *Empire of Style,* 47–51.
8 For more about the particular fish tally pictured in Figure 2—a bronze inscribed not to a member of court, but to a bearer in a Türgesh vassal principality—see V. A. Belyaev and S. V. Sidorovich, "Tang Tallies of Credence Found at Ak-Beshim Ancient Site," *Numismatique asiatique: Revue de la Société de Numismatique Asiatique* 33 (2020): 41–56, especially 49–51. Note: While my brother Harry expressed his desire to include an image of a Tang fish tally here, he died before selecting a specific image and securing permission to use it. I wish to thank V. A. Belyaev for his generosity in granting permission to reproduce the image in Figure 2. –Dr. N. Amos Rothschild
9 For more on the turtle tally pictured in Figure 3 (as well as another, similar tally recovered from the Ak-Beshim site in Kyrgystan), see Belyaev and Sidorovich, "Tang Tallies of Credence Found at Ak-Beshim," especially 47–8. Like the fish tally

NOTES

in Figure 3, these particular turtle tallies were owned not by court members, but by "notable representatives of the Türkic tribe, [on] whom, in accordance with the practice of the time, the Tang court bestowed [an honorary] rank" (48). Note: My brother Harry wished to include an image of a Zhou turtle tally here, but he died before selecting a specific image and securing permission to use it. I wish to thank V. A. Belyaev for his generosity in granting permission to reproduce the images in Figure 3. –Dr. N. Amos Rothschild

10   *JTS* 45.1954.
11   Short for Wu Zetian, Wu Zhao.
12   Unable to fathom this jest.
13   The Censorate's main building was a terrace or pavilion.
14   An Adjutant Stork is a bald-pated lesser stork.
15   Graham Sanders, in *Words Well Put: Visions of Poetic Competence in Chinese Tradition* (Cambridge, MA: Harvard University Asia Center, 2006), 209–12, examines a variation of this passage. Arguing that the passage displays her incapacity to grasp poetic nuance and can be understood as a grotesque parody of literati tradition of the "erudite Traditionalist" expounding principles of statecraft to the ruler, Sanders notes that Zhang Yuanyi "has to play the role of the exegete," explaining the homophone to Wu Zhao.
16   Duke Ling of Wei was a ruler during the late Spring and Autumn Era (d. 492 BC). His name is a pun for "Duke who Protects the Spirit (Coffin)."
17   People of Lingnan were thought to be swarthy and smaller in stature. This reflects a bias or prejudice of taller, sturdier northerners.
18   Clearly a mocking epithet, as Zhu Qianyi, by all accounts a repulsive and uncouth fellow who resembled a surly and slovenly short-order cook at a greasy spoon diner, was the very antithesis of the elegant and graceful women bearing this title, who served meals within the inner quarters.
19   Sanders, *Words Well Put*, 211.
20   Nanchang is in Jiangxi; it is part of Hongzhou prefecture. In Chapter 9, there is an anecdote from *Court and Country* set in Hongzhou, where Zhang Zhuo encounters a *pipa* diviner. Perhaps on the same occasion he met the "Suckling Calf." The timing is not clear, as He Ruojin does not appear in any of the official histories.
21   The first part of this account—about Du Jingxian—does not show up in the passed-down version of *Court and Country*, but does appear (and cites *Court and Country* as its source) in Tao Zongyi's collection of miscellany, *Tales from Beyond the City Walls*, which includes a number of anecdotes about anomalies and stories of bizarre supernatural events.
22   *JTS* 90.2911; *XTS* 116.4241.
23   "Left Charioteering Archer" is an alternative name with archaic military roots for the vice director of the Department of State Affairs. See Hucker, *A Dictionary of Official Titles in Imperial China*, 394–95.
24   Gan Bao, *In Search of the Supernatural*, trans. Kenneth DeWoskin and J. I. Crump (Stanford, CA: Stanford University Press, 1996), chapter 8, 108–09.
25   Robert Harrist Jr., "The Legacy of Bole: Physiognomy of Horses in Chinese Painting," *Artibus Asiae* 57.1/2 (1997): 136–37.
26   John Knobloch and Jeffery Riegel (trans.), *The Annals of Lü Buwei* (Stanford: Stanford University Press, 2000), 9.220, 25.633; also see Madeline Spring, *Animal Allegories in T'ang China* (New Haven: American Oriental Society, 1993), 105. There are numerous passages in early texts like the *Spring and Autumn Annals*, the *Annals of the Warring States*, and the *Huainanzi* that attest to Bole's superior talents.

NOTES

27 *The Annals of Lü Buwei*, 24.609.
28 Wu Zhao's title as emperor, adopted in October 690, during the early years of her Zhou dynasty.
29 *ZZTJ* 207.6551. For biographies of Di Renjie, see *JTS* 89.2885–96, *XTS* 115.4207–14; for an account of his service with Wu Zhao, see McMullen, "The Real Judge Dee: Ti Jen-Chieh and the T'ang Restoration of 705," 1–81, and Rothschild, "Rhetoric, Ritual and Support Constituencies in the Political Authority of Wu Zhao, China's Only Woman Emperor," (PhD diss., Brown University, 2003), 269–79.
30 Campany, *The Chinese Dreamscape*, defines glyphomancy as "the interpretive procedure involved converting a dream scene or image into a graph, then analyzing the graph into parts to reveal the dream's meaning" (103). Forte, in *Political Propaganda* (302, fn. 223) also translates this passage.
31 Li Rizhi's biography (*JTS* 188.4926–27) indicates that after passing the examinations, he started out as a low-level official in the Ministry of Justice at the beginning of Wu Zhao's Zhou dynasty. Unlike the "Cruel Officials" (see Chapter 3), he was known for limiting and moderating punishments.
32 *TPGJ* 176.1310.
33 *ZZTJ* 204.6459–60.
34 *TPGJ* 162.1168–69. *Records of the Censorate* (*Yushitai ji* 御史台記) was compiled by Han Wan 韓琬 in the late Tang; the passage is contained in this later Song source. *ZZTJ* 204.6460 also mentions that the skies cleared when the eleventh-hour amnesty was read.
35 The "mutual resonance of Heaven and Earth" is discussed in greater detail in Chapter 8.
36 *XTS* 4.90, 106.4043. Also see the passages in Chapter 3 on Gong Siye and Zhang Siming, men who were also implicated for helping Xu Jingzhen, the younger brother of 684 rebel leader Xu Jingye. Xu Jingzhen was fleeing to the northeast into the territory of the Tujue Turks when he was captured. Upon investigation, he divulged many names!
37 *TPGJ* 121.853.
38 Keith Knapp, *Selfless Offspring: Filial Children and Social Order in Medieval China* (Honolulu: University of Hawaii Press, 2005), 3.
39 *The T'ang Code, Volume One: General Principles*, translated and introduced by Wallace Johnson (Princeton: Princeton University Press, 1979), 61–82.
40 Archaic title from the Zhou dynasty of antiquity for the Minister of War, resuscitated by Wu Zhao.
41 From *Taiping yulan* 太平御覽 [Imperial Readings of the Taiping Era], Li Fang 李昉 (Beijing: Zhonghua, 1995; hereafter *TPYL*), 411.1899.
42 *TPYL* 414.1910.
43 In the year 711.
44 The passage comes from *TPGJ* 493.4050. Cited from *Miscellaneous Records from the Pine Window* (*Songchuang zalu* 松窗雜綠), a one-chapter late Tang text usually attributed to Li Jun 李濬.
45 *Shangshu zhengyi* 尚書正義, in *Shisan jing zhu shu*, ed. Li Xueqin (Beijing: Beijing University Press, 1999), 10.249. Young Su Ting is quoting Fu Yue, the wise advisor of Wu Ding, the penultimate and last good ruler of the Shang dynasty.
46 *Shangshu Zhengyi*, 11.279. "Dissecting the heart" is a reference to the notorious King Zhou, last ruler of the Shang dynasty, cutting open the heart of minister Bi Gan to

NOTES

see if the heart of a sage had seven openings; "breaking the ankles" is a reference to the same tyrant having the ankles of a man who walked across an icy river barefoot in mid-winter broken to see if the man's bones were the same as other ankles.
47 In the vicinity of Huangshan, in the southeast of modern-day Anhui province.
48 *JTS* 185.4819.
49 He Qiao was an official in the Jin dynasty (fl. late third cent.). His biography in *Jin shu* 晉書 [History of Jin], comp. Fang Xuanling 房玄齡 (Beijing: Zhonghua, 1997; hereafter *JS*), 45.1283–84, remarks upon the great wealth of the He family.
50 A notorious cruel official serving under Emperor Wu of Han (r. 141–86 BC).
51 Hucker, *Dictionary of Official Titles*, remarks that the Three Dukes was "a collective reference to dignitaries who were officially considered the three paramount aides of the ruler and held the highest possible ranks" (399).
52 The Crown Prince Jiemin is Li Chongjun, Emperor Zhongzong's third son. He was not the child of Empress Wei. He was named Crown Prince in the seventh month 706 (*ZZTJ* 208.6604), and staged a coup to seize the throne in 707. He failed, though he killed Wu Zhao's nephew Wu Sansi in the process (*ZZTJ* 208.6611–12).
53 Two officials from the Western Han celebrated for their loyalty.
54 Wu Zhao's nephew Wu Sansi.
55 For Li Zhaode's biography in the official Tang histories, see *XTS* 117.4255–57 and *JTS* 87.2853–59.
56 For Wei Yuanzhong's biography in the official Tang histories, see *XTS* 122.4339–49 and *JTS* 2945–55.

CHAPTER 3

1 In his remonstrance to Wu Zhao, court official Zhu Jingze metaphorically refers to the cruel officials as "teeth and horns" (*yajiao* 牙角). Part of the text of his plea is contained in Zhu's biography (*JTS* 90.2914): "Yesterday's clever plans have become today's straw dogs. There is a difference between methods used by a ruler to secure power and those used to maintain power. Get rid of these treacherous teeth and horns, blunt the keen edge of vileness and slander, block up the source of implication and entrapment, sweep away all traces of the clique, that the people can be at ease and content! How would this not be joyous?" Below, I use this phrase several times to characterize these cruel officials.
2 Donald Wyatt, review of *Emperor Wu Zhao and Her Pantheon of Devis, Divinities, and Dynastic Mothers*, by N. Harry Rothschild, *Journal of Religion and Violence* 4.2 (2016): 231–32.
3 William Nienhauser Jr., "A Re-Examination of the 'Biographies of the Reasonable Officials' in the *Records of the Grand Historian*," *Early China* 16 (1991): 215; from *SJ* 130.3318.
4 Sima Qian, *Selections from Records of the Grand Historian*, selected by Po-Hsiang Wang, translated by Yang Hsien-yi and Gladys Yang (Beijing: Foreign Languages Press, 1979), 460–61.
5 *SJ* 122.3154.
6 Fitzgerald, *The Empress Wu*, 115–17. Wu Chao is a different Romanization of Wu Zhao.
7 Doran, *Transgressive Typologies*, 192.
8 Ibid., 192.

NOTES

9. Doran, "Insatiable Women," 425.
10. She removed her son, the once and future emperor, from the throne in 684. This was his title.
11. Fitzgerald, *The Empress Wu*, 115.
12. The first half of "Biographies of Cruel Officials" (*JTS* 186.4837–50) is devoted entirely to Wu Zhao's reign. For the purposes of this chapter, I have included a number of Wu Zhao's henchmen whom I deemed to be "cruel officials" who might not have cleared Sima Qian's bar for inclusion in an official biography.
13. Archaic name of the Ministry of Justice that Wu Zhao lifted from the Zhou dynasty of old.
14. An office in the Chancellery, a bureau that reviewed policy and advised the ruler.
15. They sent a memorial (*biao* 表), an official petition to the emperor, in this instance one outlining Jiang Rong's alleged crimes.
16. *XTS* 209.5908.
17. This seems to be an effort to presume familiarity with the mourning Wang family. Perhaps Fifth Wang is one of Wang Ju's siblings.
18. *TPGJ* 126.891–92.
19. Ibid.
20. *TPGJ* 268.2106–07.
21. This image of Yu Qianlou is from *Twenty-four Paragons of Filial Piety*, a Qing Dynasty album of 51 leaves of paintings and calligraphy. The image is reproduced here courtesy of the Metropolitan Museum of Art. Note: My brother Harry wished to include an image of Yu Qianlou here, but he died before selecting a specific image and securing permission to use it. The inscription in the painting's upper righthand corner translates as "When Yu of the Southern Qi tasted the feces, his heart was put at ease." While these words may seem hard to reconcile with the story in the *History of the Liang Dynasty* quoted above, Professor Keith Knapp, an expert on filial piety stories, explains that "there were often a couple of versions of these popular stories. [...] For most readers and viewers, Yu Qianlou shows the height of his filiality by tasting his father's feces, which is why most illustrations focus on that action" (private email exchange). —Dr. N. Amos Rothschild
22. *Liang shu* 梁書 [History of the Liang Dynasty], comp. Yao Cha 姚察 (Beijing: Zhonghua, 1997), 47.650–51. Translation draws on Ma Boying, *A History of Medicine in Chinese Culture, Vol. I* (Singapore: World Scientific, 2020), 506. Ma claims that this "truly disgusting" method of diagnosis is not of Chinese origin and comes "from India and other places that faeces were taken as a medicine."
23. *Beishi* 北史 [History of the Northern Dynasties], ed. Li Yanshou 李延壽 (Beijing: Zhonghua, 1997; hereafter *BS*), 84.2837; *Sui Shu* 隋書 [History of the Sui], Wei Zheng 魏徵 (Beijing: Zhonghua, 1996; hereafter *SS*), 72.1667.
24. *JTS* 186.4848–50.
25. This passage has been abridged. I have not translated parts about Ji Xu's involvement in securing the amnesty of the living adherents of Li Zhen, who had rebelled and been executed back in 688 prior to Wu Zhao assuming the throne.
26. *Hamlet* 3.4.209.
27. Nienhauser, "A Re-Examination of the 'Biographies of the Reasonable Officials,'" 215.
28. This is a reference to Wu Zhao, although at the time Wu Zhao ordered the construction of this box, she was grand dowager-regent, and not yet emperor.

NOTES

29 *ZZTJ* 203.6437–38.
30 *XTS* 4.89; *ZZTJ* 204.6459.
31 According to *XTS 4.89*, these men are brothers, so his surname should read Gong Siming.
32 This name is wrong. It should be Xu Jingzhen. See *XTS* 4.89.
33 See Suo Yuanli's biography for more detail: *JTS* 186.4843–44. See Chapter 8 for more on the tendency of Zhang Zhuo and other literati to bestialize or animalize non-Chinese peoples.
34 *ZZTJ* 204.6472.
35 *Chunqiu zuozhuan zhengyi*, ed. Li Xueqin (Beijing: Beijing University Press, 2000), 29.834. Cited from another source in commentary from the fourth year of Duke Xiang of Lu (569 BC).
36 Wang was the husband of the Dingan princess, Zhongzong's third daughter.
37 *JTS* 186.4853–54, where he is included in the second half of the chapter on "Cruel Officials." All eleven men in the first half are from Wu Zhao's era.
38 It is implicit that the spirits, foxes, and forest sprites were played by men colluding with the "cruel officials" to pretend to present "evidence" or testimony of the victim's guilt from the spirit realm.
39 Robert Buswell and Donald Lopez, *The Princeton Dictionary of Buddhism* (Princeton: Princeton University Press, 2014), 695 and 1018.
40 Professor Alice Laborde, in Kristina Lindgrin, "Professor Offers Dissenting Opinion on Marquis de Sade," *L.A. Times*, 15 July 1991.
41 See Albert Cohen, *Delinquent Boys: Culture of the Gang* (Glencoe, IL: Free Press, 1955).

CHAPTER 4

1 Hucker, *A Dictionary of Official Titles in Imperial China*, 32. There were also commanderies (*jun* 郡) along the frontier, often placed under military government, though these were discontinued in the early Tang, when they were replaced by garrisons (Hucker, 200). Also see *Dictionary of the Ben Cao Gang Mu, Vol. II: Geographical and Administrative Designations*, eds. Hua Linfu, Paul Buell, and Paul Unschuld (Berkeley: University of California Press, 2017), 15–17.
2 Denis Twitchett, "Introduction," in *The Cambridge History of China, vol. 3: Sui and T'ang China*, eds. Twitchett and Fairbank (Cambridge: Cambridge University Press, 1979), 13.
3 For more on this three-part tax system, see Twitchett, *Financial Administration under the T'ang Dynasty*, 24–25.
4 *TPGJ* 171.1255–56.
5 In northern Henan, along the Wei River, which gives the prefecture its name.
6 *TPGJ* 263.2057.
7 Modern-day Kaifeng.
8 *XTS* 107.4077 and 116.4239.
9 *TPGJ* 328.2609.
10 *TPGJ* 254.1980.
11 It is hard to determine the gender of this slave. As the slave seems to be ensconced in the domestic household, I am assuming that she is female.
12 A prefecture in modern-day Guangzhou.
13 Hucker, *Dictionary of Official Titles in Imperial China*, 31.

NOTES

14 In the southeast of modern-day Hebei, just north of Hengshui.
15 The commemorative statue was roughly 8 inches tall.
16 Using this phrase, an advisor cautioned Emperor Taizong during a mounted archery outing in the early Tang; *JTS* 75.2638.
17 Edward Slingerland, *Confucius, The Analects: With Selections from Traditional Commentaries* (Indianapolis: Hackett, 2003), 238.
18 For a brief bio of Li Ming, see *JTS* 76.2666.
19 I provide the characters here because the name of the prince is romanized in the same way as that of his brother, Li Xian 李顯, the Emperor Zhongzong.
20 Li Xian was deposed in 680, banished to a prefecture in northern Sichuan, and quietly eliminated when the purge of Li princes began in earnest in 684. Li Ming was one of the early victims. Actually, there is strong evidence that indicates that Li Xian was not Wu Zhao's son, but the child of her sister. For an account of the escalating tensions between mother and son, see *Wu Zhao: China's Only Woman Emperor*, 73–75; Guisso, *Politics of Legitimation*, 23–24.
21 Sima Qian's *Records of the Grand Historian* dedicates a full chapter to these righteous assassins. Also see Yuri Pines, "A Hero Terrorist: Adoration of Jing Ke Revisited," *Asia Major* 21.2 (2008): 1–34.
22 *XTS* 129.4482.
23 Li Shizhen, *Ben Cao Gang Mu, Vol. IX: Fowls, Domestic and Wild Animals, Human Substances*, trans. Paul Unschuld (Berkeley: University of California Press, 2021), 1012–14.
24 Keith N. Knapp, "Chinese Filial Cannibalism: A Silk Road Import?" in *China and Beyond in the Medieval Period: Cultural Crossings and Inter-Regional Connections*, eds. Dorothy C. Wong and Gustav Heldt (Amherst, NY: Cambria Press, 2014), 137.
25 Li Shizhen, *Ben Cao Gang Mu, Vol. IX*, 1013.
26 It is not clear from the passage why Chen Yuanguang became enraged. Perhaps it was that the military subordinate served the wine clumsily, perhaps it was because as a soldier he hesitated to pour wine for the guests.
27 Hugh Clark, *The Sinitic Encounter in Southeast China through the First Millennium CE* (Honolulu: University of Hawaii Press, 2016), 120–22.
28 A local military officer entrusted with protection of a district. Lin'an was a district within Hangzhou.
29 *Guanzi. Political, Economic, and Philosophical Essays from Early China: A Study and Translation*, translated and annotated by W. Allyn Rickett (Princeton: Princeton University Press, 1985), 428.
30 *XTS* 195.5577.
31 Hongjie Wang, "'Wolves Shepherding the People': Cruelty and Violence in the Five Dynasties," in *Behaving Badly in Early and Medieval China*, 189–207.
32 Mo Yan, *Republic of Wine*, trans. Howard Goldblatt (New York: Arcade Books, 2000), 75–85. Also see Goldblatt, "Forbidden Food: The 'Saturnicon' of Mo Yan," *World Literature* 74.3 (2000): 75–84.
33 See Knapp, "Chinese Filial Cannibalism," 135–37. In "Forbidden Food," Goldblatt remarks that "irrespective of the approbation given to [the self-mutilating act of feeding one's own flesh to kin as a filial act] [...] in Confucian society, the fact remains that it constitutes the ingestion of the body of another human being, who may or may not die as a result, and represents the sort of cannibalistic traditions that Lu Xun saw as China's shame" (485, fn.30). Lu Xun, an early twentieth century

NOTES

novelist–intellectual, was a harsh critic of the manner in which Confucian morality cannibalized the young.
34 Key Ray Chong, *Cannibalism in China* (Wakefield, NY: Longwood Academic, 1990), 1–2.
35 *ZZTJ* 192.6053–54.
36 Jack Chen, *The Poetics of Sovereignty: On Emperor Taizong of the Tang Dynasty* (Cambridge, MA: Harvard University Press, 74–76). The terse description above does not do justice to Chen's intricate and nuanced argument.

CHAPTER 5

1 The first part of this passage—about the advance of the Turks in 703 during a total solar eclipse and their subsequent retreat during a total lunar eclipse—can be found in Chapter 7.
2 Though some of these figures also served as officials, they are better known for their ingenuity as craftsmen.
3 *TPGJ* 211.1614–15.
4 Both Forte, *Mingtangs and Buddhist Utopias*, 109, and Joseph Needham, Wang Ling, and Derek De Solla Price, *Heavenly Clockwork: The Great Astronomical Clocks of Medieval China* (Cambridge, UK: Cambridge University Press, 2008), 82, translate this passage.
5 Needham, Ling, and Price, *Heavenly Clockwork*.
6 For extensive context on the significance of this prototypical mechanical clock, this regulated zodiac-wheel, see Antonino Forte, *Mingtangs and Buddhist Utopias*, 109–17.
7 Li Yuanjia (618–688) was the eleventh son of Tang founding emperor Gaozu. For his biography, see *JTS* 64.2427–28. He is a child of a consort from the Yuwen 宇文 clan (*XTS* 79.3539).
8 E. R. Truitt, *Medieval Robots: Mechanism, Magic, Nature, and Art* (Philadelphia: University of Pennsylvania Press, 2015), 1–3.
9 For a comparative (if later chronological) framework, see Truitt, *Medieval Robots*, Chapter 6, "The Clockwork Universe," 141–53.
10 Twitchett, *Financial Administration under the T'ang Dynasty*, 86–87.
11 Wang and Zhao, *Wu Zetian pingzhuan*, second edition (Xi'an: Sanqin, 2000), 280.
12 *JTS* 94.2998.
13 Chen, *Empire of Style*, 7 and 127.
14 Ibid., 9.
15 Robert Marks, *China: Its Environment and History* (Boston: Rowman and Littlefield, 2012), 141 and 166–67.
16 *ZZTJ* 202.6400. Chen Jinhua, *Philosopher, Practitioner, Politician: The Many Lives of Fazang (643–712)* (Leiden: Brill, 2007), 187 fn. 33, translates the passage, discusses the man's identity, and situates the proposed undertaking in broader context.
17 The Shit King's gentleman visitor, Lu Jingyang, does not appear in either of the Tang histories, though someone with a very similar name served Wu Zhao's grandson, Emperor Xuanzong, as Minister of Works. In *JTS* 9.221 there is a minister named Lu Jingrong 陸景融, instead of Lu Jingyang 陸景暘.
18 *TPGJ* 243.1875.
19 Part of greater Luoyang, to the west of the city proper; at the beginning of the Tang, a county.

NOTES

20 Qiang Ning, *Art, Religion, and Politics in Medieval China: The Dunhuang Cave of the Zhai Family* (Honolulu: University of Hawai'i Press, 2004), 125.
21 Michael Loewe, *Everyday Life in Early Imperial China during the Han Period* (Hackett: Indianapolis, 2005), 142.
22 *ZZTJ* 21.687.
23 Benn, *Daily Life in the Tang*, 159.
24 *TPGJ* 226.1737–38.
25 Anne Kinney, *Representations of Childhood and Youth in Early China* (Stanford, CA: Stanford University Press, 2004), 43–44; also see the larger chapter, "The Precocious Child," 33–52.
26 It is possible that this is a reference to Li Yuanjia, the eleventh son of Tang founder Gaozu—whom we encountered earlier in this chapter as the possessor of several pieces of brilliant artisanship—but I can find no source that definitively indicates this talented child comes from the imperial Li family.
27 There is no real biographical information on Xue. I base my identification of Xue as a "poet-courtier" upon the single poem credited to him in *QTS* 45.553–54. Even this anthology mentions his transcendent skill at pitch-pot.
28 Virginia Bower and Colin Mackenzie, "Pitchpot: The Scholar's Arrow-throwing Game," in *Asian Games: The Art of Contest*, eds. Finkel and Mackenzie (New York: Asia Society, 2004), 275.
29 See Constance Cook and Ke Heli, "From Bone to Bamboo: Number Sets and Mortuary Ritual," *Journal of Oriental Studies* 41.1 (2006): 15–16.
30 Bower and Mackenzie, "Pitchpot," 275. This image of an ink rubbing of two men playing pitch pot is from *Zhongguo Meishu quanji huihuapian* 18: *Huaxiangshi xiangzhuan*. Shanghai: Shanghai renmin meishu chubanshe, 1988. The original stone relief carving is held at Nanyang Stone-carved Art Museum. Special thanks to Professor Han Yuxiang for his help in securing permission to reproduce the image here.
31 Ibid., 277.
32 *Lî Kî: The Book of Rites XI-XLVI*, trans. James Legge (Oxford: Clarendon Books, 1885), Chapter 37, 397–401. Curiously, it was the responsibility of the guest to furnish the "referee," perhaps to avoid too much of a home court advantage for the host.
33 *JTS* 29.1066.
34 *JTS* 47.2045.
35 *JTS* 199.5320.
36 Michael Lerner, "Map Room: The Spread of Backgammon and Parchisi," *World Policy Journal* (2012): 16–17. There were, Andrew Lo contends, "a rich variety of games of the backgammon type" in sixth- and seventh-century China, some with indigenous roots, others "imports transmitted along the Silk Road from the West." See "Double Sixes, Holding Spears, and the Long March: Games of the Backgammon Family in China," in *Asian Games*, 97. See Lo, 100, for Song and Yuan sources citing Indian origin.
37 Yui Suzuki, "Twanging Bows and Throwing Rice: Warding off Evil in Medieval Japanese Birth Scenes," *Artibus Asiae* 74.1 (2014): 33, from Helen Craig McCullough, trans., *Ōkagami, the Great Mirror: Fujiwara Michinaga (966–1027) and His Times* (Princeton: Princeton University Press, 1980), 136–37. Also see Stewart Cullin, "The Japanese Game of Suguroku," *The Brooklyn Museum Quarterly* 7.4 (1920): 213–33.
38 *XTS* 115.4212. David McMullen, "The Real Judge Dee: Ti Jen-Chieh and the T'ang Restoration of 705," 70, also remarks upon this dream and the response of court ministers.

NOTES

39 *JTS* 51.2172.
40 *XTS* 42.1090.
41 Lo, "Double Sixes, Holding Spears, and the Long March," 97. A Yuan-era poem describes the pieces as resembling "clothes-beaters" (99).
42 Jiang Yonglin, "In the Name of 'Taizu': The Construction of Zhu Yuanzhang's Legal Philosophy and Chinese Cultural Identity in the 'Veritable Records of Taizu,'" *T'oung Pao* 96 (2010): 422 fn. 32.
43 *TPGJ* 171.1257.
44 Xiangzhou was seated in modern-day Xiangyang, Hubei.
45 Qianzhou was situated south of Lake Boyang in modern-day Jiangxi.
46 A county within Qianzhou.
47 Arthur Waley, "The Chinese Cinderella Story," *Folklore* 58 (1947): 226–38. Waley identifies "Ye Xian" as the earliest iteration of the Cinderella story.
48 Five ounces.
49 32 pounds!
50 A largely residential ward named after a monastery constructed there at the dawn of the Tang dynasty. See Victor Xiong, *Sui-Tang Chang'an: A Study in the Urban History of Medieval China* (Ann Arbor: Center for Chinese Studies, University of Michigan, 2000), 314.
51 He is sometimes known as Rickshaw Boy; one of the recent translations of the novel is Lao She, *Rickshaw Boy: A Novel*, trans. Howard Goldblatt (New York: Harper Perennial Modern Chinese Classics, 2010).
52 Li Shizhen, *Ben Cao Gang Mu, Vol. II: Waters, Fires, Soils, Metals, Jades, Stones, Minerals, Salts*, translated and annotated by Paul Unschuld (Berkeley: University of California Press, 2021), 8.252.
53 *Ben Cao Gang Mu, Vol. II*, 8.252.
54 Southern Shandong/northern Jiangsu.
55 I cannot find any record of Guo Chun and Wang Sui serving in any official capacity during the Tang, so I have placed these two passages in this chapter on "Common People." In the case of Guo Chun, local officials were sent to investigate, which also suggests he came from the ranks of the commoners.

CHAPTER 6

1 *Comprehensive Discussions in White Tiger Hall (Baihu tong* 白虎通), Paul Goldin trans., in *Images of Women in Chinese Thought and Culture: Writings from the pre-Qin Period through the Song Dynasty*, ed. Robin Wang (Indianapolis: Hackett, 2003), 173.
2 Yang Lien-sheng, "Female Rulers in Imperial China," *Harvard Journal of Asian Studies* 23 (1960–61): 48.
3 David Hall and Roger Ames, "Sexism, with Chinese Characteristics," in *The Sage and the Second Sex* (Chicago: Open Court, 2000), 84.
4 Yenna Wu, *The Chinese Virago: A Literary Theme* (Cambridge: Harvard University Council on East Asian Studies, 1995), 20.
5 Guisso, *Women in China: Current Directions in Historical Scholarship* (Youngstown, NY: Philo Press, 1981), 60.
6 *Liji zhengyi* 禮記正義, annotated and with commentary by Li Xueqin (Beijing: Beijing University Press, 2000), 27.836.
7 For more on the relative lack of restriction on women in the early Tang, see Gao Shiyu, "A *Fixed* State of Affairs and Mis-Positioned Status: Gender Relations

during the Sui, Tang and Five Dynasties," in *The Chalice and the Blade*, eds. Min and Gao (Beijing: Academy of Social Sciences, 1995), 270–314; Duan Tali 段塔麗. *Tangdai funü diwei yanjiu* 唐代婦女地位研究 [Research on the Position of Women in the Tang Dynasty] (Beijing: Renmin chubanshe, 2000), 124–26. See also, Jennifer Jay, "Imagining Matriarchy: 'Kingdoms of Women' in Tang China," *Journal of the American Oriental Society* 116 (1996): 220–29; Jay, "Vignettes of Chinese Women in Tang Xi'an (618–906): Individualism in Wu Zetian, Yang Guifei, Yu Xuanji, and Li Wa," *Chinese Culture* 31.1 (1990), 77–89. In *Women in Tang China* (Boston: Rowman and Littlefield, 2020), Bret Hinsch cautions against providing too sunny a forecast for Tang women, noting that the story is complicated: women did not "comprise a unitary group" and "complex and fluctuating" social and political conditions alternatingly "favored and limited female autonomy" (7).

8   Gao Shiyu, "A Fixed State of Affairs and Mis-positioned Status," 292–93. Most famously, in the early seventh century, the Turkish empress of Emperor Sui Yangdi refused to allow him to have any concubines. When he commented upon the exquisite hands of a palace maid, the empress had the girl's hands cut off and served at his next meal.

9   Benn, *Daily Life in Traditional China: The Tang Dynasty*, 107–13.

10 Chen, *Empire of Style*, 7.

11 James T.C. Liu, "Polo and Cultural Change: From T'ang to Sung China," *Harvard Journal of Asiatic Studies* 45.1 (1985): 203–24; Rong Xinjiang 榮新江, "Nüban nanzhuang: Sheng Tang funü xingbie yishi" 女扮男裝:盛唐婦女性別意識 [Donning Male Attire: Gender Consciousness of Women in the High Tang] Abstracts and Papers from the Tang Women's Studies Conference (Beijing University, 2001), 320–44.

12 Gao Shiyu, "A Fixed State of Affairs and Mis-positioned Status," 311.

13 In some sources like *Storied Poems* this story is set in the Tang in 689, a year before Wu Zhao inaugurated the Zhou. In *Court and Country*, it is set in the Zhou. In the *Comprehensive Mirror* (*ZZTJ* 206.6518), Qiao's death and clan eradication occurred in 697.

14 Jade Disc is referred to as a bi 婢, a slave girl or a lesser concubine.

15 This story is set in Wu Zhao's capital, Luoyang, which has a Southern Market. Chang'an does not.

16 Also see *Sui-Tang jiahua* 隋唐嘉話, comp. Liu Su 劉餗 from *Tang-Song shiliao biji congkan* 唐宋史料筆記叢刊 (Beijing: Zhonghua, 1997), 39; *TPGJ* 274.2158–59.

17 Doran, *Transgressive Typologies*, 204–05. Doran discusses this story in *Court and Country* and other sources rather extensively (202–05).

18 Sanders, *Words Well Put*, 267–68.

19 *JTS* 190.5012. Here and in an extensive telling in the late Tang *Storied Poems* (*Benshi shi* 本事詩), written by Meng Qi 孟棨, as well as in other sources, Jade Disc (Biyu 碧玉) is known by the sobriquet Yaoniang 窈娘, the Demurely Coy Maiden; Sanders translates the passage from *Storied Poems* (1.2) in *Words Well Put*, 265.

20 Timothy Wai Keung Chan, "Dedication and Identification in Wang Bo's Compositions on the Gallery of Prince Teng," *Mounumenta Serica* 50 (2002): 240, c.f. *JTS* 64.2436.

21 This passage is also translated in Chan, "Dedication and Identification in Wang Bo's Compositions on the Gallery of Prince Teng," 240.

22 *JS* 96.2511.

NOTES

23 Hinsch, *Women in Tang China*, 110.
24 Anne Kinney, *Exemplary Women of Early China: The Lienü zhuan of Liu Xiang* (New York: Columbia University Press, 2014), 4.14: 83–84.
25 *XTS* 205.5817.
26 For Fang Xuanling's extensive biography, see *JTS* 66.2459–67.
27 The word for jealous (*du* 妒) contains the woman radical (*nü* 女), indicating that, linguistically and culturally, this was thought of as an innate female characteristic. From the Eastern Han forward, jealousy was one of the seven justifications for a man to divorce (or expel, these seven justifications were called the "seven expulsions" (*qichu* 七出)); see Sun Xiao and Pan Shaoping, "Order and Chaos: The Social Positions of Men and Women in the Qin, Han, and Six Dynasties Period," in *The Chalice and the Blade*, ed. Gao Shiyu (Beijing: Academy of Social Science, 1995), 257.
28 *TPGJ* 272.2145.
29 A ward with both residences and businesses situated to the northeast of the Northern Market on the northern side of the Luo River.
30 See *The Annals of Lü Buwei*, 14.329, from "Harmonious Relations" (*Yuhe* 遇合).
31 I am not sure which Chu ruler was fond of pickled celery.
32 Norman Ho, "Confucian Jurisprudence in Action: Pre-Tang Dynasty Panwen (Written Legal Judgments)," *Washington International Law Journal* 22.1 (2013): 105 fn. 165, has translated a long account on Chu statesman, Qu Dao, and his son Qu Jian, from the Spring and Autumn era (sixth cent. BC); c.f. Narrative of States (*Guoyu* 國語), "Narratives of Chu" (Chuyu).
33 Literally, "sheep dates." Father of Confucian disciple Zengzi, Zeng Xi's fondness for sheep dates is mentioned in the *Mencius* (7B.36), trans. D.C. Lau (New York: Penguin, 1970), 202.
34 Meng Lingxiu was a local official in Wuxing (near modern-day Huzhou, Zhejiang), when Liu Yong visited him. For more on scab-eating Liu Yong, see *Song shu* 宋書 [History of the Liu Song Dynasty], comp. Shen Yue 沈約 (Beijing: Zhonghua, 1997), 42.1308. An official in the Southern Song dynasty, Liu Yong felt that addictive scabs had a delectable fishy flavor akin to abalone; he whipped subordinates and people under his jurisdiction without due cause to produce more wounds that would scab over. One time, to the shock and revulsion of a friend he was visiting, he picked up a scab fallen from the friend's ankle and wolfed it down!
35 A medical treatment that involved using moxa to cauterize certain points of the body to improve the flow of *qi* and cure maladies. This treatment sometimes leaves a scar.
36 It is not clear where this story about the honey-and-ant-guzzling Emperor Mingdi (r. 466–472) of the Liu Song dynasty comes from. It also appears in later texts.
37 This saying "chasing the stench across the sea" comes from *Lushi Chunqiu*, "Harmonious Relations"; see *The Annals of Lü Buwei*, 14.329. There is a story about a man who reeks so horribly that his family, relatives, and acquaintances can't bear to be anywhere near him. Distraught, he goes to the sea to isolate himself; however, there is something about his pungent reek that titillates a primal nasal chord of the fisherfolk, prompting them to follow the man around the waters.
38 Hinsch, *Women in Tang China*, 11.
39 Part of Jizhou in the southeastern part of modern Hebei. Officially, this was no longer a county name in the Tang.
40 A coastal southeastern city in modern-day Zhejiang.
41 Confucius, *The Analects*, D.C. Lau trans. (New York: Penguin, 1979), 95, VIII.20.

NOTES

42 Lisa Raphals, "A Woman Who Understood the Rites," in *Confucius and the Analects: New Essays*, ed. Bryan Van Norden (New York: Oxford University Press, 2002), 275–76. Raphals shows that Jing Jiang's renown predated Liu Xiang's 劉向 (79–8 BC) Western Han dynasty *Biographies of Exemplary Women* (*Lienü zhuan* 列女傳); *Narrative of States* (*Guoyu* 國語) from the early Warring States era includes eight passages on Lady Ji of Lu, many of which illustrate the powerful moral suasion that she, as a widowed mother, exercised over her son Wenbo. She also instructed him on proper ceremonial deportment in hosting guests. Also see Zhou Yiqun, *Festivals, Feasts, and Gender Relations in Ancient China and Greece* (New York: Cambridge University Press, 2010), 245–47.

43 Raphals, *Sharing the Light: Representations of Women and Virtue in Early China* (Albany: SUNY Press, 1998), 6. The second chapter of this book, "Women as Prescient Counselors," is full of many more examples from early China of women who acted as shadow ministers—counseling, teaching, admonishing, offering strategy, or otherwise advising men (rulers, husbands, sons) in high or influential positions.

44 This event, also recorded in *ZZTJ* 206.6534, occurred in 698.

45 *XTS* 205.5822.

46 *JTS* 187.4877.

47 *JTS* 51.2172.

48 There is also a shorter version of this incident in the Princess Yicheng's brief biography in *XTS* 83.3653.

49 Wu, *The Chinese Virago*, 73.

50 Giorgio Sperati, "Amputation of the Nose Throughout History," *Acta Otorhinolaryngol Italia* 29 (2009): 44–50: Patricia Skinner, "The Gendered Nose and Its Lack: 'Medieval' Nose-Cutting and Its Modern Manifestations," *Journal of Women's History* 26 (2014): 45–67.

51 Emperor Zhongzong's reduced princely title during much of his banishment, between 684 and 698.

52 Wei Xuanzhen's wife came from the eminent Cui 崔 family.

53 "Filial and Harmonious" was part of Emperor Zhongzong's posthumous title, indicating that this passage was written after his death in 710.

54 A Wei 阿韋 is yet another familiar, contemptuous nickname sometimes used for Empress Wei, who was implicated in the poisoning and death of her husband, Zhongzong, in 710. It means something like "Ol' Lady Wei" or "Missy Wei."

55 Zhou Rengui had previously presented the head of the Ning family chieftain to Empress Wei. This act of personal loyalty marked Zhou as part of her extended group of supporters. Therefore, the general was executed in 710 when Empress Wei was removed from power and killed.

56 Fitzgerald, *The Empress Wu*, 113.

57 *ZZTJ* 203.6417; *JTS* 87.2843–44.

58 *JTS* 6.116, 87.2844.

59 *ZZTJ* 208.6603.

60 *ZZTJ* 208.6603–04. The passage below from *Court and Country* appears in Hu Sanxing's 胡三省 "examined discrepancies" (*kao yi* 考異), a commentary on the text from the early Yuan dynasty.

61 *ZZTJ* 208.6603–04. In 710, after Empress Wei reportedly poisoned husband Zhongzong and tried to rule as grand dowager through a feckless son, she was killed in a coup. As a member of her clique and a Wei loyalist, Zhou Rengui was killed as well.

NOTES

62 *JTS* 7.142.
63 For a very different perspective on these campaigns to eradicate the Ning clan of Liao or Man "southern barbarians," see Catherine Churchman, *The People Between the Rivers: The Rise and Fall of a Bronze Drum Culture, 200–750 AD* (Lanham, MD: Rowman and Littlefield, 2016), esp. Chapter 7, "The Last of the Bronze Drum Chiefs: The Rise and Fall of Great Families," 169–201. The Nings are one of these last great families from this Bronze Drum Culture.

CHAPTER 7

1 Kam Louie, *Theorising Chinese Masculinity: Society and Gender in China* (Cambridge, UK: Cambridge University Press, 2002), 4, has engaged in a thoughtful gendered examination of the civil–military "dyad" of masculinity in traditional China; the civil lineage stems from Confucius, the martial lineage from Guan Yu.
2 It first appears in Sima Qian's *Records of the Historian* (*SJ* 97.2699).
3 *YYZZ*, 1.2. See also Image 7.1. Also see Pan Yihong, "Integration of the Northern Ethnic Frontiers in Tang China," *Chinese Historical Review* 19 (2012): 14–15. The painting pictured in Figure 6 is a Ming dynasty representation of Emperor Taizong, courtesy of the National Palace Museum.
4 Hucker, *A Dictionary of Official Titles in Imperial China*, 34.
5 *QTW* 172.1757. For more on the debate in Wu Zhao's court of how best to manage the Tibetan threat, see Wang Zhenping, *Tang China in Multi-Polar Asia: A History of Diplomacy and War* (Honolulu: University of Hawaii Press, 2013), 279–80.
6 *XTS* 110.4111–29; *JTS* 109.3287–3301.
7 Abramson, *Ethnic Identity in Tang China*, xvii–xviii.
8 *ZZTJ*, chapters 201–202.
9 Skaff, *Sui-Tang China and Its Turko-Mongol Neighbors*, 89–90.
10 Wang, *Tang China in Multi-Polar Asia*, 86–88; Evelyn Rawski, *Early Modern China and Northeast Asia: Cross-border Perspectives* (Cambridge: Cambridge University Press, 2015), 35–36.
11 *ZZTJ* 205.6482.
12 Ning Chia, "Women in Frontier Politics: Heqin," in *Presence and Presentation: Women in the Chinese Literate Tradition*, ed. Sherry Mou (New York: St. Martin's Press, 1999), 39–76. Ning Chia describes this diplomatic practice of marrying Chinese princesses and Inner Asian nomadic leaders in the following fashion: "Heqin women's experience is full of paradox: their impressive courage and deep sorrow, their great contribution and immense tragedy, and their loyalty to two political entities and painful isolation in personal life. Their tearful tales, however, accompanied their general success in frontier politics. It has been stated that *heqin* intermarriage was the best means of cultural communication between the Chinese Empire and the Inner Asian powers" (66).
13 *ZZTJ* 205.6509–10.
14 The Ministry of Spring is an alternative name for the Ministry of Rites; Wu Zhao used the archaic names of bureaucratic institutions from the Zhou dynasty of old.
15 For an example of one of these songs wishing a ruler a long life and a long reign, see Charles Hartman, "Stomping Songs: Words and Image," *Chinese Literature: Essays, Articles, and Reviews* 17 (1995): 19–21.
16 *ZZTJ* 206.6515–16.

17. *Zhouli zhushu* (Beijing: Beijing University Press, 2000), 14.352.
18. He is also known as Zhang Renyuan 張仁愿 because the *dan* 亶 in his name was a homophone for the *dan* 旦 in the personal name of Emperor Ruizong, under whom the general served, and thus was taboo.
19. Pan Yihong, *Son of Heaven and the Heavenly Qaghan: Sui-Tang China and Its Neighbors* (Bellingham, WA: Western Washington University, 1997), 270.
20. *JTS* 93.2981. Both Tang histories have biographies for Zhang Renyuan; see *JTS* 2981–82, *XTS* 111.4151–53.
21. Pan Yihong, *Son of Heaven and the Heavenly Qaghan*, 241–42.
22. Skaff, *Sui-Tang China and Its Turko-Mongol Neighbors*, 193, notes that Cao Huaishun was likely Sogdian, one of the many non-Chinese generals serving in the early Tang and Wu-Zhou militaries.
23. For more on this tactical othering to assert (or in this case, reclaim, after suffering a rout) one's own masculinity, see Laura Levine, "Men in Women's Clothing: Anti-Theatricality and Effeminization from 1579 to 1642," *Criticism* 28.2 (1986): 121–43, and the work of R. W. Connell (and subsequent criticism of that work) on hegemonic masculinity.
24. *TPGJ* 191.1436.
25. *ZZTJ* 203.6432.
26. *XTS* 5.119, 32.843. In this source, Sun Quan is mentioned as one of the leaders in the campaign against the Xi and the Khitan. For this campaign in a broader context, see Pan Yihong, *Son of Heaven and the Heavenly Qaghan*, 273.
27. Louie, *Theorising Chinese Masculinity*, 22–24.
28. Luo Guanzhong, *Three Kingdoms*, trans. Moss Roberts (Beijing: Foreign Languages Press, 1995), Vol. I.1.12.
29. Seven feet tall!
30. Melonport was located on the northern bank of the Yangzi, in Jiangsu.
31. *TPGJ* 192.1441.
32. *JTS* 5.105, 196.5224. At this juncture, Song Lingwen was a vice commandant (*langjiang* 郎將), leading elite troops at the capital, Chang'an.
33. This Buddhist temple was located in Chang'an. See Chen Jinhua, "The Multiple Roles of the Twin Chanding Monasteries in Sui-Tang Chang'an," *Studies in Chinese Religions* 1.4 (2015): 344–56. The Chanding temples played host to an imperial outing, housed artistic marvels, and held festivals celebrating Buddhist relics within.
34. A coastal county in modern-day North Vietnam on the fringes of the empire.
35. *JTS* 191.5095.
36. Timothy Barrett, review of *Medieval Chinese Warfare, 300–900*, by David Graff, *Bulletin of the School of Oriental and African Studies* 66.1 (2003): 128.
37. Yingzhou includes Hejian, a small city in modern-day Hebei famous for its donkey meat. In the early Tang and during Wu Zhao's reign, the region was officially known as Hejian Commandery instead of Yingzhou prefecture, though, as this passage from *Court and Country* shows, many people still called it Yingzhou. Gaoyang and Boye, mentioned later in this passage, are counties within this administrative unit. See Victor Xiong, *Historical Dictionary of Medieval China* (Lanham, MD: Scarecrow Press, 2009), 627.
38. A general amnesty usually accompanied the declaration of a new reign era.
39. Ji Yougong 計有功, *Tangshi jishi* 唐詩紀事 [Records on Tang Poetry], chapter 80, https://ctext.org/wiki.pl?if=en&chapter=409780&remap=gb#p39 (accessed 10 March 2020).

NOTES

40 *YYZZ*, continued in Chapter 4, 246.
41 For instance, see the initial posts in https://www.reddit.com/r/army/comments/7zyoio/things_to_keep_you_from_becoming_bored_to_death/ (accessed 9 March 2121).
42 It is not entirely clear that Yuan Sizhong was a military officer. The title he bears could be either military or civil. For more on his title—*lushi canjun* 錄事參軍—see Hucker, *Dictionary of Official Titles*, 323. Outside of this passage, I cannot locate any further trace of Yuan Sizhong or his father, Yuan Ping.

CHAPTER 8

1 Clae Waltham trans., *Shu Ching* (Chicago: Henry Regnery, 1971), "The Tribute of Yu," 52–53.
2 *Liji zhengyi*, 5.136.
3 Marks, *China: Its Environment and History*, 4.
4 Chen Sanping, *Multicultural China in the Early Medieval Ages* (Philadelphia: University of Pennsylvania Press, 2012), Chapter 1, "Legacy," 4–38, contends that the "core Tuoba [Türk] and other Xianbei descent" of the imperial family was an "open secret" (4–5). For more on the role of the divine Lord Lao in the founding and legitimation of the Tang, see *XTS* 70.1956 for the claimed lineage; also see Anna Seidel, "The Image of the Perfect Ruler in Early Taoist Messianism: Laozi and Li Hung," *History of Religions* 9 (1969–1970): 244; Woodbridge Bingham, *Founding of the Tang Dynasty* (New York: Octagon Books, 1970), 118.
5 Ibid., 36. I have added the brackets.
6 Chen, *Empire of Style*, 92 and 94.
7 For more context, see Rothschild, "Sumozhe Suppressed, Huntuo Halted: An Investigation into the Nature and Stakes of the Cold-Splashing Festal Sogdian Dramas Performed in Early Eighth Century China," *Frontiers of Chinese History* 12.2 (2017): 277.
8 Wang Zhenping, *Tang China in Multi-Polar Asia*, 1–2.
9 Modified from Arthur Waley trans., *Monkey* (New York: Grove Press, 1970), 125.
10 Zhao and Wang, *Wu Zetian pingzhuan*, 292.
11 *THY* 100.1798.
12 Chen Jo-shui, "Empress Wu and Proto-Feminist Sentiments in T'ang China," in *Imperial Rulership and Cultural Change in Traditional China*, eds. Frederick Brandauer and Chih-chieh Huang (Seattle: University of Washington Press, 1994), 83–85.
13 Gaozong and Wu Zhao jointly performed the *feng* and *shan* rites on Mount Tai in 666. See *ZZTJ* 201.6346, *JTS* 5.89–90, and 23.888; also Wechsler, *Offerings of Jade and Silk*, 184–85.
14 In *ZZTJ* (201.6391, 6393), it is recorded that in the seventh month an imperial edict announced the Two Sages would hold the rite at Mount Song on the winter solstice. Because of Turkish rebellion, the celebration of the *feng* and *shan* was called off in the eleventh lunar month.
15 Though Zhang Zhuo places the Tibetan delay after the Turkish delay, and both Tang histories and the *Comprehensive Mirror* mention Tibetan incursions in 680, both the *THY* (7.101) and the *ZZTJ* (201.6379) indicate that the Two Sages planned a *feng* and *shan* back in 676; the former source indicates that Tibetan incursions that year delayed the rite.

NOTES

16. The cancelation due to illness is also recorded in the *THY* 7.102 and *JTS* 5.111.
17. Twitchett, *Financial Administration under the T'ang Dynasty*, 75.
18. Unlike the "barbarians" whose border incursions and invasions are also referenced in this paragraph, Xu Jingye was one of the Li princes who rebelled against Wu Zhao in 684. Bozhou and Yuzhou were flashpoints in the domestic uprisings against Wu Zhao during her regency led by princes from the Li family of Tang dynasts.
19. Dong Zhongshu 董仲舒 (179–104 BC), the famous Han dynasty Confucian scholar–statesmen, helped systematize and amplify the idea of "mutual responsiveness between Heaven and man."
20. Confucius, trans. by Andrew Plaks, *Ta Hsüeh and Chung Yung* (The Highest Order of Cultivation and On the Practice of the Mean) (New York: Penguin Classics, 2003), 53, entry 32.
21. Joseph Needham, "Human Laws and Laws of Nature in China and the West (II): Chinese Civilization and the Laws of Nature," *Journal of the History of Ideas* 12.2 (1951): 201.
22. John Major, *Heaven and Earth in Early Han Thought: Chapters Three, Four, and Five of the Huainanzi* (Albany: SUNY Press, 1993), 225.
23. Wang Aihe, *Cosmology and Political Culture in Early China* (Cambridge: Cambridge University Press, 2000), 130 and 191–92.
24. Wang Yu-ch'uan, "An Outline of the Central Government of the Former Han Dynasty," *Harvard Journal of Asiatic Studies* 12.1 (1949): 164–65.
25. Mark Elvin, "Who Was Responsible for the Weather? Moral Meteorology in Late Imperial China," *Osiris*, 2nd series, 13 (1998): 213–14.
26. Skaff, *Sui-Tang China and Its Turko-Mongol Neighbors*, 43–44, 48–51; Pan Yihong, *The Son of Heaven and the Heavenly Qaghan*, 262–63.
27. Abramson, *Ethnic Identity in Tang China*, 29.
28. Zhenyuan is a county in Haozhou prefecture (modern-day Henan) on the site of the putative birthplace of Laozi, the legendary sage–founder of Daoism. Shortly after performing the *feng* and *shan* sacrifices on Mount Tai, the Two Sages bestowed this name on the county in 666, as they headed homeward from the ceremony. See Hu Sanxing commentary in *ZZTJ* 201.6347.
29. Hucker, *Dictionary of Titles in Imperial China*, 425.
30. *TPGJ* 258.2015.
31. For more on the Qidan in the early Tang and, more specifically their rebellion of 696–97, see Chen Jinhua, "Fazang, the Holy Man," *Journal of the International Association of Buddhist Studies* 28.1 (2005): 38–40; Guisso, *Wu Tse-t'ien and the Politics of Legitimation in Tang China*, 138–43; Pan Yihong, *Son of Heaven and the Heavenly Khan*, 265–69; Victor Xiong, *Historical Dictionary of Medieval China*, 405–406. Skaff refers to the Khitan as one of several "Mongolic-speaking tribal unions that periodically united or feuded with each other, the Sui, the Tang, Türks, and Uighur" (38). He remarks the Wu Zhao's utilization of Qapaghan to subdue the Khitan was a two-fold military error: she never placed Qapaghan under supervision of a Chinese general and she used "a more distant khanate" to attack a "neighboring one" (49).
32. Chen, "Fazang, the Holy Man," 37.
33. *ZZTJ* 205.6506–07. In this source, the gorge is called Xiashi 硤石 instead of Yellow Roebuck.
34. Phoenix Hall was the archaic Zhou name for the Secretariat that Wu Zhao had adopted. Li Zhaode was a chief minister in the Secretariat, a branch concerned with

NOTES

recommending policy decisions and "drafting documents in which imperial decisions were issued" (Hucker, *A Dictionary of Official Titles in Imperial China*, 29).

35 See Li Zhaode's biography, *JTS* 87.2853–59.
36 *ZZTJ* 206.6519.
37 *ZZTJ* 206.6514–15. A footnote from commentator Hu Sanxing (206.6515) attributed to *Court and Country* is the source of the third fragment in this subsection.
38 This fragment also appears in the commentary by Hu Sanxing in *ZZTJ* 206.6521.
39 Guisso, *Wu Tse-t'ien and the Politics of Legitimation*, 112.
40 For Tang-Koguryo relations, see Guisso, *Wu Tse-t'ien and the Politics of Legitimation*, 112–25; Rothschild, "The Koguryan Connection: The Quan (Yon) Family in the Establishment of Wu Zhao's Political Authority," *China Yongu: The Journal of Chinese Studies of Pusan National University* 14.1 (2008): 199–234; David Graff, *Medieval Chinese Warfare, 300–900* (New York: Routledge, 2002), 195–201.
41 Edward Schafer, *The Golden Peaches of Samarkand: A Study of T'ang Exotics* (Berkeley: University of California Press, 1963), 44.
42 *JTS* 5.104 indicates that in 678 Guo held the position of Secretarial Drafter.
43 A residential ward in the northwest quadrant of Chang'an. See Victor Xiong, *Sui-Tang Chang'an*, 227.
44 To corroborate the sense that this story is intended to be about clever officials solving mysteries, in *Miscellaneous Records*, this story is placed in the chapters featuring "Brilliant Investigators," *TPGJ* 171.1256.
45 Kim Pusik, *The Silla Annals of the Samguk Sagi*, trans. Edward Schulz and Hugh H.W Kang, with Daniel Kane (Gyeonggi-do, Korea: Academy of Korean Sciences Press, 2013), 7.238–40. See also *ZZTJ* 202.6378
46 For a summary of the Sogdian people and culture, see Cristoph Baumer, *The History of Central Asia: Age of the Silk Roads*, Vol. 2 (London: I.B. Tauris, 2014), 221–54, "VII. The Sogdians." Rong Xinjiang's 榮新江 *Zhonggu Zhongguo yu Sute Wenming* 中古中國與粟特文明 [Medieval China and Sogdian Culture] (Beijing: Sanlian, 2014), 22–63, features two chapters that analyze the Sogdian diaspora throughout north and south China, respectively. Étienne De la Vaissière, *Sogdian Traders: A History*, trans. James Ward (Leiden: Brill, 2005), devotes a chapter (119–57) to China within what he calls a larger Sogdian "commercial empire" that developed between 350 and 750.
47 Chen, *Multicultural China in the Early Middle Ages*, 102.
48 Marc Abramson, *Ethnic Identity in Tang China*, 87–88.
49 Sogdian religion, like culture, was a bricolage.
50 Xiong, *Historical Dictionary of Medieval China*, 221.
51 Schafer, *The Golden Peaches of Samarkand*, 4.
52 Albert Dien, *Six Dynasties Civilization* (New Haven: Yale University Press, 2007), 285. For another nuanced treatment of the valences of *hu*, see Shao-yun Yang's, "The Semantic Context of Word Play with the Label Hu 胡 in Anecdotes about the Tang," unpublished paper, https://denison.academia.edu/ShaoyunYang/Papers, accessed 4 April 2015. Reflecting the change in the meaning of *Hu* over time, Yang also remarks that, "*Hu* is more complicated because its primary referent shifted over time from northern steppe nomads (Han period) to "Western" Central Asians, especially Sogdians (Tang), and then back to steppe nomads (Song to Qing), in *The Way of the Barbarians: Redrawing Ethnic Boundaries in Tang and Song China* (Seattle: University of Washington Press, 2019), 166 fn. 28.

NOTES

53 This porcelain camel and groom are held at the New Luoyang City Museum, Henan, China. Photo credit belongs to Gary Lee Todd, Ph.D.
54 Translation from Picken ed., *Music from the Tang Court, Vol. 2*, 11.
55 Pénélope Riboud, "Priests and Other Xian 祆 Ritual Performers in Medieval China," *Early Medieval China* 25 (2019): 106.
56 Laurence Picken ed., *Music from the Tang Court, Vol. 2* (Cambridge: Cambridge University Press, 1985), 7–12, and *Music from the Tang Court, Vol. 4* (Cambridge: Cambridge University Press, 1987), 1–9.
57 A city block north of the Luo River and to the west of the Imperial City.
58 A number of contemporary scholars have noted this passage. Riboud, "Priests and Other Xian 祆 Ritual Performers in Medieval China," 109–10, has also translated it. Ge Chengyong's "A Comparative Study of Two Stone Steles Unearthed in the Two Capitals of the Tang Dynasty, Xi'an and Luoyang," in *From the Oxus River to the Chinese Shores: Studies on East Syriac Christianity in Central Asia and China*, eds. Li Tang and Dietmar Winkler (Zurich: Verlag, 2013), 165, identifies the *hu* in the passage as identifying Zoroastrian "Hu people." Benn, in *Daily Life in Traditional China*, 162, identifies them as Persian Manicheans.
59 Set along the early stages of the Silk Road, Liangzhou, the city mentioned in the second passage, had long been a center of Sogdian culture; see de la Vassière, *Sogdian Traders*, 136.
60 Riboud, "Priests and Other Xian 祆 Ritual Performers in Medieval China," 110–11 also translates this passage. I would like to thank Victor Mair for the incredibly helpful suggestions he offered in translating and contextualizing both of these passages (email correspondence 17 March 2021).
61 Touraj Daryaee and Soodabeh Malekzayeh, "The Performance of Pain and Remembrance in Late Ancient Iran," *Silk Road* 12 (2014): 57–64; and Livil Mikhail Iancu, "Self-Mutilation, Multiculturalism, and Hybridity: Herodotus on the Karians in Egypt," *Anatolia Antiqua* 25 (2017): 59–60.
62 Riboud, "Priests and Other Xian 祆 Ritual Performers in Medieval China," 111–12.
63 Ibid., 112.
64 *SS* 7.149.
65 Edwin Pulleyblank, "Jihu: Indigenous Inhabitants of Shaanbei and Western Shanxi," in *Opuscula Altaica: Essays Presented in Honor of Henry Schwarz*, eds. Edward H. Kaplan and D.W. Whisenant (Seattle: University of Washington Press, 1994), 510.
66 For a more comprehensive vantage of the Bai Tieyu uprising, see Rothschild, "Emerging from the Cocoon: Ethnic Revival, Lunar Radiance, and the Cult of Liu Sahe in the Jihu Uprising of 682–83," *Annali* 65.1 (2005): 257–82; also see April Hughes, *Worldly Saviors and Imperial Authority in Medieval Chinese Buddhism* (Honolulu: University of Hawaii Press), 50. For more on the Jihu, see Pulleyblank, "Jihu: Indigenous Inhabitants of Shaanbei and Western Shanxi," 498–530.
67 *TPGJ* 238.1833.
68 Erica Brindley, "Hairstyle and Yue Identity in Chinese Texts," in *Imperial China and its Southern Neighbors*, eds. Victor Mair and Liam Kelley (Singapore: Institute of Southeast Asian Studies, 2020), 18–21. Brindley also analyzes other characteristics associated with unbound hair, such as purity of spirit, connection to the natural world, youthfulness, insanity, and numinous power.
69 Ibid., 37.
70 Chen Sanping, "'Godly Worm' and the 'Literati Prism' of Chinese Sources," *Journal of the American Oriental Society* 139.2 (2019): 417. Chen explains that "traditional

NOTES

Chinese literature still represents the leading primary source in Sinology and related studies. This is not only due to the enormity of its volume, but can also be more consequentially attributed to the simple fact that, as far as received primary sources are concerned, for a long time the educated Confucian gentry monopolized almost all genres of writing, not the least historiography, in East Asia. The inherent gentry bias of traditional written sources, though long recognized, still permeates much of modern scholarship. More often than not, we are looking at China's past through a 'literati prism.'" In this article, Chen remarks that this "literati prism" distorts historiography and "gentrifies" popular tradition (429).

71 Marks, China, *Its Environment and History*, 113; "Wet-Rice Cultivation," 113–16.
72 Even today, many of the prefectures and counties in the Wuxi area are "autonomous" regions for the Miao, Tujia, and Dong minorities.
73 For more on Jayadevī in Champa, see Trudy Jacobsen, *Lost Goddesses: The Denial of Female Power in Cambodian History* (Singapore: NAIS, 2008), 23–26, and "Autonomous Queenship in Cambodia, 1st–9th Centuries AD," *Journal of the Royal Asiatic Society* 13.3 (2003): 140–42, and O. W. Walters, "North-western Cambodia in the Seventh Century," *Bulletin of School of Oriental and African Studies* 37.2 (1974): 357–75.
74 Li Li 李莉, "Sichuan Fengjiexian fengxiangxia yaguanzang" 四川奉节县风箱峡崖棺葬, *Wenwu* 文物 (1978.7): 89–90.
75 Lewis, *China's Cosmopolitan Empire*, 155; Xiong, *Historical Dictionary of Medieval China*, 316.
76 Schafer, "Tang," Food in Chinese Culture," 101.
77 Charles Higham, *The Bronze Age of Southeast Asia* (Cambridge, UK: Cambridge University Press, 1996), 90–103.
78 Camphor.
79 *JTS* 197.5271–72; *XTS* 222.6301. See *JTS* 197.5269 for fine cotton *karpāsa* (Skt.) cloth *gubei* 古貝 clothing of Linyi, upon which the clothing of Champa is reportedly modeled. The point—perhaps borrowed from Zhang Zhuo—about abstaining from alcohol to avoid licentiousness, except with one's spouse within one's own home, also appears in these official histories. Also see Geoffrey Goble, "Maritime SE Asia: The View from Sui-Tang China," *Nalanda-Sririjawa Center Working Papers* 16 (2014): 1–19. For more on the identification of *gubei* as cotton cloth, see Paul Pelliot, *Notes on Marco Polo I, Ouvrage posthume* (Paris: Imprimerie Nationale Librarie Adrien-Maisonneuve, 1959), 433–42, part of an impressive 90-page study on foreign terms for cotton. This is the Chinese name for the tribute item sometimes brought from South and Southeast Asia.

CHAPTER 9

1 Wechsler, *Offerings of Jade and Silk*, 234.
2 David McMullen, "Bureaucrats and Cosmology: The Ritual Code of T'ang China," in *Rituals of Royalty: Power and Ceremonial in Traditional Societies*, eds. David Cannadine and Simon Price (Cambridge, UK: Cambridge University Press, 1987), 186.
3 Peter Gregory and Patricia Ebrey, "The Religious and Historical Landscape," in *Religion and Society in T'ang and Song China*, ed. Ebrey and Gregory (Honolulu: University of Hawaii Press, 1993), 12. For the original conception of these three elite traditions as mountain peaks growing from "an indistinct mass of popular beliefs and practices," see Erich Zürcher, "Buddhist Influence on Early Taoism: A Survey of Scriptural Evidence," *T'oung Pao* 66 (1980): 146.

NOTES

4   Rhoads Murphey, *East Asia: A New History*, 4th edition (New York: Pearson Longman, 2007), 45.
5   A prefecture seated in modern-day Nanchang, Jiangxi.
6   A figure from remote antiquity renowned for his longevity.
7   See, for instance, Lao Tzu, Lau trans., *Tao Te Ching* (New York: Penguin Classics, 1963), 85 (I. 28).
8   Timothy Barrett, *Taoism under the T'ang* (London: Wellsweep, 1996), 11–45.
9   For a more extensive account of Hu Chao's career and his service in Wu Zhao's court, see Rothschild, "Rhetoric, Ritual and Support Constituencies," 227–34. See also Edward Schafer, "The Restoration of the Shrine of Wei Hua-tsun at Lin-ch'uan in the Early Eighth Century," *Journal of Oriental Studies* 15 (1977): 124–37, and Russell Kirkland, "Huang Ling-wei: A Taoist Priestess in T'ang China," *Journal of Chinese Religions* 19 (1991): 47–73.
10 For more on Kou Qianzhi and his potent influence on the Northern Wei dynasty, see Richard Mather, "K'ou Ch'ien-chih and the Taoist Theocracy of the Northern Wei," in *Facets of Taoism: Essays in Chinese Religion*, eds. Welch and Seidel (New Haven: Yale University Press, 1979), 103–22, and Livia Kohn, "Kou Qianzhi," in *The Routledge Encyclopedia of Taoism*, 601–602.
11 Forte, *Political Propaganda and Ideology*, 329–30, also translates this passage.
12 See Forte, *Political Propaganda and Ideology in China*, 309–12, "The Inscription of Kou Qianzhi, the Daoist Master of Song Peak," part of Dunhuang document S6502. For other sources—some of them likely drawing on Zhang Zhuo—see *ZZTJ* 203.6421, *JTS* 185.4800.
13 Because Zhang Zhuo refers to Ruizong's posthumous name, we know that this passage comes from after Ruizong's death (13 July 716).
14 Russell Kirkland, "Ye Fashan," in *The Routledge Encyclopedia of Taoism*, ed. Fabrizio Predagio (New York: Routledge, 2008), 1154–55; Russell Kirkland and Livia Kohn, "Daoism in the Tang (618–907)," in *Daoism Handbook*, ed. Livia Kohn (Leiden: Brill, 2004), 342–43.
15 As a relatively young adept, Ye Fashan was at this monastery from 656 to 661.
16 Franciscus Verellen, *Imperiled Destinies: The Daoist Quest for Deliverance in Medieval China* (Cambridge: Harvard University Asia Center, 2019), 289.
17 Part of Gaozong's posthumous title.
18 Li Shizhen, *Ben Cao Gang Mu, Volume VIII: Clothes, Utensils, Worms, Insects, Amphibians, Animals with Scales, Animals with Shells* (Berkeley: University of California Press, 2021), 38.91.
19 The Shady Mountains run along the southeastern fringe of the Gobi Desert in Inner Mongolia and Hebei.
20 Rothschild, *Wu Zhao: China's Only Woman Emperor*, 74–75; *JTS* 191.5097.
21 Legge translation of *Analects* II.16, from *The Chinese Classics, Vol. I: The Analects, The Greater Learning, and The Doctrine of the Mean* (London: Trubner, 1861), 14.
22 René Grousset, *In the Footsteps of the Buddha* (London: Routledge and Sons, 1932), 276.
23 Forte has translated and analyzed most of this passage. See *Mingtangs and Buddhist Utopias*, 77–79.
24 Zhang Zhuo.
25 Zhang Qian was a scribe or administrative aide (*changshi* 長史) in Wu Zhao's era.
26 King Yu is Yu the Great (Da Yu 大禹), a culture hero whose relentless digging of channels saved China from a primordial flood in the legendary Xia dynasty. He is

NOTES

not originally a Buddhist figure, but sometimes came to be considered a bodhisattva as folk culture mingled indigenous Chinese beliefs and the Buddhist faith. The pool in front of the temple of King Yu was probably not a designated pool for the release of redeemed creatures.

27 *Ben Cao Gangmu*, Vol. VIII, 43.538–39.
28 An official of the central government who oversees local government around the empire.
29 For a far more nuanced understanding of these palace chapels (*neidaochang* 那道場), see Chen Jinhua, "The Tang Buddhist Palace Chapels," *Journal of Chinese Religions* 32.1 (2004): 100–73. Chen references this passage (128).
30 Kenneth Ch'en, *Buddhism in China* (Princeton: Princeton University Press, 1964), 278.
31 Scholars have also shown that this occasion can also be considered a *pañcavārṣika* (*wuzhe dahui* 無遮大會), a Buddhist "festival without barriers." The implications are that there are no limitations on charitable donations, no barriers between social classes, and boundless reverence for the Buddha. See Chen Jinhua, "*Pañcavārṣika* Assemblies in Liang Wudi's Buddhist Palace Chapel," *Harvard Journal of Asiatic Studies* 66.1 (2006): 43–103; Max Deeg, "Origins and Development of the Buddhist Pañcavārṣika, Part II: China, *Saṃbhāṣā* : *Nagoya Studies in Indian Culture and Buddhism* 18 (1997): 67–90, and Rothschild, "Zhuanlun wang, yishi yu huozai: Wu Zhao yu 694 nian de wuzhedahui" 轉輪王、儀式、及火災：武曌与 694 年的無遮大會 [Cakravartin, Ceremony, and Conflagration: Wu Zhao and the Pañcāvarṣika of 694], in *Qianling wenhua yanjiu* 7 (2012), 101–13.
32 Forte, *Mingtangs and Buddhist Utopias*, 85, discusses the "inserted hemp" technique. He also translates the first part of this passage on p. 86.
33 *Court and Country* erroneously records it as the fifth month.
34 In the Tang, the Gold and Silver Workshop was part of the Directorate for Imperial Manufactories. See Hucker, *Dictionary of Titles in Imperial China*, 168.
35 There is also a lengthy account of this event in *ZZTJ* 205.6499–6501.
36 For a comparative study, see William Kelly, "Incendiary Actions: Fires and Firefighting in the Shogun's Capital and the People's City," in *Edo and Paris: Urban Life and the State in the Early Modern Era*, ed. James McClain (Ithaca, NY: Cornell University Press, 1994), 310–31.
37 *SS* 62.1483–84.
38 *ZZTJ* 205.6499; *JTS* 22.865.
39 *JTS* 22.865.
40 This translation is based on the rendering of Charles Hartman, in "Stomping Songs: Word and Image," *Chinese Literature: Essays, Articles, Reviews* 17 (1995): 15. Lewis Hodous, in *Folkways of China* (London: Arthur Probsthrain, 1929), 44, loosely translates this passage and references this event in his chapter "The Lantern Festival."
41 Paul Kroll, "The Representation of the Mantic Arts in the High Culture of Medieval China," in *Coping with the Future: Theories and Practices of Divination in East Asia*, ed. Michael Lackner (Leiden: Brill, 2017), 99. "Gradually diminishing" does not mean non-existent. Kroll argues that while, on the level of high/elite culture, divination became a less "prominent aspect of life, it was still an element to be reckoned with" (100); he provides numerous examples of different divinatory practices that continued into the Tang.
42 Campany, *The Chinese Dreamscape*, 70.

NOTES

43. In the Yonghui era, Zhang Zhuo would not have been born yet. This may be a copyist's error for the Yonglong era (680–681)—although by this later date Zhang Zhuo would no longer have been a child and the prediction would not make sense.
44. *JTS* 191.5093–94.
45. Turtle (*gui* 龜) is a homophone for eminence (*gui* 貴).
46. Jessey Choo, "Historicized Ritual and Ritualized History—Women's Lifecycle in Late Medieval China (600–1000)" (Princeton University diss., 2009), 205–06, also translates this passage. Choo remarks that this is evidence that "divination results were delivered in the form of a verse couplet" (206), though it remained the task of the diviner to apprehend the meaning of the verse.
47. Guisso, "The reigns of empress Wu, Chung-tsung and Jui-tsung," 294–97.
48. In southern Hebei, seat of ancient Jizhou.
49. Kristofer Schipper and Franciscus Verellen eds., "Zhang Zun," in *The Taoist Canon: A Historical Companion the Daozong* (Chicago: University of Chicago Press, 2004), 1243. Also see Aat Vervoorn, "The Life of Zhang Zun," *Monumenta Serica* 38 (1988–89): 69–94.
50. *ZZTJ* 205.6497.
51. *XTS* 116.4243, *JTS* 90.2912.
52. The archaic alternative name of the Secretariat in Wu Zhao's era.
53. A prefecture seated in modern-day Chongqing.
54. He was wearing the purple robes (*zishan* 紫衫) donned by military officers instead of the purple gown (*zipao* 紫袍) designated for chief ministers.
55. Campany, *The Chinese Dreamscape*, 75–77; 82–84.
56. Ibid., 98.
57. Northwest of Ji'nan in modern-day Shandong.
58. Stephan Kory, "Presence in Variety: De-Trivializing Female Diviners in Medieval China," *Nan Nü* 18 (2016): 42, analyzes and partially translates this passage.
59. Xiong, *Sui-Tang Chang'an*, 184–85.
60. Kory, "Presence in Variety," 42, analyzes and partially translates this passage. This study shows that there was a wide range (in terms of social standing, geographical distribution, religious affiliation, etc.) of female diviners in medieval China.
61. Luo Manling 羅曼玲, "Tangdai xiaoshuo Zhong yishixingtai yiyi de 'yao'" 唐代小说中意识形态意义的'妖,' *Beijing daxue xuebao* 50.6 (2013): 100. For more on the Buddhist monk Huifan, see Chen Jinhua, "A Complicated Figure with Complex Relationships: The Monk Huifan and Early Tang Saṃgha-state Interactions," in *The Middle Kingdom and the Dharma Wheel*, ed. Thomas Jülch (Leiden: Brill, 2020), 140–221. Huifan was an Indian or Central Asian monk who was deeply insinuated in imperial politics. Ultimately, he was executed in the aftermath of a failed plot, along with Wu Zhao's daughter, the Taiping Princess, and other conspirators to murder Xuanzong in 713.
62. Midnight.
63. A division of the imperial bodyguards.
64. *TPGJ* 285.2271. There are four chapters and more than forty entries for practitioners of *huanshu*.
65. *TPGJ* 238.1830.
66. *XTS* 3.76. Changzhou was seated in today's Changzhou in Jiangsu.
67. This was the last, relatively low-ranking office that Luo Binwang held as an official under Gaozong.

NOTES

68 *JTS* 67.2491. This oath appears in the biography of Li Jingye, the rebel leader in the uprising against Wu Zhao in 684, and in Luo Binwang's polemic mentioned in the following footnote. For more on Luo Binwang, see Volker Klöpsch, "Lo Pin-wang's Survival: Traces of a Legend," *T'ang Studies* 6 (1988): 77–97. Luo Binwang did not make it to the end of the year.
69 *QTW* 199.2009–10. Luo Binwang's polemic also appears in *JTS* 67.2490–91 and is excerpted in *ZZTJ* 203.6421–22.
70 *TPGJ* 231.1769.
71 Near Shijiazhuang in modern-day Hebei.
72 Lippiello, *Auspicious Omens and Miracles in Ancient China*, 135–39; Keith Knapp, *Selfless Offspring*, 233 fn. 82. In the late Tang however, after a white hare was captured in an imperial palace, a diviner pronounced that the creature was an inauspicious omen, as white was a funerary color (*XTS* 35.923).
73 *XTS* 219.6179; the Malgal presented pelts of white hares to Xuanzong on numerous occasions.
74 The *yi* 逸 of Xiaoyi contains the character for hare (*tu* 兔).
75 *ZZTJ* 204.6446.
76 *XTS* 209.5910. The troublemaker later rose to become a censor in Wu Zhao's court and was disparagingly called the "White Hare Censor."
77 The site for meetings of an inner council of high officials.
78 Jingyun and Guangzheng are gates on the southern wall of the Palatine City of Wu Zhao's Eastern Capital Luoyang. The Jingyun Gate is an interior gate and the Guangzheng Gate is the outer gate set to the west of the central Yingtian Gate. See *TPYL* 183.891, from Wei Shu's *New Records of the Two Capitals* (*Liangjing xinji* 兩京新記), a work compiled shortly after Wu Zhao's era.
79 *ZZTJ* 205.6497 and 6502; *JTS* 90.2924.
80 Sun Yinggang, "Imagined Reality: Urban Space and Sui-Tang Beliefs in the Underworld," *Studies in Chinese Religions* 1.4 (2015): 384, also translates this passage.
81 Gaozong. Great Emperor (*Dadi* 大帝) was part of his posthumous title.
82 There is a record of Xu Ziru serving in the Changshou era (692–693), early in Wu Zhao's Zhou dynasty. He died working on editing Sima Qian's *Records of the Historian*—the prototype for all of the subsequent state histories (*JTS* 189.4953–54).
83 Fang Qi, *Elegy of a River Shaman*, trans. N. Harry Rothschild and Meng Fanjun (Portland, ME: Merwin Asia, 2016), 154–55.
84 The precise context of Bohai is not clear. It may be a reference to a county established in modern-day Binzhou 濱州, Shandong during Wu Zhao's reign as grand dowager (688). However, Bohai may also be a reference to Balhae, the multiethnic kingdom of Chinese, Malgal, Khitan, and former Koguryans in the northeast that emerged during Wu Zhao's Zhou dynasty. Gao was a common Koguryan surname.
85 *TPGJ* 368.2931.

CHAPTER 10

1 Marks, *China, Its Environment and History*, 3.
2 Schafer, "The Conservation of Nature under the T'ang Dynasty," *Journal of the Social and Economic History of the Orient* 5.3 (1962): 299–300. In the quote, I have changed Wade-Giles Romanization to *pinyin*.
3 Mark Elvin, *Retreat of the Elephants: An Environmental History of China* (New Haven: Yale University Press, 2004), 5.

NOTES

4   *QTW* 519.5277. Liang Su 梁肅 is citing the *Zuo zhuan*, from the sixth year of Duke Cheng of Lu 魯成公 (585 BC).
5   Schafer, "The Conservation of Nature under the Tang Dynasty," 279–80.
6   Marks, *China, Its Environment and History*, 103–11.
7   Ibid., 119–20.
8   Matthew Somers, "Time, Space, and Structure in the Consolidation of the T'ang Dynasty (617–700)," *Journal of Asian Studies* 45.5 (1986): 971–94; Mark Lewis, *China's Cosmopolitan Empire*, 5–8.
9   Twitchett, *Financial Administration under the T'ang*, 13.
10 Edward Schafer, *The Vermilion Bird*, 228.
11 The story is related in Shi Nai'an and Luo Guanzhong, *Outlaws of the Marsh*, trans. Sidney Shapiro (Beijing: Foreign Language Press, 1993), Chapter 23, 457–75.
12 See *Fang Qi, Elegy of a River Shaman*. The Miao people in the southwest also have a tiger cult. See Schafer, *The Vermilion Bird*, 11.
13 Spring, *Animal Allegories in T'ang China*, 61–63. Lai Hu 來鵠 mentions these rites in his "Discourse on Cats and Tigers" (*Maohu shuo* 貓虎説), written in the late Tang.
14 *XTS* 35.923.
15 Benn, *Daily Life in Traditional China*, 238.
16 The Prince of Guo is Tang founding emperor Gaozu's fifteenth son, Li Feng 李鳳.
17 Li Qianli, a member of the imperial family and grandson of Taizong who attached himself to Wu Zhao, presented auspicious omens betokening Heaven's sanction of her rule in order to avoid her purge of the Li princes. He is mentioned in passing by court wag Zhang Yuanyi in Chapter 2.
18 The creature is cataloged in Li Shizhen, *Ben Cao Gang Mu*, Vol. IX, 655. Though this medical compendium comes from the late Ming dynasty, in describing this creature its author cites the same text—*Illustrations of Auspicious Omens*—mentioned in Zhang Zhuo's passage. Figure 8 is a Qing dynasty woodblock print from Chen Menglei's *Gujin tushu jicheng* (Comprehensive Corpus of Illustrations and Books from Ancient Times to the Present).
19 Wang Yongping 王永平, "Tang Gaozong, Wu Zetian shiqi yu Linyi de guanxi" 唐高宗、武則天時期与林邑的關系 [Foreign Relations with Champa during the reigns of Tang Gaozong and Wu Zetian], "Conference Proceedings from the 11th Conference of the Wu Zetian Research Association," supplemental essay, 4–5.
20 Rothschild, *Emperor Wu Zhao and Her Pantheon of Devis, Divinities, and Dynastic Mothers*, 195–202.
21 Elvin, *Retreat of the Elephants*, 9. Elvin remarks that "Chinese farmers and elephants do not mix."
22 Ibid., 15.
23 Wang Yongping, "Tang Gaozong, Wu Zetian shiqi yu Linyi de Guanxi," 3.
24 *TPYL* 890.3955.
25 *XTS* 47.1217.
26 A county located in southwestern Hubei or northern Hunan.
27 Schafer, *The Vermilion Bird*, 83 and 231. He opines that xingxing may either be the hoolock gibbon or the black gibbon.
28 Pei Yan 裴炎, "Inscription on Gibbons," *QTW* 168.1712–13. He is citing Li Daoyuan's early sixth century *Annotations on the Classic of Waterways* (*Shuijing zhu* 水經註) and other earlier sources. Also see Schafer, *Golden Peaches of Samarkand*, 209.

NOTES

29 Lewis, *China's Cosmopolitan Empire*, 54.
30 Schafer, *Vermilion Bird*, 223; *Golden Peaches of Samarkand*, 73–75, c.f. *Bencao Gangmu*, chapter 50. Schafer notes that yellow cows, descended from the zebu, likely came from the South. Also see Spring, *Animal Allegories in T'ang China*, 77–94.
31 *TPGJ* 447.3652. Translation from Rania Huntington, *Alien Kind: Foxes and Late Imperial Chinese Narrative* (Cambridge: Harvard University Asia Center, 2003), 1.
32 Xiaofei Kang, "The Fox [*hu* 狐] and the Barbarian [*hu* 胡]: Unraveling Representations of the Other in Late Tang Tales," *Journal of Chinese Religions* 27.1 (1999): 35–36 and 59. Kang concludes that there is a consonance between foxes (*hu*) and foreigners (*hu*), both linguistically (they are homophones) and socially: "Tang literati were frequently fascinated by the marginal and the foreign, but they also perceived these forces as threats to their social prestige and cultural superiority. They appreciated the various entities symbolized by the fox as exotic and transitory, but despised and exorcised them when they attempted to cross the threshold of acceptability" (59). See also Huntington, *Alien Kind*, "Species History, Genre History," 7–33.
33 Kang, "The Fox and the Barbarian," also translates this passage (38).
34 Huntington, *Alien Kind*, 4.
35 Goushi was a short, flat-topped hill 30 kilometers west of the imposing Mount Song. For more on the significance of this hill during Wu Zhao's time, see Rothschild, *Emperor Wu Zhao and Her Pantheon*, 158–60.
36 Huntington, *Alien Kind*, 11. Huntington refers to this passage but does not translate it.
37 In Lingnan, in the remote south.
38 Li Shizhen, *Ben Cao Gang Mu*, vol. IX, 797.
39 Rebecca Doran, "The Cat Demon, Gender, and Religious Practice: Towards Reconstructing a Chinese Cultural Pattern," *Journal of the American Oriental Society* 135.4 (2015): 689–707.
40 Doran, "Insatiable Women and Transgressive Authority," 90–91.
41 Timothy Barrett and Mark Strange, "Walking by Itself: The Singular History of the Chinese Cat," in *Animals through Chinese History: Earliest Times to 1911*, eds. Roel Sterckx, Martina Siebert, and Dagmar Schäfer (Cambridge, UK: Cambridge University Press, 2020), 87.
42 This passage is incomplete in *Court and Country* (see 1.18 and 1.26 fn. 50). Doran, "The Cat Demon," has partially translated this passage, which appears in more complete form in *TPGJ* 139.1004.
43 Barrett and Strange, "Walking by Itself," 90, have translated this passage. I have drawn heavily upon their rendering.
44 For more on Xue Jichang's career, see his biography in *XTS* 120.4314 and *JTS* 185.4804–05.
45 Ibid., 89.
46 Li Shizhen, *Ben Cao Gang Mu*, Vol. IX, 799.
47 The *New Tang History* borrowed Zhang Zhuo's account, almost verbatim (*XTS* 35.922).
48 For more on the Mandate of Heaven, see Sarah Allen, *The Heir and the Sage: Dynastic Legend in Early China* (San Francisco: Chinese Materials Center, 1981), 3; John Chinnery, "The Role of the State," in *China: Empire and Civilization*, ed. Edward Shaughnessy (Oxford: Oxford University Press, 2005), 45; Jiang Yonglin, *The Mandate of Heaven and the Great Ming Code* (Seattle: University of Washington Press, 2011): 25; Hughes, *Worldly Saviors and Imperial Authority in Medieval Chinese Buddhism*, 3.

NOTES

49 This brief account is part of a longer paragraph in *Court and Country* that also includes accounts of foxes plundering the mansion of Wu Zhao's favorites, the Zhangs—examined in the subsection on foxes in this chapter. These two accounts were paired because both the unnatural fowl and uncanny foxes are represented as manifestations of the censure of Heaven and nature because of Wu Zhao's disruption of proper cosmic biorhythms.
50 *Shangshu Zhengyi*, "Mu shi" 牧誓, 11.285.
51 See, for instance, *XTS* 4.87–89 and 34.880 and 889.
52 See also Rothschild, "Wu Zhao's Remarkable Aviary," 81–82.
53 *JTS* 6.122.
54 Liu Su, *Sui-Tang jiahua* (Beijing: Zhonghua, 1997), 46. For more on the specific context of the Taiping Princess's pond, see Doran, *Transgressive Typologies*, 170–71. Doran convincingly argues that, rather than understanding this action as a genuine effort to accumulate Buddhist merit and save sentient animals, Zhang Zhuo and others wrote the story (and others) into a wider narrative of wanton destruction and wasteful exploitation of the natural world perpetrated by Wu Zhao and the generation of powerful "transgressive" women that succeeded her.
55 See Rothschild, "Wu Zhao's Remarkable Aviary," 79–80.
56 Of Ruzhou prefecture, Henan.
57 Lippiello, *Auspicious Omens and Miracles in Ancient China*, 33 and 138–39. Lippiello identifies white crows, pheasants, swallows, sparrows, and pigeons as auspicious signs of good rulers, though she does not mention the magpie.
58 Doran, *Transgressive Typologies*, 167–82.
59 This translation follows Doran, *Transgressive Typologies*, 173. Chen, *Empire of Style*, 52, also translates this passage and mentions the Anle Princess's sartorial marvel and the "game of emulation" that it prompted as an example of the "aesthetic play" that Chen deems "one of the key features of the Tang fashion system."
60 Schafer, "The Conservation of Nature under the T'ang Dynasty," 301–02.
61 This bird's name is the title of a verse by the celebrated Tang poet Du Fu. Stephen Owen renders this bird of a hundred tongues as a "shrike." However, the tendency of the shrike or butcher bird to impale its prey on thorns is precisely the sort of detail that Zhang Zhuo would relish incorporating in his account. The bird in this passage from *Court and Country* comes in spring and eats earthworms, behavior more representative of a mockingbird or robin. See Du Fu, *The Poetry of Du Fu*, Vol. I, trans. Stephen Owen, eds. Paul Kroll and Ding Xiang Warner (Boston: De Gruyter, 2015), 207.
62 *Ben Cao Gang Mu*, Vol. II, 7.168.
63 *TPGJ*, chapters 464–72.
64 Schafer, *The Divine Woman: Dragon Ladies and Rain Maidens* (San Francisco: North Point Press, 1980), 166.
65 Though this may be the later organization of Chen Jiru, who compiled the inherited six-chapter version of *Court and Country* in his late Ming dynasty *Secret Satchel from the Hall of Precious Colors*.
66 This river is Himalayan run-off leading to the confluence of the Red River and Da River in Phu Tho province (where Fengzhou prefecture is located) in northern Vietnam.
67 Dazhou, Sichuan.
68 Modern-day Jinan, Shandong.

NOTES

69 Mount Guzhu is in Huzhou prefecture of modern-day Zhejiang, to the immediate west of Lake Tai 太湖.
70 Schafer, *Vermilion Bird*, 216, refers to this snake as the "Requiter of Wrongs."
71 Schafer, *Golden Peaches of Samarkand*, 192–93, translates a similar passage from Liu Xun's 劉恂 tenth-century geographical treatise on the Southland, *Lingbiao lüyi* 嶺表綠異 (Record of Extraordinary Things in Lingnan).
72 Schafer, *Vermilion Bird*, 216–17. Schafer mentions this technique of staking down pythons alive. *Ben Cao Gang Mu*, Vol. VIII, 43.578–86, lists the medicinal properties of other parts of the python as well.
73 *Ben Cao Gang Mu*, Vol. VIII, 581–83.
74 Anne Birrell trans., *The Classic of Mountains and Seas* (New York: Penguin, 1999), 202; see Book XVII, 185–86, for the textual account.
75 This is a local Red River (Chishui 赤水), not to be confused with the larger Red River (Honghe 紅河) in southern China and SE Asia.
76 *JTS* 37.1350, *ZZTJ* 203.6442. *QTW* 235.2371 has the text of the minister's critical memorial.
77 Region south of the middle and lower Yangzi; see Xiong, *Historical Dictionary of Medieval China*, 647.
78 *TPGJ* 407.3289.
79 For a comparison of these two "man-shaped" roots, see Stephen Fulder, *The Book of Ginseng: And Other Chinese Herbs for Vitality* (Rochester, Vermont: Healing Arts Press, 1993), 106–07.
80 Wu, *The Chinese Virago*, 238 fn. 103, mentions this story.
81 These are two counties on the eastern side of Bingzhou prefecture.
82 *The Annals of Lü Buwei*, 12.263–64.
83 Donald Holzman, "The Cold Food Festival in Early Medieval China," *Harvard Journal of Asiatic Studies* 46.1 (1986): 51–79. Also see Ian Chapman's translation of the section on the Cold Food Festival from the *Record of the Year and Seasons of Jing-Chu* (*Jing-Chu suishi ji* 荊楚歲時記) in *Early Medieval China: A Sourcebook*, eds. Wendy Swartz, Robert Campany, Yang Lu, and Jessey Choo (New York: Columbia University Press, 2014), 477–78; and Lewis Hodous, "The Feast of Cold Food," in *Folkways of China*, 86–91.
84 *JTS* 89.2887.
85 Aina Jushi 艾衲居士, "Jie Zhitui Sets Fire to His Jealous Wife," translated by Mei Chun and Lane J. Harris, in *Idle Talk under a Bean Arbor* (*Doupeng xianhua* 豆棚閒話) (Seattle: University of Washington Press, 2017), 9–22.
86 A flowering perennial native to northern and eastern China sometimes known as the bellflower.
87 A flowering plant native to China, the Chinese foxglove (or rehmannia) is now widely known for its healing and medicinal properties.
88 A rare first-person reference.
89 Arsenic sulfide.
90 Wang Chong, *Lunheng* 論衡, chapter 23, "A Discussion of Toxins" (*yan du* 言毒). See Alfred Forke trans., *Lun-Heng, Part I: Philosophical Essays of Wang Ch'ung* (London: Luzac and Company, 1907), 300–01. Forke renders *yege* 冶葛 as "wild dolichos" rather than heartbreak grass.
91 This recipe is contained in *Cures for Fifty-two Ailments*, the aforementioned text recovered at Mawangdui in Changsha. See Chang Huang, Jiankang Liang, Li Han,

NOTES

Juntian Liu, Mengyun Yu, and Baixiao Zhao, "Moxibustion in Early Chinese Medicine and Its Relation to the Origin of Meridians: A Study on the Unearthed Literatures," *Evidence-based Complementary and Alternative Medicine* (2017): 3–4.
92   Benn, *Daily Life in Traditional China*, 206–07.
93   Edward Schafer, "Tang," in *Food in Chinese Culture: Anthropological and Historical Perspectives*, ed. K. C. Chang (New Haven: Yale University Press, 1977), 95–97. Betel nuts also have unfortunate carcinogenic properties unrecognized at the time.
94   Guizhou.
95   *Ben Cao Gang Mu*, Vol. VIII, 43.615–16, contains a detailed description of this pit viper.
96   Giant rat snake.

AFTERNOTE

1   For a more detailed account of terms like *xiaoshuo* or *zhiguai* see Campany, *Strange Writing*, 129–33 and 151–52.
2   Forte, *Mingtang and Buddhist Utopias*, 77.
3   Hong Mai, *Rongzhai xubi*, Chapter 12.
4   Xiaofei Tian, "Tales from Borderland: Anecdotes in Early Medieval China," in *Idle Talk*, 38.
5   Ellen Cong Zhang, "'To Be Erudite in Miscellaneous Knowledge': A Study of Song (960–1279) *Biji* Writing," 44.
6   Shields, "Gossip, Anecdote, and Literary History," 125.
7   Luo Manling, "Remembering Kaiyuan and Tianbao: The Construction of Mosaic Memory in Medieval Historical Miscellanies," *T'oung Pao*, second series, 97 (2011): 269–70.
8   Carrie Reed, "Motivation and Meaning of a 'Hodge-Podge': Duan Chengshi's *Youyang zazu*," *Journal of the American Oriental Society* 123.1 (2003): 121–22 and 145.
9   Ma Xueqin, "Zhang Zhuo shengping jingli ji shengzu nian kaoshi," 62.

Bibliography

PRE-MODERN SOURCES (INCLUDING TRANSLATIONS)

Baihu tong 白虎通. [*Comprehensive Discussions in White Tiger Hall*], translated by Paul Goldin. In *Images of Women in Chinese Thought and Culture: Writings From the Pre-Qin Period Through the Song Dynasty*, edited by Robin Wang, 170–76. Indianapolis: Hackett, 2003.

Beishi 北史. [History of the Northern Dynasties], 100 Chapters, compiled by Li Yanshou 李延壽 (7th cent.). Beijing: Zhonghua shuju 中華書局, 1997.

Bencao gangmu 本草綱目. Li Shizhen 李時珍, 52 Chapters. See *Ben Cao Gang Mu, Vol. II: Waters, Fires, Soils, Metals, Jades, Stones, Minerals, Salts*, translated and annotated by Paul Unschuld. Berkeley: University of California Press, 2021; *Ben Cao Gang Mu, Vol. VIII: Clothes, Utensils, Worms, Insects, Amphibians, Animals With Scales, Animals With Shells*, translated and annotated by Paul Unschuld. Berkeley: University of California Press, 2021; *Ben Cao Gang Mu, Vol. IX: Fowls, Domestic and Wild Animals, Human Substances*, translated and annotated by Paul Unschuld. Berkeley: University of California Press, 2021.

Cefu yuangui 冊府元龜. [Storehouse of the Original Tortoise], 1000 Chapters, compiled by Wang Qinruo 王欽若. Beijing: Zhonghua shuju, 1994.

Chaoye jianzai 朝野僉載. [Collected Records From Court and Country], 6 Chapters, Zhang Zhuo 張鷟. In *Tang-Song shiliao biji congkan* 唐宋史料筆記叢刊. Beijing: Zhonghua shuju, 1997.

Chunqiu zuozhuan zhengyi 春秋左傳正義. [The Spring and Autumn Annals and Chronicles of Zhou]. In *Shisan jing zhu shu*, edited by Li Xueqin. Beijing: Beijing University Press, 2000.

Da Tang Xinyu 大唐新語. [New Words From the Great Tang], 12 Chapters, Liu Su 劉肅. In *Tang-Song shiliao biji congkan*. Beijing: Zhonghua shuju, 1997.

Daxue 大學 [Greater Learning] and Zhong Yong 中庸 [Doctrine of the Mean], *Confucius. Ta Hsüeh and Chung Yung* (The Highest Order of Cultivation and on the Practice of the Mean), translated by Andrew Plaks. New York: Penguin Classics, 2003.

Daodejing 道德經. *Tao Te Ching*, 2 Chapters, Laozi, translated by D. C. Lau. London: Penguin Books, 1963.

Doupeng xianhua 豆棚閒話. [*Idle Talk Under a Bean Arbor*]. Aina Jushi 艾衲居士. *Idle Talk Under a Bean Arbor*, translated by Mei Chun and Lane J. Harris. Seattle: University of Washington Press, 2017.

Du Fu 杜甫. *The Poetry of Du Fu, Vol. I*, translated by Stephen Owen, Paul Kroll, and Ding Xiang Warner. Boston: De Gruyter, 2015.

Guanzi 管子. *Political, Economic, and Philosophical Essays From Early China: A Study and Translation*, translated and annotated by W. Allyn Rickett. Princeton: Princeton University Press, 1985.

BIBLIOGRAPHY

Guilin fengtu ji 桂林風土記. [*Record of the Customs and Geography of Guilin*], 1 Chapter, Mo Xiufu 莫休夫. https://ctext.org/wiki.pl?if=gb&chapter=78667.

Han shu 漢書. [History of the Han Dynasty], 100 Chapters, Ban Gu 班固 and Ban Biao 班彪. Beijing: Zhonghua, 1996.

Huainanzi 淮南子, Liu An 劉安. Heaven and Earth in Early Han Thought: *Chapters Three, Four, and Five of the Huainanzi*, translation and commentary by John Major. Albany: SUNY Press, 1993.

Jin shu 晉書. [History of the Jin Dynasty], 130 Chapters, compiled by Fang Xuanling 房玄齡. Beijing: Zhonghua shuju, 1997.

Jinghua yuan 鏡花緣. Li Ruzhen 李汝珍, *Destinies of Flowers in the Mirror*, translated by Lin Tai-yi. Berkeley: University of California Press, 1965.

Jiu Tang shu 舊唐書. [Old Tang History], 200 Chapters, compiled by Liu Xu 劉煦. Beijing:Zhonghua shuju, 1997.

Li ji 禮記. [Book of Rites]. Liji zhengyi 禮記正義. In Shisan jing zhu shu, edited by Li Xueqin. Beijing: Beijing University Press, 1999; also see Lî Kî: The Book of Rites, translated by James Legge. Oxford: Clarendon Books, 1885.

Liang shu 梁書. [History of the Liang Dynasty], 56 Chapters, compiled by Yao Cha 姚察. Beijing: Zhonghua shuju, 1997.

Lienü zhuan 列女傳. [Biographies of Exemplary Women], 8 Chapters, Liu Xiang 劉向. See Anne Kinney, *Exemplary Women of Early China: The Lienü zhuan of Liu Xiang*. New York: Columbia University Press, 2014.

Lun yu 論語. *The Analects, Confucius*, translated by D. C. Lau. New York: Penguin, 1979; *Confucius, the Analects: With Selections From Traditional Commentaries*, translated by Edward Slingerland. Indianapolis: Hackett, 2003; *The Chinese Classics, Vol. I: The Analects, the Greater Learning, and the Doctrine of the Mean*, translated by James Legge. London: Trubner, 1861.

Lunheng 論衡. Wang Chong 王充, 30 Chapters. *Lun-Heng, Part I: Philosophical Essays of Wang Ch'ung*, translated by Alfred Forke. London: Luzac and Company, 1907.

Lüshi chunqiu 呂氏春秋, John Knoblock, and Jeffery Riegel (trans.). *The Annals of Lü Buwei*. Stanford: Stanford University Press, 2000.

Mencius 孟子. translated by D. C. Lau. New York: Penguin, 1970.

Nan Qi shu 南齊書. [History of the Southern Qi Dynasty], 60 Chapters, compiled by Xiao Zixian 蕭子顯. Beijing: Zhonghua shuju, 1997.

Ōkagami. The Great Mirror: Fujiwara Michinaga (966–1027) and His Times, translated by Helen Craig McCullough. Princeton, NJ: Princeton University Press, 1980.

Quan Tangshi 全唐詩. [Complete Anthology of Tang Poetry], 900 Chapters, compiled by Peng Dingqiu 彭定求. Beijing:Zhonghua shuju, 1995.

Quan Tangwen 全唐文. [Complete Anthology of Tang Prose], 1000 Chapters, compiled by Dong Gao 董誥. Beijing:Zhonghua shuju, 1996.

Rongzhai xubi 容齋續筆. [Continued Jottings of Rongzhai], 16 Chapters, Hong Mai 洪邁, https://ctext.org/wiki.pl?if=gb&res=696035.

Ruyijun zhuan 如意君傳. Xu Changling 徐昌齡, Charles Stone, translation and critical annotation, *The Fountainhead of Chinese Erotica: The Lord of Perfect Satisfaction*. Honolulu: University of Hawaii Press, 2003.

Samguk Sagi 三國史記. Kim Pusik 金富軾. *The Silla Annals of the Samguk Sagi*, translated by Edward Schulz, Hugh H. W. Kang, and Daniel Kane. Gyeonggi-do, Korea: Academy of Korean Sciences Press, 2013. Chapters 1–12 of *Samguk sagi*.

Sancai tuhui 三彩圖會. 106 Chapters. Wang Qi 王圻. Taibei: Chengwen, 1970.

BIBLIOGRAPHY

Sanguo yanyi 三國演義, 100 Chapters. Luo Guanzhong 羅貫中, *Three Kingdoms*, translated by Moss Roberts. Beijing: Foreign Languages Press, 1995.

Shangshu zhengyi 尚書正義. [The Book of History and Orthodox Commentaries]. In *Shisan jing zhu shu*, edited by Li Xueqin. Beijing: Beijing University Press, 1999.

Shanhai jing 山海經. [*Classic of Mountains and Seas*], translated by Ann Birrell. New York: Penguin Books, 1999.

Shi ji 史記. [Records of the Grand Historian], 130 Chapters, compiled by Sima Qian 司馬遷. Beijing: Zhonghua shuju, 1995. See also *Historical Records*, translated by Raymond Dawson. New York: Oxford University Press, 1994; and *Selections From Records of the Grand Historian*. Selected by Po-Hsiang Wang, translated by Yang Hsien-yi and Gladys Yang. Beijing: Foreign Languages Press, 1979.

Shisan jing zhu shu 十三經注疏. [The Thirteen Classics With Annotations and Commentaries], Chief editor Li Xueqin 李學勤. Beijing: Beijing University Press, 1999.

Shuihu zhuan 水滸傳. Shi Nai'an 施耐庵 and Luo Guanzhong 羅貫中, 100 Chapters. *Outlaws of the Marsh*, translated by Sidney Shapiro. Beijing: Foreign Language Press, 1993.

Shujing 書經. *Shu Ching*, translated by Clae Waltham. Chicago: Henry Regnery, 1971.

Song shi 宋史 [History of the Song Dynasty], Tuo Tuo 脫脫, 496 Chapters. Beijing: Zhonghua, 1997.

Song shu 宋書 [History of the Liu Song Dynasty], 100 chapters, compiled by Shen Yue 沈約. Beijing: Zhonghua shuju, 1997.

Soushen ji 搜神記. Gan Bao 干寶. In *Search of the Supernatural*, 20 Chapters, translated by Kenneth DeWoskin and J. I. Crump. Stanford, CA: Stanford University Press, 1996.

Sui Shu 隋書. [History of the Sui Dynasty], 85 Chapters, compiled by Wei Zheng 魏徵. Beijing: Zhonghua shuju, 1996.

Sui-Tang jiahua 隋唐嘉話. [Splendid Stories of the Sui and Tang], 3 Chapters, compiled by Liu Su 劉餗, from *Tang-Song shiliao biji congkan*. Beijing: Zhonghua shuju, 1997.

Taiping guangji 太平廣記. [Miscellaneous Records of the Taiping Era], 500 Chapters, compiled by Li Fang 李昉. Beijing: Zhonghua shuju, 1996.

Taiping yulan 太平御覽 [Imperial Readings of the Taiping Era], 1000 Chapters, compiled by Li Fang. Beijing: Zhonghua shuju, 1995.

Tang Dengke jikao 唐登科記考. [Study of *Records of Examination Candidates in the Tang*], 10 Chapters, Xu Song 徐松, https://ctext.org/wiki.pl?if=gb&res=892992.

Tang huiyao 唐會要. [Essential Institutions of the Tang], 100 Chapters, compiled by Wang Pu 王溥. Beijing: Zhonghua shuju, 1998.

Tang liangjing chengfang kao 唐兩京城坊考. [A Study of the Walled Cities and Wards of the Two Tang Capitals], 5 Chapters, compiled by Xu Song. Beijing: Zhonghua shuju, 1985.

Tanglü 唐律. *The T'ang Code, Volume One: General Principles*, translation and commentary by Wallace Johnson. Princeton: Princeton University Press, 1979.

Tangshi jishi 唐詩紀事. [Records on Tang Poetry], 81 Chapters, compiled by Ji Yougong 計有功. https://ctext.org/wiki.pl?if=en&res=438234&remap=gb.

Tongdian 通典 [Comprehensive Manual of Institutions], 200 Chapters, compiled by Du You 杜佑. Beijing: Zhonghua shuju, 1996.

Wei shu 魏書. [History of the Wei Dynasty], 114 Chapters, compiled by Wei Shou 魏收. Beijing: Zhonghua shuju, 1995.

Xin Tang shu 新唐書. [New History of the Tang], 225 Chapters, compiled by Ouyang Xiu 歐陽修. Beijing: Zhonghua shuju, 1997.

BIBLIOGRAPHY

Xiyou ji 西遊記, 100 Chapters. *Monkey*, translated by Arthur Waley. New York: Grove Press, 1970.

Youxian ku 游仙窟. *Zhang Zhuo, Dwelling of a Playful Goddess: China's First Novelette*, translated and commentary by Howard Levy. Japan: Dai Nippon Insatsu Tokyo, 1965.

Youyang zazu 酉陽雜俎. [Miscellaneous Morsels From Youyang], 20 Chapters Plus 10 Additional Chapters. *Duan Chengshi* 段成式. Shenyang: Wanjuan Publishing, 2020.

Zhouli [Rites of Zhou] 周禮. Zhouli zhushu 周禮注疏. In *Shisan jing zhu shu*, edited by Li Xueqin. Beijing: Beijing University Press, 1999.

Zhuangzi 莊子. Burton Watson, trans. *The Complete Works of Zhuangzi*. New York: Columbia University Press, 2013.

Zizhi tongjian 資治通鑒. [Comprehensive Mirror for the Advancement of Governance], 294 Chapters, compiled by Sima Guang 司馬光; Commentary by Hu Sanxing 胡三省 from the Yuan edition. Beijing: Zhonghua shuju, 1995.

MODERN SOURCES

Abramson, Marc. *Ethnic Identity in Tang China*. Philadelphia: University of Pennsylvania Press, 2008.

Allen, Sarah. *The Heir and the Sage: Dynastic Legend in Early China*. San Francisco: Chinese Materials Center, 1981.

Bao, Shanben. "Liu Piao, the Grand Princess." In *Biographical Dictionary of Chinese Women, Antiquity Through the Sui (1600 BCE–618 CE)*, edited by Lily Xiao Hong Lee and A.D. Stefanowska, 166 68. London: Routledge, 2015.

Barrett, Timothy. "Review of *Medieval Chinese Warfare, 300–900*, by David Graff." *Bulletin of the School of Oriental and African Studies* 66.1 (2003): 128–29.

———. *Taoism Under the T'ang*. London: Wellsweep, 1996.

———. *The Woman Who Discovered Printing*. New Haven: Yale University Press, 2008.

Barrett, Timothy, and Mark Strange. "Walking by Itself: The Singular History of the Chinese Cat." In *Animals Through Chinese History: Earliest Times to 1911*, edited by Roel Sterckx, Martina Siebert, and Dagmar Schäfer, 84–98. Cambridge, UK: Cambridge University Press, 2020.

Baumer, Cristoph. *The History of Central Asia: Age of the Silk Roads*, Vol. 2. London: I.B. Tauris, 2014.

Belyaev, V. A., and S. V. Sidorovich. "Tang Tallies of Credence Found at Ak-Beshim Ancient Site." *Numismatique asiatique: Revue de la Société de Numismatique Asiatique* 33 (2020): 41–56.

Benn, Charles. *Daily Life in Traditional China: The Tang Dynasty*. Westport, CT: Greenwood Press, 2002.

Bingham, Woodbridge. *Founding of the Tang Dynasty*. New York: Octagon Books, 1970.

Bower, Virginia, and Colin Mackenzie. "Pitchpot: The Scholar's Arrow-Throwing Game." In *Asian Games: The Art of Contest*, edited by K. Finkel and Colin Mackenzie, 275–81. New York: Asia Society, 2004.

Brindley, Erica. "Hairstyle and Yue Identity in Chinese Texts." In *Imperial China and its Southern Neighbors*, edited by Victor Mair and Liam Kelley, 16–42. Singapore: Institute of Southeast Asian Studies, 2020.

Buswell, Robert, and Donald Lopez. *The Princeton Dictionary of Buddhism*. Princeton: Princeton University Press, 2014.

BIBLIOGRAPHY

Campany, Robert. *Strange Writing: Anomaly Accounts in Early Medieval China*. Albany: SUNY Press, 1996.

———. *The Chinese Dreamscape, 300 BCE–800AD*. Cambridge: Harvard Asia Center, 2020.

———. "The Meaning of Cuisines of Transcendence in Late Classical and Early Medieval China." *T'oung Pao*, 2nd Series, 91 (2005): 1–57.

Chan, Timothy Wai Keung Chan. "Dedication and Identification in Wang Bo's Compositions on the Gallery of Prince Teng." *Mounumenta Serica* 50 (2002): 215–55.

Chang, Huang, Jiankang Liang, Li Han, Juntian Liu, Mengyun Yu, and Baixiao Zhao. "Moxibustion in Early Chinese Medicine and Its Relation to the Origin of Meridians: A Study on the Unearthed Literatures." *Evidence-based Complementary and Alternative Medicine* (2017): 1–9.

Chapman, Ian. "Festival and Ritual Calendar: Selections From the *Record of the Year and Seasons of Jing-Chu* (Jing-Chu suishi ji 荊楚歲時記)." In *Early Medieval China: A Sourcebook*, edited by Wendy Swartz, Robert Campany, Yang Lu, and Jessey Choo, 468–93. New York: Columbia University Press, 2014.

Chen, BuYun. *Empire of Style: Silk and Fashion in Tang China*. Seattle: University of Washington Press, 2019.

Chen, Jack. "Introduction." In *Idle Talk: Gossip and Anecdotes in Traditional China*, edited by Jack Chen and David Schaberg, 1–15. Berkeley: University of California Press, 2012.

———. *The Poetics of Sovereignty: On Emperor Taizong of the Tang Dynasty*. Cambridge, MA: Harvard University Press.

Chen, Jack, and David Schaberg, eds. *Idle Talk: Gossip and Anecdotes in Traditional China*. Berkeley: University of California Press, 2012.

Chen, Jinhua. "A Complicated Figure with Complex Relationships: The Monk Huifan and Early Tang Saṃgha-State Interactions." In *The Middle Kingdom and the Dharma Wheel*, edited by Thomas Jülch, 140–221. Leiden: Brill, 2020.

———. "Fazang, the Holy Man." *Journal of the International Association of Buddhist Studies* 28.1 (2005): 11–84.

———. "More Than a Philosopher; Fazang as a Politician and Miracle Worker." *History of Religions* 42.4 (May 2003): 320–58.

———. "*Pañcavārṣika* Assemblies in Liang Wudi's Buddhist Palace Chapel." *Harvard Journal of Asiatic Studies* 66.1 (2006): 43–103.

———. *Philosopher, Practitioner, Politician: The Many Lives of Fazang*. Leiden: Brill, 2007: 643–712.

———. "Tang Buddhist Palace Chapels." *Journal of Chinese Religions* 32 (2004): 101–73.

———. "The Multiple Roles of the Twin Chanding Monasteries in Sui-Tang Chang'an." *Studies in Chinese Religions* 1.4 (2015): 344–56.

Chen, Jo-shui. "Empress Wu and Proto-Feminist Sentiments in T'ang China." In *Imperial Rulership and Cultural Change in Traditional China*, edited by Frederick Brandauer and Chih-chieh Huang, 77–114. Seattle: University of Washington Press, 1994.

Chen, Sanping. "Godly Worm" and the "Literati Prism" of Chinese Sources." *Journal of the American Oriental Society* 139.2 (2019): 417–31.

———. *Multicultural China in the Early Medieval Ages*. Philadelphia: University of Pennsylvania Press, 2012.

Ch'en, Kenneth. *Buddhism in China*. Princeton, NJ: Princeton University Press, 1964.

Chinnery, John. "The Role of the State." In *China: Empire and Civilization*, edited by Edward Shaughnessy, 44–55. Oxford: Oxford University Press, 2005.

BIBLIOGRAPHY

Chong, Key Ray. *Cannibalism in China*. Wakefield, NY: Longwood Academic, 1990.

Choo, Jessey. *Historicized Ritual and Ritualized History—Women's Lifecycle in Late Medieval China*. Princeton University Dissertation, 2009: 600–1000.

Churchman, Catherine. *The People Between the Rivers: The Rise and Fall of a Bronze Drum Culture, 200–750 AD*. Lanham, MD: Rowman and Littlefield, 2016.

Clark, Hugh. *The Sinitic Encounter in Southeast China Through the First Millennium CE*. Honolulu: University of Hawaii Press, 2016.

Cohen, Albert. *Delinquent Boys: Culture of the Gang*. Glencoe, IL: Free Press, 1955.

Cook, Constance, and Ke Heli. "From Bone to Bamboo: Number Sets and Mortuary Ritual." *Journal of Oriental Studies* 41.1 (2006): 1–40.

Cullin, Stewart. "The Japanese Game of Suguroku." *The Brooklyn Museum Quarterly* 7.4 (1920): 213–33.

Darayaee, Touraj, and Soodabeh Malekzayeh. "The Performance of Pain and Remembrance in Late Ancient Iran." *Silk Road* 12 (2014): 57–64.

de la Vaissière, Étienne. *Sogdian Traders: A History*. Leiden: Brill, 2005.

Deeg, Max. "Origins and Development of the Buddhist Pañcavārṣika, Part II: China." *Saṃbhāṣā: Nagoya Studies in Indian Culture and Buddhism* 18 (1997): 67–90.

Dien, Albert. *Six Dynasties Civilization*. New Haven: Yale University Press, 2007.

Dien, Dora Shu-fang. *Empress Wu Zetian in Fiction and in History: Female Defiance in Confucian China*. New York: Nova Science Publishers Inc, 2003.

Doran, Rebecca. *Insatiable Women and Transgressive Authority: Constructions of Gender and Power in Early Tang China*. Ph.D. Dissertation, Harvard University, 2011.

———. "The Cat Demon, Gender, and Religious Practice: Towards Reconstructing a Chinese Cultural Pattern." *Journal of the American Oriental Society* 135.4 (2015): 689–707.

———. *Transgressive Typologies: Constructions of Gender and Power in Early Tang China*. Cambridge, MA: Harvard University Asia Center, 2016.

Duan, Tali 段塔麗. *Tangdai funü diwei yanjiu* 唐代婦女地位研究 [Research on the Position of Women in the Tang Dynasty]. Beijing: Renmin chubanshe, 2000.

Ebrey, Patricia Buckley, ed. *Chinese Civilization: A Sourcebook*, 2nd edition. New York: The Free Press, 1993.

Elvin, Mark. *Retreat of the Elephants: An Environmental History of China*. New Haven: Yale University Press, 2004.

———. "Who Was Responsible for the Weather? Moral Meteorology in Late Imperial China." *Osiris*, 2nd Series 13 (1998): 213–37.

Fang, Qi. *Elegy of a River Shaman*, translated by N. Harry Rothschild and Meng Fanjun. Portland, ME: Merwin Asia, 2016.

Finkel, Irving, and Colin McKenzie, eds. *Asian Games: The Art of Contest*. New York: Asia Society, 2004.

Fitzgerald, C. P. *The Empress Wu*. Melbourne: Cheshire, 1955.

Forte, Antonino. *Mingtang and Buddhist Utopias in the History of the Astronomical Clock: The Tower, the Statue and the Armillary Sphere Constructed by Empress Wu*. Rome: Italian Institute of East Asian Studies, 1988.

———. *Political Propaganda and Ideology in China at the End of the Seventh Century: Inquiry into the Nature, Authors and Function of Dunhuang Document S.6502 Followed by an Annotated Translation*, 2nd edition. Kyoto: Scuola Italiana di Studi sull'Asia Orientale, 2005.

Fracasso, Ricardo. "The Nine Tripods of Empress Wu." In *Tang China and Beyond*, edited by Antonino Forte, 85–96. Kyoto: Italian School of East Asian Studies, 1988.

Fulder, Stephen. *The Book of Ginseng: And Other Chinese Herbs for Vitality*. Rochester, Vermont: Healing Arts Press, 1993.

BIBLIOGRAPHY

Gao, Shiyu. "A *Fixed* State of Affairs and Mis-Positioned Status: Gender Relations During the Sui, Tang and Five Dynasties." In *The Chalice and the Blade*, edited by Min and Shiyu Gao, 270–314. Beijing: Academy of Social Sciences, 1995.

Ge, Chengyong. "A Comparative Study of Two Stone Steles Unearthed in the Two Capitals of the Tang Dynasty, Xi'an and Luoyang." In *From the Oxus River to the Chinese Shores: Studies on East Syriac Christianity in Central Asia and China*, edited by Li Tang and Dietmar Winkler, 161–76. Zurich: Verlag, 2013.

Goble, Geoffrey. "Maritime SE Asia: The View From Sui-Tang China." *Nalanda-Sririjawa Center Working Papers* 16 (2014): 1–19.

Goldblatt, Howard. "Forbidden Food: The "Saturnicon" of Mo Yan." *World Literature* 74.3 (2000): 75–84.

Graff, David. *Medieval Chinese Warfare, 300–900*. New York: Routledge, 2002.

Gregory, Peter, and Patricia Ebrey. "The Religious and Historical Landscape." In *Religion and Society in T'ang and Song China*, edited by Patricia Ebrey and Peter Gregory, 1–44. Honolulu: University of Hawaii Press, 1993.

Grousset, René. *In the Footsteps of the Buddha*. London: Routledge and Sons, 1932.

Guisso, Richard. "The Reigns of the Empress Wu, Chung-tsung and Jui-tsung." In *The Cambridge History of China, Vol. 3: Sui and T'ang China*, edited by Denis Twitchett and John Fairbank, 290–332. Cambridge, UK: Cambridge University Press, 1979.

———. *Women in China: Current Directions in Historical Scholarship*. Youngstown, NY: Philo Press, 1981.

———. *Wu Tse-t'ien and the Politics of Legitimation in T'ang China*. Bellingham: Western Washington University Press, 1978.

Guo Dianchen 郭殿忱. "Shenzhou tangxian Zhang Zhuo ji qi 'Yong yan' shi kaoshi" 深州唐賢張鷟及其 '咏燕' 詩考釋. *Hengshui xueyuan xuebao* 衡水學院學報 17.3 (2015): 68–70.

Hall, David, and Roger Ames. "Sexism, With Chinese Characteristics." In *The Sage and the Second Sex*, edited by Li Chenyang, 75–95. Chicago: Open Court.

Han, Ting 韓婷, and Zhang Jinxi 張金铱. "Zhang Zhuo ji qi Chaoye qianzai kaoshi" 張鷟及其朝野僉載考釋. *Hefei gongye daxue xuebao* 合肥工業大學學報 30.2 (2016): 73–79.

Harrist, Robert, Jr. "The Legacy of Bole: Physiognomy of Horses in Chinese Painting." *Artibus Asiae* 57.1/2 (1997): 35–154.

Hartman, Charles. "Stomping Songs: Words and Image." *Chinese Literature: Essays, Articles, and Reviews* 17 (1995): 1–49.

Herbert, P. A. *Examine the Honest, Appraise the Able*. Faculty of Asian Studies Monograph, New Series, No. 10. Canberra: Australia National University, 1988.

Higham, Charles. *The Bronze Age of Southeast Asia*. Cambridge, UK: Cambridge University Press.

Hinsch, Bret. *Passions of the Cut Sleeve: The Male Homosexual Tradition in China*. Berkeley: University of California Press, 1992.

———. "Textiles and Female Virtue in Early Imperial Chinese Historical Writings." *Nan nü* 5.2 (2003): 170–202.

———. *Women in Early Imperial China*. Lanham, MD: Rowman and Littlefield, 2002.

———. *Women in Tang China*. Boston: Rowman and Littlefield, 2020.

Hiraoka Takeo 平岡武夫. *Todai no koyomi* 唐代の暦 [The Tang Calendar]. Shanghai: Shanghai guji, 1990.

Ho, Norman. "Confucian Jurisprudence in Action: Pre-Tang Dynasty *Panwen* (Written Legal Judgments)." *Washington International Law Journal* 22.1 (2013): 49–111.

BIBLIOGRAPHY

Ho Peng, Yoke. *Chinese Mathematical Astrology: Reaching Out for the Stars.* London: Routledge, 2003.

Hodous, Lewis. *Folkways of China.* London: Arthur Probsthrain, 1929.

Holzman, Donald. "The Cold Food Festival in Early Medieval China." *Harvard Journal of Asiatic Studies* 46.1 (1986): 51–79.

Hu, Ji 胡戟. "Tangdai duliang heng yu mouli zhidu" 唐代度量衡與畝里制度. *Xibei daxue xuebao* 4 (1980): 34–41.

———. *Wu Zetian benzhuan* 武則天本傳 *[Essential Biography of Wu Zetian].* Xi'an: Shaanxi Shifan daxue chubanshe, 1998.

Hua, Linfu, Paul Buell, and Paul Unschuld, eds. *Dictionary of the Ben Cao Gang Mu, Vol. II: Geographical and Administrative Designations.* Berkeley: University of California Press, 2017.

Huang, Guangren 黃光任. *Nühuang Wu Zhao* 女皇武曌. Xi'an: Shaanxi luyou chubanshe, 2000.

Hucker, Charles. *A Dictionary of Official Titles in Imperial China.* Stanford: Stanford University Press, 1985.

Hughes, April. *Worldly Saviors and Imperial Authority in Medieval Chinese Buddhism.* Honolulu: University of Hawaii Press.

Huntington, Rania. *Alien Kind: Foxes and Late Imperial Chinese Narrative.* Cambridge: Harvard University Asia Center, 2003.

Iancu, Livil Mikhail. "Self-Mutilation, Multiculturalism, and Hybridity: Herodotus on the Karians in Egypt." *Anatolia Antiqua* 25 (2017): 57–67.

Idema, Wilt, and Beata Grant. *The Red Brush: Writing Women of Imperial China.* Cambridge, MA: Harvard University Asia Center, 2004.

Jacobsen, Trudy. "Autonomous Queenship in Cambodia, 1st–9th Centuries." *Journal of the Royal Asiatic Society* 13.3 (2003): 357–75.

———. *Lost Goddesses: The Denial of Female Power in Cambodian History.* Singapore: NAIS, 2008.

Jay, Jennifer. "Imagining Matriarchy: "Kingdoms of Women" in Tang China." *Journal of the American Oriental Society* 116 (1996): 220–29.

———. "Vignettes of Chinese Women in Tang Xi'an (618–906): Individualism in Wu Zetian, Yang Guifei, Yu Xuanji, and Li Wa." *Chinese Culture* 31.1 (1990): 77–89.

Jia, Jinhua. "A Study of the *Jinglong Wenguan ji.*" *Monumenta Serica* 47 (1999): 209–36.

Jiang, Yonglin. "In the Name of "Taizu": The Construction of Zhu Yuanzhang's Legal Philosophy and Chinese Cultural Identity in the 'Veritable Records of Taizu.'" *T'oung Pao* 96 (2010): 408–70.

———. *The Mandate of Heaven and the Great Ming Code.* Seattle: University of Washington Press, 2011.

Kang, Xiaofei. "The Fox [hu 狐] and the Barbarian [hu 胡]: Unraveling Representations of the Other in Late Tang Tales." *Journal of Chinese Religions* 27.1 (1999): 35–67.

Kelly, William. "Incendiary Actions: Fires and Firefighting in the Shogun's Capital and the People's City." In *Edo and Paris: Urban Life and the State in the Early Modern Era,* edited by James McClain, 310–31. Ithaca, NY: Cornell University Press, 1994.

Kinney, Anne. *Chinese Views of Childhood.* Honolulu: University of Hawaii Press, 1995.

———. *Representations of Childhood and Youth in Early China.* Stanford: Stanford University Press, 2004.

Kirkland, Russell. "Huang Ling-wei: A Taoist Priestess in T'ang China." *Journal of Chinese Religions* 19 (1991): 47–73.

BIBLIOGRAPHY

———. "Ye Fashan." In *The Routledge Encyclopedia of Taoism*, edited by Pregadio, 1154–55. New York: Routledge, 2008.

Kirkland, Russell, and Livia Kohn. "Daoism in the Tang (618–907)." In *Daoism Handbook*, edited by Livia Kohn, 339–83. Leiden: Brill, 2004.

Klein, Esther Sunkyung. *The History of the Historian: Perspectives on the Authorial Roles of Sima Qian*. Princeton University, Ph.D. Dissertation, 2010.

Klöpsch, Volker. "Lo Pin-wang's Survival: Traces of a Legend." *T'ang Studies* 6 (1988): 77–97.

Knapp, Keith, and Keith N. Knapp, "Chinese Filial Cannibalism: A Silk Road Import?" In *China and Beyond in the Medieval Period: Cultural Crossings and Inter-Regional Connections*, editd by Dorothy C. Wong and Gustav Heldt, 135–49. Amherst, NY: Cambria Press, 2014.

———. *Selfless Offspring: Filial Children and Social Order in Medieval China*. Honolulu: University of Hawaii Press, 2005.

Kohn, Livia. "Kou Qianzhi." In *The Routledge Encyclopedia of Taoism*, edited by Fabrizio Pregadio, 601–02. New York: Routledge, 2011.

Kory, Stephan. "A Remarkably Resonant and Resilient Tang-Dynasty Augural Stone: Empress Wu's *Baotu*." *T'ang Studies* 26 (2008): 99–124.

———. "Presence in Variety: De-Trivializing Female Diviners in Medieval China." *Nan Nü* 18 (2016): 3–48.

Kroll, Paul. "The Representation of the Mantic Arts in the High Culture of Medieval China." In *Coping With the Future: Theories and Practices of Divination in East Asia*, edited by Michael Lackner, 99–125. Leiden: Brill, 2017.

———. "True Dates of Reign Periods in the Tang Dynasty." *T'ang Studies* 2 (1984): 25–32.

Lao, She. *Rickshaw Boy: A Novel*, translated by Howard Goldblatt. New York: Harper Perennial Modern Chinese Classics, 2010.

Lee, Isabelle. "Touhu: Three Millennia of the Chinese Arrow Vase and the Game of Pitch-pot." *Transactions of the Oriental Ceramic Society* 56 (1991–92): 13–27.

Lee, Lily Xiao Hong, and A. D. Stefanowska, eds. *Biographical Dictionary of Chinese Women, Antiquity Through Sui, 1600 BC–618 AD*. Armonk, NY: ME Sharpe, 2007.

Lerner, Michael. "Map Room: The Spread of Backgammon and Parchisi." *World Policy Journal* (2012): 16–17.

Levine, Laura. "Men in Women's Clothing: Anti-Theatricality and Effeminization From 1579 to 1642." *Criticism* 28.2 (1986): 121–43.

Lewis, Mark Edward. *China's Cosmopolitan Empire: The Tang Dynasty*. Cambridge, MA: Harvard University Press, 2009.

Li Li 李莉. "Sichuan Fengjiexian fengxiangxia yaguanzang" 四川奉节县风箱峡崖棺葬. *Wenwu* 文物 7(1978): 89–91.

Lin, Yutang 林語堂. *Wu Zetian zhuan* 武則天傳. Xi'an: Shaanxi shifan daxue chubanshe, 2005.

Lindgrin, Kristina. "Professor Offers Dissenting Opinion on Marquis de Sade." *L.A. Times*, 15 July 1991.

Lippiello, Tiziana. *Auspicious Omens and Miracles in Ancient China: Han, Three Dynasties, and Six Kingdoms*. Sankt Augustin, Germany: Steyler Verlag, 2001.

Liu, James T.C. "Polo and Cultural Change: From T'ang to Sung China." *Harvard Journal of Asiatic Studies* 45.1 (1985): 203–24.

Lo, Andrew. "Double Sixes, Holding Spears, and the Long March: Games of the Backgammon Family in China." In *Asian Games: The Art of Contest*, edited by K. Finkel and Colin Mackenzie, 97–104. New York: Asia Society, 2004.

BIBLIOGRAPHY

Loewe, Michael. *Everyday Life in Early Imperial China During the Han Period.* Hackett: Indianapolis.

Louie, Kam. *Theorizing Chinese Masculinity: Society and Gender in China.* Cambridge, UK: Cambridge University Press, 2002.

Lu, Simian 呂思勉. *Sui-Tang-Wudai shi* 隋唐五代史. Shanghai: Shanghai guji, 1984.

Luo, Manling 羅曼玲. "Remembering Kaiyuan and Tianbao: The Construction of Mosaic Memory in Medieval Historical Miscellanies." *T'oung Pao*, Second Series 97 (2011): 263–300.

———. "Tangdai xiaoshuo Zhong yishixingtai yiyi de "yao"" 唐代小说中意识形态意义的'妖.'" *Beijing daxue xuebao* 北京大學學報 50.6 (2013): 97–105.

Ma, Boying. *A History of Medicine in Chinese Culture, Vol. I.* Singapore: World Scientific, 2020.

Ma, Xueqin 馬雪芹. "Zhang Zhuo shengping jingli ji shengzu nian kaoshi" 張鷟生平經歷生卒年考釋. *Hebei daxue xuebao* 河北大學學報 24.3 (2001): 62–64.

Major, John. *Heaven and Earth in Early Han Thought: Chapters Three, Four, and Five of the Huainanzi.* Albany: SUNY Press, 1993. (see *Huainanzi*).

Marks, Robert. *China: Its Environment and History.* Boston: Rowman and Littlefield, 2012.

Mather, Richard. "K'ou Ch'ien-chih and the Taoist Theocracy of the Northern Wei." In *Facets of Taoism: Essays in Chinese Religion*, edited by H. Welch and A. Seidel, 103–22. New Haven: Yale University Press, 1979.

McMullen, David. "Bureaucrats and Cosmology: The Ritual Code of T'ang China." In *Rituals of Royalty: Power and Ceremonial in Traditional Societies*, edited by David Cannadine and Simon Price, 181–237. Cambridge, UK: Cambridge University Press, 1987.

———. *State and Scholars in T'ang China.* New York: Cambridge University Press, 1988.

———. "The Real Judge Dee: Ti Jen-Chieh and the T'ang Restoration of 705." *Asia Major* 6/1, 3rd Series (1993): 1–81.

Min, Jiayin, ed. *The Chalice and the Blade in Chinese Culture.* Beijing: Academy of Social Sciences, 1995.

Mo, Yan. *Republic of Wine*, translated by Howard Goldblatt. New York: Arcade Books, 2000.

Moule, A. C. *The Rulers of China, 221 BC to AD 1949.* New York: Frederick A. Praeger, 1957.

Murphey, Rhoads. *East Asia: A New History*, 4th edition. New York: Pearson Longman, 2007.

Needham, Joseph. "Human Laws and Laws of Nature in China and the West (II): Chinese Civilization and the Laws of Nature." *Journal of the History of Ideas* 12.2 (1951): 194–230.

Needham, Joseph, Wang Ling, and Derek De Solla Price. *Heavenly Clockwork: The Great Astronomical Clocks of Medieval China.* Cambridge, UK: Cambridge University Press, 2008.

Nienhauser, William, Jr. "A Re-Examination of the "Biographies of the Reasonable Officials in the *Records of the Grand Historian*." *Early China* 16 (1991): 209–33.

Ning, Chia. "Women in Frontier Politics: Heqin." In *Presence and Presentation: Women in the Chinese Literate Tradition*, edited by Sherry Mou, 39–76. New York: St. Martin's Press, 1999.

Ning, Qiang. *Art, Religion, and Politics in Medieval China: The Dunhuang Cave of the Zhai Family.* Honolulu: University of Hawai'i Press, 2004.

Pan, Yihong. "Integration of the Northern Ethnic Frontiers in Tang China." *Chinese Historical Review* 19 (2012): 3–26.

BIBLIOGRAPHY

———. *Son of Heaven and the Heavenly Qaghan: Sui-Tang China and Its Neighbors*. Bellingham: Western Washington University Press, 1997.

Pelliot, Paul. *Notes on Marco Polo I, Ouvrage Posthume*. Paris: Imprimerie Nationale Librarie Adrien-Maisonneuve, 1959.

Peng, Xinwei. *A Monetary History of China*, Vol. 1, translated by Edward Kaplan. Bellingham: Western Washington University, 1993.

Pettit, J. E. E. "The Erotic Empress: Fantasy and Sovereignty in Chinese Temple Inscriptions." *T'ang Studies* 26 (2008): 125–42.

Picken, Laurence, ed. *Music From the Tang Court, Vol. 2*. Cambridge: Cambridge University Press, 1985.

———. *Music From the Tang Court, Vol. 4*. Cambridge: Cambridge University Press, 1987.

Picken, Laurence E. R., and Noël J. Nickson, *Music From the Tang Court 7: Some Ancient Connections Explored*. Cambridge, UK: Cambridge University Press, 2000.

Pines, Yuri. "A Hero Terrorist: Adoration of Jing Ke Revisited." *Asia Major* 21.2 (2008): 1–34.

Pulleyblank, Edwin G. "Jihu: Indigenous Inhabitants of Shaanbei and Western Shanxi." In *Opuscula Altaica: Essays Presented in Honor of Henry Schwarz*, edited by E. H. Kaplan and D. W. Whisenant, 498–530. Seattle: University of Washington Press, 1994.

Qian, Tony. "Classical Learning and the Law: Erudition as Persuasion in the *Dragon Sinews, Phoenix Marrows Judgments* of Zhang Zhuo." *Tang Studies* 35.1 (2017): 20–50.

Qiang, Fang. "Hot Potatoes: Chinese Complaint Systems From Early Times to the Late Qing (1898)." *Journal of Asian Studies* 68.4 (2009): 1105–35.

Qiang, Fang, and Xiaobing Li, eds. *Corruption and Anti-Corruption in Modern China*, edited by Fang Qiang and Xiaobing Li. London: Lexington Books, 2019.

Raphals, Lisa. "A Woman Who Understood the Rites." In *Confucius and the Analects: New Essays*, edited by Bryan Van Norden, 275–302. New York: Oxford University Press, 2002.

———. *Sharing the Light: Representations of Women and Virtue in Early China*. Albany: SUNY Press, 1998.

Rawski, Evelyn. *Early Modern China and Northeast Asia: Cross-border Perspectives*. Cambridge: Cambridge University Press, 2015.

Reed, Carrie. "Motivation and Meaning of a "Hodge-Podge": Duan Chengshi's *Youyang zazu*." *Journal of the American Oriental Society* 123.1 (2003): 121–45.

Riboud, Pénélope. "Priests and Other Xian 祆 Ritual Performers in Medieval China." *Early Medieval China* 25 (2019): 100–20.

Rideout, J.K. "The Rise of Eunuchs During the T'ang Dynasty, Part I." *Asia Major* (New Series) 1 (1949–50): 53–72.

———. "The Rise of Eunuchs During the T'ang Dynasty, Part II." *Asia Major* (New Series) 3 (1952): 42–58.

Roberts, Chris. *Heavy Words Lightly Thrown: The Reason Behind the Rhyme*. New York: Gotham Books, 2006.

Rong, Xinjiang 榮新江. "Nüban nanzhuang: Sheng Tang funü xingbie yishi" 女扮男裝:盛唐婦女性別意識 [Donning Male Attire: Gender Consciousness of Women in the High Tang], 320–44. Abstracts and Papers From the Tang Women's Studies Conference, Beijing University, 2001.

———. *Zhonggu Zhongguo yu Sute Wenming* 中古中國與粟特文明 [Medieval China and Sogdian Culture]. Beijing: Sanlian, 2014.

Rong, Zhaozu 容肇祖. "Tang Zhang Zhuo shiji kao" 唐張鷟事跡考. *Lingnan xuebao* 嶺南學報 6.4 (1941): 129–39.

BIBLIOGRAPHY

Rothschild, N. Harry. "An Inquiry into Reign Era Changes Under Wu Zhao, China's Only Female Emperor." *Early Medieval China* 12 (2006): 123–49.

———. "Beyond Filial Piety: *Biographies of Exemplary Women* and Wu Zhao's New Paradigm of Political Authority." *T'ang Studies* 23–4 (2005–6): 149–68.

———. "Emerging from the Cocoon: Ethnic Revival, Lunar Radiance, and the Cult of Liu Sahe in the Jihu Uprising of 682–683." *Annali* 65 (2005): 257–82.

———. *Emperor Wu Zhao and Her Pantheon of Devis, Divinities, and Dynastic Mothers*. New York: Columbia University Press, 2015.

———. "Empress Wu." In *Chief Consultant*, edited by John Makeham. China: The World's Oldest Living Civilization, 212–15. Lane Cove, AU: Global Book Publishing, 2008.

———. ""Her Influence Great, Her Merit Beyond Measure": A Translation and Initial Investigation of the Epitaph of Shangguan Wan'er." *Studies in Chinese Religion* 1.2 (2015): 131–48.

———. *Rhetoric, Ritual and Support Constituencies in the Political Authority of Wu Zhao, China's Only Woman Emperor*. Ph.D. Dissertation, Brown University, 2003.

———. "Severing Grandma's Phallus: A Gendered Re-examination of the Raising and Razing of Female Emperor Wu Zhao's Axis of the Sky." *Journal of Left History* 21.2 (2018): 51–72.

———. "Sovereignty, Virtue and Crisis Management: Prime Minister Yao Chong's Proactive Handling of the Locust Plague of 715–6." *Journal of Environmental History* 17.4 (2012): 783–812.

———. "*Sumozhe* Suppressed, *Huntuo* Halted: An Investigation into the Nature and Stakes of the Cold-Splashing Festal Sogdian Dramas Performed in Early Eighth Century China." *Frontiers of Chinese History* 12.2 (2017): 262–300.

———. "The Koguryan Connection: The Quan (Yon) Family in the Establishment of Wu Zhao's Political Authority." *China Yongu: The Journal of Chinese Studies of Pusan National University* 14.1 (2008): 199–234.

———. "Wu Zetian." In *Routledge Encyclopedia of Chinese History*, 673–74. Abingdon, UK: Routledge, 2017.

———. "Wu Zhao." In *The Berkshire Encyclopedia of Chinese Biography*, 571–84. Great Barrington, MA: Berkshire Publishing, 2014.

———. "Wu Zhao and the Queen Mother of the West." *Journal of Daoist Studies* 3 (2010): 29–56.

———. *Wu Zhao: China's Only Woman Emperor*. New York: Longman World Biography Series, 2008.

———. "Wu Zhao's Remarkable Aviary." *Southeast Review of Asian Studies* 27 (2005): 71–88.

———. "Zhuanlun wang, yishi yu huozai: Wu Zhao yu 694 nian de wuzhedahui" 轉輪王、儀式、及火災：武曌与694年的無遮大會 [Cakravartin, Ceremony, and Conflagration: Wu Zhao and the Pañcāvarṣika of 694]. *Qianling wenhua yanjiu* 7 (2012), 101–13.

Sanders, Graham. "I Read They Said He Sang What He Wrote: Orality, Writing, and Gossip in Tang Poetry Anecdotes." In *Idle Talk: Gossip and Anecdotes in Traditional China*, edited by Jack Chen and David Schaberg, 88–106. Berkeley: University of California Press, 2012.

———. *Words Well Put: Visions of Poetic Competence in Chinese Tradition*. Cambridge, MA: Harvard University Asia Center, 2006.

Schafer, Edward. "The Conservation of Nature under the T'ang Dynasty." *Journal of the Social and Economic History of the Orient* 5.3 (1962): 279–308.

BIBLIOGRAPHY

———. *The Divine Woman: Dragon Ladies and Rain Maidens*. San Francisco: North Point Press, 1980.
———. *Pacing the Void*. Berkeley: University of California Press, 1977.
———. "Tang." In *Food in Chinese Culture: Anthropological and Historical Perspectives*, edited by K. C. Chang, 85–140. New Haven: Yale University Press, 1977.
———. *The Golden Peaches of Samarkand*. Berkeley: University of California Press, 1963.
———. "The Restoration of the Shrine of Wei Hua-tsun at Lin-ch'uan in the Early Eighth Century." *Journal of Oriental Studies* 15 (1977): 124–37.
———. *The Vermilion Bird: T'ang Images of the South*. Berkeley: University of California Press, 1967.
Schipper, Kristofer, and Franciscus Verellen, eds. "Zhang Zun." In *The Taoist Canon: A Historical Companion the Daozong*, 1243. Chicago: University of Chicago Press, 2004.
Schneewind, Sarah. *A Tale of Two Melons: Emperor and Subject in Ming China*. Indianapolis: Hackett Publishing, 2006.
Sen, Tansen. *Buddhism, Diplomacy and Trade*. Honolulu: University of Hawaii Press, 2003.
Seidel, Anna. "The Image of the Perfect Ruler in Early Taoist Messianism: Laozi and Li Hung." *History of Religions* 9 (1969–70): 216–47.
Shields, Anna. "Gossip, Anecdote, and Literary History: Representations of the Yuanhe Era in Tang Anecdote Collections." In *Idle Talk: Gossip and Anecdotes in Traditional China*, edited by Jack Chen and David Schaberg, 107–31. Berkeley: University of California Press, 2012.
Skaff, Jonathan. *Sui-Tang China and Its Turko-Mongol Neighbors*. New York: Oxford University Press, 2012.
Skinner, Patricia. "The Gendered Nose and Its Lack: "Medieval" Nose-Cutting and Its Modern Manifestations." *Journal of Women's History* 26 (2014): 45–67.
Smith, Adam. "The Chinese Sexagenary Cycle and Ritual Foundations of the Calendar." In *Calendars and Years II: Astronomy and Time in the Ancient and Medieval World*, edited by John Steele, 1–37. Oxford: Oxbow Books, 2010.
Somers, Matthew. "Time, Space, and Structure in the Consolidation of the T'ang Dynasty (617–700)." *Journal of Asian Studies* 45.5 (1986): 971–994.
Sperati, Giorgio. "Amputation of the Nose Throughout History." *Acta Otorhinolaryngol Italia* 29 (2009): 44–50.
Spring, Madeline. *Animal Allegories in T'ang China*. New Haven: American Oriental Society, Vol. 36, 1993.
Stone, Charles. *The Fountainhead of Chinese Erotica*. Honolulu: University of Hawaii Press, 2003.
Sun, Xiao, and Shaoping Pan. "Order and Chaos: The Social Positions of Men and Women in the Qin, Han, and Six Dynasties Period." In *The Chalice and the Blade*, edited by Gao Shiyu, 226–69. Beijing: Academy of Social Science, 1995.
Sun, Yinggang. "Imagined Reality: Urban Space and Sui-Tang Beliefs in the Underworld." *Studies in Chinese Religions* 1.4 (2015): 375–416.
Suzuki, Yui. "Twanging Bows and Throwing Rice: Warding off Evil in Medieval Japanese Birth Scenes." *Artibus Asiae* 74.1 (2014): 17–41.
Tan, Qixiang 譚其驤, ed. *Zhongguo lishi* dituji 中國歷史地圖集 [Chinese Historical Atlas], Vols. 8. Beijing: Zhongguo ditu chubanshe, 1996.
Tong, Jowen R. *Fables for the Patriarchs: Gender Politics in Tang Discourse*. Lanham, MD: Rowman and Littlefield, 2000.
Truitt, E. R. *Medieval Robots: Mechanism, Magic, Nature, and Art*. Philadelphia: University of Pennsylvania Press, 2015.

BIBLIOGRAPHY

Twitchett, Denis. *Financial Administration Under the T'ang Dynasty* (2nd ed.). Cambridge: Cambridge University Press, 1970.

———. "Introduction." In *The Cambridge History of China, Vol. 3: Sui and T'ang China*, edited by D. Twitchett and J. K. Fairbank, 1–47. Cambridge: Cambridge University Press, 1979.

———. *The Writing of Official History Under the T'ang*. New York: Cambridge University Press, 1992.

Twitchett, Denis, and Howard Wechsler. "Kao-tsung (reign 649–683) and the Empress Wu: The Inheritor and the Usurper." In *Cambridge History of China, Vol. 3: Sui and Tang China, 589–906, Part I*, edited by D. Twitchett and J. K. Fairbank, 242–89. Cambridge: Cambridge University Press, 1979.

Twitchett, Denis, and John Fairbank, eds. *Cambridge History of China, Vol. 3: Sui and Tang China, 589–906, Part I*. Cambridge: Cambridge University Press, 1979.

Verellen, Franciscus. *Imperiled Destinies: The Daoist Quest for Deliverance in Medieval China*. Cambridge: Harvard University Asia Center, 2019.

Vervoorn, Aat. "The Life of Zhang Zun." *Monumenta Serica* 38 (1988–89): 69–94.

Vitiello, Giovanni. *The Libertine's Friend: Homosexuality and Masculinity in Late Imperial China*. Chicago: University of Chicago Press, 2011.

Waley, Arthur. "The Chinese Cinderella Story." *Folklore* 58 (1947): 226–38.

Wallace, Leslie. "Wild Youths and Fallen Officials: Falconry and Moral Opprobrium in Early Medieval China." In *Behaving Badly in Early and Medieval China*, edited by N. Harry Rothschild and L. Wallace, 122–34. Honolulu: University of Hawai'i Press, 2017.

Wang, Aihe. *Cosmology and Political Culture in Early China*. Cambridge: Cambridge University Press, 2000.

Wang, Eugene. *Shaping the Lotus Sutra: Buddhist Visual Culture in Medieval China*. Seattle: University of Washington Press, 2005.

Wang, Hongjie. *Power and Politics in Tenth Century China: The Former Shu Regime*. Amherst, New York: Cambria Press, 2011.

Wang, Shuanghuai. "Wu Zetian yu kuli de guanxi" 武則天與酷吏的關係 [The Relationship Between Wu Zetian and Her "Cruel Officials"]. In *Wu Zetian yanjiu lunwenji* 武則天研究論文記, edited by Zhao and Li, 177–86. Taiyuan: Shanxi guji, 1998.

Wang, Shuanghuai, and Zhao Wenrun. *Wu Zetian pingzhuan* 武則天評傳 [A Critical Biography of Wu Zetian]. Xi'an: Sanqin chubanshe, 1993.

———. *Wu Zetian pingzhuan* (2nd ed.). Xi'an: Sanqin, 2000.

Wang, Yongping 王永平. "Tang Gaozong, Wu Zetian shiqi yu Linyi de guanxi 唐高宗、武則天時期与林邑的關系 [Foreign Relations With Champa During the Reigns of Tang Gaozong and Wu Zetian]. In *Conference Proceedings from the 11th Conference of the Wu Zetian Research Association, Supplemental Essay*, Guangyuan, 2013.

Wang, Yu-ch'uan. "An Outline of the Central Government of the Former Han Dynasty." *Harvard Journal of Asiatic Studies* 12.1 (1949): 134–87.

Wang, Zhenping. *Tang China in Multi-Polar Asia: A History of Diplomacy and War*. Honolulu: University of Hawaii Press, 2013.

———. *Offerings of Jade and Silk: Ritual and Symbol in the Legitimization of the T'ang*. New Haven: Yale University Press, 1985.

BIBLIOGRAPHY

Wechsler, Howard. "The Founding of the T'ang Dynasty: Kao-tsu (Reign 618–626)." In *The Cambridge History of China, Vol.3: Sui and T'ang China, 589–906, Part I*, edited by D. Twitchett and J. Fairbank, 150–87. Cambridge, UK: Cambridge University Press, 1979.

Wolters, O.W. "North-western Cambodia in the Seventh Century." *Bulletin of the School of African and Oriental Studies* 37.2 (1974): 355–84.

Wright, Arthur. *The Sui Dynasty: The Unification of China, AD 581–617*. New York: Alfred A. Knopf, 1978.

Wu, Yenna. *The Chinese Virago: A Literary Theme*. Cambridge: Harvard University Council on East Asian Studies, 1995.

Wu, Zetian yanjiuhui 武則天研究會 [Wu Zetian Research Association]. "Di 11 jie Wu Zetian yanjiuhui, huiyi taolun lunwenji" 第11屆武則天研究會,會議討論文集 Conference Proceedings from the 11th Conference of the Wu Zetian Research Association, Guangyuan, 2013.

Wyatt, Donald. Review of *Emperor Wu Zhao and Her Pantheon of Devis, Divinities, and Dynastic Mothers*, by N. Harry Rothschild. *Journal of Religion and Violence* 4.2 (2016): 229–33.

Xiong, Victor Cunrui. *Historical Dictionary of Medieval China*. Lanham, MD: Scarecrow Press, 2009.

———. *Sui-Tang Chang'an: A Study in the Urban History of Medieval China*. Ann Arbor: Center for Chinese Studies, University of Michigan, 2000.

Yang, Lien-sheng. "Female Rulers in Imperial China." *Harvard Journal of Asian Studies* 23 (1960–61): 47–61.

Yang, Shao-yun. "The Semantic Context of Word Play With the Label Hu 胡 in Anecdotes About the Tang." Unpublished Paper, https://denison.academia.edu/ShaoyunYang/Papers, accessed 4 April 2015.

———. *The Way of the Barbarians: Redrawing Ethnic Boundaries in Tang and Song China*. Seattle: University of Washington Press, 2019.

Yao, Ping. "Historicizing Great Bliss: Erotica in Tang China (618–907)." *Journal of the History of Sexuality* 22.2 (2013): 207–29.

———. "Tang Women in the Transformation of Buddhist Filiality." In *Gendering Chinese Religion: Subject, Identity, and Body*, edited by Jinhua Jia, Xiaofei Kang, and Ping Yao, 25–46. Albany: SUNY Press, 2014.

Zhang, Ellen Cong. "'To Be Erudite in Miscellaneous Knowledge': A Study of Song (960–1279) Biji Writing." *Asia Major*, Third Series, 25.2 (2012): 43–77.

Zhang, Zhibin, and Paul Unschuld, eds. *Dictionary of the Ben Cao Gang Mu, Vol. I: Chinese Historical Illness Terminology*. Berkeley: University of California Press, 2015.

Zheng, Jinsheng, Nalini Kirk, Paul Buell, and Paul Unschuld, eds. *Dictionary of the Ben Cao Gang Mu, Vol. III: Persons and Literary Sources*. Berkeley: University of California Press, 2018.

Zhou, Yiqun. *Festivals, Feasts, and Gender Relations in Ancient China and Greece*. New York: Cambridge University Press, 2010.

Zürcher, Erik. "Buddhist Influence on Early Taoism: A Survey of Scriptural Evidence." *T'oung Pao* 66 (1980): 84–147.

———. "Foreword." In *Lippiello, Auspicious Omens and Miracles in Ancient China: Han, Three Dynasties, and Six Kingdoms*, 10–12. Sankt Augustin, Germany: Steyler Verlag, 2001.

Index

Page numbers followed with "n" refer to endnotes.

Abramson, Marc 137, 157
achillomancy 185–86
acrobatics 109
albino magpie 210
Altaic legacy 164
Anle Princess 44, 68, 210–11
artisans 101–4
artists 101–4
ash calligraphy 102
aviary 208–12

Ba, kingdom of 168
backgammon 112–13
bad officials 90–93; *see also* cruel officials
Bai (Bo) Juyi 163
Bai Tieyu 155, 165–67, 177
Ban Zhao (Lady of Handsome Fairness Ban) 44
barbarians 151–52, 266n18; animalizing 156–58; incursions 155–56
Barrett, Timothy 146
Benn, Charles 29, 109
bestiary: cats 205–7; cattle 203; elephants 200–202; foxes 203–5; gibbons 202; rabbits 207–8; tigers 198–99
"bird of 100 tongues" (*baishe*) 211–12
birds 208–12
Blacktooth Changzhi 137–38
Boast Father 215
bodhisattva 177
Bohai 273n84
Bole (Sun Yang) 56
Book of History 63, 151, 208
Brindley, Erica 167
Buddhism 15, 171, 177, 179
Buddhist Lantern Festival 108
Buddhists 176–82
burial practices, Southland 167–69

BuYun Chen 152

Cai Heng 3
Campany, Robert 12–13, 183, 187
cannibalism 97–98
Cao Huaishun 142–43
Cao Renjie 159
cats 205–7
cattle 203
Champa 168–69
Chan 178
Chang'an 106–7, 198, 216
Chang'e 192
chastity 125
Chen Anping 187
Chen BuYun 46, 106, 120
Chen Cangqi 116–17
Chen Huaiqing 114–15, 219–20
Chen, Jack 12
Chen Lingying 139
Chen Ximin 54
Chen Yuanguang 92, 96
Chen Zangqi 97
Cheng Xingmou 7
child acrobats 109
child prodigy 109–10
Chrysopelea 214
Chuan Huangzhong 199
citizen's arrest 113–14
Clark, Hugh 96
Classic of Mountains and Seas (*Shanhaijing*) 215
Cohen, Albert 86
comet 155–56
common people: artists, artisans, and craftsmen 101–4; games and gamers 110–13; hospitality of 99–100; merchants 104–8; other vignettes of 113–18; peasant-farmers 99–101; performers 108–10

INDEX

Confucianism 61, 109, 119, 171–72, 182
Confucius 176
craftsmen 101–4
crested mynahs 209
cruel officials 59–61, 63, 68, 71–74, 224, 253n1; after Wu Zhao's era 82–85; Empress Wei 83; Empress Wei (Traitor Wei, Commoner Wei, Miss Wei, Missy Wei) 37–38, 40, 42–44, 83, 112, 130–32, 180, 210; end of 80–82; Guo Ba 77–78; Lai Junchen 38, 40, 66–68, 73–74, 77–78, 80–83, 85–86, 160; Li Quanjiao 6–7, 84–85; Suo Yuanli 81–82; Wang Xu 84–85; Wu Sansi 35, 37–38, 44, 66–69, 83, 112; Wu Yizong 39, 50–53, 75–78, 80, 128, 140, 157; Zhou Xing 60–61, 74–75, 81–82, 85
Cui Hun 62
Cui Jian 123–24
Cui Jing 128
Cui Rizhi 65
Cui Rong 42
Cui Shi 40–41
Cui Wu 116
Cui Xuansheng 7

Dangxiang 138
Daoism 171–73
Daoists 172–76
day laborer 114
Deng You 91
Di Renjie 35, 58–59, 66, 68, 112, 187, 218
Dien, Al 162
Ding Yuguo 67
Director of the Court of Watches 6
divination 183–88
Dong Xingcheng 113–14
Dong Yan 40–41
Dongfang Zha 51
Dora Shu-fang Dien 31
Doran, Rebecca 31, 41, 43, 72, 122, 205–6, 210
Dou Zhifan 92–93
Double Ears (Duke Wen of Jin) 217–18
Dragon-son Liu 189–90
Du Jingquan (Du Yuanfang) 186, 191
Du Jingxian 53–54
Duan Chengshi 13, 225
Duan Jin 76
Duan Zan 76
Duke Mu of Qin 55–56
duplicitous sorcerers 189–90

Elegy of a River Shaman (Fang Qi) 194–95
elephants 200–202
Ellen Cong Zhang 12, 223
Elvin, Mark 155, 197
Empress Wang 16, 19, 25, 191
Empress Wei (Traitor Wei, Commoner Wei, Miss Wei, Missy Wei) 37–38, 40, 42–44, 83, 112, 130–32, 180, 210
ethnic Other 157
examination system 45, 57, 90
Extensive Records of the Taiping Era (*Taiping guangji*, Li Fang) 13, 59, 61, 77, 88, 90, 143, 189–90, 196, 212, 245n49

faith healers 114; false 190
Fan Qinben 173
Fan Wen 173
Fang Xuanling 125–26
female slave 121–23
feng 153–54
Feng Yi 193
Feng Zidu 40–41
filial cannibalism 97–98
filial piety 61–64, 117–18
fish 212–14
Fitzgerald, C. P. 72, 74, 131
folk wisdom 100–101
Forte, Antonino 103, 223
Four Barbarians 149, 151
foxes 203–5

game: Backgammon 112–13; of pitch-pot 110–12
Gan Bao 55
Gao Jun 62
Gao Rui 129–30
Gao Shiyu 120
Gao Yi 195–96
gaoshou 54
Gaozong 15–16, 19, 25, 68, 123, 154, 161, 173, 176, 194, 206–7, 218
gender 120; anarchy 34, 72, 83, 184
gibbons 202
glyphomancy 58, 252n30
Gong Siming 81
Gong Siye 81
good officials 59–61
goose 208–9
Grannie He 188
Grannie Lai 188–89
Grotto of a Playful Goddess (*Youxianku*, Zhang Zhuo) 10–11

INDEX

Grousset, René 176
Gu Zong 46, 102
Guan Yu 144
Guanyin 38, 178
Guisso, Richard 119, 160
Guo Ba 77–78
Guo Chun 117–18
Guo Wujing 91
Guo Zhengyi 161

Halys pit viper 221
Han Linggui 75–76
Han Xun 213
He Axiao 157
He Dayuan 105–7
He Qiao 66
He Ruojin 53
Heichi Changzhi 137
Helan Minzhi 42, 44
hen 208
heterodox teachings 179
High Carts: *see* Tiele (High Carts)
Hinsch, Bret 127
Hong Mai 12, 223
hospitality of common people 99–100
Hou Zhiyi 62
hu 162–63, 267n52
Hu Chao 172–73
Hu Liang 133
Hu Yuanli 50
Huifan 189
Huntington, Rania 204
Huo Guang 41

illegitimate Zhou 14, 19
Ilterish Khan (Ashina Gumalu) 157
Immortal Medicine Li 187
"Imperial Capital" (Luo Binwang), *The* 191

Jack Chen 98
Jade Disc 121–23, 133
Jealous Girl 217–18
Ji Mao 128
Ji Xi 35
Ji Xianzhi 57
Ji Xu 35–36, 51, 53, 78, 80, 128–29
Jiang Chen 60
Jiang Chong 66
Jiang Rong 74–75
Jiannan Circuit 209–10
Jie Zhitui 217–18
Jihu 165–67
Jingle County Princess 51

Judgments on Dragon Sinew and Phoenix Marrow (*Longjin fengsui*, Zhang Zhuo) 11
junzi 94

Kam Louie 144
karmic retribution 132–33
Khitan: *see* Qidan (Khitan)
King Min of Qi 127
King of Champa 222
Kinney, Anne 109
Knapp, Keith 61
Koguryans 160–62
Kong Luqiu 50
Kory, Stephen 189
Kou Qianzhi 173–74, 183
Kroll, Paul 182
Kuafu 215

Laborde, Alice 85
Lai Junchen 38, 40, 66–68, 73–74, 77–78, 80–83, 85–86, 160
landscape 215–16
Lao Ai 38–39
Laozi (Li Er) 151, 172
Levy, Howard 7, 10–11, 14
Li Chengjia 205
Li Chongfu 249n57
Li Chongjun 253n52
Li Cide 189–90
Li Fang 13, 212, 243n8, 245n49
Li Feng 89
Li Hong 16, 88–89, 199–200
Li Huaibi 157
Li Ji (Xu Ji) 184–85, 190
Li Jiegu 158–59
Li Jin 88
Li Jingxuan 142–43, 146
Li Jingye (Xu Jingye) 60, 74, 80–81, 155, 185, 190–91, 252n36, 266n18, 273n68
Li Jingzhen 184
Li Jinxing 138
Li Jinzhong 155, 158
Li Liangbi 157–58
Li Longfan 5
Li Longji 6
Li Ming 95–96
Li Ningdao 94
Li Qianli 50, 199
Li Qiao 63–64, 67–68
Li Quanjiao 6–7, 84–85
Li Rizhi 7, 59, 63
Li Ruoxu 7
Li Ruzhen 19

INDEX

Li Shizhen 96
Li Ti 116
Li Xiang 30, 35, 90
Li Xiaoyi 192
Li Yuanjia 103–4
Li Yuanying (Prince of Teng) 123–25
Li Zhaode 50, 66, 68, 86–87, 159–60, 186
Li Zhe 91
Li Zhen 177
Li Zheng 114
Liang Wudi 181
Liang Xuzhou 7
Liao 132–33, 168
licentious cults 179
Lin Yutang 31
Lingnan 168–69; crested mynahs 209; fauna and flora of 220–22; natural toxins 219; snakes 214, 221–22; wee turtles of 221
Lippiello, Tiziana 26
literati-officials 7, 220
Liu Chong 195
Liu Jiao 109
Liu Jing 175
Liu Jingyang 209
Liu Kezhuang 42
Liu Qing 91
Liu Rengui 54–55, 107, 142
Liu Sahe 166
Liu Xiangshu 142
Liu Xu 19
Liu Yao 124
Liu Yong 127
Lo, Andrew 113
local examinations 90
local officials 87–89; bad 90–93; humorless 89–90; inept and foolish 93–94; lawless frontier 94–95; stingy 91–92; worse 95–98
Lu Jingyang 107
Lu Renjie 50–51, 64–65
Lu Shide 51, 66, 68
Lu Xian 58
Lu Xun 256n33
Lu Yuanfang 75
Lu Yuqing 89–90
Lü Zhiwei 50
Luo Binwang 191
Luo Hei(hei) 29–30
Luo Hui 107
Luo Manling 189, 224
Luo Wuzheng 50
Luoyang 105–6, 153, 198

Ma Jipu 50–51
Ma Renjie 155, 158–59
Ma Xiantong 5
Ma Xueqin 225
Ma Zhiji 179
McMullen, David 20, 171
Madame He 133
Madame Lu 125–26
Madame Zhao 184
Malgal: *see* Mohe (Malgal)
Man 167–68
Mao Jun 109
maple trees 216–17
Marks, Robert 151, 167, 197
Marquis de Sade 85
Master Ding 177–78
Master Xue: *see* Xue Huaiyi
Melville, Herman 2
Meng Lingxiu 127
merchants 104–8
Ming Chongyan 175–76
Minhuai (Crown Prince of Jin) 124
Mo Yan 97
Mohe (Malgal) 137–38, 153
moral meteorology 155
Mount Felicity 216
moxibustion 220
Mrs. Zheng 124
mud guppies or loaches 213
Myriad Acres Slope 213

natural toxins and cures 219–20
Needham, Joseph 103, 155
nepotism 34–39
New Tang History 23, 125, 190, 199
Nienhauser, William 80
Ning family 131, 262n55
non-Han generals 137–38

Old Tang History (Zhang Zhuo) 9, 23, 48, 74, 78, 145, 218
omens 24–27
oneiromancy 187
Ouyang Xiu 20

palace intimates 31
Pan Chan 113
parrots 209
patriarchal system 119
patrimonial generosity 138
peasant-farmers 99–101
Pei Feishu 107
Pei Guang 60

INDEX

Pei Gui 184
Pei Min 143–44
Pei Shaoye 143–44
Pei Xuan 130
Pei Yan 202
Pei Ziyi 194
Pei Ziyun 88
Peng Botong 144–46
Peng Xianjue 24
Pengzu 172
physiognomy 184–85
pipa divination 183, 187–88
pitch-pot 110–12
policy of appeasement 135
precocity 109
prognostication 184–85
Pure Consort Xiao 25
python bile 215

Qapaghan, Khan of the Tujue Turks 5, 138–42, 152, 156, 158, 160
Qi Li Longfan 5
Qi Lianyao 78, 80
Qian, Tony 7
Qian Weidao 3
Qiang 148
Qiang Ning 108
Qiao Shu 124
Qiao Zhizhi 121–23, 128, 133
Qibi 31
Qidan (Khitan) 27, 153, 157–60; uprising of 696–697 158–60
Quan Longxiang 146–49

rabbits 207–8
Raphals, Lisa 129
red-billed chough 211
Reed, Carrie 225
religious frauds 189–90
Ren Zhengli 89
Ren Zhengming 92, 95–96
Riboud, Pénélope 164
Rideout, J. K. 38
Ruizong (Emperor) 6, 63, 182

Sakyamuni 177
salt penalty 140
Sanders, Graham 53, 122
savage cruelty of Wu Yizong 75–77
Schafer, Edward 161–63, 169, 197–98, 202
Schneewind, Sarah 26
self-mutilation 125

shan 153–54
Shangguan Wan'er 41, 43–44
Shazha Zhongyi 137
Shen Quanjiao 56–57
Shen Yue 26
Shen Zirong 57
Shi Chong 122
Shields, Anna 12, 223–24
Sichuan region 212–13
signs 25–26; *see also* symbols
Sima Guang 20
Sima Qian 71–72, 80
snakes 214–15, 221–22
social mobility 128–29
Sogdians 162–65
Song Lingwen 145–46
Song Yun 83
Song Zhiti 145–46
Song Zhiwen 42, 77, 83, 145–46
Song Zhixun 83
southern borderlands 220–22
Southland 167–69
Spring of the Jealous Woman 217–18
street performers 108
Su Gui 63–64
Su Ting 63
Su Weidao 50
Su Zheng 52
suguroku 112
Sun Chan'gao 93
Sun Quan 143
Sun Simiao 116
Sun Wanrong 50, 155, 157–60
Suo Yuanli 81–82
supernatural 190; realm 192–96
symbols 24–25

Taiping Princess 178, 192–93, 209–10
Taizong 98, 126, 135, 138, 165
Tang Boruo 51
Tao Zongyi 13
Tenth Lady 10–11
terrestrial displacement 216
"Three Kindling Gatherers" 116
Tian Yi 78
Tibetans 137–38, 142, 152, 154
Tiele (High Carts) 137
tigers 198–99
Tony Qian 12
Truitt, E. R. 104
Tujue Turks 138–42, 152–53, 156–58, 160
Tumor-Ridden Su 126–27
Twitchett, Denis 87

unfilial piety 61–64; *see also* filial piety

van Gulik, Robert 58

Wallace, Leslie 32
Wang Fangqing 50
Wang Gao 143
Wang Huifeng 124
Wang Jing 88
Wang Jingrong 194–95
Wang Jishan 53–54
Wang Ju 75, 103
Wang Qiuli 29–30
Wang Sui 117
Wang Tongjiao 83
Wang Xiaojie 155, 159–60
Wang Xingzai 99–100
Wang Xu 84–85
Wang Yuquan 155
Wang Zhenping 152
Wang Zhu 78
water dragon 213
watery tribes 212–14
Wei Chang 161–62
Wei Hao 99
Wei Ling 211
Wei Xuanzhen 131–32
Wei Yuanzhong 34, 67–68, 77–78
Wei Zhigu 243n7
wen culture 148
White, Jade 161–62
"white special" 213
Wu Chengsi 35–36, 121–23, 192
Wu Ding 252n45
Wu Sansi 35, 37–38, 44, 66–69, 83, 112
Wu Shihuo 26
Wu Shikai 67
Wu Song 199–200
Wu Xiwu 50
Wu Yizong 39, 50–53, 75–78, 80, 128, 140, 157
Wu Zhao 2–5; Buddhism and 15, 18, 176–82, 209; comic savagery of Zhang Yuanyi 49–53; cruel officials of (*see* cruel officials); Daoism 172, 176; Di Renjie's interpretation of 58; dreams and 58, 112; fearlessness 28–29; filial and unfilial piety 61–64; good officials 59–61; hangers-on of 40–41; as intemperate grannie 28; kinsmen and relatives 34–42; local officials of 87–98; male favorites 29–34; merchants and 104–5; military affairs and foreign relations 18, 151–53; military generals of 137–38; natural world and 197–98; perspective of the center 64–65; physiognomy and 184; power of symbols and omens in 24–27, 58, 190–94, 200, 206, 208, 210, 216; and Qapaghan Khan 139–41, 158, 160; reign as emperor 14–20; "religious frauds" and 172, 189; satirical nicknames 53–55; signs of status and service 46–48; system of ranking 45–46, 48; Tang gender norms and 15, 31, 34, 39, 41, 72, 119–20, 184, 208, 210–11; transgressive women after 42–44; Xue Huaiyi and Zhang brothers 29–34; *yin-yang* divination and 182–84, 186; Zhang Zhuo's assessments of ministers 65–69; Zhang Zhuo's representation of 20–23, 156, 172, 183–4, 200
Wuping County 202
Wuxi region 167–68; snake in 221–22
Wyatt, Donald 71

Xi 143–44
Xiao Quan 115
Xiaofei Tian 223
Xie You 95
Xin Chengsi 143–44
xingxing 202
Xiong, Victor 162
Xiongnu 141, 157, 166
Xu (Li) Jingye 60, 74, 80–81, 155, 185, 190–91, 252n36, 266n18, 273n68
Xu (Li) Jingzhen 81, 184, 252n36
Xu Yougong 67–68
Xu Zhen 81
Xu Ziru 194
Xuanwu 47–48
Xuanzong (Emperor) 6–8, 13, 18, 59, 63, 83, 174
Xue Huaiyi 30, 34, 38, 40, 77, 177, 180–81
Xue Jichang 206
Xue Shenhuo 110
Xue Zhen 97

Yan Banqian 9
Yan (Zhuang) Junping 185–86
Yan Shengqi 92
Yan Zhiwei 139–40
Yang Chuyu 210
Yang Lien-sheng 119
Yang Qizhuang 76

INDEX

Yang Wulian 103
Yang Xuanji 189
Yang Yuanliang 114
Yangzi River Valley 168, 198–99, 216, 221
Yao Chong 7–8
Yao Ping 10
Ye Fashan 174–75
Yellow River Valley 200
Yellow Roebuck Gorge 158–59
Yenna Wu 119, 130
Yi Shentong 55
Yicheng Princess 130
yin-yang divination 183–84
Yu Qianlou 78
Yu Sixuan 80–81
Yuan Banqian 9
Yuan Bensong 51
Yuan Jia 110
Yuan Sizhong 149
Yuan Tiangang 184
Yuan Zhihong 67

Zen 178
Zeng Xi 127
Zengzi 261n33
Zhang brothers: *see* Zhang Changzong; Zhang Yizhi
Zhang Changling 42
Zhang Changqi 33, 210
Zhang Changyi 32–33
Zhang Changzong 30–34, 40, 42, 68, 205
Zhang Chong 102
Zhang Chujin 59–61
Zhang Cong 62
Zhang Heng 45–46
Zhang Huaisu 95–96
Zhang Jian 204
Zhang Jian (Zhang Zhuo's grandson) 242n3
Zhang Jingzang 184–85
Zhang Qian 178
Zhang Qizhen 62
Zhang Rendan 141
Zhang Ruzi 52
Zhang Sengyou 101
Zhang Shiqi 67
Zhang Shizhi 67
Zhang Sigong 28–29
Zhang Siming 81
Zhang Tinggui 7

Zhang Xi 209
Zhang Xiwang 193
Zhang Xuanyu 155, 158–59
Zhang Yizhi 30–34, 37, 40, 42, 68, 77, 83, 147, 149, 204–5
Zhang You 206
Zhang Yuanyi 49–53, 77, 140
Zhang Yue 42
Zhang Zhuo (Zhang Wencheng), Master Who Drifts then Rests 16–17, 23, 34–35, 40, 43, 49, 53–54, 56–57, 59, 62, 64–65, 76, 78, 83, 86, 91, 93, 95, 97–98, 115–17, 127, 135, 137, 146, 148–49, 152, 154–55, 160, 164–69, 171–74, 176–77, 181–85, 187–92, 200, 207–8, 210, 214–17, 220, 223–24; assessments of ministers in Wu Zhao's court 65–69; death sentence 7–8; exile 7; life and official career 2–9; literary career 9–14; literary judgments 11–12; representation of Wu Zhao in *Court and Country* 20–22
Zhang Zu 192
Zhangsun Wuji 152
Zhao Kuo 50
Zhao Luwen 67–68
Zhao Wenhui 159
Zhao Xuanjing 179
Zhao Yanxi 220
Zheng Yin 40, 68
Zhongshu, Dong 155
Zhongzong 17, 34, 43, 63–64, 81, 83, 112, 131–32, 173, 175
Zhou Fang 113
Zhou Rengui 131–33
Zhou Xing 60–61, 74–75, 81–82, 85
Zhou Yunyuan 192–93
Zhou Zigong 194
Zhu Qianyi 26–27, 50–51, 126–28
Zhu Qinming 55
Zhu Suihou 116
Zhuang 9
Zhuangzi 3
Zong Chuke 38
Zoroastrian rites 164
Zoroastrianism 162, 164
Zou Luotuo (Camel Zou) 115
Zu Zhenjian 185
Zuo Fen 44
Zürcher, Erik 25

www.ingramcontent.com/pod-product-compliance
Lightning Source LLC
Chambersburg PA
CBHW021136230426
43667CB00005B/137